C by Dissection

Fourth Edition

The Essentials of C Programming

Original editon, entitled C BY DISSECTION: THE ESSENTIALS OF C PROGRAMMING, 4th Edition, 0201713748 by KELLEY, AL; POHL, IRA, published by Pearson Education, Inc, publishing as Addison-Wesley, Copyright © 2001

ISBN 978-89-450-7213-9

C by Dissection

Fourth Edition

The Essentials of C Programming

Al Kelley / Ira Pohl

University of California, Santa Cruz

Addison Wesley Longman

Boston San Francisco New York
London Toronto Sydney Tokyo Singapore Madrid
Mexico City Munich Paris Cape Town Hong Kong Montreal

Other Publications by Al Kelley and Ira Pohl

Al Kelley and Ira Pohl have authored of a series of books together published by Addison-Wesley and Benjamin Cummings on the C programming language:

A Book on C: An Introduction to Programming in C
C by Dissection
Turbo C: The Essentials of C Programming

Ira is also coauthor with Charlie McDowell of the Addison-Wesley publication:

Java by Dissection: The Essentials of Java Programming

Ira is the sole author of Addison-Wesley or Benjamin Cummings publications:

C++ for C Programmers
C++ for Pascal Programmers
C++ for Fortran Programmers
Turbo C++
Object-Oriented Programming Using C++
C++ Distilled

Ira's first book, coauthored with Alan Shaw, was a pioneering text on computer science (Computer Science Press, 1981):

The Nature of Computation: An Introduction to Computer Science

About Al Kelley

Al Kelley, Ph.D., is an emeritus faculty at the University of California at Santa Cruz, where he was a professor of mathematics. Al's research interests include computational mathematics, center and subcenter manifolds, Hamiltonian mechanics, nonlinear ordinary differential equations and optimization.

He has lectured at the Institute of Mathematics, Ukrainian Academy of Sciences, Kiev; the Fifth International Congress on Nonlinear Oscillations in Kiev; the Institute for Advanced Study, Princeton; and was a participant in US-USSR Exchange Program under the auspices of the National Academy of Sciences.

About Ira Pohl

Ira Pohl, Ph.D., is a professor of computer science at the University of California, Santa Cruz. He has more than 30 years of experience as a software methodologist. His teaching and research interests are in the areas of artificial intelligence, programming languages, practical complexity problems, heuristic search methods, deductive algorithms, and educational and social issues. He originated error analysis in heuristic search methods and deductive algorithms.

He has lectured at Berkeley, Stanford, the Vrije University in Amsterdam, the Courant Institute, Edinburgh University in Scotland, and Auckland University in New Zealand.

When not programming, he enjoys riding bicycles in Aptos, California, with his wife, Debra, and daughter, Laura.

To Our Wives

Preface

Today, the ANSI C programming language is widely used throughout the world in both academia and industry. In many educational institutions it is the language of choice for a first programming course and for a language to be used for computer science instruction. A key reason for this is that C has drifted down the curriculum from more advanced courses to more introductory courses. Further, C comes with many useful libraries, and it is supported by sophisticated integrated environments. Improvements in ANSI C remedy a number of deficiencies found in traditional C, such as weak typing rules. These improvements, coupled with C's broadened impact as a language of choice for systems, graphics, and databases, make it a critical choice in teaching programming and computer science.

C by Dissection presents a thorough introduction to the programming process by carefully developing working programs to illuminate key features of the C programming language. Program code is explained in an easy-to-follow careful manner throughout. The code has been tested on several platforms and is obtainable from the Internet site *aw.com.*

The code in *C by Dissection* can be used with most C systems, including those found in operating systems such as MacOS, MS-DOS, OS/2, UNIX, and Windows.

Dissections

This book presents readers with a clear and thorough introduction to the programming process by carefully developing working C programs using the method of *dissection.* Dissection is a unique pedagogical tool first developed by the authors in 1984 to illuminate key features of working code. A dissection is similar to a structured walk-through of the code. Its intention is to explain to the reader newly encountered programming elements and idioms as found in working code. Programs and functions are explained in an easy-to-follow step-by-step manner. Key ideas are reinforced throughout by use in different contexts.

No Background Assumed

This book assumes no programming background and can be used by students and first-time computer users. Experienced programmers not familiar with C will also benefit from the carefully structured presentation of the C language. For student use, the book is intended as a first course in computer science or programming.

It is suitable for a CS1 course or beginning programming course for other disciplines. Each chapter presents a number of carefully explained programs that lead the student in a holistic manner to ever-improving programming skills. From the start, the student is introduced to complete programs, and at an early point in the text is introduced to writing functions as a major feature of structured programming. The function is to the program as the paragraph is to the essay. Competence in writing functions is the hallmark of the skilled programmer and hence is emphasized. Examples and exercises are plentiful in content and level of difficulty. They allow instructors to pick assignments appropriate to their audience.

Special Features

This fourth edition of *C by Dissection: The Essentials of C Programming* incorporates a number of special features:

- Up-to-date ANSI C used throughout, such as function prototypes
- "Moving to C++" sections at the end of each chapter to help with a transition to object-oriented C++
- Early explanation of multifile programs to enable the programmer to write properly modular code and produce and use libraries
- Early explanation of simple recursion to reflect its earlier introduction in beginning computer science courses
- Coverage of program correctness and type safety
- In-depth explanation of functions and pointers, because these concepts are typically stumbling blocks for the beginner
- Discussion of two-dimensional arrays reflecting C's increasing use by scientists and engineers
- Recursion treated in depth, reflecting C's increasing use by computer scientists for implementing sophisticated algorithms
- Optional C++ and Java exercises
- Bitwise operators in an appendix, improving the presentation of mainstream language features

Chapter Features

Each chapter contains the following pedagogical elements:

Dissections. Each chapter has several important example programs. Major elements of these programs are explained by the method of dissection. This step-by-step discussion of new programming ideas helps the reader encountering these ideas for the first time to understand them.

Programming Style and Methodology. Programming style and methodology is stressed throughout. Important concepts, such as structured branching statements, nested flow of control, top-down design, and structured programming, are presented early in the book. A consistent and proper coding style is adopted from the beginning with careful explanation as to its importance and rationale. The coding style used in the book is one commonly used by working programming professionals in the C community. Because C supports function prototypes and strong type checking, this style is adhered to throughout.

Working Code. Right from the start, the student is introduced to full working programs. With the executable code, the student can better understand and appreciate the programming ideas under discussion. Many programs and functions are explained through dissections. Variations on programming ideas are often presented in the exercises.

Common Programming Errors. Many typical programming bugs, along with techniques for avoiding them, are described. Much of the frustration of learning a programming language is caused by encountering obscure errors. Many books discuss correct code but leave the reader with a trial-and-error process for finding out about bugs. This book explains how typical errors in C are made and what must be done to correct them.

System Considerations. C is available on almost any computer and under most operating systems, but there are occasional differences in behavior from one system to another. This book describes such differences. Also, there are differences in behavior between ANSI C and traditional C, and these are described as well. All the programs have been tested, usually in a number of different environments. The book emphasizes writing portable system-independent code.

Moving to C++. At the end of each chapter is an optional section that describes the programming elements needed to move to C++. Exercises supporting these sections are included as well. For the most part, C is a subset of the C++ programming language, and many students first learn C before going on to C++. The text aids this natural migration. For the reader who wishes a complete mastery of C++ programming, the text is readily paired with *C++ for C Programmers, Third Edition* by Ira Pohl (Addison Wesley Longman, Inc., Reading, MA, 1999, ISBN 0-201-39519-3).

Summary. At the end of each chapter we present a succinct list of points that were covered in the chapter. This list serves as a review for the reader, reinforcing the new ideas that were presented in the chapter.

Exercises. The exercises at the end of each chapter test the student's knowledge of the language. Many exercises are intended to be done interactively while reading the text. This encourages self-paced instruction by the reader. In addition to exercising features of the language, some exercises look at a topic in more detail, and others extend the reader's knowledge to an advanced area of use.

Classroom Usage

This book can be used as a text in a one-semester course that teaches students how to program. Chapters 1 through 10 cover the C programming language through the use of arrays, pointers, and strings. A second-semester course can be devoted to more advanced data types, file processing, and software engineering, as covered in Chapters 11 through 15. In a course designed for students who already have some knowledge of programming, not necessarily in C, the instructor can cover all the topics in the text. This book can also be used as a text in other computer science courses that require the student to use C.

Interactive Environment

This book is written explicitly for an interactive environment. Experimentation via keyboard and screen is encouraged throughout. For PCs, there are many vendors that supply interactive C/C++ systems, including Borland, IBM, Metroworks, Microsoft, and Symantec.

Professional Use

While intended for the beginning programmer, *C by Dissection: The Essentials of C Programming* is a friendly introduction to the entire language for the experienced programmer as well. In conjunction with *A Book on C, Fourth Edition,* by Al Kelley and Ira Pohl (Addison Wesley Longman, Inc., Reading, MA, 1998, ISBN 0-201-18399-4), the computer professional will gain a comprehensive understanding of the language, including key points concerning its use under MS-DOS and UNIX. As a package, the two books offer an integrated treatment of the C programming language and its use that is unavailable elsewhere. Furthermore, in conjunction with *C++ for C Programmers, Third Edition,* by Ira Pohl or *Object-Oriented Programming Using C++, Second Edition,* by Ira Pohl (Addison Wesley Longman, Inc., Reading, MA, 1997, ISBN 0-201-89550-1), the student or professional is also given an integrated treatment of the object-oriented language C++.

ANSI C Standard

The acronym ANSI stands for "American National Standards Institute." This institute is involved in setting standards for many kinds of systems, including programming languages. In particular, ANSI Committee X3J11 is responsible for setting the standard for the programming language C. In the late 1980s, the committee created draft standards for what is known as "ANSI C" or "standard C." By 1990, the committee had finished its work, and the International Standardization Organization (ISO) approved the standard for ANSI C as well. Thus ANSI C, or ANSI/ISO C, is an internationally recognized standard.

The ANSI C standard specifies the form of programs written in C and establishes how these programs are to be interpreted. The purpose of the standard is to promote portability, reliability, maintainability, and efficient execution of C language programs on a variety of machines. All major C compilers follow the ANSI C standard.

Acknowledgments

Our special thanks go to John dePillis, who developed the original cartoons for this edition. Our thanks also to Debra Dolsberry, who acted as the chief technical editor for much of the material in this book. In addition, she was largely responsible for using FrameMaker to create files suitable for typesetting this book. Our special thanks also go to Robert Field, who acted as the technical editor for the first edition. He provided many useful insights on programming practice and methodology.

We would like to thank the following reviewers who commented on the suggested updates and added features found throughout this edition of the book: Dr. N. W. Campbell, University of Bristol, United Kingdom; Hubert Chen, Cornell University; Muralidharan Narayanan, Kansas State University; Dr. Lawrence (Pete) Petersen, Texas A&M University; Mike Quinn, Oregon State University; and Suba Varadaraja, Ohio State University

We would also like to thank Maite Suarez-Rivas, Senior Acquisitions Editor, for her enthusiasm, support, and encouragement; and we would like to thank Pat Mahtani, Diane Freed, and Lisa Hogue for their careful attention to the production of this book.

Al Kelley
Ira Pohl
University of California, Santa Cruz

Contents

Chapter 1

Writing an ANSI C Program

This chapter introduces the reader to the ANSI C programming world. Some general ideas on programming are discussed, and a number of elementary programs are thoroughly explained. The basic ideas presented here become the foundation for more complete explanations that occur in later chapters. An emphasis is placed on the basic input/output functions of C. Getting information into and out of a machine is the first task to be mastered in any programming language.

C uses the functions `printf()` and `scanf()` extensively for output and input, respectively. The use of both of these functions is explained. Other topics discussed in this chapter include the use of variables to store values and the use of expressions and assignments to change the value of a variable. The chapter also includes a discussion of the `while` statement. An example is presented to show how a `while` statement provides for repetitive action.

Throughout this chapter and throughout the text many examples are given. Included are many complete programs, which often are dissected. This allows the reader to see in detail how each construct works. Topics that are introduced in this chapter are seen again in later chapters, with more detailed explanation where appropriate. This spiral approach to learning emphasizes ideas and techniques essential for the C programmer.

Each chapter ends with a section called "Moving to C++." C++ is largely a superset of C. By learning C++ you are also learning the kernel language of C. A follow-on book, *C for C++ Programmers,* second edition, by Ira Pohl, teaches the rest of C++ that is not found here. Also, most chapters have exercises that are based on Java programs. Java is partly based on C. However, unlike C++, some C concepts do not work in Java or have a different meaning. Increasingly, people coming to programming in C have started from a Java background, such as that found in the companion volume, *Java by Dissection,* by Ira Pohl and Charlie McDowell. The modern programmer needs to be comfortable in all three C-based languages.

1.1 Getting Ready to Program

Programs are written to instruct machines to carry out specific tasks or to solve specific problems. A step-by-step procedure that accomplishes a desired task is called an *algorithm.* Thus programming is the activity of communicating algorithms to computers. We are all used to giving instructions to someone in English and having that person carry out the instructions. The programming process is analogous, except that machines have no tolerance for ambiguity and must have all steps specified in a precise language and in tedious detail.

The Programming Process

1 Specify the task.

2 Discover an algorithm for its solution.

3 Code the algorithm in C.

4 Test the code.

A computer is a digital electronic machine composed of three main components: processor, memory, and input/output devices. The processor is also called the *central processing unit,* or *CPU.* The processor carries out instructions that are stored in the memory. Along with the instructions, data is also stored in memory. The processor typically is instructed to manipulate the data in some desired fashion. Input/output devices take information from agents external to the machine and provide information to those agents. Input devices are typically terminal keyboards, disk drives, and tape drives. Output devices are typically terminal screens, printers, disk drives, and tape drives. The physical makeup of a machine can be quite complicated, but the user need not be concerned with the details. The operating system on a machine looks after the coordination of machine resources.

The *operating system* consists of a collection of special programs and has two main purposes. First, the operating system oversees and coordinates the resources of the machine as a whole. For example, when a file is created on a disk, the operating system takes care of the details of locating it in an appropriate place and keeping track of its name, size, and date of creation. Second, the operating system provides tools to users, many of which are useful to the C programmer. Two of these tools are of paramount importance: the text editor and the C compiler.

We assume the reader is capable of using a text editor to create and modify files containing C code. C code is also called *source code,* and a file containing source code is called a *source file.* After a file containing source code (a program) has been created, the C compiler is invoked. This process is system-dependent. (See Section 1.11, "Writing and Running a C Program," on page 27.) For example, on some systems we can invoke the compiler with the command

```
cc pgm.c
```

where *pgm.c* is the name of a file that contains a program. If there are no errors in *pgm.c*, this command produces an *executable file*—one that can be run, or executed. Although we think of this as compiling the program, what actually happens is more complicated.

In Chapter 14, "Software Tools," we discuss the compilation process in more detail. Here, we just want to mention the basics. When we compile a simple program, three separate actions occur: first the preprocessor is invoked, then the compiler, and finally the loader. The preprocessor modifies a copy of the source code by including other files and by making other changes. (In Section 1.5, "The Use of #define and #include," on page 13, we discuss the preprocessor further.) The compiler then translates this into *object code*, which the loader then uses to produce the final executable file. A file that contains object code is called an *object file*. Object files, unlike source files, usually are not read by humans. When we speak of compiling a program, we really mean invoking the preprocessor, the compiler, and the loader. For a simple program this is all done with a single command.

After the programmer writes a program, it has to be compiled and tested. If modifications are needed, the source code has to be edited again. Thus part of the programming process consists of the cycle

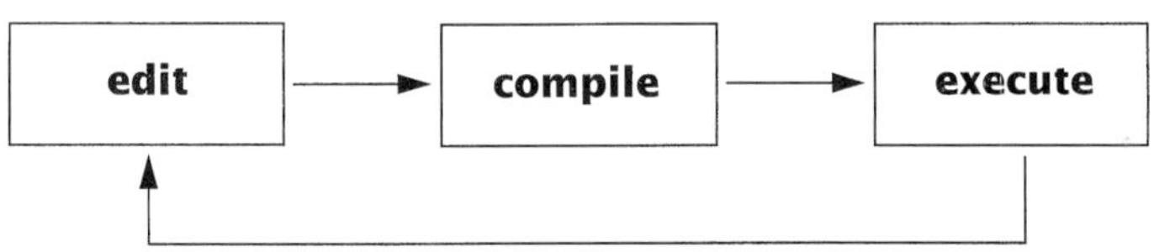

When the programmer is satisfied with the program performance, the cycle ends.

1.2 A First Program

A first task for anyone learning to program is to print on the screen. Let us begin by writing the Kernighan and Ritchie program that prints the phrase "Hello, world!" on the screen. The complete program is

```
/* The traditional first program in honor of
   Dennis Ritchie who invented C at Bell Labs in 1972  */

#include <stdio.h>

int main(void)
{
   printf("Hello, world!\n");
   return 0;
}
```

Using the text editor, the programmer types this into a file ending in *.c*. The choice of a file name should be mnemonic. Let us suppose *hello.c* is the name of the file in which the program has been written. When this program is compiled and executed, it prints on the screen

```
Hello, world!
```

The Most Popular Phrase in Computer Programming—the Rest of the Story.

Dissection of the hello Program

■
```
/* The traditional first program in honor of
   Dennis Ritchie who invented C at Bell Labs
   in 1972 */
```

These three lines are a comment. Text that is bracketed by the starting symbol pair `/*` and the ending symbol pair `*/` is ignored by the compiler. It serves as documentation for the human reader of the program.

■ `#include <stdio.h>`

Lines that begin with a `#` are called *preprocessing directives*. They communicate with the preprocessor. This `#include` directive causes the preprocessor to include a copy of the standard header file *stdio.h* at this point in the code. This header file is provided by the C system. The angle brackets around `<stdio.h>` indicate that this file is to be found in the "usual place," which is system-dependent. We have included this file because it contains information about the `printf()` function.

■ `int main(void)`

Every program has a function named `main`, where execution begins. The parentheses following `main` indicate to the compiler that it is a function. The keyword `int` declares the return type to be integer valued. The keyword `void` indicates the function takes no arguments.

■ `{`

A left brace begins the body of each function. A corresponding right brace must end the function. Our style is to place these braces on separate lines at the left margin. Braces are also used to group statements together.

■ `printf()`

The C system contains a standard library of functions that can be used in programs. This is a function from the library that prints on the screen. We included the header file *stdio.h* because it provides certain information to the compiler about the function `printf()`—namely, its function prototype. (Function prototypes are discussed in Section 4.4, "Function Prototypes," on page 131.)

■ `printf("Hello, world!\n");`

This is the function `printf()` being called, or *invoked*, with a single argument—namely, the string

```
"Hello, world!\n"
```

A string constant in C is a series of characters surrounded by double quotes. This string is an argument to the function `printf()`, which controls what is to be printed. The two characters \n at the end of the string (read "backslash n") represent a single character called *newline*. It is a nonprinting character and its effect is to advance the cursor on the screen to the beginning of the next line. Notice that this line ends with a semicolon. All declarations and statements in C end with a semicolon.

■ `return 0;`

The integer value zero is returned by `main()` to the operating system. Zero means the program completed successfully. Nonzero values are used to tell the operating system that `main()` has been unsuccessful.

■ `}`

This right brace matches the left brace above and ends the function `main()`.

The function `printf()` acts to continuously print across the screen. It moves to a new line when a newline character is read. The screen is a two-dimensional display that prints from left to right and top to bottom. To be readable, output must appear properly spaced on the screen.

Let us rewrite our program to make use of two `printf()` statements. Although the program looks different, its output is the same.

```
#include <stdio.h>

int main(void)
{
   printf("Hello, ");
   printf("world!\n");
   return 0;
}
```

Notice that the string used as an argument to the first `printf()` statement ends with a blank character. If the blank were not there, the words `Hello world!` would have no space between them in the output.

As a final variation to this program, let us add the phrase "Hello, universe!" and print the statements on two lines.

```
#include <stdio.h>

int main(void)
{
   printf("Hello, world!\n");
   printf("Hello, universe!\n");
   return 0;
}
```

When we execute this program, the following appears on the screen:

```
Hello, world!
Hello, universe!
```

Notice that the two `printf()` statements in the body of `main()` could be replaced by the single statement

```
printf("Hello, world!\nHello, universe!\n");
```

The availability of useful functions like `printf()` in the standard library is a powerful feature of C. Although technically the standard library is not part of the C language, it is part of the C system. Because the functions in the standard library are available wherever a C system is found, programmers routinely use them.

1.3 Variables, Expressions, and Assignments

Our first program illustrated the use of `printf()` for output. In our next program we want to illustrate the use of variables to manipulate integer values. Variables are used to store values. Because different kinds of variables are used to store different kinds of data, the type of each variable must be specified. To illustrate our ideas, we write a program based on the wreck of the ship *Hesperus*. This calamity at sea, which was made famous in a poem by Henry Wadsworth Longfellow, occurred off the reef of Norman's Woe near Gloucester, Massachusetts, in 1839. The waters off the reef are about 7 fathoms deep. In the program we convert this depth to other units of measure. Here is the algorithm that our program uses.

Algorithm for the *Hesperus*

1 Assign the number of fathoms to a variable.

2 Convert fathoms to feet and store in a variable.

3 Convert feet to inches and store in a variable.

4 Print the different units of measure neatly on the screen.

In writing the C code, we have to choose an appropriate set of variables. In this case integer variables are a natural choice. We have to make sure that our conversion expressions use the right constants and output must be convenient to read.

```
#include <stdio.h>

int main(void)
{
   int   inches, feet, fathoms;

   fathoms = 7;
   feet = 6 * fathoms;
   inches = 12 * feet;
   printf("Wreck of the Hesperus:\n");
   printf("Its depth at sea in different units:\n");
   printf("   %d fathoms\n", fathoms);
   printf("   %d feet\n", feet);
   printf("   %d inches\n", inches);
   return 0;
}
```

When we compile this program and run it, here is what appears on the screen:

```
Wreck of the Hesperus:
Its depth at sea in different units:
   7 fathoms
   42 feet
   504 inches
```

Dissection of the depth Program

- `#include <stdio.h>`

In any program that uses `printf()`, we include the standard header file *stdio.h*. We will see later why the compiler wants this file.

- ```
  int main(void)
  {
     int   inches, feet, fathoms;
  ```

The first line within the body of the function `main()` is a declaration. The variables `inches`, `feet`, and `fathoms` are declared to be of type `int`, one of the fundamental types in C. A variable of type `int` can take on integer values. All variables in a program must be declared before they can be used. Declarations, as well as statements, end with a semicolon.
  ```

■
```
fathoms = 7;
```

This is an assignment statement. The equal sign = is the basic assignment operator in C. The value of the expression on the right side of the = symbol is assigned to the variable on the left side. Here, the constant expression on the right side is 7. That value is assigned to the variable `fathoms`.

■
```
feet = 6 * fathoms;
inches = 12 * feet;
```

These are assignment statements. Because 1 fathom is equal to 6 feet, to convert a given number of fathoms to an equivalent number of feet, we must multiply by 6. The asterisk symbol * is the multiplication operator. The value of the expression `6 * fathoms` is assigned to the variable `feet`. Because the current value of the variable `fathoms` is 7, the expression `6 * fathoms` has the value 42, and this value is assigned to `feet`. To convert feet to inches, we must multiply by 12. The value of the expression `12 * feet` is assigned to the variable `inches`.

■
```
printf("   %d fathoms\n", fathoms);
```

This `printf()` statement has two arguments:

`"   %d fathoms\n"` and `fathoms`

Note that they are separated by a comma. The first argument in a `printf()` function is always a string, called the *control string*. In this example the control string contains the conversion specification `%d`. A conversion specification is also called a *format*. The format `%d` causes the value of the expression in the second argument, in this case the variable `fathoms`, to be printed in the format of a decimal integer. Ordinary characters in a control string—that is, characters not comprising a format—are simply printed on the screen. Notice that the control string in this example begins with three blank spaces, causing the line being printed to be indented. The remaining `printf()` statements in the program are similar to this one.

In C, all variables must be declared before they are used in expressions and statements. The general form of a simple program is

```
preprocessing directives

int main(void)
{
    declarations

    statements
}
```

At the top of the file we might have preprocessing directives such as `#include` lines. In the body of `main()`, the declarations must come before the statements. The declarations tell the compiler what kind of data can be stored in each of the variables. This enables the compiler to set aside the appropriate amount of memory to hold the data. We have already seen the use of integer data. Shortly, we discuss character data and floating data. The statements in the program carry out the desired computations and display information on the screen.

A variable name, also called an *identifier*, consists of a sequence of letters, digits, and underscores, but it may not begin with a digit. Identifiers should be chosen to reflect their use in the program. In this way they serve as documentation, making the program more readable. After variables have been declared, they can be assigned values and used in expressions.

Certain keywords, also called *reserved words*, cannot be used by the programmer as names of variables. Examples of keywords are `char`, `int`, and `float`. In Chapter 2, "Lexical Elements, Operators, and the C System," we present a table of all the keywords. Other names are known to the C system and normally would not be redefined by the programmer. The name `printf` is an example. Because it is the name of a function in the standard library, it usually isn't used as the name of a variable.

Expressions typically are found on the right side of assignment operators and as arguments to functions. The simplest expressions are just constants, such as 6 and `12`, which were both used in the previous program. The name of a variable alone can be considered an expression, and meaningful combinations of operators with variables and constants are also expressions.

Among the many operators in C are the binary arithmetic operators,

```
+    -    *    /    %
```

used for addition, subtraction, multiplication, division, and modulus, respectively. These are called *binary* operators because they act on two operands, as in the expression

```
a + b
```

Here, the operator + is acting on the two operands `a` and `b`. An expression such as this has a value that depends on the values of `a` and `b`. For example, if `a` has value 1 and `b` has value 2, the expression `a + b` has value 3.

In C, an integer expression divided by another integer expression yields an integer value. Any fractional part is discarded. Thus 1/2 has value 0, 7/2 has value 3, 18/4 has value 4, and 29/5 has value 5. Division by zero is not allowed. If a and b are int variables and one (or both) of them is negative, the value of a/b is system-dependent (see exercise 5 on page 35).

Most beginning programmers are not familiar with the modulus operator %. As we shall see, it has many uses in programming. The expression a%b yields the remainder after a is divided by b. For example, because 5 divided by 3 is 1 with a remainder of 2, the expression 5%3 has value 2. In a similar fashion, 7%4 has value 3, 12%6 has value 0, 19%5 has value 4, and 33%7 has value 5. In the expression a%b the value of b cannot be zero, because this would lead to division by zero. The modulus operator can act only on integer expressions, whereas all the other arithmetic operators can act on both integer and floating expressions. As with the division operator, if either operand of the modulus operator is negative, the value of the operation is system-dependent (see exercise 5 on page 35).

The keyword char stands for "character." Variables and constants of type char are used to manipulate characters. Constants of type char are written within single quotes, as in 'A' and '1' and '+'. Here is a simple example.

```
#include <stdio.h>

int main(void)
{
   char   c;

   c = 'A';
   printf("%c\n", c);       /* the letter A is printed */
   return 0;
}
```

The output of this program is the letter A followed by a newline character. First the variable c is declared to be of type char. Then c is assigned the value 'A'. Finally, the printf() statement causes printing to occur. Notice that the control string in the argument list for printf() contains the format %c. This causes the variable c in the second argument to be printed in the format of a character.

In ANSI C, there are three floating types: float, double, and long double. They are used to manipulate real numbers, also called *floating* numbers or *floating-point* numbers. Floating constants such as 1.069, 0.003, and 7.0 are all of type double, not float. We express this idea by saying that double is the *working floating type* in C. A constant of type float is created by adding an F suffix, as in 1.069F. Similarly, a constant of type long double is created by adding an L suffix, as in -7.0L. Note carefully that the floating constant 7.0 and int constant 7 are different. Although their conceptual values are the same, their types are different, causing them to be stored differently in a machine. The technical details concerning float and double are discussed in Chapter 6, "The Fundamental Data Types."

Let us next give a simple illustration of the use of floating-point constants and variables in a program.

```
#include <stdio.h>

int main(void)
{
   float   x, y;

   x = 1.0;
   y = 2.0;
   printf("The sum of x and y is %f.\n", x + y);
   return 0;
}
```

The output of this program is

```
The sum of x and y is 3.000000.
```

First the variables `x` and `y` are declared to be of type `float`. Then `x` and `y` are assigned the floating values `1.0` and `2.0`, respectively. It is no problem that these constants are of type `double` and the variables are of type `float`. Floating types can be freely mixed in expressions and assignments. The control string in the first argument to `printf()` contains the format `%f`. This causes the value of the expression `x + y` in the second argument to be printed in the format of a floating number with six digits to the right of the decimal point.

The division of floating values works as expected. For example, the floating expression `7.0/2.0` has 3.5 for its value. In contrast, the `int` expression `7/2` has the value 3 because, with integer division, any remainder is discarded. In a floating expression, division by zero is either disallowed or results in a value that is not a number (see exercise 11 on page 37).

The modulus operator % works with integer expressions only. If `x` and `y` are variables of type `float` or `double`, an expression such as `x % y` is not allowed.

Typically, an assignment statement is composed of a variable on the left side followed by an equal sign = followed by an expression on the right side. The expression can be simple or complicated and can contain function calls. Constants and ordinary expressions are not allowed on the left side of an =. We can write

```
a = b + c;
```

but not

```
a + b = c;   /*assignment to this expression not allowed*/
2 = c;       /*assignment to constant is not allowed*/
```

1.4 Initialization

When variables are declared, they may also be initialized. For example, consider the declarations

```
char   c = 'A';
int    i = 1;
```

The variable `c` is declared to be of type `char`, and its value is initialized to `'A'`. The variable `i` is declared to be of type `int`, and its value is initialized to `1`. As another example of initialization, the *depth* program can be rewritten as follows:

```
#include <stdio.h>

int main(void)
{
   int   inches, feet, fathoms = 7;

   feet = 6 * fathoms;
   .....
```

Whether a variable is initialized depends on its intended use in a program. Typically, constants or constant expressions are used to initialize a variable. We could have written

```
int   inches, feet, fathoms = 3 + 4;
```

but not

```
int   inches, feet = 6 * fathoms, fathoms = 7;
```

The variable `fathoms` cannot be used before it has been declared; the C language does not have look-ahead capability. In exercise 6 on page 35, we point out a situation where it makes sense to use a constant expression as an initializer.

1.5 The Use of #define and #include

When the C compiler is invoked, the preprocessor does its work first. Just before compilation takes place, the preprocessor modifies the source code being passed to the compiler. For example, files may be included, and specified character strings in the source code may be changed into other specified strings. The lines in a program that give commands to the preprocessor are called *preprocessing directives*, and they begin with a pound sign, #. A common programming style is to write the # at the left margin.

We have already used the preprocessing directive

```
#include <stdio.h>
```

This scheme supports the use of standard libraries that are portable across systems. Such code is reusable and easily maintained.

With a preprocessing directive of the form

```
#include <filename>
```

the preprocessor looks for the file only in standard places. In UNIX systems, the standard header files such as *stdio.h*, *math.h*, *string.h*, and *stdlib.h* are typically found in */usr/include*. In general, where the standard header files are stored is system-dependent.

Another form of the `#include` facility is given by

```
#include "filename"
```

This causes the preprocessor to replace the line with a copy of the contents of the named file. A search for the file is made first in the current directory and then in other system-dependent places. There is no restriction on what an include file can contain. In particular, it can contain other preprocessing directives that are, in turn, expanded by the preprocessor.

Some examples of `#define` directives:

```
#define   LIMIT   100
#define   PI      3.14159
```

If these preprocessing directives occur at the top of a file that is being compiled, the preprocessor first changes all occurrences of the identifier `LIMIT` to `100` and all occurrences of the identifier `PI` to `3.14159`. Whatever is in a string constant remains unchanged. Thus the preprocessor changes

```
printf("PI = %f\n", PI);    to    printf("PI = %f", 3.14159);
```

Because the identifier `PI` is replaced everywhere by `3.14159`, it is called a *symbolic constant.*

The use of symbolic constants in a program makes it more readable. More importantly, if a constant has been defined symbolically by the `#define` facility and then used throughout a program, it can easily be changed later, if necessary. For example, if we write

```
#define   LIMIT   100
```

then use LIMIT throughout thousands of lines of code to symbolically represent the constant 100, it is easy to change the code later. If we want to redefine the symbolic constant LIMIT from 100 to 10000, all we have to do is to change the preprocessing directive to

```
#define   LIMIT   10000
```

This automatically updates all the code; to update the executable file produced by the program, we have to recompile it.

A #define line can occur anywhere in a program. It affects only those lines in the file that come after it. Normally, all #define directives are placed at the beginning of the file, just after any #include directives. By convention, identifiers that are to be changed by the preprocessor are written in capital letters.

We illustrate the use of a symbolic constant in the next section in the program that computes area.

1.6 The Use of printf() and scanf()

The function printf() is used for printing formatted output. Similarly, the function scanf() is used for reading formatted input. These functions are in the standard library and are available for use wherever a C system resides. Both printf() and scanf() are passed a list of arguments that can be thought of as

control_string and *other_arguments*

where *control_string* is a string that may contain conversion specifications, or formats. A conversion specification begins with a % character and ends with a conversion character. For example, in the format %d, the letter d is the conversion character.

The Use of printf()

As we have already seen, the format %d is used to print the value of an expression as a decimal integer. In a similar fashion, %c is used to print the value of an expression as a character, %f is used to print the value of a floating expression, and %s is used to print a string. The formats in a control string are used to determine how the other arguments are to be printed. Formats that are appropriate for the arguments should be used. Consider

```
printf("Get set: %s %d %f %c%c\n",
       "one", 2, 3.33, 'G', 'O');
```

The arguments to `printf()` are separated by commas. In this example there are six arguments:

```
"Get set: %s %d %f %c%c\n"    "one"    2    3.33    'G'    'O'
```

The first argument is the control string. The formats in the control string are matched with the other arguments. In this example the `%s` corresponds to `"one"`, the `%d` corresponds to `2`, the `%f` corresponds to `3.33`, the first `%c` corresponds to `'G'`, and the second `%c` corresponds to `'O'`. Each format in a control string specifies how the value of its corresponding argument is to be printed. When executed, the above `printf()` statement causes

```
Get set: one 2 3.330000 GO
```

to be printed. Sometimes it is convenient to write a long `printf()` statement on more than one line. Here is an example that illustrates how we can do this:

```
printf("%s%s\n",
   "This statement will print ",
   "just one very long line of text on the screen.");
```

The following table describes how the conversion characters in formats affect their corresponding arguments.

printf() conversion characters	
Conversion character	**How the corresponding argument is printed**
c	as a character
d	as a decimal integer
e	as a floating-point number in scientific notation
f	as a floating-point number
g	in the e-format or f-format, whichever is shorter
s	as a string

When an argument is printed, the *place* where it is printed is called its *field* and the number of characters in its field is called its *field width.* The field width can be specified in a format as an integer occurring between the % and the conversion character. Thus the statement

```
printf("%c%3c%7c\n", 'A', 'B', 'C');
```

prints

```
A  B      C
```

First the A is printed. Then the B is printed in a field of three characters; because the B requires only one space, the other two spaces are blanks. Then the C is printed in a field of seven characters; because the C requires only one space, the other six spaces are blanks.

For floating values, we can control the *precision*, as well as the field width. The precision is the number of decimal digits printed to the right of the decimal point. In a format of the form %*m.n*f, the field width is specified by *m*, and the precision is specified by *n*. With a format of the form %*m*f, only the field width is specified. With a format of the form %.*n*f, only the precision is specified. The following statements illustrate these ideas:

```
printf("Some numbers: %.1f %.2f %.3f\n", 1.0, 2.0, 3.0);
printf("More numbers:%7.1f%7.2f%7.3f\n", 4.0, 5.0, 6.0);
```

Here is the output:

```
Some numbers: 1.0 2.00 3.000
More numbers:     4.0    5.00   6.000
```

To understand the output, you have to count the spaces carefully. The printf() function allows the programmer to print neatly on the screen. Nonetheless, getting printout to look right can be very tedious.

The Use of scanf()

The function scanf() is analogous to the function printf() but is used for input rather than output. Its first argument is a control string with formats that correspond to the various ways the characters in the input stream are to be interpreted. After the control string, the other arguments are *addresses*. The address of a variable is the place in memory where that variable is stored. (Addresses and pointers are explained in detail in Chapter 8, "Functions, Pointers, and Storage Classes.") The symbol & represents the *address operator*. In the example

```
scanf("%d", &x);
```

the format %d causes input characters typed at the keyboard to be interpreted as a decimal integer, and causes the value of the decimal integer to be stored at the address of x.

When the keyboard is used to input values into a program, a sequence of characters is typed, and a sequence of characters is received by the program. This sequence is called the *input stream*. If "123" is typed, the person typing it may think of it as a decimal integer, but the program receives it as a sequence of characters. The scanf() function can be used to convert strings of decimal digits, such as 123, into integer values and store them in the appropriate place.

The following table describes the effects of the conversion characters in formats used with the function scanf().

scanf() conversion	
Conversion character	**How characters in the input stream are converted**
c	character
d	decimal integer
f	floating-point number (float)
lf	floating-point number (double)
Lf	floating-point number (long double)
s	string

Caution: With printf(), the %f format is used to print either a float or a double. With scanf(), the %f format is used to read in a float, and %lf is used to read in a double. (We will you again about this later in Section 1.10, "Common Programming Errors," on page 26.)

Let us write a program in which the user is prompted to input her initials followed by her age. We use the scanf() function to read the input characters typed on the keyboard, to convert them to appropriate values, and to store the values at specified addresses.

```
#include <stdio.h>

int main(void)
{
   char   first, middle, last;
   int    age;

   printf("Input your three initials and your age:  ");
   scanf("%c%c%c%d", &first, &middle, &last, &age);
   printf("\nGreetings %c.%c.%c.  %s %d.\n",
      first, middle, last,
      "Next year your age will be", age + 1);
   return 0;
}
```

Notice carefully that the arguments passed to scanf() are

```
"%c%c%c%d"     &first     &middle     &last     &age
```

The first argument is the control string. Each format in the control string corresponds to one of the remaining arguments. More explicitly, the first format is a %c, and it corresponds to &first, which is the first argument following the control string; the second format is a %c, and it corresponds to &middle, which is the second argument following the control string; and so forth. After the control string, all the arguments passed to scanf() must be addresses. The address operator & applied to a variable yields its address.

Suppose we execute the preceding program and input CBD and 19 when prompted. Here is what appears on the screen:

```
Input your three initials and your age:  CBD  19 Greetings
C.B.D.  Next year your age will be 20.
```

When reading in numbers, scanf() skips white space (blanks, newlines, and tabs), but when reading in a character, white space is *not* skipped. Thus the program does not run correctly with the input CB D. Instead, the third character is read in as a blank, a perfectly good character, and then scanf() attempts to interpret the character D as a decimal integer, causing the program to misbehave.

The preceding program is not robust. After all, if the user is asked to type in initials, the program should accept white space between them. This can easily be done in C with the help of string variables, a topic that we cover in Chapter 10, "Strings and Pointers."

In our next program we use a #define preprocessing directive to define a symbolic constant. Then we use scanf() to read in a value from the keyboard and printf() to print on the screen. In this program we are particularly concerned with the %lf and %f formats.

```
#include <stdio.h>
#define   PI   3.141592653589793

int main(void)
{
   double   radius;

   printf("\n%s\n\n%s",
      "This program computes the area of a circle.",
      "Input the radius:  ");
   scanf("%lf", &radius);
   printf("\n%s\n%s%.2f%s%.2f%s%.2f\n%s%.5f\n\n",
      "Area = PI * radius * radius",
      "     = ", PI, " * ", radius, " * ", radius,
      "     = ", PI * radius * radius);
   return 0;
}
```

Suppose we execute this program and input `2.333` when prompted. Then the following appears on the screen:

```
This program computes the area of a circle.
Input the radius:  2.333
Area = PI * radius * radius
     = 3.14 * 2.33 * 2.33
     = 17.09934
```

A manual calculation shows that $3.14 \times 2.33 \times 2.33$ equals 17.046746, which does not agree with the result printed by our program. The reason for this is that `PI` and `radius` are printed with only two digits to the right of the decimal point, whereas their values in memory have more precision.

Note carefully that we used a `%lf` format in the control string that reads in a `double` in the call to `scanf()`. If we change the type of the variable `radius` from `double` to `float`, we must change the `%lf` to `%f`; no change would be necessary in the control string used in the call to `printf()`. The `lf` in the format `%lf` stands for "long float." In traditional C, the type `long float` was synonymous with `double`. In ANSI C, the type `long float` does not exist although some implementations still accept it.

Another difference between `printf()` and `scanf()` concerns the `int` value returned by each of these functions. When `printf()` is called, the number of characters printed is returned, whereas when `scanf()` is called, the number of successful conversions is returned. In Section 1.8, "Problem Solving: Computing Sums," on page 23, we illustrate a typical use of the value returned by `scanf()`. Although programmers rarely use the value returned by `printf()`, it certainly is easy to do so (see exercise 18 on page 39).

For complete details concerning `printf()`, `scanf()`, and related functions, see Chapter 13, "Input/Output and Files."

1.7 The `while` Statement

Statements in a program are normally executed one after another. This is called *sequential flow of control.* C provides the `while` statement to perform a repetitive action instead of a sequential flow of control.

Counting, adding, searching, sorting, and other tasks often involve doing something over and over. In this section we illustrate how a `while` statement can be used to perform a repetitive action. In so doing, we also reiterate many of the other ideas already presented in this chapter.

The following program uses a `while` statement to add the consecutive integers from 1 to 10. In the dissection that follows, we explain how the `while` statement works.

```
#include <stdio.h>

int main(void)
{
   int   i = 1, sum = 0;

   while (i <= 10) {
      sum = sum + i;
      i = i + 1;
   }
   printf("Sum = %d\n", sum);
   return 0;
}
```

Dissection of the add_ten Program

- ```
  int   i = 1, sum = 0;
  ```

The variables `i` and `sum` are declared to be of type `int` and are initialized to `1` and `0`, respectively.

- ```
  while (i <= 10) {
     sum = sum + i;
     i = i + 1;
  }
  ```

This whole construct is a `while` statement, or `while` loop. First the expression `i <= 10` is evaluated. One reads this as "`i` is less than or equal to `10`." Because the current value of `i` is 1, the expression is *true*, causing execution of the statements between the braces `{` and `}`. The variable `sum` is assigned the old value of `sum` plus the value of `i`. Because the old value of `sum` is 0 and `i` is 1, `sum` is assigned the value 1. The variable `i` is assigned the old value of `i` plus 1. Because the old value of `i` is 1, `i` is assigned the value 2. We have now gone through the loop once. Now the program reevaluates the expression `i <= 10`. Because `i` has the value 2, the expression is still *true*, causing execution of the loop again. At the end of the second time through the loop, the value of `sum` is 1 + 2, and `i` is 3. Because `i <= 10` is still *true*, the loop is executed again. At the end of the third time through, the value of `sum` is 1 + 2 + 3, and the value of `i` is 4. This process continues until `i` has the value 11, when expression `i <= 10` is *false*. When this happens, the body of the loop is skipped, and the next statement after the `while` statement is executed.

- ```
  printf("Sum = %d\n", sum);
  ```

This `printf()` statement causes `Sum = 55` to be printed.
  ```

A `while` loop has the general form

`while` (*expression*)
  statement

where *statement* can be a single statement or a group of statements enclosed between the braces { and }. A group of statements enclosed in braces is called a *compound statement.* In C, a compound statement can go anywhere that a statement can go.

1.8 Problem Solving: Computing Sums

Programming is problem solving with the help of a computer. Many problems require the use of a particular problem-solving pattern, or technique, to arrive at their solution. In the following program we use *iteration* to solve our problem. Iteration is repeated action. Computers are champion iterators, readily performing tens of millions of repetitions quickly and rapidly.

We want to write a program that repeatedly adds numbers that are typed in by the user. Here is our algorithm to accomplish this.

Algorithm for Computing Sum

1 Initialize the two variables `cnt` and `sum`.

2 Prompt the user for input.

3 Repeatedly read in data, increment `cnt`, and add to `sum`.

4 Finally, print the values of `cnt` and `sum`.

The `while` statement is one of three kinds of constructs provided in C to perform iterative actions. In our solution, we use the value returned by `scanf()` to control the action of a `while` statement. This allows the user of the program to type in an arbitrary amount of data. In the dissection that follows, we explain the mechanisms in detail.

```
/* Sums are computed. */
#include <stdio.h>

int main(void)
{
   int     cnt = 0;
   float   sum = 0.0, x;

   printf("The sum of your numbers will be computed\n\n");
   printf("Input some numbers:  ");
   while (scanf("%f", &x) == 1) {
      cnt = cnt + 1;
      sum = sum + x;
   }
   printf("\n%s%5d\n%s%12f\n\n","Count:", cnt,"  Sum:", sum);
   return 0;
}
```

Dissection of the find_sum Program

■ `scanf("%f", &x) == 1`

The symbols == represent the equal operator. An expression such as `a == b` tests to see whether the value of `a` is equal to the value of `b`. If it is, then the expression is *true*; if not, the expression is *false*. For example, `1 == 1` is *true*, and `2 == 3` is false. The `scanf()` function is being used to read in characters typed by the user, to convert those characters to a value of type `float`, and to place the value at the address of `x`. If `scanf()` is successful in doing this, one successful conversion has been made, and the value 1 is returned by the function. If, for some reason, the conversion process fails, the value 0 is returned; if no more data is available, the value -1 is returned.

Thus the expression

```
scanf("%f", &x) == 1
```

tests to see whether `scanf()` succeeded in its task. If it did, the expression is *true*; otherwise, it is *false*.

■
```
while (scanf("%f", &x) == 1) {
   cnt = cnt + 1;
   sum = sum + x;
}
```

We can think of this as

```
while (scanf() succeeds in making a conversion) {
    .....
```

As long as the expression `scanf("%f", &x) == 1` is *true*, the body of the `while` loop is executed repeatedly. Each time through the loop, `scanf()` reads in characters, converts them to a number, and places the value of the number at the address of `x`. Then `cnt` is assigned the old value of `cnt` plus 1, and `sum` is assigned the old value of `sum` plus `x`. Thus `cnt` keeps a count of the numbers entered so far, and `sum` keeps a running total of those numbers. When does the process stop? Either of two things can happen. First, the user may type in something that cannot be converted to a `float`. Suppose, for example, a letter is typed instead of a digit. Then `scanf()`, failing to make a successful conversion, returns the value 0, which in turn causes the expression

```
scanf("%f", &x) == 1
```

to be *false*. The process also stops if the user indicates to the program that all the data has been entered. To do this, the user must type an end-of-file signal; this signal is system-dependent. In UNIX, a carriage return followed by a control-d is the typical way to effect an end-of-file signal. In MS-DOS, a control-z must be typed instead.

■ `printf("\n%s%5d\n%s%12f\n\n","Count:", cnt,"  Sum:", sum);`

Suppose this program is executed and the numbers

```
1.1  2.02  3.003  4.0004  5.00005
```

are entered, followed by a newline and an end-of-file signal. Here is what appears on the screen:

```
The sum of your numbers will be computed

Input some numbers:  1.1  2.02  3.003  4.0004  5.00005

Count:    5
  Sum:   15.123449
```

If you carefully count spaces, you will see that the value of `cnt` has been printed in a field of five characters and that `sum` has been printed in a field of 12 characters. This was caused by the `%5d` and `%12f` formats. Notice that the digits printed for the sum are wrong beyond the third decimal place (see exercise 17 on page 38).

1.9 Style

A good coding style is essential to the art of programming. It facilitates the reading, writing, and maintenance of programs. A good style uses white space and comments so that the code is easier to read and understand, and is visually attractive. The proper use of indentation is crucial, as it indicates to the reader the intended flow of control. For example, in the construct

```
while (expression)
    statement
```

the indentation of *statement* indicates that its execution is under the control of the `while` loop. Another important stylistic point is to choose names for variables that convey their use in the program to further aid understanding. A good style avoids error-prone coding habits.

In this text we are following the Bell Labs industrial programming style. In column 1 we place all `#include`s, `#define`s, `main()`s, and braces `{` and `}` that begin and end the body of `main()`.

```
#include <stdio.h>
#include <stdlib.h>

#define   GO   "Let's get started."

int main(void)
{
   .....
}
```

The declarations and statements in the body of `main()` are indented three spaces. This visually highlights the beginning and end of the function body. There is one blank line following the `#include`s, one following the `#define`s, and one between the declarations and statements in the body of `main()`.

An indentation of two, three, four, five, or eight spaces is common. We use three spaces. Whatever is chosen as an indentation should be used consistently. To heighten readability, we put a blank space on each side of the binary operators. Some programmers do not bother with this, but it is part of the Bell Labs style.

There is no single agreed upon "good style." As we proceed through this text, we often point out alternate styles. Once you choose a style, you should use it consistently. Good habits reinforce good programming. *Caution:* Beginning programmers sometimes think they should dream up their own distinctive coding style. This should be avoided. The preferred strategy is to choose a style that is already in common use.

1.10 Common Programming Errors

When you first start programming, you make many frustrating simple errors. One such error is to leave off a closing double quote character to mark the end of a string. When the compiler sees the first ", it starts collecting all the characters that follow as a string. If the closing " is not present, the string continues to the next line, causing the compiler to complain. Error messages vary from one compiler to another. Here is one possibility:

```
Unterminated string or character constant
```

Another common error is to misspell a variable name or forget to declare it. Compilers readily catch this kind of error and properly inform you of what is wrong. However, if you misspell the name of a function, such as `prinf()` instead of `printf()`, the compiler informs you that the function cannot be found. If you do not notice that the error message refers to `prinf` instead of `printf`, you may be quite mystified (see exercise 4 on page 34).

Even elementary errors, such as forgetting to place a semicolon at the end of a statement or leaving off a closing brace, can result in rather mystifying error messages from compilers. As you become more experienced, some of the error messages produced by your compiler will begin to make sense. Exercise 4 on page 34, suggests some programming errors you may want to introduce on purpose in order to experiment with the error message capability of your compiler.

Both `printf()` and `scanf()` use a control string that can contain conversion specifications, or formats. The `%f` format is used with `printf()` to print either a `float` or a `double`. But with `scanf()`, a `%f` is used to read in a `float`, and a `%lf` is used to read in a `double`. It is a common programming error to forget to use `%lf` when using `scanf()` to read in a `double`. Most compilers cannot catch this error, so your program runs but produces incorrect results.

Another common programming error is to forget that a format in a `printf()` statement of the form `%`*m.n*`f` uses *m* to specify the field width. For example, to specify two decimal digits to the left of the decimal point and three to the right, do *not* use `%2.3f`. Instead, use `%6.3` to account for all the digits plus the decimal point itself.

Perhaps the most common error of all when using `scanf()` is to omit the address operator &. If you write

```
scanf("%d%d", a, b);        instead of        scanf("%d%d", &a, &b);
```

your compiler probably does not catch the error. Instead, you are more likely to get a run-time error that is difficult to debug.

1.11 System Considerations

In this section we discuss a number of topics that are system-dependent. We begin with the mechanics of writing and running a C program.

Writing and Running a C Program

The precise steps you have to follow to create a file containing C code and to compile and execute it depend on three things: the operating system, the text editor, and the compiler. However, in all cases the general procedure is the same. We first describe in some detail how it is done in a UNIX environment. Then we discuss how it is done in an MS-DOS environment.

In the discussion that follows we use the *cc* command to invoke the C compiler. In reality, however, the command depends on the compiler that is being used. For example, if we were using the command line version of the Borland C compiler, we would use the command *bcc* instead of *cc*. (For a list of C compilers, see the table in Section 14.3, "The C Compiler," on page 475.)

Steps for Writing and Running a C Program

1 Using an editor, create a text file—say *pgm.c*—that contains a C program. The name of the file must end with *.c*, indicating that the file contains C source code. For example, to use the *vi* editor on a UNIX system, we would give the command

```
vi pgm.c
```

To use an editor, the programmer must know the appropriate commands for inserting and modifying text.

2 Compile the program. This can be done with the command

```
cc pgm.c
```

The *cc* command invokes the preprocessor, the compiler, and the loader in turn. The preprocessor modifies a copy of the source code according to the preprocessing directives and produces what is called a *translation unit.* The compiler translates the translation unit into object code. If there are errors, the programmer must start again at step 1, editing the source file. Errors that occur at this stage are called *syntax errors* or *compile-time errors.* If there are no errors, the loader uses the object code produced by the compiler, along with object code obtained from various libraries provided by the system, to create the executable file *a.out.* The program is now ready to be executed.

3 Execute the program. This is done with the command

```
a.out
```

Typically, the program completes execution, and a system prompt reappears on the screen. Any errors that occur during execution are called *run-time* errors. If, for some reason, the program needs to be changed, the programmer must start again at step 1.

If we compile a different program, the file *a.out* is overwritten and its contents lost. If the contents of the executable file *a.out* are to be saved, the file must be moved or renamed. Suppose we give the command

```
cc hello.c
```

This causes executable code to be written automatically into *a.out.* To save this file, we can give the command

```
mv a.out hello
```

This moves *a.out* to *hello.* Now the program can be executed with the command

```
hello
```

In UNIX, it is common practice to give the executable file the same name as the corresponding source file, except to drop the *.c* suffix. If we wish, we can use the *-o* option to direct the output of the *cc* command. For example, the command

```
cc -o hello hello.c
```

causes the executable output from *cc* to be written directly into *hello*, leaving intact whatever is in *a.out.*

Different kinds of errors can occur in a program. Syntax errors are caught by the compiler, whereas run-time errors manifest themselves only during program execution. For example, if an attempt to divide by zero is encoded into a program, a run-time error may occur when the program is executed (see exercises 10 and 11 on page 37). An error message produced by a run-time error is not very helpful for finding the trouble.

Let us now consider the MS-DOS environment. Here, some other text editor would most likely be used. Some C systems, such as Borland C, have both a command line environment and an integrated environment. The integrated environment includes both the text editor and the compiler. In MS-DOS, the executable output produced by a C compiler is usually written to a file that has the same name as the source file, but with the extension *.exe* instead of *.c*. Suppose, for example, we are using the command line environment in Borland C. If we give the command

bcc hello.c

then the executable code is written to *hello.exe*. To execute the program, we give the command

hello.exe

or, equivalently,

hello

To invoke the program, we do not need to type the *.exe* extension. If we wish to rename this file, we can use the *rename* command.

Interrupting a Program

The user may want to interrupt, or kill, a program that is running. For example, the program may be in an infinite loop. (In an interactive environment it is not necessarily wrong to use an infinite loop in a program.) Throughout this text we assume that the user knows how to interrupt a program. In MS-DOS and in UNIX, a control-c is commonly used to effect an interrupt. On some systems a special key, such as *delete* or *rubout*, is used. Make sure you know how to interrupt a program on your system.

Typing an End-of-File Signal

When a program is taking its input from the keyboard, it may be necessary to type an end-of-file signal for the program to work properly. In UNIX, this is done by typing a carriage return followed by a control-d. In MS-DOS, a control-z is typed instead (see exercise 19 on page 39).

Redirection of the Input and the Output

Many operating systems, including MS-DOS and UNIX, can redirect the input and output. To understand how this works, first consider the UNIX command

ls

This command causes a list of files and directories to be written to the screen. (The comparable command in MS-DOS is *dir*.) Now consider the command

ls > temp

The symbol > causes the operating system to redirect the output of the command to the file *temp*. (In MS-DOS, the file name needs an extension.) What was written to the screen before is now written to the file *temp*.

Our next program is called *dbl_out*. It can be used with redirection of both the input and the output. The program reads characters from the standard input file, which is normally connected to the keyboard, and writes each character twice to the standard output file, which is normally connected to the screen.

```
#include <stdio.h>

int main(void)
{
   char   c;

   while (scanf("%c", &c) == 1) {
      printf("%c", c);
      printf("%c", c);
   }
   return 0;
}
```

If we compile the program and put the executable code in the file *dbl_out*, then, using redirection, we can invoke this program in any of four ways:

dbl_out
dbl_out < infile
dbl_out > utfile
dbl_out < infile > outfile

Used in this context, the symbols < and > can be thought of as arrows (see exercise 19 on page 39).

Some commands are not meant to be used with redirection. For example, the *ls* command does not read characters from the keyboard. Therefore, it makes no sense to redirect the input to the *ls* command; because it does not take keyboard input, there is nothing to redirect.

1.12 Moving to C++

Most C programs run without change on a C++ compiler. So, by learning C, you are already learning C++. This section introduces C++ style I/O. Whereas *stdio.h* is used in the C++ community, the C++ I/O library is *iostream.h*.

```
/* hello program in C++, using iostream IO.
    Note the use of endl to create a newline.
*/

#include <iostream.h>
   int main(void) {

   cout << "Hello, world!" << endl;
   return 0;         //This is optional
}
```

The identifier `cout` represents the screen. The insertion operator << is used to place the string literal "`Hello, world!`" into the output stream. The I/O manipulator `endl` acts to flush the output and moves to a new line. In C++ programs it is appropriate to omit `return 0` because it is implicitly inserted in the program.

The next program computes the greatest common divisor of two integers. The integers are input from the keyboard.

```
/* Greatest common divisor program.*/

#include  <iostream.h>

int main(void)
{
   int  m, n, r;

   cout << "\nPROGRAM Gcd C++";
   cout << "\nEnter two integers: ";
   cin >> m >> n;
   cout << "\nGCD(" << m << ", " << n << ") = " ;
   while (n != 0) {
      r = m % n;
      m = n;
      n = r;
   }
   cout << m << endl;
}
```

The identifier `cin` is the standard input stream normally associated with keyboard input. The first typed-in value is converted to an integer value placed in the variable `m`. The second typed-in value is placed in `n`. Notice how this input expression is intuitive and simpler than a corresponding use of `scanf()`. A key feature of this library is that formats are unnecessary. Input and output using *iostream.h* is type-safe.

Summary

- An algorithm is a computational procedure consisting of elementary steps. Programming is the art of communicating algorithms to computers.

- A simple program consists of preprocessing directives and the function `main()`. The body of the function is made up of declarations and statements written between the braces { and }. All variables must be declared. The declarations must occur before the statements.

- The simplest expressions consist of just a constant, a variable, or a function call. In general, expressions consist of combinations of operators and other expressions. Most expressions have values. The assignment operator = is used to assign the value of an expression to a variable.

- When a variable is declared, it may also be initialized. Typically, constants or constant expressions are used as initializers.

- When source code is compiled, the preprocessor does its work first. Lines that begin with a # are called *preprocessing directives*. The programmer uses preprocessing directives to give commands to the preprocessor. Typically, the `#include` and `#define` directives are placed at the top of the file. A `#define` directive affects only the lines in the file that occur after it.

- A preprocessing directive of the form

  `#define` *identifier* *replacement_string*

  causes the preprocessor to change every occurrence of *identifier* to *replacement_string* before compilation takes place.

- In traditional C, the # that begins a preprocessing directive must begin in column 1. In ANSI C, the # can be preceded by blanks and tabs.

- The `printf()` function in the standard library is used for output. The arguments to this function consist of a control string followed by other arguments. The control string consists of ordinary text intermixed with conversion specifications, or formats. The ordinary text is simply printed, whereas a format causes the value of an associated argument to be printed according to the instructions embodied in the format. A format begins with a % and ends with a conversion character.

- The `scanf()` function in the standard library is used for input. It is analogous to `printf()`. Both functions take a variable number of arguments, the first one being a control string. For `printf()`, the other arguments are expressions and for `scanf()`, they are addresses. The expression &v has as its value the address of v.

- Statements are ordinarily executed sequentially. The special flow-of-control statements, such as a `while` statement, can alter the sequential execution of a program.

Exercises

1 Write on the screen the words

```
she sells sea shells by the seashore
```

(a) all on one line, (b) on seven lines, and (c) inside a box.

2 Here is part of a program that begins by having the user input three integers:

```
#include <stdio.h>

int main(void)
{
   int   a, b, c, sum;

   printf("Input three integers:  ");
   .....
```

Complete the program so that when the user executes it and types in 2, 3, and 7, this is what appears on the screen:

```
Input three integers:  2  3  7
Twice the sum of your integers plus 7 is 31  ---  bye!
```

3 The following program writes a large letter *I* on the screen:

```
#include <stdio.h>

#define   HEIGHT   17

int main(void)
{
   int   i = 0;

   printf("\n\nIIIIIII\n");
   while (i < HEIGHT) {
      printf("  III\n");
      i = i + 1;
   }
   printf("IIIIIII\n\n\n");
   return 0;
}
```

Execute this program so you understand its effect. Write a similar program that prints a large letter *C* on the screen.

4 The purpose of this exercise is to help you become familiar with some of the error messages produced by your compiler. You can expect some error messages to be helpful and others to be less so. First check to see that the following program compiles with no error messages:

```
#include <stdio.h>

int main(void)
{
   int   a = 1, b = 2, c = 3;

   prinf("Some output:  %d %d %d\n", a, b, c, c)
   return 0;
}
```

Now introduce each of the following programming errors in turn, compile the program, and record the error messages generated:

Change the first comma in the declaration to a semicolon.
Change `printf` to `prinf`.
Remove the second " in the control string.
Replace the list a, b, c by a, b, c, c.
Remove the semicolon at the end of the `printf()` statement.
Remove the closing brace.

5 In this exercise we want to investigate how the operators / and % work with negative integer operands. If a and b are of type `int` and either a or b is negative, the value of a/b is system-dependent. For example, 7/-2 has value -3 on some machines and -4 on others. Also, the sign of a%b is system-dependent, but on all ANSI C systems it is guaranteed that

`(a / b) * b + a % b` has the value `a`

What happens on your system? Write an interactive program that contains the following code:

```
int   a, b;

printf("Input two nonzero integers:  ");
scanf("%d%d", &a, &b);
printf("%s%4d\n%s%4d\n%s%4d\n%s%4d\n%s%4d\n",
   "          a =", a,
   "          b =", b,
   "      a / b =", a / b,
   "      a % b =", a % b,
   "ANSI check =", (a / b) * b  +  a % b  -  a);
```

6 Write an interactive program that asks the user to input the length and width of a rectangular lawn. The dimensions should be in yards. Your program should compute the area of the lawn in square yards, square feet, and square inches (and in square meters, too, if you are ambitious). Print all the information neatly on the screen. Use the following declaration:

```
int   cv_factor = 36 * 36; /*conversion:sq in per yrd */
```

An equivalent declaration is

```
int   cv_factor = 1296;   /* conversion: sq in per yrd */
```

but because most people know that there are 36 inches in a yard, the first declaration is preferable. One can tell at a glance that the right conversion factor is being used. *Caution:* If your lawn is large and you are working on a small machine, you may not get the right number of square inches, even though you wrote a correct program. There are limitations on the size of an integer that can be stored in an `int` (see Chapter 6, "The Fundamental Data Types").

7 Here is part of an interactive program that computes the value of some coins. The user is asked to input the number of half dollars, quarters, dimes, and so on.

```
#include <stdio.h>

int main(void)
{
   int   h,         /* number of half dollars */
         q,         /* number of quarters     */
         d,         /* number of dimes        */
         n,         /* number of nickels      */
         p;         /* number of pennies      */
   .....

   printf("Value of your change will be computed.\n\n");
   printf("How many half dollars do you have?  ");
   scanf("%d", &h);
   printf("How quarters do you have?  ");
   scanf("%d", &q);
   .....
```

Complete the program, causing it to print out relevant information. For example, you may want to create output that looks like this:

```
You entered:     0 half dollars
                 3 quarters
                 2 dimes
                17 nickels
                 1 pennies
The value of your 23 coins is equivalent to 181 pennies.
```

Notice that `pennies` is plural, not singular as it should be. After you learn about the `if-else` statement in Chapter 3, "Flow of Control," you can modify your program so that its output is grammatically correct.

8 Modify the program that you wrote in the previous exercise so that the last line of the output looks like this:

```
The value of your 23 coins is $1.81
```

Hint: Declare `value` to be a variable of type `float`, and use the format `%.2f` in your `printf()` statement.

9 The function `scanf()` returns the number of successful conversions as an `int`. Consider the statement

```
printf("%d\n", scanf("%d%d%d", &a, &b, &c));
```

When this statement is executed, an integer is printed. What are the possible values for the integer? Explain. *Hint:* Write a test program and execute it using redirection. If you do not use redirection, input and output can be intermixed on the screen and cause confusion. When `scanf()` receives an end-of-file signal, the value -1 is returned.

10 The purpose of this exercise is to find out what happens on your system when a run-time error occurs. Try the following code:

```
int   a = 1, b = 0;
printf("Division by zero: %d\n", a / b);
```

On a UNIX system you might get a *core dump.* That is, the system might create a file named *core* that contains information about the state of your program just before it ended abnormally. This file is not meant to be read by humans. A debugger can use the core dump to give you information about what your program was doing when it aborted. (Do not leave core dumps lying around. Because they are rather large, they eat up valuable disk space.)

11 On some systems, dividing by a floating zero does not result in a run-time error. On other systems it does. Try the following code:

```
double   x = 1.0, y = -1.0, z = 0.0;
printf("Division by zero:  %f  %f\n", x / z, y / z);
```

What happens on your system? If `Inf` or `NaN` gets printed, you can think of the value as "infinity" or "not a number."

12 Except for a `printf()` statement, the following program is complete. It uses integer division and the modulus operator to convert seconds to minutes and seconds.

```
/* Convert seconds to minutes and seconds. */

#include <stdio.h>

int main(void)
{
   int   input_value, minutes, seconds;

   printf("Input the number of seconds:  ");
   scanf("%d", &input_value);
   minutes = input_value / 60;
   seconds = input_value % 60;
   printf(.....);
   return 0;
}
```

Complete the program by writing an appropriate `printf()` statement. For example, if 123 is entered after the prompt, the program might print the line

```
123 seconds is equivalent to 2 minutes and 3 seconds
```

13 Modify the program that you completed in the previous exercise so that seconds are converted to hours, minutes, and seconds. For example, if 7384 is entered after the prompt, your program might print the line

```
7384 seconds is equivalent to 2 hours, 3 minutes and 4
seconds
```

14 Repetitive action is essential to most programs. Therefore, a programmer must know precisely how a `while` loop works. Study the following code in detail, writing down what you think will be printed. Then write a test program to check your answer.

```
int   i = 1, sum = 0;

while (i < 10) {
   sum = sum + i;
   i = i + 1;
   printf("sum = %d   i = %d\n", sum, i);
}
```

15 Do two variations of the program you wrote in the previous exercise. For the first variation, the line

```
sum = sum + i;
```

should be replaced by

```
sum = sum + 2 + i;
```

For the second variation, the line should be replaced by

```
sum = (sum / 3) + (i * i);
```

16 How is an end-of-file signal entered at the keyboard on your system? Experiment with the *find_sum* program to see that the program terminates when an inappropriate character or an end-of-file signal is typed. What happens when the program is executed and no numbers are entered?

17 Unlike integer arithmetic, floating arithmetic need not be exact. Very small errors can occur in computations with floating data. Moreover, the errors are system-dependent. Often this is of no concern to the user. With the data that we used as input for the *find_sum* program, the sum had an error in the sixth

decimal place. Modify the program so that the variable `sum` is a `double` instead of a `float`. Because a `double` usually (but not always; see Chapter 6, "The Fundamental Data Types") represents real numbers more accurately than a `float` does, the result may be more accurate with the same input. Check to see if this is the case on your machine.

18 In ANSI C, the `printf()` function returns the number of characters printed as an `int`. To see how this works, write a small program containing the following lines:

```
int   cnt;
cnt = printf("abc\n");
printf("%d\n", cnt);
```

What integer is printed? Replace the string `"abc\n"` by the following string:

```
"\tMontana!\n\n\tIt really is big sky country!\n\n"
```

Now what integer is printed? Write down your answer, then run your program to verify it. *Hint:* Do not forget that newlines and tabs are counted too.

19 As with many new ideas, you can best understand redirection by experimenting with it. Write the program *dbl_out* that we presented in the section "Redirection of the Input and the Output," on page 30, in a file named *dbl_out.c*. After you have compiled and executed the program so that you understand its effects, try the following commands:

```
dbl_out < dbl_out.c
dbl_out < dbl_out.c > temp
```

The following command is of special interest:

```
dbl_out > temp
```

This command causes characters that are typed in at the keyboard to be written to the file *temp*, provided you type an end-of-file signal when you are finished. What happens if instead of typing an end-of-file signal, you type a control-c to kill the program?

20 In this exercise we want to use the *dbl_out* program used in the prior exercise. First give the command

```
dbl_out
```

then type in abc followed by a carriage return. What is printed on the screen depends on how your operating system is configured. Normally, the operating system waits for a complete line to be typed in before processing the characters. If this is the case, you can see aabbcc printed on the next line on the screen. If UNIX is available to you, give the command

stty cbreak

Now the operating system reads each character as it is typed. Try the command *dbl_out* again, and type in abc followed by a carriage return. What appears on the screen? Explain. *Hint:* Characters typed on the keyboard are normally echoed on the screen. You may want to experiment further by giving the command

stty -echo

which turns off the echoing. When you are finished with this exercise, you should give the command

stty -cbreak echo

to return the operating system to its normal state. *Caution:* With echoing turned off, you cannot see what you are doing!

21 C++: Recode the *Hesperus* program in Section 1.3, "Variables, Expressions, and Assignments," on page 8, to use cout.

22 C++: Write a general program that takes as an input the depth in fathoms and converts it to feet and inches.

23 C++: Improve the previous program by writing it as a loop that continues to take various inputs until a negative number is entered.

24 C++: Write a program that illustrates the type-safety of C++ I/O. Code a program that inputs and outputs both integers and doubles. Then see what happens when you input a value such as 2.99 to an integer variable and to a double variable. Output both variables. What is printed?

Chapter 2

Lexical Elements, Operators, and the C System

In this chapter we explain the lexical elements of the C programming language. C is a language. Like other languages, it has an alphabet and rules for putting together words and punctuation to make correct, or legal, programs. These rules are the *syntax* of the language. The program that checks on the legality of C code is called the *compiler.* If there are errors, the compiler prints error messages and stops. If there are no errors, then the source code is legal and the compiler translates it into object code, which in turn is used by the loader to produce an executable file.

When the compiler is invoked, the preprocessor does its work first. For that reason we can think of the preprocessor as being built into the compiler. On some systems this is actually the case, whereas on others the preprocessor is separate. This is of no concern to us in this chapter. We have to be aware, however, that we can get error messages from the preprocessor as well as from the compiler (see exercise 24 on page 74). Throughout this chapter, we use the term *compiler* in the sense that, conceptually, the preprocessor is built into the compiler.

A C program is a sequence of characters that is converted by a C compiler to object code, which in turn is converted to a target language on a particular machine. On most systems the target language is a form of machine language that can be run or interpreted. For this to happen, the program must be syntactically correct. The compiler first collects the characters of the program into *tokens,* which can be thought of as the basic vocabulary of the language.

In ANSI C, there are six kinds of tokens: keywords, identifiers, constants, string constants, operators, and punctuators. The compiler checks that the tokens can be formed into legal strings according to the syntax of the language. Most compilers are very precise in their requirements. Unlike human readers of English, who are able to understand the meaning of a sentence with an extra punctuation mark or a misspelled word, a C compiler fails to provide a translation of a syntactically incorrect program, no matter how trivial the error. Hence the programmer must learn to be precise in writing code.

The programmer should strive to write code that is understandable by other programmers as well. A key part in doing this is producing well-commented code with meaningful identifier names. In this chapter we illustrate these concepts.

" HMMM. THE COMPUTER CAN'T DIRECTLY PROCESS MY C PROGRAM. I'LL HAVE TO COMPILE MY PROGRAM FIRST. COMPILING WILL CREATE TOKENS FROM MY C CODE, THEN TRANSLATE THOSE TOKENS INTO TARGET CODE FOR MY PARTICULAR PROCESSOR."

2.1 Characters and Lexical Elements

A C program is first constructed by the programmer as a sequence of characters; these are shown in the following table.

Characters that can be used in a program	
lowercase letters	a b c ..... z
uppercase letters	A B C ..... Z
digits	0 1 2 3 4 5 6 7 8 9
other characters	+ - * / = ( ) { } [ ] < > ' " !
	@ # $ % & _ | ^ ~ \ . , ; : ?
white space characters	*blank*, *newline*, *tab*, etc.

These characters are collected by the compiler into syntactic units called *tokens.* Let us look at a simple program and informally pick out some of its tokens before we go on to a strict definition of C syntax.

```
/* Read in two scores and print their sum. */

#include <stdio.h>

int main(void)
{
   int   score_1, score_2, sum;

   printf("Input two scores as integers:  ");
   scanf("%d%d", &score_1, &score_2);
   sum = score_1 + score_2;
   printf("%d + %d = %d\n", score_1, score_2, sum);
   return 0;
}
```

Lexical Dissection of the sum Program

- ```
  /* Read in two scores and print their sum. */
  ```

Comments are delimited by /* and */. The compiler first replaces each comment with a single blank. Thereafter, the compiler either disregards white space or uses it to separate tokens.

- ```
  #include <stdio.h>
  ```

This is a preprocessing directive that causes the standard header file *stdio.h* to be included. We have included it because it contains the function prototypes for `printf()` and `scanf()`. A function prototype is a kind of declaration. The compiler needs function prototypes to do its work.

- ```
  int main(void)
  {
     int   score_1, score_2, sum;
  ```

The compiler groups these characters into four kinds of tokens. The function name `main` is an identifier, and the parentheses `()` immediately following `main` are an operator. They tell the compiler that `main` is a function. The characters , { and ; are punctuators; `int` is a keyword; `score_1`, `score_2`, and `sum` are identifiers.
  ```

The compiler uses the white space between int and score_1 to distinguish the two tokens. We cannot write

```
intscore_1, score_2, sum; /*wrong: white space necessary */
```

On the other hand, the white space following a comma is superfluous. We could have written

```
int   score_1,score_2,sum;
```

but not

```
int   score_1score_2sum;
```

The compiler would consider score_1score_2sum an identifier.

■
```
printf("Input two scores as integers:  ");
scanf("%d%d", &score_1, &score_2);
```

The names printf and scanf are identifiers, and the parentheses following them tell the compiler that they are functions. After the compiler has translated the C code, the loader attempts to create an executable file. If the code for printf() and scanf() has not been supplied by the programmer, it is taken from the standard library. A programmer normally would not redefine these identifiers. A series of characters enclosed in double quotes is a string constant, as in

```
"Input two scores as integers:  "
```

The compiler treats this as a single token and provides space in memory to store the string. The character & in &score_1 and &score_2 is the address operator. The compiler treats it as a token. Even though the characters & and a are adjacent to each other, the compiler treats each as a separate token. We could have written

```
&  score_1  ,  &  score_2      or      &score_1,&score_2
```

but not

```
&score_1 &score_2        /* the comma is missing */
score_1&, &score_2       /* & requires operand on the right
*/
```

The comma is a punctuator.

■ `sum = score_1 + score_2;`

The characters = and + are operators. White space here is ignored, so we could have written

```
sum=score_1+score_2;
```

or

```
sum    =    score_1    +    score_2 ;
```

but not

```
s    u    m  =  score_1  +  score_2;
```

If we had done so, each letter on this line would have been treated by the compiler as a separate identifier. Because not all of these identifiers have been declared, the compiler would complain. Even if they were declared, the expression `s u` isn't legal.

The compiler either ignores white space or uses it to separate elements of the language. The programmer uses white space to provide more legible code. To the compiler, program text is implicitly a single stream of characters, but to the human reader it is a two-dimensional tableau.

2.2 Comments

Comments are arbitrary strings of symbols placed between the delimiters /* and */. Comments are not tokens. The compiler changes each comment into a single blank character. Thus comments are not part of the executable program. We have already seen examples such as

```
/* a comment */      /*** another comment ***/       /*****/
```

Another example is

```
/*
 *   A comment can be written in this fashion
 *   to set it off from the surrounding code.
 */
```

The following illustrates one style that gives prominence to comments:

```
/*****************************
*   If you wish, you can    *
*   put comments in a box.  *
*****************************/
```

Comments are used by the programmer as a documentation aid. The aim of documentation is to explain clearly how the program works and how it is to be used. Sometimes a comment contains an informal argument demonstrating the correctness of the program.

Comments should be written simultaneously with program text. Some programmers insert comments as a last step, but there are two problems with this. The first is that once the program is running, the tendency is either to omit or abbreviate the comments. The second is that ideally the comments should serve as running commentary, indicating program structure and contributing to program clarity and correctness. They cannot do this if they are inserted after the coding is finished.

2.3 Keywords

Keywords are explicitly reserved words that have a strict meaning as individual tokens in C. They cannot be redefined or used in other contexts.

Keywords				
auto	do	goto	signed	unsigned
break	double	if	sizeof	void
case	else	int	static	volatile
char	enum	long	struct	while
const	extern	register	switch	
continue	float	return	typedef	
default	for	short	union	

Some implementations may have additional keywords. These vary from one implementation, or system, to another.

As an example, here are some of the additional keywords in Borland C.

Additional keywords for Borland C						
asm	cdecl	far	huge	interrupt	near	pascal

Compared to other major languages, C has only a small number of keywords. Ada, for example, has 63 keywords. It is a characteristic of C that it does a lot with relatively few special symbols and keywords.

2.4 Identifiers

An identifier is a token that is composed of a sequence of letters, digits, and the special character _ which is called an *underscore.* A letter or underscore must be the first character of an identifier. In most implementations of C the lower- and uppercase letters are treated as distinct. It is good programming practice to choose identifiers that have mnemonic significance so that they contribute to the readability and documentation of the program. Some examples of identifiers are

```
k
_id
iamanidentifier2
so_am_i
```

but not

```
not#me          /* special character # not allowed */
101_south       /* must not start with a digit */
-plus           /* do not mistake - for _ */
```

Identifiers are created to give unique names to various objects in a program. Keywords can be thought of as identifiers that are reserved to have special meaning in the C language. Identifiers such as `scanf` and `printf` are already known to the C system as input/output functions in the standard library. These names normally would not be redefined. The identifier `main` is special, in that C programs always begin execution at the function called `main`.

One major difference among operating systems and C compilers is the length of discriminated identifiers. On some older systems, an identifier with more than eight characters is accepted, but only the first eight characters are used. The remaining characters are simply disregarded. On such a system, for example, the variable names

`i_am_an_identifier`   and   `i_am_an_elephant`

are considered the same.

In ANSI C, at least the first 31 characters of an identifier are discriminated. Many C systems discriminate more (see Section 2.15, "System Considerations," on page 67).

Good programming style requires the programmer to choose names that are meaningful. If you were to write a program to figure out various taxes, you might have identifiers such as `tax_rate`, `price`, and `tax`, so that the statement

```
tax = price * tax_rate;
```

would have an obvious meaning. The underscore is used to create a single identifier from what would normally be a string of words separated by spaces. Meaningfulness and avoiding confusion go hand in hand with readability to constitute the main guidelines for a good programming style.

Caution: Identifiers that begin with an underscore can conflict with system names. Only systems programmers should use such identifiers. As an example, consider the identifier `_iob`, which is often defined as the name of an array of structures in *stdio.h.* If a programmer tries to use `_iob` for some other purpose, the compiler may complain, or the program may misbehave. Applications programmers are best advised to use identifiers that do not begin with an underscore. Furthermore, using two consecutive underscores in any position in an identifier is restricted to system use.

2.5 Constants

As we have seen in some simple introductory programs, C manipulates various kinds of values. Whole numbers like `0` and `17` are examples of integer constants, and fractional numbers like `1.0` and `3.14159` are examples of floating constants. Like most languages, C treats integer and floating constants differently. In Chapter 6, "The Fundamental Data Types," we discuss in detail how C understands numbers. Also, there are character constants such as `'a'`, `'b'`, and `'+'`. Character constants are written between single quotes, and, as we shall see in Chapter 6, "The Fundamental Data Types," they are closely related to integers. Some character constants are of a special kind, such as the newline character, written `'\n'`. The backslash is the escape character, and we think of `\n` as "escaping the usual meaning of `n`." Even though `\n` is written with the two characters `\` and `n`, it represents a single character called *newline.*

In addition to the constants that we have already discussed, there are enumeration constants in C. We discuss these along with the keyword `enum` in Chapter 7, "Enumeration Types and `typedef`." Integer constants, floating constants, character constants, and enumeration constants are all collected by the compiler as tokens. Because of implementation limits, constants that are syntactically expressible may not be available on a particular machine. For example, an integer may be too large to be stored in a machine word.

Decimal integers are finite strings of decimal digits. Because C provides octal and hexadecimal integers as well as decimal integers, we have to be careful to distinguish between the different kinds of integers. For example, `17` is a decimal integer constant, `017` is an octal integer constant, and `0x17` is a hexadecimal integer constant. (See Chapter 6, "The Fundamental Data Types," for further discussion.) Also, negative constant integers like `-33` are considered constant expressions. Some examples of constant decimal integers are

```
0
77
123456789000            /* too large for the machine? */
```

but not

```
0123                    /* an octal integer */
-49                     /* a constant expression */
123.0                   /* a floating constant */
```

Although we have used integer constants such as 144 and floating constants such as 39.7, their meaning in terms of type, along with details concerning memory requirements and machine accuracy, is complicated enough to require a thorough discussion. We do this in Chapter 6, "The Fundamental Data Types."

2.6 String Constants

A sequence of characters enclosed in a pair of double quote marks, such as "abc", is a string constant, or a string literal. It is collected by the compiler as a single token. In Chapter 10, "Strings and Pointers," we see that string constants are stored by the compiler as arrays of characters. String constants are always treated differently from character constants. For example, "a" and 'a' are not the same.

Note that a double quote mark " is just one character, not two. If the character " itself is to occur in a string constant, it must be preceded by a backslash character \. If the character \ is to occur in a string constant, it too must be preceded by a backslash. Some examples of string constants are

```
"a string of text"
""                              /* the null string */
"     "                         /* a string of blank characters */
"   a = b + c;    "             /* nothing is executed */
"   /* this is not a comment */    "
"a string with double quotes \" within"
"a single backslash \\ is in this string"
```

but not

```
/* "this is not a string" */
"and
neither is this"
```

Character sequences that would have meaning if outside a string constant are just a sequence of characters when surrounded by double quotes. In the previous examples, one string contains what appears to be the statement `a = b + c;` but because it occurs inside double quotes, it is explicitly this sequence of characters.

Two string constants that are separated only by white space are concatenated by the compiler into a single string. Thus

`"abc" "def"` is equivalent to `"abcdef"`

String constants are treated by the compiler as tokens. As with other constants, the compiler provides the space in memory to store string constants. We emphasize this point again in Chapter 10, "Strings and Pointers."

2.7 Operators and Punctuators

In C, there are many special characters with particular meanings. Examples include the arithmetic operators

```
+     -     *     /     %
```

which stand for the usual arithmetic operations of addition, subtraction, multiplication, division, and modulus, respectively. Recall that in mathematics the value of *a* modulus *b* is obtained by taking the remainder after dividing *a* by *b*. Thus, for example, 5%3 has the value 2, and 7%2 has the value 1. (For a discussion of % with negative operands, see Chapter 1, "Writing an ANSI C Program," and particularly exercise 5 on page 35.) In a program, operators can be used to separate identifiers. Although typically we put white space around binary operators to heighten readability, this is not required.

```
a+b           /* this is the expression a plus b */
a_b           /* this is a 3-character identifier */
```

Some symbols have meanings that depend on context. For example, consider the % symbol in the two statements

`printf("%d", a);` and `a = b % 7;`

The first % symbol is the start of a conversion specification, or format, whereas the second % symbol represents the modulus operator.

Examples of punctuators include parentheses, braces, commas, and semicolons. Consider the following code:

```
int main(void)
{
   int   a, b = 2, c = 3;
   a = 17 * (b + c);
   .....
```

The parentheses immediately following `main` are treated as an operator. They tell the compiler that `main` is the name of a function. After this, the symbols `{ , ; (` and `)` are punctuators. Operators and punctuators are collected by the compiler as tokens, and along with white space, they serve to separate language elements.

Some special characters are used in many contexts, and the context itself can determine which use is intended. For example, parentheses are sometimes used to indicate a function name; at other times they are used as punctuators. Another example is given by the expressions

```
a + b          ++a          a += b
```

All of these expressions use + as a character, but ++ is a single operator, as is +=. Having the meaning of a symbol depend on context makes for a small symbol set and a terse language.

2.8 Precedence and Associativity of Operators

Operators have rules of *precedence* and *associativity* that determine precisely how expressions are evaluated. Because expressions inside parentheses are evaluated first, parentheses can be used to clarify or change the order in which operations are performed. Consider the expression

```
1 + 2 * 3
```

In C, the operator * has higher precedence than +, causing the multiplication to be performed first, followed by the addition. Hence the value of the expression is 7. An equivalent expression is

```
1 + (2 * 3)
```

On the other hand, because expressions inside parentheses are evaluated first, the expression

```
(1 + 2) * 3
```

is different; its value is 9. Now consider the expressions

`1 + 2 - 3 + 4 - 5` is equivalent to `(((1 + 2) - 3) + 4) - 5`

Because the binary operators + and - have the same precedence, the associativity rule "left to right" is used to determine how it is evaluated. This means the operations are performed from left to right. Thus they are equivalent expressions.

"ASHLEY, I DON'T CARE WHAT THE MANUAL SAYS. I THINK THERE ARE SOME OPERATORS THAT JUST SHOULD NOT ASSOCIATE WITH EACH OTHER."

The following table gives the rules of precedence and associativity for some of the operators of C. In addition to the operators we have already seen, the table includes operators that are discussed later in this chapter.

Operator precedence and associativity	
Operator	**Associativity**
() ++ (*postfix*) -- (*postfix*)	left to right
+ (*unary*) - (*unary*) ++ (*prefix*) -- (*prefix*)	right to left
* / %	left to right
+ -	left to right
= += -= *= /= *etc.*	right to left

All the operators on a given line, such as *, /, and %, have equal precedence with respect to one another, but have higher precedence than all the operators that occur on the lines below them. The associativity rule for all the operators on a given line appears on the right side of the table.

Whenever we introduce new operators, we give their rules of precedence and associativity, and often we encapsulate the information by augmenting this table. These rules are essential information for every C programmer.

In addition to the binary plus, which represents addition, there is a unary plus; both are represented by a plus sign. The same is true for the minus sign. The unary plus was introduced with ANSI C; there is no unary plus in traditional C, only unary minus.

From the preceding table we see that the unary operators have higher precedence than binary plus and minus. In the expression

```
- a * b - c
```

the first minus sign is unary, and the second binary. Using the rules of precedence, we see that

```
((- a) * b) - c
```

is an equivalent expression.

2.9 Increment and Decrement Operators

The increment operator ++ and decrement operator -- are unary operators with the same precedence as the unary plus and minus, and they associate from right to left. Both ++ and -- can be applied to variables but not to constants or ordinary expressions. Moreover, the operators can occur in either prefix or postfix position, with different results. Some examples are

```
++i
cnt--
```

but not

```
777++           /* constants cannot be incremented */
++(a * b - 1)   /* cannot increment ordinary expressions */
```

Each of the expressions `++i` and `i++` has a value; moreover, each causes the stored value of `i` in memory to be incremented by 1. The expression `++i` causes the stored value of `i` to be incremented first, with the expression then taking as its value the new stored value of `i`. In contrast, the expression `i++` has as its value the current value of `i`; then the stored value of `i` is incremented. The following code illustrates the situation:

```
int   a, b, c = 0;
a = ++c;
b = c++;
printf("%d %d %d\n", a, b, ++c);      /* 1 1 3 is printed */
```

In a similar fashion, `--i` causes the stored value of `i` in memory to be decremented by 1 first, with the expression then taking this new stored value as its value; with `i--`, the value of the expression is the current value of `i`, and then the stored value of `i` in memory is decremented by 1.

Note carefully that ++ and -- cause the value of a variable in memory to be changed. The operator +, on the other hand, does not do this. An expression such as `a + b` has a value that, when evaluated, leaves the values of the variables `a` and `b` unchanged. These ideas are expressed by saying that the operators ++ and -- have a *side effect*; not only do these operators yield a value, but they also change the stored value of a variable in memory (see exercise 20 on page 73).

In some cases we can use ++ in either prefix or postfix position with the same result. For example, each of the statements

```
++i;     and     i++;
```

is equivalent to

```
i = i + 1;
```

In simple situations, one can consider ++ and -- as operators that provide concise notation for incrementing and decrementing a variable. In other situations, careful attention must be paid as to whether prefix or postfix position is desired. Prefix operators are the preferred style, as they are less prone to misuse.

Declarations and initializations		
`int   a = 1, b = 2, c = 3, d = 4;`		
Expression	**Equivalent expression**	**Value**
`a * b / c`	`(a * b) / c`	0
`a * b % c + 1`	`((a * b) % c) + 1`	3
`++ a * b - c --`	`((++ a) * b) - (c --)`	1
`7 - - b * ++ d`	`7 - ((- b) * (++ d))`	17

2.10 Assignment Operators

To change the value of a variable, we have already used assignment statements such as

```
a = b + c;
```

Unlike other languages, C treats = as an operator. Its precedence is lower than all the operators we have discussed so far, and its associativity is right to left. In this section we explain in detail the significance of this.

To understand = as an operator, let us first consider + for the sake of comparison. The binary operator + takes two operands, as in the expression `a + b`. The value of the expression is the sum of the values of `a` and `b`. By comparison, a simple assignment expression is of the form

variable = *right_side*

where *right_side* is itself an expression. Notice that a semicolon placed at the end would have made this an assignment statement. The assignment operator = has the two operands *variable* and *right_side*. The value of *right_side* is assigned to *variable*, and that becomes the value of the assignment expression as a whole. To illustrate this, consider the statements

```
b = 2;
c = 3;
a = b + c;
```

where the variables are all of type `int`. By making use of assignment expressions, we can condense this to

```
a = (b = 2) + (c = 3);
```

The assignment expression `b = 2` assigns the value 2 to the variable `b`, and the assignment expression itself takes on this value. Similarly, the assignment expression `c = 3` assigns the value 3 to the variable `c`, and the assignment expression itself takes on this value. Finally, the values of the two assignment expressions are added, and the resulting value is assigned to `a`.

Although this example is artificial, there are many situations in which assignment occurs naturally as part of an expression. A frequently occurring situation is multiple assignment. Consider the statement

```
a = b = c = 0;
```

Because the operator = associates from right to left, an equivalent statement is

```
a = (b = (c = 0));
```

First `c` is assigned the value 0, and the expression `c = 0` has value 0. Then `b` is assigned the value 0, and the expression `b = (c = 0)` has value 0. Finally, `a` is assigned the value 0, and the expression `a = (b = (c = 0))` has value 0. Many languages do not use assignment in such an elaborate way. C is different in this respect.

In addition to =, there are other assignment operators, such as += and -=. An expression such as

```
k = k + 2
```

adds 2 to the old value of `k` and assign the result to `k`, and the expression as a whole has that value. The same task is accomplished by the expression

```
k += 2
```

The following table contains all the assignment operators.

Assignment operators						
=	+=	-=	*=	/		
=	%=	>>=	<<=	&=	^=	|=

All these operators have the same precedence, and they all have right-to-left associativity. The semantics is specified by

variable *op*= *expression*

which is equivalent to

variable = *variable* *op* (*expression*)

with the exception that if *variable* is itself an expression, it is evaluated only once. When dealing with arrays, this is an important technical point (see exercise 15 on page 333). Note carefully that an assignment expression such as

`j *= k + 3` is equivalent to `j = j * (k + 3)`

rather than

```
j = j * k + 3
```

The following table illustrates how assignment expressions are evaluated.

Declarations and initializations			
`int    i = 1, j = 2, k = 3, m = 4;`			
Expression	**Equivalent expression**	**Equivalent expression**	**Value**
`i += j + k`	`i += (j + k)`	`i = (i + (j + k))`	6
`j *= k = m + 5`	`j *= (k = (m + 5))`	`j = (j * (k = (m + 5)))`	18

Even though assignment statements sometimes resemble mathematical equations, the two notions are distinct and should not be confused. The mathematical equation

$$x + 2 = 0$$

does not become an assignment statement when you type

```
x + 2 = 0;        /* wrong */
```

The left side of the equal sign is an expression, not a variable, and this expression may not be assigned a value. Now consider the assignment statement

```
x = x + 1;
```

The current value of x is assigned the old value of x plus 1. If the old value of x is 2, the value of x after execution of the statement is 3. Observe that as a mathematical equation,

$$x = x + 1$$

is meaningless; after subtracting x from both sides of the equation, we obtain

$$0 = 1$$

Although they look alike, the assignment operator in C and the equal sign in mathematics are not comparable.

2.11 An Example: Computing Powers of 2

To illustrate some of the ideas presented in this chapter, we write a program that prints on a line some powers of 2. Here is the program:

```
/* Some powers of 2 are printed. */

#include <stdio.h>

int main(void)
{
   int   exponent = 0, power_of_two = 1;

   while (++exponent <= 10)
      printf("%5d", power_of_two *= 2);
   printf("\n");
   return 0;
}
```

The output of the program is

```
    2    4    8   16   32   64  128  256  512 1024
```

Dissection of the pow_of_2 Program

■ /* Some powers of 2 are printed. */

Programs often begin with a comment that explains the intent or the use of the program. If the program is large, the comment may be extensive. The compiler treats comments as white space.

■ #include <stdio.h>

The header file *stdio.h* contains the function prototype for the printf() function. This is a kind of declaration for printf(). The compiler needs it to work correctly.

■ int   exponent = 0, power_of_two = 1;

The variables exponent and power_of_two are declared to be of type int. They are initialized to 0 and 1, respectively.

■ while (++exponent <= 10)

As long as the value of the expression ++exponent is less than or equal to 10, the body of the while loop is executed. The first time through the loop the expression ++exponent has the value 1; the second time through the loop ++exponent has the value 2; and so forth. Thus the body of the loop is executed 10 times.

■ `printf("%5d", power_of_two *= 2);`

The body of the `while` loop consists of this statement. The string constant `"%5d"` is passed as the first argument to the `printf()` function. The string contains the format `%5d`, which indicates that the value of the expression `power_of_two *= 2` is to be printed as a decimal with field length 5.

■ `power_of_two *= 2`

This assignment expression is equivalent to

```
power_of_two = power_of_two * 2
```

which causes the old value of `power_of_two` to be multiplied by 2 and the resulting value to be assigned to `power_of_two`. The value assigned to `power_of_two` is the value of the assignment expression as a whole. The first time through the loop, the old value of `power_of_two` is 1, and the new value is 2; the second time through the loop, the old value of `power_of_two` is 2, and the new value is 4, and so forth.

2.12 The C System

The C system consists of the C language, the preprocessor, the compiler, the library, and other tools useful to the programmer, such as editors and debuggers. In this section we discuss the preprocessor and the library. For details about functions in the standard library, see Appendix A, "The Standard Library."

The Preprocessor

Lines that begin with a # are called *preprocessing directives.* These lines communicate with the preprocessor. In traditional C, preprocessing directives were required to begin in column 1. In ANSI C, this restriction has been removed. Although a # may be preceded on a line by white space, it is still a common programming style to start preprocessing directives in column 1.

We have already made use of preprocessing directives such as

`#include <stdio.h>` and `#define PI 3.14159`

Another form of the `#include` facility is given by

`#include "`*filename*`"`

This causes the preprocessor to replace the line with a copy of the contents of the named file. A search for the file is made first in the current directory and then in other system-dependent places. With a preprocessing directive of the form

```
#include <filename>
```

the preprocessor looks for the file only in the "other places" and not in the current directory.

Because `#include` directives commonly occur at the beginning of the program, the include files that they refer to are called *header files*, and `.h` is used to end the file name. This is a convention, not a preprocessor requirement. There is no restriction on what an include file can contain. In particular, it can contain other preprocessing directives that are expanded by the preprocessor in turn. Although files of any type may be included, it is considered poor programming style to include files that contain code for function definitions (see Chapter 5, "Character Processing").

On UNIX systems the standard header files such as *stdio.h* are typically found in the directory */usr/include*. On Borland systems they might be found in the directory *\bc\include*. In general, the location of the standard `#include` files is system-dependent. All of these files are readable, and programmers, for a variety of reasons, have occasion to read them.

One of the primary uses of header files is to provide function prototypes. For example, *stdio.h* contains the following lines:

```
int   printf(const char *format, ...);
int   scanf(const char *format, ...);
```

These are the function prototypes for the `printf()` and `scanf()` functions in the standard library. Roughly speaking, a function prototype tells the compiler the types of the arguments that get passed to the function and the type of the value that gets returned by the function. Before we can understand the function prototypes for `printf()` and `scanf()`, we need to learn about the function definition mechanism, pointers, and type qualifiers. These ideas are presented in later chapters. The main point that we are making here is that header files are often included because they contain the function prototypes of functions that are being used. The compiler needs the function prototypes to do its work correctly.

The Standard Library

The standard library contains many useful functions that add considerable power and flexibility to the C system. Many of the functions are used extensively by all C programmers, whereas other functions are used more selectively. Most programmers become acquainted with functions in the standard library on a need-to-know basis.

Programmers usually are not concerned about the location on the system of the standard library, because the library contains compiled code that is unreadable to humans. It can happen that the standard library is made up of more than one file. The mathematics library, for example, is conceptually part of the standard library, but it typically exists in a separate file. Whatever the case, the system knows where to find the code that corresponds to functions from the standard library, such as `printf()` and `scanf()`, that the programmer has used. However, even though the system provides the code, it is the responsibility of the programmer to provide the function prototype. This is usually accomplished by including appropriate header files.

Caution: Do not mistake header files for the libraries themselves. The standard library contains object code of functions that have already been compiled. The standard header files do not contain compiled code.

To illustrate the use of a function in the standard library, let us show how `rand()` can be used to generate some randomly distributed integers. In later chapters we have occasion to use `rand()` to fill arrays and strings for testing purposes. Here, we use it to print some integers on the screen.

```
/*Printing random numbers. */

#include <stdio.h>
#include <stdlib.h>

int main(void)
{
   int   i, n;

   printf("\n%s\n%s",
    "Some randomly distributed integers will be printed.",
    "How many do you want to see?  ");
   scanf("%d", &n);
   for (i = 0; i < n; ++i) {
      if (i % 6 == 0)
       printf("\n");
      printf("%9d", rand());
   }
   printf("\n");
   return 0;
}
```

Suppose we execute the program and type 11 when prompted. Here is what appears on the screen:

```
Some randomly distributed integers will be printed.
How many do you want to see?  11

    16838     5758    10113    17515    31051     5627
    23010     7419    16212     4086     2749
```

Dissection of the prn_rand Program

- ```
  #include <stdio.h>
  #include <stdlib.h>
  ```

These header files are included because of the function prototypes they contain. In particular, the function prototype

```
int   rand(void);
```

is in *stdlib.h*. It tells the compiler that `rand()` is a function that takes no arguments and returns an `int` value. Rather than include *stdlib.h*, we could just as well supply this line ourselves, either at the top of the file or as a declaration inside `main()`.

- ```
  printf("\n%s\n%s",
     "Some randomly distributed integers will be printed.",
     "How many do you want to see?  ");
  scanf("%d", &n);
  ```

A prompt to the user is printed on the screen. The characters typed in by the user are received by `scanf()`, converted into the format of a decimal integer, and placed at the address of `n`.

- ```
  for (i = 0; i < n; ++i) {
     .....
  }
  ```

This is a `for` loop. It is equivalent to

```
i = 0;
while (i < n) {
   .....
   ++i;
}
```

Another way to write this program would be to initialize `i` to zero and then use the construct

```
while (i++ < n) {
   .....
}
```

Note carefully that `i++ < n` is different from `++i < n` (see exercise 10 on page 71).
```

■
```
if (i % 6 == 0)
   printf("\n");
```

The operator == is the "is equal to" operator. If *expr1* and *expr2* are two expressions with the same value, the expression *expr1* == *expr2* is *true*; otherwise it is*false*. In Chapter 4, "Functions and Structured Programming," we see that == has lower precedence than %. Thus

`i % 6 == 0`   is equivalent to   `(i % 6) == 0`

The effect of this is that starting with the first time through the loop, and every sixth time thereafter, the expression as a whole is *true*. Whenever the expression is *true*, a newline character is printed.

■
```
printf("%9d", rand());
```

Every time through the loop, the value returned by the call to `rand()` is printed in the format of a decimal integer. The width of the field where the integer is printed is 9 characters.

2.13 Style

Each of the statements

`++i;`   and   `i++;`

increments the stored value of `i` in memory by 1. No use is made of the value of the expression; only the side effect of the operator ++ is being used. In this simple example, it is a matter of personal taste whether `++i` or `i++` is used. We prefer prefix operators. As part of a more complicated expression, only one of `++i` or `i++` may be appropriate. The two expressions do not have the same value.

A correct style strives for code that is readable. Although the statement

```
x = (y = 2) + (z = 3);
```

is both correct and concise, it is not as readable as

```
y = 2;
z = 3;
x = y + z;
```

It is important not to condense code just for the sake of using less space. Readability is an attribute that should not be sacrificed.

If we want to add 7 to the variable `a`, we can write either

```
a += 7;        or        a = a + 7;
```

Although the choice is largely a matter of taste, professional programmers definitely favor the first.

Commenting style is crucial to program readability. There is no one correct style. Comments, properly used, allow others to understand both what the program does and how it works. Both individuals and organizations should adopt and consistently stay with a given commenting style. Style becomes habit, and good habits reinforce good programming practice.

Comments should occur at the top of the program and at the head of major structural groupings within the source code. Short comments should occur to the right of individual statements when the effect of the statement is not obvious.

The lead comment should be visually set off and should include information such as the name of the organization, the programmer's name, the date, and the purpose of the program.

```
/*
 *   Organization:  SOCRATIC SOLUTIONS (Trade Mark)
 *   Programmer:    Constance B. Diligent
 *   Date:          19 April 1993
 *
 *   Purpose:       Birthday greetings
 */

#include <stdio.h>

int main(void)
{
   printf("\nHAPPY BIRTHDAY TO YOU!\n\n");
   return 0;
}
```

Although in practice the overcommenting of code almost never occurs, comments, nevertheless, should not clutter the program. Comments should illuminate what the program is doing. For example,

```
tax = price * rate;      /* sales tax formula */
```

gives insight into the program, but

```
tax = price * rate;      /* multiply price by rate */
```

is redundant and therefore useless. It is very important to choose identifiers that describe their own use and thereby avoid extraneous commenting.

2.14 Common Programming Errors

The programming errors discussed in this section are chiefly syntactic. These errors are caught by the compiler, and in general they keep the compiler from producing an executable output file.

Consider the following code contained in the file *exmpl_1.c.* Because the code is not syntactically correct, error and warning messages is produced when we compile it. The exact form of the messages vary from one compiler to another, but in general the content of the messages is similar.

```
#include <stdio.h>

int main(void)
{
   int   a = 1, b = 2, c = 3;

   x = a + b;
   printf("x = %d\n", x);
   return 0;
}
```

Suppose we compile this program on a Borland C system, using the *bcc* command. Here are some of the messages that are produced:

```
Error EXMPL_1.C 7: Undefined symbol 'x' in function main
Warning EXMPL_1.C 9: 'c' is assigned a value that is never used
Warning EXMPL_1.C 9: 'b' is assigned a value that is never used
 .....
```

The name of the file containing the code is listed, along with the line number in which the error occurs. The integrated environment *tc* highlights the line the error occurs in, so that the programmer can immediately use the editor to correct that line. The error is easily understood; namely, x is used but not declared. The first warning message is appropriate but the second is not. It is a spurious warning that is the result of an earlier problem—namely, x being undeclared.

Let us consider another example. Unless you are an experienced programmer, you might not see the errors at first glance.

```
#include <stdio.h>

int main(void)
{
   int    a, b = 2, c = 3;       /* a, b, and c will be used
                                    to illustrate arithmetic/*

   a = (4 * b + 5 * c) / 6
   printf("a = %d   b = %d   c = %d\n", a, b, c);
   return 0;
)
```

Again, a raft of messages are produced by the compiler, some of them spurious.

```
Error EXMPL_2 12: Unexpected end of file in comment started
        on line 5 in function main
Error EXMPL_2 13: Compound statement missing } in function main
Warning EXMPL_2 13: 'c' is assigned a value that is never used
          in function main
 .....
```

What has happened is that the comment starting on line 5 is never closed. The first error message indicates this. Note that because the compiler was unable to find a closing } to end the program, the line numbering in the messages is spurious. Also, a spurious warning about c is produced. Compilers frequently produce this type of misleading advice. Automatic error detection by the compiler is no substitute for great care in program preparation.

After the programmer fixes one error, the compiler may uncover other. This would happen in the preceding program because a semicolon is missing at the end of the line preceding the `printf()` statement.

Most compilers have options that specify the kinds of warnings they produce. As a general rule, the warning level should be set as high as possible. Consider the following code:

```
#include <stdio.h>

main(void)
{
   printf("Try me!\n");
   return 0;
}
```

Because the option *-w* sets the highest warning level for the Borland compiler, we give the command

bcc -w try_me.c

The following warning is produced:

```
Warning TRY_ME.C 6: Function should return a value
                    in function main
```

This warning disappears if we change

`main()` to `void main(void)`

This tells the compiler that `main()` is a function that takes no arguments and returns no values. The Borland compiler is happy with this, but for technical reasons a lot of other compilers still complain. We discuss this issue later in more detail (see Section 4.16, "System Considerations," on page 157). *Warning:* The *-w* option on some compilers turns all warnings off! The kinds of options and how they are invoked vary from one compiler to another.

2.15 System Considerations

ANSI C has both a unary minus and unary plus, but traditional C has only a unary minus. If you are writing portable code that has to run on a traditional compiler as well as on an ANSI C compiler, you should not use the unary plus operator.

The floating type `long double` is not available in traditional C. Because the type is new to ANSI C, many compilers treat a `double` and a `long double` the same way. With time, this should change.

One major difference among operating systems and C compilers is the length of discriminated identifiers, both internal and external. Examples of internal identifiers are macro names and ordinary variables. On some systems an internal identifier with more than eight characters is accepted, but only the first eight characters are used. The remaining characters are simply disregarded. On such a system, for example, the following variable names are considered the same.

`cafeteria_1` and `cafeteria_2`

Typical examples of external identifiers are the names of functions in the standard library, such as `printf` and `scanf`, and the names of files. In MS-DOS, file names are restricted to eight characters plus a three-letter extension. On a given system, a programmer learns the length of discriminated identifiers by experimenting, reading the manual, or asking someone. This is not a problem. On the other hand, if a programmer is writing C code to run on a spectrum of systems, the limitations of all the systems must be known and respected. In ANSI C, the compiler must discriminate among at least 31 characters of an internal identifier, and the system as a whole must discriminate among at least six characters of an external identifier. Many systems discriminate more.

2.16 Moving to C++

C++ has a rest-of-line comment symbol //. This is an improvement over C's bracketed comment symbols, as it is less erro-prone and more convenient.

```
//The circumference and area of a circle.
//              by
//          Cottage Consultants - LMP & DJD
//             V 2.3

const double pi = 3.14159; //pi to 6 significant digits
```

C++ allows declarations to be intermixed with executable statements. We continue this example.

```
#include <iostream.h>       //standard C++ IO library

int main()
{
   while (true) {              //infinite loop - control-C exits;
true is a bool
      cout << "\nENTER radius: ";  //prompt
      double r;             //C++ allows declarations inside block
      cin >> r;                    //input
      double diam = 2 * r;         //declare and initialize
      cout << "\nDiameter = " << diam;
      cout << "\nArea = " << pi * r * r;
      cout << "\nCircumference = " << pi * diam<< endl;
   }
   return 0;  //this may be omitted; return 0 is understood
}
```

By allowing declarations to be intermixed with executable statements, C++ lets you place the declaration next to the first use of a variable. This can avoid initialization errors.

C++ has approximately twice the number of keywords of C. Although legal, it is poor practice to use C++ keywords as identifiers in C programs. Some of the keywords C++ uses are: `private`, `public`, and `protected` for data hiding; `catch`, `try`, and `throw` for exception handling; `new` and `delete` for memory management; and `class` and `template` for defining data types.

Summary

- Tokens are the basic syntactic units of C. They include keywords, identifiers, constants, string constants, operators, and punctuators. White space, along with operators and punctuators, can serve to separate tokens. For this reason, white space, operators, and punctuators are collectively called *separators*. White space, other than serving to separate tokens, is ignored by the compiler.

- Comments are enclosed by the bracket pair `/*` and `*/` and are treated as white space by the compiler. They are critical for good program documentation. Comments should assist the reader to both use and understand the program.

- A keyword, also called a *reserved word*, has a strict meaning. There are 32 keywords in C. They cannot be redefined.

- Identifiers are tokens that the programmer uses chiefly to name variables and functions. They begin with a letter or underscore and are chosen to be meaningful to the human reader.

- Some identifiers are already known to the system because they are the names of functions in the standard library. These include the input/output functions `scanf()` and `printf()` and mathematical functions such as `sqrt()`, `sin()`, `cos()`, and `tan()`.

- Constants include various kinds of integer and floating constants, character constants such as `'a'` and `'#'`, and string constants such as `"abc"`. All constants are collected by the compiler as tokens.

- String constants such as `"deep blue sea"` are arbitrary sequences of characters, including white space characters, that are placed inside double quotes. A string constant is stored as an array of characters, but it is collected by the compiler as a single token. The compiler provides the space in memory needed to store a string constant. Character constants and string constants are treated differently. For example, `'x'` and `"x"` are not the same.

- Operators and punctuators are numerous in C. The parentheses following `main()` are an operator; they tell the compiler that `main` is a function. The parentheses in the expression `a * (b + c)` are punctuators. The operations inside the parentheses are done first.

- In C, the rules of precedence and associativity for operators determine how an expression gets evaluated. The programmer needs to know them.

- The increment operator ++ and the decrement operator -- have a side effect. In addition to having a value, an expression such as `++i` causes the stored value of `i` in memory to be incremented by 1.

- The operators ++ and -- can be used in both prefix and postfix position, possibly with different effects. The expression `++i` causes `i` to be incremented in memory, and the new value of `i` is the value of the expression. The expression `i++` has as its value the current value of `i`, and then `i` is incremented in memory.

- In C, the assignment symbol is an operator. An expression such as `a = b + c` assigns the value of `b + c` to `a`, and the expression as a whole takes on this value. Although the assignment operator in C and the equal sign in mathematics look alike, they are not comparable.

- Many useful functions are available in the standard library. When a library function is used, the corresponding function prototype can be obtained by including the appropriate standard header file.

Exercises

1 Is `main` a keyword? Explain.

2 List five keywords and explain their use.

3 Give examples of three types of tokens.

4 Which of the following are not identifiers and why?

```
3id       o_no_o_no      00_go     star*it     __yes
1_i_am    one_i_aren't   me_to-2   xYshouldI   int
```

5 Design a standard form of introductory comment that gives a reader information about who wrote the program and why.

6 Take a symbol such as + and illustrate the different ways it can be used in a program.

7 ANSI C does not provide for the nesting of comments although many compilers do. Try the following line on your compiler and see what happens:

```
/* This is an attempt /* to nest */ a comment. */
```

8 Write an interactive program that converts pounds and ounces to kilograms and grams. Use symbolic constants that are defined before `main()`.

9 This question illustrates one place where white space around operators is important. Because both + and ++ are operators, the expression `a+++b` can be interpreted as either

```
a++ + b        or        a + ++b
```

depending on how the plus symbols are grouped. Normally, the first two pluses would be grouped and passed to the compiler to see if this were syntactically correct. Write a short program to see which interpretation is made by your compiler.

10 For the *pow_of_2* program in Section 2.11, "An Example: Computing Powers of 2," on page 58, explain what the effect would be if the expression `++i` were changed to `i++`.

11 Study the following code and write down what you think it prints. Then write a test program to check your answers.

```
int   a, b = 0, c = 0;
a = ++b + ++c;
printf("%d %d %d\n", a, b, c);
a = b++ + c++;
printf("%d %d %d\n", a, b, c);
a = ++b + c++;
printf("%d %d %d\n", a, b, c);
a = b-- + --c;
printf("%d %d %d\n", a, b, c);
```

12 What is the effect in the following statement if some, or all, of the parentheses are removed? Explain.

```
x = (y = 2) + (z = 3);
```

13 First complete the entries in the table that follows. After you have done this, write a program to check that the values you entered are correct.

Declarations and initializations		
`int a = 2, b = -3, c = 5, d = -7, e = 11, f = -3;`		
Expression	**Equivalent expression**	**Value**
`a / b / c`	`(a / b) / c`	`0`
`7 + c * -- d / e`	`7 + ((c * (-- d)) / e)`	
`2 * a % - b + c + 1`		
`39 / - ++ e - + 29 % c`		
`a += b += c += 1 + 2`		
`7 - + ++ a % (3 + f)`	*error, why?*	

14 Consider the following code:

```
int   a = 1, b = 2, c = 3;
a += b += c += 7;
```

Write an equivalent statement that is fully parenthesized. What are the values of the variables a, b, and c? First write down your answer; then write a test program to check it.

15 A good programming style is crucial to the human reader, even though the compiler sees only a stream of characters. Consider the following program:

```
int main(void
){float qx,
zz,
tt;printf("gimme 3"
);scanf
(   "%f%f        %f",&qx,&zz
,&tt);printf("averageis=%f",(qx+tt+zz)/3.0);
return 0;}
```

Although the code is not very readable, it should compile and execute. Test it to see if it does. Then completely rewrite the program. Use white space and comments to make it more readable and well documented. *Hint:* Include a header file and choose new identifiers to replace qx, zz, and tt.

16 The integers produced by the function rand() all fall within the interval [0, *n*], where *n* is system-dependent. In ANSI C, the value for *n* is given by the symbolic constant RAND_MAX, which is defined in the standard header file *stdlib.h*. Of course, an incomplete ANSI C system may fail to make this symbolic constant available. Is it available on your system? Write a program to find out.

17 The function rand() returns values in the interval [0, RAND_MAX] (see the previous exercise). If we declare the variable median and initialize it to have the value RAND_MAX/2, then rand() returns a value that is sometimes larger than median and sometimes smaller. On average, however, there should be as many values that are larger as there are values that are smaller than the median. Test this hypothesis. Write a program that calls rand(), say 500 times, inside a for loop, increments the variable plus_cnt every time rand() returns a value larger than median, and increments the variable minus_cnt every time rand() returns a value less than median. Each time through the for loop, print out the value of the difference of plus_cnt and minus_cnt. This difference should oscillate near zero. Does it?

18 Rewrite the *prn_rand* program in Section 2.12, "The Standard Library," on page 61, so that the integers printed are in the interval [0, 100]. *Hint:* Use the modulus operator. How many numbers do you have to print before you see the value 100? (If you do not see it, you have done something wrong.)

19 Rewrite the *prn_rand* program to make use of the construct

```
while (i++ < n) {
    .....
}
```

After you get your program running and understand its effects, rewrite the program, changing

```
i++ < n     to     ++i < n
```

Now the program behaves differently. To compensate for this, rewrite the body of the while loop so the program behaves exactly as it did before.

20 The value of an expression such as ++a + a++ is system-dependent. This is because the side effects of the increment operator ++ can take place at different times. This is both a strength of C, because compilers can do what is natural at the machine level, and a weakness, because such an expression is system-dependent and the expression has different values on different machines. Experienced C programmers recognize expressions such as this to be potentially dangerous and do not use them. Experiment with your machine to see what value is produced by ++a + a++ after a has been initialized to zero. Does your compiler warn you that the expression is dangerous?

21 Libraries on a UNIX system typically end in *.a*, which is mnemonic for "archive." Libraries in MS-DOS typically end in *.lib*. See if you can find the standard C libraries on your system. These libraries are not readable. On a UNIX system you can give a command such as

```
ar t /lib/libc.a
```

to see all the titles of the objects in the library.

22 In both ANSI C and traditional C, a backslash at the end of a line in a string constant has the effect of continuing it to the next line. For example:

```
"by using a backslash at the end of the line \
a string can be extended from one line to the next"
```

Write a program that uses this construct. Many screens have 80 characters per line. What happens if you try to print a string with more than 80 characters?

23 In ANSI C, a backslash at the end of *any* line is supposed to have the effect of continuing it to the next line. This can be expected to work in string constants and macro definitions on any C compiler, either ANSI or traditional (see the previous exercise). However, not all ANSI C compilers support this in a more general way. After all, except in macro definitions, this construct gets little use. Does your C compiler support this in a general way? Try the following:

```
#\
include <stdio.h>
mai\
n()
{
   print\
f("Will this \
work?\n");
}
```

24 When you invoke the compiler, the system first invokes the preprocessor. In this exercise we want to deliberately make a preprocessing error, just to see what happens. Try the following program:

```
#incl <stdixx.h>

int main(void)
{
   printf("Try me.\n");
   return 0;
}
```

What happens if you change `#incl` to `#include`?

25 C++: Recode the program for computing powers of two in C++.

26 C++: Rewrite the *prn_rand* program so that the integers printed are in the interval [0, M]. Make the integer M an input to the program that is prompted for and input using `cin`.

27 Java: Here is a program to compute the area of a rectangle:

```
// SimpleInput.java-reading numbers from the keyboard
//Java by Dissection:  page 27
import tio.*;    // use the package tio

class SimpleInput {
  public static void main (String[] args) {
    int width, height, area;

    System.out.println("type two integers for" +
            " the width and height of a box");
    width = Console.in.readInt();
    height = Console.in.readInt();
    area = width * height;
    System.out.print("The area is ");
    System.out.println(area);
  }
}
```

Convert this program to C. Note how `scanf()` is used in place of the method `readInt()` found in the package *tio*. The method `readInt()` was developed for *Java by Dissection* to provide simple terminal input/output. One advantage of Java is that there is no need for format control in `println()`. Thus Java I/O is typesafe. In C, the programmer has to be very careful when writing format control strings for both `printf()` and `scanf()`.

28 A further advantage of Java is that this program produces the same answer regardless of what machine the code is run on. Java types are machine-independent. C types are system-dependent and may vary across different machines. This is especially important when using floating types such as double. The above code can be changed to be double as follows:

```
import tio.*;      // use the package tio

class SimpleInputDouble {
  public static void main (String[] args) {
    double width, height, area;

    System.out.println("type two integers for" +
                       " the width and height of a box");
    width = Console.in.readDouble();
    height = Console.in.readDouble();
    area = width * height;
    System.out.print("The area is ");
    System.out.println(area);
  }
}
```

Write this program in C. See if the Java and C program give the same results on the machine you use.

Chapter 3

Flow of Control

Statements in a program are normally executed one after another. This is called *sequential flow of control.* Often we want to alter the sequential flow of control to provide for a choice of action or the repetition of an action. We can use `if`, `if-else`, and `switch` statements to select among alternative actions and `while`, `for`, and `do` statements to achieve iterative actions. We explain these flow-of-control constructs in this chapter. We start with a discussion of the relational, equality, and logical operators. We also discuss the compound statement, which is used to group together statements that are to be treated as a unit.

3.1 Relational, Equality, and Logical Operators

Here are the operators most often used to affect flow of control.

<table>
<tr><th colspan="3">Relational, equality, and logical operators</th></tr>
<tr><td rowspan="4">Relational operators</td><td><code>less than</code></td><td><</td></tr>
<tr><td><code>greater than</code></td><td>></td></tr>
<tr><td><code>less than or equal to</code></td><td><=</td></tr>
<tr><td><code>greater than or equal to</code></td><td>>=</td></tr>
<tr><td rowspan="2">Equality operators</td><td><code>equal to</code></td><td>==</td></tr>
<tr><td><code>not equal to</code></td><td>!=</td></tr>
<tr><td rowspan="3">Logical operators</td><td><code>(unary) negation</code></td><td>!</td></tr>
<tr><td><code>logical and</code></td><td>&&</td></tr>
<tr><td><code>logical or</code></td><td>||</td></tr>
</table>

We begin with a thorough discussion of them. These operators are used in expressions that we think of as being *true* or *false*. We explain how *true* and *false* are implemented in C.

Just like other operators, the relational, equality, and logical operators have rules of precedence and associativity that determine precisely how expressions involving these operators are evaluated. These rules are shown in the following table.

Operator precedence and associativity	
Operators	**Associativity**
`()` `++` *(postfix)* `--` *(postfix)*	left to right
`+` *(unary)* `-` *(unary)* `++` *(prefix)* `--` *(prefix)*	right to left
`*` `/` `%`	left to right
`+` `-`	left to right
`<` `<=` `>` `>=`	left to right
`==` `!=`	left to right
`&&`	left to right
`||`	left to right
`?:`	right to left
`=` `+=` `-=` `*=` `/=` *etc*	right to left
`,` *(comma operator)*	left to right

The `!` operator is unary. All the other relational, equality, and logical operators are binary. They all operate on expressions and yield either the `int` value 0 or the `int` value 1. The reason for this is that in the C language, *false* is represented by any zero value and *true* is represented by any nonzero value. Some examples of expressions that can be used to represent *false* are an `int` expression having the value 0, a floating expression having the value 0.0, the null character `'\0`, (see Chapter 5, "Character Processing") and the `NULL` pointer (see Chapter 8, "Functions, Pointers, and Storage Classes"). Similarly, any expression with a nonzero value can be used to represent *true*. Intuitively, an expression such as `a < b` is either *true* or *false*. In C, this expression yields the `int` value 1 if it is *true* or the `int` value 0 if it is *false*.

3.2 Relational Operators and Expressions

The relational operators

```
<    >    <=    >=
```

are all binary. They each take two expressions as operands and yield either the `int` value 0 or the `int` value 1. Some examples are

```
a < 3
-1.1 >= (2.2 * x + 3.3)
a < b < c     /* syntactically correct, but confusing */
```

but not

```
a =< b        /* out of order */
a < = b       /* space not allowed */
a >> b        /* this is a shift expression */
```

Consider a relational expression such as `a < b`. If `a` is less than `b`, then the expression has the `int` value 1, which we think of as being *true*. If `a` is not less than `b`, the expression has the `int` value 0, which we think of as being *false*. Observe that the value of `a < b` is the same as the value of `a - b < 0`. Because the precedence of the relational operators is less than that of the arithmetic operators,

`a - b < 0`   is equivalent to   `(a - b) < 0`

The usual arithmetic conversions occur in relational expressions (see Chapter 6, "The Fundamental Data Types").

Let *a* and *b* be arbitrary arithmetic expressions. The following table shows how the value of *a* - *b* determines the values of relational expressions.

Values of relational expressions				
a - b	**a < b**	**a > b**	**a <= b**	**a >= b**
positive	0	1	0	1
zero	0	0	1	1
negative	1	0	1	0

The following table illustrates the use of the rules of precedence and associativity to evaluate relational expressions.

Declarations and initializations		
`int i = 1, j = 2, k = 3;` `double x = 5.5, y = 7.7;`		
Expression	**Equivalent expression**	**Value**
`i < j - k`	`i < (j - k)`	0
`- i + 5 * j >= k + 1`	`((- i) + (5 * j)) >= (k + 1)`	1
`x - y <= j - k - 1`	`(x - y) <= ((j - k) - 1)`	1
`x + k + 7 < y / k`	`((x + k) + 7) < (y / k)`	0

3.3 Equality Operators and Expressions

The equality operators == and != are binary operators that act on expressions. They yield either the `int` value 0 or the `int` value 1. Some examples are

```
ch == 'A'
count != -2
x + y == 2 * z - 5
```

but not

```
a = b               /* an assignment expression */
a = = b - 1         /* space not allowed */
(x + y) =! 44       /* syntax error: equivalent to (x+y)=(!44) */
```

Intuitively, an equality expression such as `a == b` is either *true* or *false*. More precisely, if `a` is equal to `b`, `a == b` yields the `int` value 1 (*true*); otherwise it yields the `int` value 0 (*false*). Note that an equivalent expression is `a - b == 0`. This is what is implemented at the machine level.

The expression `a != b` illustrates the use of the "not equal to" operator. It is evaluated in a similar fashion, except that the test here is for inequality rather than for equality. The operator semantics is given by the following table.

Values of equality expressions		
a - b	**a == b**	**a != b**
zero	1	0
nonzero	0	1

The next table shows how the rules of precedence and associativity are used to evaluate some expressions with equality operators.

Declarations and initializations		
`int i = 1, j = 2, k = 3;`		
Expression	**Equivalent expression**	**Value**
`i == j`	`j == i`	0
`i != j`	`j != i`	1
`i + j + k == - 2 * - k`	`((i + j) + k) == ((- 2) * (- k))`	1

3.4 Logical Operators and Expressions

The logical operator ! is unary, and the logical operators && and || are binary. Each of these operators, when applied to expressions, yields either the `int` value 0 or the `int` value 1.

Logical negation can be applied to an expression of arithmetic or pointer type. If an expression has a zero value, its negation yields the `int` value 1. If the expression has a nonzero value, its negation yields the `int` value 0.

Some examples are

```
!a
!(x + 7.7)
!(a < b || c < d)
```

but not

```
a!          /* out of order */
a != b      /* != is the token for "not equal" operator */
```

The following table gives the semantics of the ! operator.

Values of negation expressions	
a	**!a**
zero	1
nonzero	0

Although logical negation is a very simple operator, there is one subtlety. The operator ! in C is unlike the *not* operator in ordinary logic. If *s* is a logical statement, then

not (*not s*) = *s*

whereas in C the value of `!!5`, for example, is 1. Because ! associates from right to left, as do all other unary operators, the expression

`!!5` is equivalent to `!(!5)`

and `!(!5)` is equivalent to `!(0)`, which has the value 1. The following table shows how some expressions with logical negation are evaluated.

Declarations and initializations		
`int i = 7, j = 7;` `double x = 0.0, y = 999.9;`		
Expression	**Equivalent expression**	**Value**
`! (i - j) + 1`	`(! (i - j)) + 1`	2
`! i - j + 1`	`((! i) - j) + 1`	-6
`! ! (x + 3.3)`	`! (! (x + 3.3))`	1
`! x * ! ! y`	`(! x) * (!(! y))`	1

The binary logical operators && and || also act on expressions and yield either the `int` value 0 or the `int` value 1. Some examples are

```
a && b
a || b
!(a < b) && c
3 && (-2 * a + 7)
```

but not

```
a &&          /* one operand missing */
a | | b       /* extra space not allowed */
a & b         /* this is a bitwise operation */
&b            /* the address of b */
```

The operator semantics are shown in the following table.

Values of bitwise expressions			
a	**b**	**a && b**	**a || b**
zero	zero	0	0
zero	nonzero	0	1
nonzero	zero	0	1
nonzero	nonzero	1	1

This table, although completely accurate, does not reflect the way programmers usually think when dealing with logical expressions. Even experienced programmers think in terms of truth values, as shown in the following table.

Truth table for && and ||			
a	**b**	**a && b**	**a || b**
F	F	F	F
F	T	F	T
T	F	F	T
T	T	T	T

The precedence of && is higher than ||, but both operators are of lower precedence than all unary, arithmetic, and relational operators. Their associativity is left to right. The next table shows how the rules of precedence and associativity are used to compute the value of some logical expressions.

Declarations and initializations		
`int    i = 3, j = 3, k = 3;` `double x = 0.0, y = 2.3;`		
Expression	**Equivalent expression**	**Value**
`i && j && k`	`(i && j) && k`	1
`x || i && j - 3`	`x || (i && (j - 3))`	0
`i < j && x < y`	`(i < j) && (x < y)`	0
`i < j || x < y`	`(i < j) || (x < y)`	1

Short-Circuit Evaluation

With expressions that contain the operands of && and ||, the evaluation process stops as soon as the outcome *true* or *false* is known. This is called *short-circuit* evaluation. It is an important property of these operators. Suppose *expr1* and *expr2* are expressions, and *expr1* has value zero. In the evaluation of the logical expression

expr1 && *expr2*

the evaluation of *expr2* does not occur because the value of the logical expression as a whole is already determined to be 0. Similarly, if *expr1* has a nonzero value, then in the evaluation of

expr1 || *expr2*

the evaluation of *expr2* does not occur because the value of the logical expression as a whole is already determined to be 1. Short-circuit evaluation is illustrated in the following code:

```
int   i, j;
i = 2 && (j = 2);
printf("%d  %d\n", i, j);                 /* 1  2 is printed */
(i = 0) && (j = 3);
printf("%d  %d\n", i, j);                 /* 0  2 is printed */
i = 0 || (j = 4);
printf("%d  %d\n", i, j);                 /* 1  4 is printed */
(i = 2) || (j = 5);
printf("%d  %d\n", i, j);                 /* 2  4 is printed */
```

Here is a simple example of how short-circuit evaluation might be used. Suppose we want to do a calculation that depends on certain conditions:

```
if (x >= 0.0 && sqrt(x) <= 7.7) {
   .....                                  /* do something */
```

If the value of x is negative, the square root of x is not taken (see exercise 20 on page 118).

3.5 The Compound Statement

A compound statement is a series of declarations and statements surrounded by braces. The chief use of the compound statement is to group statements into an executable unit. When declarations come at the beginning of a compound statement, it is called a *block* (see Chapter 8, "Functions, Pointers, and Storage Classes"). In C, wherever it is syntactically correct to place a statement, it is also syntactically correct to place a compound statement. *A compound statement is itself a statement.*

An example of a compound statement is

```
{
   a = 1;
   {
      b = 2;
      c = 3;
   }
}
```

Note that in this example there is a compound statement within a compound statement. An important use of the compound statement is to achieve the desired flow of control in `if`, `if-else`, `while`, `for`, `do`, and `switch` statements.

3.6 The Empty Statement

The empty statement is written as a single semicolon. It is useful where a statement is needed syntactically but no action is required semantically. As we shall see, this is sometimes useful in flow-of-control constructs such as `if-else` and `for` statements.

An expression followed by a semicolon is called an *expression statement.* The empty statement is a special case of the expression statement. Some examples of expression statements are

```
a = b;                  /* an assignment statement */
a + b + c;              /* legal, but no useful work done */
;                       /* an empty statement */
printf("%d\n", a);      /* a function call */
```

3.7 The `if` and `if-else` Statements

The general form of an `if` statement is

```
if (expr)
   statement
```

If *expr* is nonzero (*true*), then *statement* is executed; otherwise *statement* is skipped, and control passes to the next statement. In the example

```
if (grade >= 90)
   printf("Congratulations!\n");
printf("Your grade is %d.\n", grade);
```

a congratulatory message is printed only when the value of `grade` is greater than or equal to 90. The second `printf()` is always executed.

Usually, the expression in an `if` statement is a relational, equality, or logical expression, but an expression from any domain is permissible. Some other examples of `if` statements are

```
if (y != 0.0)
   x /= y;
if (a < b && b < c) {
   d = a + b + c;
   printf("Everything is in order.\n");
}
```

but not

```
if  b == a              /* parentheses missing */
   area = a * a;
```

Where appropriate, compound statements should be used to group a series of statements under the control of a single `if` expression. The following code consists of two `if` statements:

```
if (j < k)
   min = j;
if (j < k)
   printf("j is smaller than k\n");
```

The code can be written in a more efficient and more understandable way by using a single `if` statement with a compound statement for its body.

```
if (j < k) {
   min = j;
   printf("j is smaller than k\n");
}
```

The `if-else` statement is closely related to the `if` statement. It has a general form given by

```
if (expr)
   statement1
else
   statement2
```

If *expr* is nonzero, then *statement1* is executed and *statement2* is skipped; if *expr* is zero, then *statement1* is skipped and *statement2* is executed. In both cases control then passes to the next statement. Consider the code

```
if (x < y)
   min = x;
else
   min = y;
printf("Min value = %d\n", min);
```

If `x < y` is *true*, then `min` is assigned the value of `x`; if it is *false*, `min` is assigned the value of `y`. Control then passes to the `printf()` statement. Here is another example of an `if-else` construct:

```
if (c >= 'a' && c <= 'z')
   ++lc_cnt;
else {
   ++other_cnt;
   printf("%c is not a lowercase letter\n", c);
}
```

but not

```
if (a != b) {
   a += 1;
   b += 2;
} ;
else                /* syntax error */
   c *= 3;
```

The syntax error occurs because the semicolon following the right brace creates an empty statement, and consequently the `else` has nowhere to attach.

Because an `if` statement is itself a statement, it can be used as the statement part of another `if` statement. Consider the code

```
if (a == 1)
   if (b == 2)
      printf("***\n");
```

This is of the form

```
if (a == 1)
   statement
```

where *statement* is the following `if` statement:

```
if (b == 2)
   printf("***\n");
```

In a similar fashion, an `if-else` statement can be used as the statement part of another `if` statement. Consider, for example,

```
if (a == 1)
   if (b == 2)
      printf("***\n");
   else
      printf("###\n");
```

Now we are faced with a semantic difficulty. This code illustrates the "dangling else" problem: It is not clear what the `else` part is associated with. Do not be fooled by the format of the code. As far as the machine is concerned, the following code is equivalent:

```
if (a == 1)
   if (b == 2)
      printf("***\n");
else
   printf("###\n");
```

The rule is that an else attaches to the nearest if. Thus the code is correctly formatted as we first gave it. It has the form

```
if (a == 1)
   statement
```

where *statement* is the if-else statement

```
if (b == 2)
   printf("***\n");
else
   printf("###\n");
```

To illustrate the use of the if and if-else statements, we write an interactive program that finds the minimum of three values entered at the keyboard.

```
/* Find the minimum of three values. */

#include <stdio.h>

int main(void)
{
   int   x, y, z, min;

   printf("Input three integers:  ");
   scanf("%d%d%d", &x, &y, &z);
   if (x < y)
      min = x;
   else
      min = y;
   if (z < min)
      min = z;
   printf("The minimum value is %d\n", min);
   return 0;
}
```

Dissection of the find_min Program

- #include <stdio.h>

The header file *stdio.h* is supplied by the system. We have included it because it contains the function prototypes for printf() and scanf().

- printf("Input three integers: ");

In an interactive environment, the program must prompt the user for input.

- ```
  scanf("%d%d%d", &x, &y, &z);
  ```

The library function `scanf()` is used to read in three integer values that are stored at the addresses of `x`, `y`, and `z`, respectively.

- ```
  if (x < y)
     min = x;
  else
     min = y;
  ```

This whole construct is a single `if-else` statement. The values of `x` and `y` are compared. If `x` is less than `y`, then `min` is assigned the value of `x`; if `x` is not less than `y`, then `min` is assigned the value of `y`.

- ```
  if (z < min)
     min = z;
  ```

This is an `if` statement. A check is made to see if the value of `z` is less than the value of `min`. If it is, then `min` is assigned the value of `z`; otherwise, the value of `min` is left unchanged.

3.8 The `while` Statement

Repetition of action is one reason we rely on computers. When there are large amounts of data, it is very convenient to have control mechanisms that repeatedly execute specific statements. In C, the `while`, `for`, and `do` statements provide for repetitive action.

Although we have already used the `while` statement, or `while` loop, in many examples, we now want to explain precisely how this iterative mechanism works. Consider a construction of the form

```
while (expr)
   statement
next statement
```

First *expr* is evaluated. If it is nonzero (*true*), then *statement* is executed, and control is passed back to the beginning of the `while` loop. The effect of this is to have the body of the `while` loop, namely *statement*, executed repeatedly until *expr* is zero (*false*). At that point, control passes to *next statement*. An example is

```
while (i <= 10) {
   sum += i;
   ++i;
}
```
```

Assume that just before this loop the value of i is 1 and the value of sum is 0. Then the effect of the loop is to repeatedly increment the value of sum by the current value of i and then to increment i by 1, as shown in the following table.

Values during while loop execution	
Number of times through the loop	**Value of sum**
first	0 + 1
second	0 + 1 + 2
third	0 + 1 + 2 + 3

After the body of the loop has been executed 10 times, the value of i is 11, and the value of the expression i <= 10 is 0 (*false*). Thus the body of the loop is not executed, and control passes to *next statement*. When the while loop is exited, the value of sum is 55. Note again that a compound statement is used to group statements together, with the compound statement itself syntactically representing a single statement.

3.9 Problem Solving: Finding Maximum Values

Programmers often have to find an item with a particular property in a collection of items. We illustrate such a task by finding the maximum value of some real numbers entered interactively at the keyboard. Our program makes use of if and while statements.

```
/* Find the maximum of n real values. */
#include <stdio.h>

int main(void)
{
   int     cnt = 0, n;
   float   max, x;

   printf("The maximum value will be computed.\n");
   printf("How many numbers do you wish to enter?  ");
   scanf("%d", &n);
   while (n <= 0) {
      printf("\nERROR: Positive integer required.\n\n");
      printf("How many numbers do you wish to enter?  ");
      scanf("%d", &n);
   }
```

```
   printf("\nEnter %d real numbers:  ", n);
   scanf("%f", &x);
   max = x;
   while (++cnt < n) {
      scanf("%f", &x);
      if (max < x)
         max = x;
   }
   printf("\nMaximum value:  %g\n", max);
   return 0;
}
```

Let us suppose we execute this program and enter 5 after the first prompt. If, after the second prompt, we enter 1.01, -3, 2.2, 7.07000, and 5, this is what appears on the screen:

```
The maximum value will be computed.
How many numbers do you wish to enter?  5
Enter 5 real numbers:  1.01  -3  2.2  7.07000  5
Maximum value:  7.07
```

Dissection of the *find_max* Program

- ```
  int     cnt = 0, n;
  float   max, x;
  ```

The variables `cnt` and `n` are declared to be of type `int`, and the variables `max` and `x` are declared to be of type `float`. We use `cnt` as a counter.

- ```
  printf("The maximum value will be computed.\n");
  ```

A line of text is printed explaining the purpose of the program. This is an important documentation aid. The program, in effect, is documenting its own output. This is good programming style.

- ```
  printf("How many numbers do you wish to enter?  ");
  scanf("%d", &n);
  ```

The user is prompted to input an integer. Then the function `scanf()` is used to store the value of the integer entered by the user at the address of `n`.
  ```

■
```
while (n <= 0) {
   printf("\nERROR: Positive integer required.\n\n");
   printf("How many numbers do you wish to enter?  ");
   scanf("%d", &n);
}
```

If `n` is negative or zero, the value of the expression `n <= 0` is 1 (*true*), causing the body of the `while` loop to be executed. An error message and another prompt are printed, and a new value is stored at the address of `n`. As long as the user enters nonpositive numbers, the body of the loop is repeatedly executed. This `while` loop provides the program with some input error correction capability. Other input errors, such as typing the letter *a* instead of a digit, still cause the program to fail. For more robust error correction, we need to look at the actual characters typed by the user. To do this we need character processing tools and strings (see Chapter 5, "Character Processing," and Chapter 10, "Strings and Pointers").

■
```
printf("\nEnter %d real numbers:  ", n);
scanf("%f", &x);
max = x;
```

The user is prompted to input `n` real numbers. The `scanf()` function uses the format `%f` to convert the input stream characters to a floating-point number and to store its value at the address of `x`. The variable `max` is assigned the value of `x`.

■
```
while (++cnt < n) {
   scanf("%f", &x);
   if (max < x)
    max = x;
}
```

Before we enter this loop, we have already picked up one value for `x`. We count it by incrementing `cnt` as we enter the loop. The first time through the loop, the expression `++cnt` has the value 1, the variable `n` has value 5, and the expression `++cnt < n` has the value 1 (*true*). Each time through the loop, we pick up another value for `x` and test to see if it is larger than the current value for `max`. If it is, we assign `x` to `max`. Control then passes back to the top of the loop, where `cnt` is incremented and a test is made to see if we need to get more values. The body of a `while` statement is a single statement, in this case a compound statement. The compound statement aids flow of control by grouping several statements to be executed as a unit.

■ `printf("\nMaximum value:  %g\n", max);`

We print the value of `max` with the `%g` format. Notice that 7.07000 was entered at the keyboard but 7.07 was printed. The `%g` format does not print extraneous zeros.

3.10 The for Statement

The `for` statement, like the `while` statement, is used to execute code iteratively. We can explain its action in terms of the `while` statement. The construction

```
for (expr1; expr2; expr3)
    statement
next statement
```

is semantically equivalent to

```
expr1;
while (expr2) {
    statement
    expr3;
}
next statement
```

provided that *expr2* is present, and that no `continue` statement is in the body of the `for` loop. From our understanding of the `while` statement, we see that the semantics of the `for` statement is the following: First *expr1* is evaluated; typically, *expr1* is used to initialize the loop. Then *expr2* is evaluated; if it is nonzero (*true*), then *statement* is executed, *expr3* is evaluated, and control passes back to the beginning of the `for` loop again, except that evaluation of *expr1* is skipped. Typically, *expr2* is a logical expression controlling the iteration. This process continues until *expr2* is zero (*false*), at which point control passes to *next statement*.

Some examples of `for` loops, or `for` statements, are

```
for (i = 1; i <= n; ++i)
    factorial *= i;
for (j = 2; k % j == 0; ++j) {
    printf("%d is a divisor of %d\n", j, k);
    sum += j;
}
```

but not

```
for (i = 0, i < n, i += 3)      /* semicolons are needed */
   sum += i;
```

Any or all of the expressions in a `for` statement can be missing, but the two semicolons must remain. If *expr1* is missing, no initialization step is performed as part of the `for` loop. The code

```
i = 1;
sum = 0;
for ( ; i <= 10; ++i)
   sum += i;
```

computes the sum of the integers from 1 to 10, and so does the code

```
i = 1;
sum = 0;
for ( ; i <= 10 ; )
   sum += i++;
```

When *expr2* is missing, the rule is that the test is always *true*. Thus the `for` loop in the code

```
i = 1;
sum = 0;
for ( ; ; ) {
   sum += i++;
   printf("%d\n", sum);
}
```

is an infinite loop.

A `for` statement can be used as the statement part of an `if`, `if-else`, `while`, or another `for` statement. Consider, for example, the construction

```
for ( ..... )
   for ( ..... )
      for ( ..... )
         statement
```

This construction as a whole is a single `for` statement. Its statement part is another `for` statement, which in turn has, as its statement part, yet another `for` statement.

In many situations, program control can be accomplished by using either a `while` or `for` statement; the choice is often a matter of taste. One major advantage of a `for` loop is that control and indexing can both be kept right at the top. Nesting the loops can facilitate the reading of code. The program in the next section illustrates this.

3.11 Problem Solving: Combinatorics

We want to consider a problem that comes from the domain of combinatorics, the art of enumerating combinations and permutations. The problem is to list all triples of nonnegative integers that add up to a given number, such as 7. Here is a program that does this.

```
/* Find triples of integers that add up to N. */

#include <stdio.h>

#define   N   7

int main(void)
{
   int   cnt = 0, i, j, k, n;

   for (i = 0; i <= N; ++i)
      for (j = 0; j <= N; ++j)
       for (k = 0; k <= N; ++k)
          if (i + j + k == N) {
             ++cnt;
             printf("%3d%3d%3d\n", i, j, k);
          }
   printf("\nCount: %d\n", cnt);
   return 0;
}
```

When we execute this program, here is some of the output that appears on the screen:

```
  0  0  7
  0  1  6
  0  2  5
  0  3  4
  .....
  6  0  1
  6  1  0
  7  0  0

Count: 36
```

Dissection of the add_to_n Program

■
```
#define   N   7
```

We use the symbolic constant N so we can more easily experiment with the program.

■
```
for (i = 0; i <= N; ++i)
    .....
```

The outermost for loop has for its statement part a for loop, which in turn has for its statement part another for loop. Instead, we could have written

```
for (i = 0; i <= N; ++i) {
    .....
}
```

However, because the body of this for statement is another for statement, the braces are not necessary.

■
```
for (j = 0; j <= N; ++j)
    for (k = 0; k <= N; ++k)
        .....
```

This is the statement part, or body, of the outermost for loop. For each outermost value of i, all values of j within the inner loop get cycled through. For each value of j, all values of k within the innermost loop get cycled through. This is similar to an odometer, where the lower digits are first cycled through before a higher digit is changed.

■
```
if (i + j + k == N) {
    ++cnt;
    printf("%3d%3d%3d\n", i, j, k);
}
```

This is the body of the innermost loop. A check is made to see if i + j + k = N. If they do, cnt is incremented and the triple of integers is printed.

3.12 Problem Solving: Boolean Variables

Boolean algebra plays a major role in the design of computer circuits. In this algebra all variables have only the values 0 or 1. Transistors and memory technologies implement zero-one value schemes with currents, voltages, and magnetic orientations. Frequently, the circuit designer has a function in mind and needs to check whether for all possible zero-one inputs the output has the desired behavior.

We use `int` variables `b1`, `b2`, . . . , `b5` to represent five boolean variables. They are allowed to take on only the values 0 and 1. A boolean function of these variables is one that returns only 0 or 1. A typical example of a boolean function is the majority function; it returns 1 if a majority of the variables have value 1, and 0 otherwise. We want to create a table of values for the functions

`b1 || b3 || b5`   and   `b1 && b2 || b4 && b5`

and for the majority function. Recall that logical expressions always have the `int` value 0 or 1.

```
/* Print a table of values for some boolean functions. */
#include <stdio.h>

int main(void)
{
   int   b1, b2, b3, b4, b5;                    /* boolean variables */
   int   cnt = 0;
   printf("\n%5s%5s%5s%5s%5s%5s%7s%7s%11s\n\n",    /* headings */
      "Cnt", "b1", "b2", "b3", "b4", "b5",
      "fct1", "fct2", "majority");
   for (b1 = 0; b1 <= 1; ++b1)
      for (b2 = 0; b2 <= 1; ++b2)
         for (b3 = 0; b3 <= 1; ++b3)
            for (b4 = 0; b4 <= 1; ++b4)
               for (b5 = 0; b5 <= 1; ++b5)
                  printf("%5d%5d%5d%5d%5d%5d%6d%7d%9d\n",
                     ++cnt, b1, b2, b3, b4, b5,
                     b1 || b3 || b5, b1 && b2 || b4 && b5,
                     b1 + b2 + b3 + b4 + b5 >= 3);
   printf("\n");
   return 0;
}
```

This program illustrates a typical use of nested `for` loops. Its output is a table of values for all possible inputs and their corresponding outputs. The circuit designer can use the table to check that the boolean functions are behaving in the required fashion. Here is some of the output of the program:

```
 Cnt   b1   b2   b3   b4   b5   fct1   fct2   majority
   1    0    0    0    0    0      0      0          0
   2    0    0    0    0    1      1      0          0
   3    0    0    0    1    0      0      0          0
 .....
```

3.13 The Comma Operator

The comma operator has the lowest precedence of all the operators in C. It is a binary operator with expressions as operands, and it associates from left to right. In a comma expression of the form

expr1 , expr2

expr1 is evaluated first, then *expr2*. The comma expression as a whole has the value and type of its right operand. An example is

```
a = 0, b = 1
```

If `b` has been declared an `int`, this comma expression has value 1 and type `int`.

The comma operator is sometimes used in `for` statements. It allows multiple initializations and multiple processing of indices. For example, the code

```
for (sum = 0, i = 1; i <= n; ++i)
   sum += i;
```

can be used to compute the sum of the integers from 1 to *n*. Carrying this idea further, we can stuff the entire body of the `for` loop inside the `for` parentheses. The previous code could be rewritten as

```
for (sum = 0, i = 1; i <= n; sum += i, ++i)
   ;
```

but not as

```
for (sum = 0, i = 1; i <= n; ++i, sum += i)
   ;
```

In the comma expression

```
++i, sum += i
```

the expression `++i` is evaluated first, and its incremented value is then added to `sum`.

Some examples of comma expressions are given in the following table.

Declarations and initializations		
`int i, j, k = 3;` `double x = 3.3;`		
Expression	**Equivalent expression**	**Value**
`i = 1, j = 2, ++ k + 1`	`((i = 1), (j = 2)), ((++ k) + 1)`	5
`k != 7, ++ x * 2.0 + 1`	`(k != 7), (((++ x) * 2.0) + 1)`	9.6

Most commas in programs do not represent comma operators. For example, the commas used to separate expressions in argument lists of functions or within initializer lists are not comma operators. If a comma operator is to be used in these places, the comma expression in which it occurs must be enclosed in parentheses.

3.14 The do Statement

The `do` statement can be considered a variant of the `while` statement. Instead of making its test at the top of the loop, it makes it at the bottom. An example is

```
do {
   sum += i;
   scanf("%d", &i);
} while (i > 0);
```

Consider a construction of the form

```
do
   statement
while (expr);
next statement
```

First, *statement* is executed, and *expr* is evaluated. If the value of *expr* is nonzero (*true*), then control passes back to the beginning of the `do` statement, and the process repeats itself. When *expr* is zero (*false*), then control passes to *next statement*.

As an example, suppose we want to read in an integer and want to insist that the integer be positive. The following code does the job:

```
do {
   printf("Input a positive integer: ");
   scanf("%d", &n);
   if (error = (n <= 0))
      printf("\nERROR: Negative value not allowed!\n\n");
} while (error);
```

As long as a nonpositive integer is entered, the user is notified with a request for a positive integer. Control exits the loop only after a positive integer has been entered.

3.15 The goto Statement

The `goto` statement is considered a harmful construct in most accounts of modern programming methodology. It causes an unconditional jump to a labeled statement somewhere in the current function. Thus it can undermine all the useful structure provided by other flow-of-control mechanisms (`if`, `if-else`, `for`, `while`, `do`, and `switch`).

Because a `goto` jumps to a labeled statement, we need to discuss this construct first. A labeled statement is of the form

label: *statement*

where *label* is an identifier. Some examples of labeled statements are

```
bye: exit(1);
L444: a = b + c;
bug1: bug2: bug3: printf("bug found\n");    /* multiple labels */
```

but not

```
333: a = b + c;      /* 333 is not an identifier */
```

Label identifiers have their own name space. This means that the same identifier can be used both for a label and a variable. This practice, however, is considered bad programming style and should be avoided.

Control can be unconditionally transferred to a labeled statement by executing a `goto` statement of the form

`goto` *label*;

An example would be

```
goto error;
  .....
error: {
   printf("An error has occurred - bye!\n");
   exit(1);
}
```

Both the `goto` statement and its corresponding labeled statement must be in the body of the same function. Here is a more specific piece of code that makes use of a `goto`:

```
while (scanf("%lf", &x) == 1) {
   if (x < 0.0)
      goto negative_alert;
   printf("%f  %f  %f\n", x, sqrt(x), sqrt(2 * x));
}

negative_alert:
   if (x < 0.0)
      printf("Negative value encountered!\n");
```

This code can be rewritten in a number of ways without using a `goto`. Here is one way:

```
while (scanf("%lf", &x) == 1 && x >= 0.0)
   printf("%f  %f  %f\n", x, sqrt(x), sqrt(2 * x));
if (x < 0.0)
   printf("Negative value encountered!\n");
```

In general, `goto` should be avoided. It is a primitive method of altering the flow of control, which is unnecessary in a richly structured language. Labeled statements and `goto`s are the hallmark of incremental patchwork program design. A programmer who modifies a program by adding `goto`s to additional code fragments soon makes the program incomprehensible.

When should a `goto` be used? A simple answer is never. Indeed, one cannot go wrong by following this advice. However, in some rare instances, which should be carefully documented, a `goto` can make the program significantly more efficient. In other cases it can simplify the flow of control. This may occur, for example, if we are in a deeply nested inner loop and we want program control to jump to the outermost level of the function.

3.16 The break and continue Statements

Two special statements,

```
break;        and        continue;
```

interrupt the normal flow of control. The `break` statement causes an exit from the innermost enclosing loop or `switch` statement (discussed in the next section). In the following example, a test for a negative argument is made, and if the test is true, a `break` statement is used to pass control to the statement immediately following the loop.

```
while (1) {
   scanf("%lf", &x);
   if (x < 0.0)
      break;            /* exit loop if x is negative */
   printf("%f\n", sqrt(x));
}

/* break jumps to here */
```

This is a typical use of `break`. What would otherwise be an infinite loop is made to terminate upon a given condition tested by the `if` expression.

The `continue` statement causes the current iteration of a loop to stop and the next iteration to begin immediately.

```
while (cnt < n) {
   scanf("%lf", &x);
   if (x > -0.01 && x < +0.01)
      continue;                 /* disregard small values */
   ++cnt;
   sum += x;
/* continue transfers control here to begin next iteration */
}
```

The `continue` statement may only occur inside `for`, `while`, and `do` loops. As the examples show, `continue` transfers control to the end of the current iteration, whereas `break` terminates the loop.

In the presence of a `continue` statement, a `for` loop of the form

```
for (expr1; expr2; expr3) {
   statements
   continue;
   more statements
}
```

is equivalent to

```
expr1;
while (expr2) {
    statements
    goto next;
    more statements
next:
    expr3;
}
```

which is different from

```
expr1;
while (expr2) {
    statements
    continue;
    more statements
    expr3;
}
```

See exercise 25 on page 119 for a convenient way to test this.

3.17 The switch Statement

The `switch` is a multiway conditional statement generalizing the `if-else` statement. The following is a typical example of a `switch` statement:

```
switch (val) {
case 1:
    ++a_cnt;
    break;
case 2:
case 3:
    ++b_cnt;
    break;
default:
    ++other_cnt;
}
```

Notice that the body of the `switch` statement in the example is a compound statement. This is so in all but the most degenerate situations. The controlling expression in the parentheses following the keyword `switch` must be of integer type (see Chapter 6, "The Fundamental Data Types"). In the example, it is just the `int` variable `val`. After the expression is evaluated, control jumps to the appropriate `case` label. The constant integral expressions following the `case` labels must all be unique. Typically, the last statement before the next `case` or `default` label is a `break` statement. If there is no `break` statement, execution "falls through" to the next statement in the succeeding case. Missing `break` statements are a frequent cause of error in `switch` statements. There may be at most one `default` label in a `switch`. Typically, it occurs last although it can occur anywhere. The keywords `case` and `default` cannot occur outside of a `switch`.

The Effect of a `switch`

1 Evaluate the `switch` expression.

2 Go to the `case` label having a constant value that matches the value of the expression found in step 1. If a match is not found, go to the `default` label; if there is no `default` label, terminate the `switch`.

3 Terminate the `switch` when a `break` statement is encountered, or by "falling off the end."

Let us review the various kinds of jump constructs that are available to us. These include the `goto`, `break`, `continue`, and `return`. The `goto` is unrestricted in its use and should be avoided as a dangerous construct. The `break` statement may be used in loops and is important to the proper structuring of the `switch` statement. The `continue` statement must be used within loops and is often unnecessary. The `return` statement must be used in functions that return values. It is discussed in Chapter 4, "Functions and Structured Programming."

3.18 Nested Flow of Control

Flow-of-control statements such as `if`, `for`, `while`, and `switch` statements can be nested within themselves and within one another. Although such nested control constructs can be quite complicated, some have a regular structure and are easily understood.

One of the more common nested flow-of-control constructs makes repeated use of `if-else` statements. Its general form is given by

```
if (expr1)
    statement1
else if (expr2)
    statement2
else if (expr3)
    statement3
  .....
else if (exprN)
    statementN
else
    default statement
next statement
```

This whole giant construction, except for *next statement*, is a single `if-else` statement. Suppose, for example, that *expr1* and *expr2* are both zero (*false*) and that *expr3* is nonzero (*true*). In this case, *statement1* and *statement2* are skipped, and *statement3* is executed; then control passes to *next statement*. No other intervening statement is executed. If we suppose that all of the expressions are zero, only *default statement* is executed. In some circumstances the execution of a default statement is not wanted. In this case a construction such as the preceding would be used, except that the two lines

```
else
    default statement
```

would not appear. *Programming tip:* If you place the more likely cases at the top of this giant `if-else` construct, your code will be more efficient because fewer expressions are computed before control passes beyond the construct.

3.19 The Conditional Operator

The conditional operator `?:` is unusual because it is a ternary operator. It takes three expressions as operands. The general form of a conditional expression is

expr1 ? *expr2* : *expr3*

First, *expr1* is evaluated. If it is nonzero (*true*), then *expr2* is evaluated, and that is the value of the conditional expression as a whole. If *expr1* is zero (*false*), then *expr3* is evaluated, and that is the value of the conditional expression as a whole. Thus a conditional expression can be used to do the work of an `if-else` statement. Consider, for example, the code

```
if (y < z)
   x = y;
else
   x = z;
```

The effect of the code is to assign to `x` the minimum of `y` and `z`. This also can be accomplished by writing

```
x = (y < z) ? y : z;
```

The parentheses are not necessary because the precedence of the conditional operator is just above assignment. Nonetheless, they help to make clear what is being tested for.

The type of the conditional expression

expr1 ? expr2 : expr3

is determined by both *expr2* and *expr3*. If they are of different types, the usual conversion rules are applied (see Chapter 6, "The Fundamental Data Types"). Note carefully that the type of the conditional expression does not depend on which of the two expressions, *expr2* or *expr3*, is evaluated.

The conditional operator `?:` has precedence just above the assignment operators, and it associates from right to left. The next table illustrates how conditional expressions are evaluated.

Declarations and initializations			
`int a = 1, b = 2;` `double x = 7.07;`			
Expression	**Equivalent expression**	**Value**	**Type**
`a == b ? a - 1 : b + 1`	`(a == b) ? (a - 1) : (b + 1)`	3	`int`
`a - b < 0 ? x : a + b`	`((a - b) < 0) ? x : (a + b)`	7.07	`double`
`a - b > 0 ? x : a + b`	`((a - b) > 0) ? x : (a + b)`	3.0	`double`

3.20 Style

Throughout this text we use the Bell Labs industrial programming style. This style embodies four key features.

Bell Labs Industrial Programming Style

1 Follow the normal rules of English, where possible, such as putting a space after a comma.

2 Put one space on each side of a binary operator to heighten readability.

3 Indent code in a consistent fashion to indicate the flow of control.

4 Place braces as indicated in the following example:

```
for (i = 0; i < n; ++i) {
   .....
}
```

The placement of braces to reflect flow of control is crucial to good programming style. The statements in the body of the loop are indented three spaces, and the closing brace } is lined up directly under the `for`. The indentation serves to visually set off those statements making up the body of the loop. The placement of the `for` above the } serves to visually mark the beginning and end, respectively, of the loop. A variation of this style would be to choose a different indentation, such as two, four, five, or eight spaces.

Another programming style is to place beginning and ending braces in the same column. Here is an example:

```
while (i < 10)
{
    .....
}
```

This is sometimes called *student style*. Which style you use is a matter of taste, and (to some extent) the power of the editor being used. Programmers who use the Bell Labs style tend to use a powerful editor that can easily find matching braces or parentheses, can indent multiple lines of code as a unit, has an autoindent feature, and so forth. For example, the *emacs* and *vi* editors in UNIX have these features.

If the body of a loop is a single statement, braces are not necessary. Nonetheless, as a matter of style, some programmers *always* use braces.

```
while (i < 10) {
    a single statement
}
```

This is an acceptable practice. The executable code produced by the compiler is just as efficient with or without the extraneous braces.

Because in C, only a small percentage of loops tend to be `do` loops, it is considered good programming style to use braces even when they are not needed. The braces in the construct

```
do {
    a single statement
} while (.....);
```

make it easier for the reader to realize this is a `do` statement rather than a `while` statement followed by an empty statement.

In many situations, either a `while` loop or a `for` loop can be used. However, if it makes sense to keep control and indexing visible at the top, then a `for` loop should be used. Otherwise, the choice is a matter of personal taste.

The following style for nested `if-else` statements is not recommended and, in fact, is seldom used:

```
if (expr1)    /* wrong style */
   statement
else if (expr2)
          statement2
      else if (expr3)
                statement3
            else if (expr3)
                       statement3
.....
```

Any variation of this style that causes the nested `if-else` statements to march across the screen is unacceptable because long chains run out of space. The horizontal space across the screen is a scarce resource.

I TOLD YOU WE LIKE OUR PROGRAMMERS TO USE NICELY INDENTED, WELL-COMMENTED CODE WHICH HAS AN EASY TO FOLLOW FLOW OF CONTROL. NO GOTOS AND NO SPAGHETTI CODE ALLOWED!

3.21 Common Programming Errors

We discuss a number of common programming errors. The first one concerns the confusion between the two expressions

```
a == b        and        a = b
```

Although they are visually similar, they are radically different in function. The expression `a == b` is a test for equality, whereas `a = b` is an assignment expression. One of the more common programming mistakes is to code something like

```
if (k = 1)
   .....
```

instead of

```
if (k == 1)
    .....
```

Because its value is 1, the assignment expression `k = 1` is always *true*. Some compilers give a warning about this; others do not. Without a warning, such an error can be quite difficult to find. Note that if we write

```
if (1 = k)
    .....
```

then the compiler certainly warns us about the error. It is not legal to assign a value to a constant. For this reason, some programmers routinely write tests of the form

constant == *expr*

This guards against the error of writing = instead of ==. A disadvantage of this style is that it does not conform to the way we ordinarily think—namely, "If `k` is equal to 1, then . . . ."

The second common programming error occurs when an expression that controls an iterative statement causes an unwanted infinite loop. Care should be taken to avoid this difficulty. For example, consider the code

```
printf("Input an integer:  ");
scanf("%d", &n);
while (--n) {
    .....
}
```

The intent is for a positive integer to be entered, its value to be stored at the address of `n`, and the body of the `while` loop to be executed repeatedly until the value of the expression `--n` is eventually zero. However, if a negative integer is assigned to `n` inadvertently, the loop becomes infinite. To guard against this possibility, the programmer should instead code

```
while (--n > 0) {
    .....
}
```

A third common programming error involves the use of an unwanted semicolon after an `if`, `while`, or `for`. Consider, for example,

```
for (i = 1; i <= 10; ++i);
   sum += i;
```

This code does not behave as expected because the semicolon at the end of the first line creates an unwanted null statement. The code is equivalent to

```
for (i = 1; i <= 10; ++i)
   ;
sum += i;
```

which clearly is not what the programmer intended. This type of bug can be very difficult to find.

Next, we want to discuss how the misuse of relational operators can lead to an unexpected result. Recall that in mathematics the expression $2 < k < 7$ means that k is greater than 2 and less than 7. We can also consider this as an assertion about k that is either *true* or *false*, depending on the value of k. For example, if k is 8, the assertion is *false*. In contrast to this, consider the following code:

```
int   k = 8;
if (2 < k < 7)
   printf("true");          /* true is printed! */
else
   printf("false");
```

The reason that the expression is *true* is straightforward. Because relational operators associate from left to right,

`2 < k < 7`   is equivalent to   `(2 < k) < 7`

Because `2 < k` is *true*, its value is 1. Thus

`(2 < k) < 7`   is equivalent to   `1 < 7`

which is obviously *true*. The correct way to write a test for both `2 < k` and `k < 7` is

`2 < k && k < 7`   which is equivalent to   `(2 < k) && (k < 7)`

because < has higher precedence than &&. The expression as a whole is *true* if and only if both operands of && are *true*.

Our final common programming error involves a test for equality that is beyond the accuracy of most machines. Here is a program that illustrates this:

```
/* An equality test that fails. */

#include <stdio.h>

int main(void)
{
   int       cnt = 0;
   double    sum = 0.0, x;

   for (x = 0.0; x != 9.9; x += 0.1) {       /* trouble! */
      sum += x;
      printf("cnt = %5d\n", ++cnt);
   }
   printf("sum = %f\n", sum);
   return 0;
}
```

Mathematically, if x starts at zero and is incremented by 0.1 repeatedly, it eventually takes on the value 9.9. The intent of the programmer is for program control to exit the for loop when that happens. However, if the test x == 9.9 is beyond the accuracy of the machine, the expression x != 9.9 is always *true*, and the program goes into an infinite loop. The programmer must remember that on any machine, floating arithmetic, unlike integer arithmetic, is not exact. To fix the problem, we can write x <= 9.9 rather than x != 9.9 (see exercise 27 on page 120).

A good programming style is to use a relational expression, if appropriate, rather than an equality expression to control a loop or an if or if-else statement. In general, this style produces code that is more robust.

3.22 System Considerations

Both the hardware and the operating system determine how numbers are represented in the machine. We want to discuss a problem that arises because floating numbers cannot be represented with infinite precision. Sometimes this can cause unexpected results. In mathematics, the relation

x < x + y   is equivalent to   0 < y

Mathematically, if y is positive, both of these relations are logically true. Computationally, if x is a floating variable with a large value, such as 7×10^{33}, and y is a floating variable with a small value, such as 0.001, then the relational expression

```
x < x + y
```

may be *false*, even though mathematically it is true. An equivalent expression is

```
(x - (x + y)) < 0.0
```

and it is this expression that the machine implements. If, in terms of machine accuracy, the values of x and x + y are equal, the expression yields the int value 0 (see exercise 6 on page 116).

Next, we want to discuss infinite loops. They sometimes occur inadvertently, but in an interactive environment the programmer may want to deliberately use an infinite loop. If so, the user has to interrupt the program to stop it. What must be typed to interrupt a program is system-dependent. In both MS-DOS and UNIX, a control-c is typically used to terminate a program. However, other operating systems may do it differently. Two conventional styles for an infinite loop are

```
while (1) {
   .....
}
```

and

```
for ( ; ; ) {
   .....
}
```

Let us suppose a programmer wishes to experiment. Rather than running a program over and over, it may be more convenient to put the essential code into an infinite loop. For example:

```
printf("Sums from 1 to n will be computed.\n\n");
for ( ; ; ) {
   printf("Input n:  ");
   scanf("%d", &n);
   sum = 0;
   for (i = 1; i <= n; ++i)
      sum += i;
   printf("sum = %d\n\n", sum);
}
```

3.23 Moving to C++

Statement types and flow of control remain the same in C++. One extension that has already been mentioned is that declarations are statements in C++ and can be intermixed with executable statements. This is especially common in loop constructions.

```
for (int i = 1, sum = 0; i <= n; ++ i)
   sum += i;
```

In this `for` statement, the declaration and initialization of `sum` and `i` are given. The variables `sum` and `i` continue to exist in the remainder of the block, just as they would have if declared at the beginning of `main()`.

ANSI C++ now allows a boolean type `bool`, so that boolean expressions may now evaluate to `true` and `false`. The type `bool` is a break with C tradition. Over the years, many schemes have been used to achieve a boolean type, such as

```
typedef int boolean;
#define true 1
#define false 0
     or
enum boolean { false, true };
```

The use of the `bool` type removes these inconsistencies. Examples of declarations are

```
bool  my_turn = false, your_true;
bool* p = &my_turn;
```

The `bool` type becomes the type returned by relational, logical, and equality expressions. The `bool` constants `true` and `false` are promotable to `1` and `0`, respectively. Nonzero values are assignment convertible to `true` and zero is assignment convertible to `false`.

Summary

- Relational, equality, and logical expressions have the `int` value 0 or 1. These expressions are used chiefly to test data to affect flow of control.

- The relational, equality, and logical operators are binary, except the negation operator `!`, which is unary. A negation expression such as `!a` has the `int` value 0 or 1. Usually, the values of `!!a` and `a` are different.

- The grouping construct `{ ····· }` is a compound statement. It allows enclosed statements to be treated as a single unit.

- An `if` statement provides a means of choosing whether or not to execute a statement. An `if-else` statement provides a means of choosing which of two statements is executed. The `else` part of an `if-else` statement associates with the nearest available `if`. This resolves the "dangling else" problem.

- One reason we use computers is to repeatedly perform certain actions. The `while`, `for`, and `do` statements provide looping mechanisms in C. The body of a `while` or `for` statement is executed zero or more times. The body of a `do` statement is executed one or more times.

- The programmer often has to choose between using a `for` or a `while` statement. Where clarity dictates that both the control and the indexing be kept visible at the top of the loop, the `for` statement is the natural choice.

- The comma operator is occasionally useful in `for` statements. Of all the operators in C, it has the lowest priority.

- The four statement types

  ```
  goto      break      continue      return
  ```

  cause an unconditional transfer of the flow of control. Except for the use of `break` statements in a `switch`, their use should be minimized.

- Avoid `goto`s; they are considered harmful to good programming.

- The `switch` statement provides a multiway conditional branch. It is useful when dealing with a large number of special cases. Typically, the `break` statement is needed for the proper functioning of a `switch`.

Exercises

1 Give equivalent logical expressions without using negation.

```
!(a > b)
!(a <= b && c <= d)
!(a + 1 == b + 1)
!(a < 1 || b < 2 && c < 3)
```

2 Complete the following table.

Declarations and initializations		
`int a = 1, b = 2, c = 3;` `double x = 1.0;`		
Expression	**Equivalent expression**	**Value**
`a > b && c < d`		
`a < ! b || ! ! a`		
`a + b < ! c + c`		
`a - x || b * c && b / a`		

3 Write a program that contains the loop

```
while (scanf("lf", &salary) == 1) {
    .....
}
```

Within the body of the while loop, compute a 23 percent federal withholding tax and a 7 percent state withholding tax and print these values along with a corresponding salary. Accumulate the sums of all salaries and taxes printed. Print these sums after the program exits the while loop.

4 What is printed when the following code executes?

```
int     a = 1, b = 2, c = 3;
float   x = 3.3, y = 5.5;

printf("%d %d\n", !  a+b/c, !a + b / c);
printf("%d %d\n", a == -b + c, a * b > c == a);
printf("%d %d\n", !!x < a + b + c, !!x + !!!y);
printf("%d %d\n", a || b == x && y, !(x || !y));
```

5 Suppose a programmer is working on a problem that requires special action if the int variable k has value 7. Consider the following code:

```
while (k = 7) {
    .....            /* do something */
    k = 0;           /* finished, exit the loop */
}
```

Contrast this with the following code:

```
if (k = 7) {
   .....               /* do something */
}
```

Both pieces of code are logically wrong. The run-time effect of one of them is so striking that the error is easy to spot, whereas the other has a subtle effect that is much harder to spot. Explain.

6 The following code is system-dependent. Nonetheless, most machines produce an answer that is logically incorrect. First explain what logically should be printed. Then test the code on your machine to see what actually is printed.

```
double   x = 1e+33, y = 0.001;
printf("%d\n", x + y > x - y);
```

What happens if you assign the value 1000 to y? Or 1 million? The point of this exercise is to emphasize that floating-point arithmetic need not approximate mathematics very well.

7 What is printed? Explain.

```
int   i = 7, j = 7;
if (i == 1)
   if (j == 2)
      printf("%d\n", i = i + j);
else
   printf("%d\n", i = i - j);
printf("%d\n", i);
```

8 The syntax error in the following piece of code does not really show up on the line indicated. Run a test program with this piece of code in it to find out which line is flagged with a syntax error. Explain why.

```
while (++i < LIMIT) do {      /* syntax error */
   j = 2 * i + 3;
   printf("j = %d\n", j);
}

   /* Many other languages require "do", but not C. */
```

9 In the following code assume that the values of `i` and `j` are not changed in the body of the loop. Can the code ever lead to an infinite loop? Explain.

```
printf("Input two integers: ");
scanf("%d%d", &i, &j);
while (i * j < 0 && ++i != 7 && j++ != 9) {
   .....      /* do something */
}
```

10 Write a program that reads in an integer value for `n` and then sums the integers from `n` to `2 * n` if `n` is nonnegative, or from `2 * n` to `n` if `n` is negative. Write the code in two versions: one using only `for` loops and the other using only `while` loops.

11 Until interrupted, the following code prints `True forever!` on the screen repeatedly. (In MS-DOS and UNIX, type a control-c to effect an interrupt.)

```
while (1)
   printf(" True forever! ");
```

Write a simple program that accomplishes the same thing, but instead of a `while` statement, use a `for` statement that has as its body an empty statement.

12 We have already explained that

```
while (1) {
   .....
}
```

is an infinite loop. What does the following code do? If you are not quite sure, try it. That is, create a program containing these lines and run it.

```
while (-33.777)
   printf("run forever, if you can");
```

13 Let *a* and *b* be arithmetic expressions. We want to establish that

`a != b` is equivalent to `!(a == b)`

Do this by completing the following table.

Values of arithmetic expressions			
a - b	**a != b**	**a == b**	**!(a == b)**
zero			
nonzero			

14 Run the program *find_max* and enter 1 when prompted. You see on the screen

```
Enter 1 real numbers:
```

This is, of course, improper English. Change the program so that `number` is printed if `n` has the value 1, and `numbers` is printed otherwise.

15 Suppose you detest even integers but love odd ones. Modify the *find_max* program so that all variables are of type `int` and only odd integers are processed. Of course, you have to explain all of this to the user via appropriate `printf()` statements.

16 What happens when you run the following code on your system? If it does not run correctly, change it so that it does.

```
double   sum = 0.0, x;

printf("%5s%15s\n", "Value", "Running sum");
printf("%5s%15s\n", "-----", "-----------");
for (x = 0.0; x != 9.9; x += 0.1) {  /*test not robust*/
   sum += x;
   printf("%5.1f%15.1f\n", x, sum);
}
```

17 Beginning programmers sometimes mix up the order of the expressions used to control a `for` loop. In the following code an attempt is being made to sum the integers from 1 to 5. What is the effect of mixing up the expressions? First, simulate what happens manually, and then write a test program to find out if you were correct.

```
int   i, sum = 0;
for (i = 1; ++i; i <= 5)
   printf("i = %d   sum = %d\n", i, sum += i);
```

18 Write an interactive program that asks the user to supply three integers *k*, *m*, and *n*, with *k* being greater than 1. Your program should compute the sum of all the integers between *m* and *n* that are divisible by *k*.

19 C++: Write the previous exercise as a C++ program.

20 This exercise gives you practice with short-circuit evaluation.

```
int   a = 0, b = 0, x;

x = 0 && (a = b = 777);
printf("%d %d %d\n", a, b, x);
x = 777 || (a = ++b);
printf("%d %d %d\n", a, b, x);
```

What is printed? First write down your answers, and then write a test program to check them.

21 C++: Write the previous exercise as a C++ program.

22 Complete the following table.

Declarations and initializations		
`int a = 1, b = 2, c = 3;`		
Expression	**Equivalent expression**	**Value**
`a && b && c`	`(a && b) && c`	
`a && b || c`		
`a || b && c`		
`a || ! b && ! ! c + 4`		
`a += ! b && c == ! 5`		

23 The semantics of logical expressions implies that the order of evaluation is critical in some computations. Which of the following expressions is most likely to be the correct one? Explain.

(a)
```
if ((x != 0.0) && ((z - x) / x * x < 2.0))
   .....
```

(b)
```
if (((z - x) / x * x < 2.0) && (x != 0.0))
   .....
```

24 A *truth table* for a boolean function is a table consisting of all possible values for its variables and the corresponding values of the boolean function itself. Previously, we created a truth table for the majority function and two other functions (see Section 3.12, "Problem Solving: Boolean Variables," on page 97). Create separate truth tables for the following boolean functions:

```
b1 || b2 || b3 || b4            !(!b1 || b2) && (!b3 || b4)
```

Use the letters `T` and `F` in your truth tables to represent *true* and *false*, respectively. *Hint:* Use a `#define` preprocessing directive to define a `BOOLEX`. Then write your program to operate on an arbitrary `BOOLEX`.

25 Here is a simple way to test the effect of a `continue` statement in the body of a `for` loop. What is printed?

```
for (putchar('1'); putchar('2'); putchar('3')) {
   putchar('4');
   continue;
   putchar('5');
}
```

26 The mathematical operation `min(x, y)` can be represented by the conditional expression

```
(x < y) ? x : y
```

In a similar fashion, using only conditional expressions, describe the mathematical operations

`min(x, y, z)` and `max(x, y, z, w)`

27 Does the nonrobust equality test program given in Section 3.21, "Common Programming Errors," on page 111, result in an infinite loop on your machine? If so, modify the program as suggested and execute it. Does it produce an answer that is close to being mathematically correct? If `x == 9.9` is never *true* as `x` is incremented in the loop, then perhaps the answer is off by an amount approximately equal to 0.1.

28 In a comma expression of the form

expr1 , *expr2*

expr1 is evaluated first, then *expr2*, and the comma expression as a whole has the value and type of its right operand. An example of a comma expression is

```
a = 1, b = 2
```

If `b` has been declared to be an `int`, then the value of this comma expression is 2 and its type is `int`. Here is a `for` loop that prints a column of even integers and a column of odd integers. Which commas are comma operators and which are not? Rewrite the code so that no comma operators are used.

```
int   i, j;

for (i = 0, j = 1; i < LIMIT; i += 2, j += 2)
   printf("%12d%12d\n", i, j);
```

29 C++: C++ now allows a boolean type. This can be simulated on a compiler that has not yet implemented this type with integer constants.

```
const int true =  1;
const int false = 0;
```

The output statement

```
cout << (expression) ? "true\t" : "false\t" ;
```

prints a boolean value. Write a program using this form of I/O to answer exercise 20 on page 118.

30 The following Java program computes an average of an unspecified number of doubles. The program uses the sentinel value 0 to stop a loop that is accumulating the read-in doubles. Convert it to C.

```
// Average.java - compute average of input values -Java by
Dissection page 74.
import tio.*;

public class Average {
  public static void main(String[] args) {
    double number;
    int count = 0;
    double runningTotal = 0;

    // initialization before first loop iteration
    System.out.println("Type some numbers, " +
        "the last one being 0");
    number = Console.in.readDouble();

    while (number != 0) {
      runningTotal = runningTotal + number;
      count = count + 1;
      // prepare for next iteration
      number = Console.in.readDouble();
    }
    System.out.print("The average of the ");
    System.out.print(count);
    System.out.print(" numbers is ");
    System.out.println(runningTotal/count);
  }
}
```

As with other Java programs that are like simple C programs, there is a `main()` method sitting inside a class. The programs differ chiefly in their use of different I/O schemes.

31 The following Java program shows some additional difference between Java and C. Convert it to C.

```
// BreakContinue.java - example of break and continue
//Java by Dissection page 80
import tio.*;

class BreakContinue {
  public static void main(String[] args) {
    int n;

    while (true) {       //seemingly an infinite loop
      System.out.print("Enter a positive integer ");
      System.out.print("or 0 to exit:");
      n = Console.in.readInt();
      if (n == 0)
        break;           // exit loop if n is 0
      if (n < 0)
        continue;        //wrong value
      System.out.print("squareroot of " + n);
      System.out.println(" = " +Math.sqrt(n));
      //continue land here at end of current iteration
    }
    //break lands here
    System.out.println("a zero was entered");
  }
}
```

A difference between C and Java is that Java has a boolean type. The control expression of an `if` or `while` statement is a boolean expression. This means that a mistake like "`if (n = 0)`" is caught syntactically by the Java compiler. The compiler in Java complains that this is an `int` expression and cannot be used as the test expression for an `if`. In C, this is not a syntax error because it means assign 0 to `n` and return the value 0, meaning *false*. In addition, the `goto` is not allowed in Java. It is allowed in C but is strongly discouraged as bad practice.

Chapter 4

Functions and Structured Programming

Structured programming is a problem-solving strategy and a programming methodology that includes the following two guidelines:

Structured Programming Guidelines

1 The flow of control in a program should be as simple as possible.

2 The construction of a program should embody top-down design.

Top-down design, also referred to as *stepwise refinement*, consists of repeatedly decomposing a problem into smaller problems. Eventually, one has a collection of small problems or tasks, each of which can be easily coded.

The function construct in C is used to write code that solves the small problems that result from this decomposition. These functions are combined into other functions and ultimately used in `main()` to solve the original problem. The function mechanism is provided in C to perform distinct programming tasks. Some functions, such as `printf()` and `scanf()`, are provided by the system; others can be written by the programmer.

We illustrate structured programming and top-down design in this chapter, but first we want to describe the function mechanism.

4.1 Function Invocation

A program is made up of one or more functions, one of them being `main()`. Program execution always begins with `main()`. When program control encounters a function name followed by parentheses, the function is *called*, or *invoked*. This means that program control passes to the function. After the function does its work, program control is passed back to the calling environment, where program execution continues. As a simple example, consider the following program, which prints a message:

```
#include <stdio.h>

void   prn_message(void);                 /* fct prototype */

int main(void)
{
   prn_message();                         /* fct invocation */
}

void prn_message(void)                    /* fct definition */
{
   printf("A message for you:  ");
   printf("Have a nice day!\n");
}
```

At the top of the file we have the `#include` preprocessing directive followed by the function prototype for `prn_message()`. The function prototype tells the compiler that this function takes no arguments and returns no values to the calling environment. Execution begins in `main()`. When program control encounters `prn_message()`, the function is called, or invoked, and program control is passed to it. After the two `printf()` statements in `prn_message()` have been executed, program control passes back to the calling environment, which in this example is in `main()`. Because there is no more work to be done in `main()`, the program ends. Although our function `prn_message()` does not return a value to the calling environment, many functions, as we shall see, do return a value.

4.2 Function Definition

The C code that describes what a function does is called the *function definition*. It has the following general form:

type function_name (parameter type list)
{
   declarations
   statements
}

Everything before the first brace comprises the *header* of the function definition, and everything between the two braces comprises the *body* of the function definition. The *type* of the function is the type of the value returned by the function. If nothing is returned, the keyword `void` is used. The *parameter type list* describes the number and types of the arguments that are passed into the function when it is invoked. If no arguments are passed in, the keyword `void` is used.

The parameters in the parameter type list are identifiers and can be used within the body of the function. Sometimes the parameters in a function definition are called *formal parameters* to emphasize their role as placeholders for actual values that are passed to the function when it is called. Upon function invocation, the value of the argument corresponding to a formal parameter is used within the body of the executing function.

To illustrate these ideas, let us rewrite the program given in Section 4.1, "Function Invocation," on page 124, so that the function `prn_message()` has a formal parameter. The parameter is used to specify how many times the message is printed.

```
#include <stdio.h>

void   prn_message(int k);

int main(void)
{
   int   how_many;

   printf("%s",
      "There is a message for you.\n"
      "How many times do you want to see it?  ");
   scanf("%d", &how_many);
   prn_message(how_many);
   return 0;
}

void prn_message(int no_of_messages)
{
   int   i;

   printf("Here is the message:\n");
   for (i = 0; i <  no_of_messages; ++i)
      printf("   Have a nice day!\n");
}
```

Dissection of the message Program

■ `#include <stdio.h>`

The standard header file *stdio.h* contains the function prototypes for `printf()` and `scanf()`. We included this file because we are using these functions. A function prototype is a kind of function definition. To do its job properly, the compiler needs to know the number and type of arguments that are passed into a function and the type of the value returned by the function. The function prototype provides this information.

■ `void   prn_message(int  k);`

This is the function prototype for the function `prn_message()`. The function type is `void`, which tells the compiler that the function does not return a value. The parameter list is `int  no_of_messages`, which tells the compiler that the function takes a single argument of type `int`.

■
```
int main(void)
{
    .....
}
```

This is the function definition for `main()`. The first line is the header to the function definition, and the lines between the two braces constitute the body of the function definition. Usually, the programmer does *not* supply a function prototype for `main()`.

■
```
printf("%s",
    "There is a message for you.\n"
    "How many times do you want to see it?  ");
scanf("%d", &how_many);
```

The call to `printf()` prompts the user to input an integer. The call to `scanf()` reads the characters typed by the user, converts those characters to a decimal value, and places the value at the address of `how_many`.

■ `prn_message(how_many);`

This statement causes the function `prn_message()` to be called, or invoked. The value of `how_many` is passed as an argument to the function.

■
```
void prn_message(int no_of_messages)
{
    .....
}
```

This is the function definition for prn_message(). The first line is the header of the function definition. Because the function does not return a value to the calling environment, the type of the function is void. The identifier no_of_messages is a parameter that is declared to be of type int. One can think of the parameter no_of_messages as representing the value of the actual argument that is passed to the function when it is called. A call to this function occurred in main() in the statement

```
prn_message(how_many);
```

In main(), suppose that the value of how_many is 2. When program control passes to prn_message(), the variable no_of_messages has this value.

■
```
void prn_message(int no_of_messages)
{
    int   i;

    printf("Here is the message:\n");
    for (i = 0; i < no_of_messages; ++i)
       printf("   Have a nice day!\n");
}
```

The code between the two braces constitutes the body of the function definition for prn_message(). If we think of no_of_messages as having the value 2, the message is printed twice. When program control reaches the end of the function, control is passed back to the calling environment.

Notice that parameters and local variables used in one function definition have no relation to those in another. For example, if the variable i had been used in main(), it would have had no relationship to the variable i in prn_message().

4.3 The return Statement

When a return statement is executed, program control is immediately passed back to the calling environment; if an expression follows the keyword return, the value of the expression is returned to the calling environment as well. This value is converted, if necessary, to the type of the function, as specified in the header to the function definition. A return statement has one of the following two forms:

```
return;
return expression;
```

Some examples are

```
return;
return 77;
return ++a;
return (a + b + c);
```

You can enclose the expression being returned in parentheses, and if the expression is complicated, it is considered good programming practice to do so.

There can be zero or more `return` statements in a function. If there is no `return` statement, control is passed back to the calling environment when the closing brace of the body is encountered. This is called "falling off the end." To illustrate the use of `return` statements, let us write a program that computes the minimum of two integers.

```
#include <stdio.h>

int   min(int a, int b);

int main(void)
{
   int   j, k, minimum;

   printf("Input two integers:  ");
   scanf("%d%d", &j, &k);
   minimum = min(j, k);
   printf("\nOf the two values %d and %d, "
          "the minumum is %d.\n\n", j, k, minimum);
   return 0;
}

int min(int a, int b)
{
   if (a < b)
      return a;
   else
      return b;
}
```

Dissection of the minimum Program

■
```
#include <stdio.h>

int   min(int a, int b);
```

We include the system header file *stdio.h* because it contains the function prototypes for `printf()` and `scanf()`. In addition to `printf()` and `scanf()`, our program uses the function `min()`, which we write ourselves. The function prototype for `min()` helps the compiler do its work.

■
```
int main(void)
{
   int   j, k, minimum;

   printf("Input two integers:  ");
   scanf("%d%d", &j, &k);
```

The variables `j`, `k`, and `minimum` are declared to be of type `int`. The user is asked to input two integers. The function `scanf()` is used to store the values in `j` and `k`.

■
```
minimum = min(j, k);
```

The values of `j` and `k` are passed as arguments to `min()`. The function `min()` returns a value, which is assigned to `minimum`.

■
```
printf("\nOf the two values %d and %d, "
       "the minumum is %d.\n\n", j, k, minimum);
```

The values of `j`, `k`, and `minimum` are printed out.

■
```
int min(int a, int b)
```

This is the header of the function definition for `min()`. The return type of the function is `int`. This means the value returned from within the function is converted, if necessary, to an `int` before it is returned to the calling environment. The parameter list

```
int a, int b
```

declares `a` and `b to be of type int`. The parameters is used in the body of the function definition.

■
```
int min(int a, int b)
{
   if (a < b)
      return a;
   else
      return b;
}
```

The code between the braces constitutes the body of the function definition for `min()`. If the value of `a` is less than the value of `b`, the value of `a` is returned to the calling environment; otherwise the value of `b` is returned.

Even small functions such as `min()` provide useful structuring to the code. If we want to modify our program so the maximum value is also computed, we can use a function `max()` to do so. We have to put its function prototype at the top of the file, call the function as appropriate in `main()`, and write its function definition at the bottom of the file. Here is the function definition:

```
int max(int a, int b)
{
   if (a > b)
      return a;
   else
      return b;
}
```

We have designed `min()` and `max()` to work with integer values. If we want these functions to work with values of type `double`, we must rewrite the functions. We rewrite `min()` and leave the rewriting of `max()` as an exercise. (See exercise 9 on page 165.) Instead of `a` and `b`, we use the parameters `x` and `y`, which is common practice when dealing with `float`s and `double`s.

```
double min(double x, double y)
{
   if (x < y)
      return x;
   else
      return y;
}
```

Even though a function returns a value, a program does not need to use it.

```
while (·····) {
   getchar();          /* get a char, do nothing with it */
   c = getchar();      /* c will be processed */
   .....
}
```

4.4 Function Prototypes

Functions should be declared before they are used. ANSI C provides for a new function declaration syntax called the *function prototype.* A function prototype tells the compiler the number and type of arguments that are to be passed to the function and the type of the value that is to be returned by the function. An example is

```
double   sqrt(double);
```

This tells the compiler that `sqrt()` is a function that takes a single argument of type `double` and returns a `double`. The general form of a function prototype is given by

type function_name (*parameter type list*) ;

The parameter type list is typically a comma-separated list of types. Identifiers are optional; they do not affect the prototype. For example, the function prototype

`void f(char c, int i);` is equivalent to `void f(char, int);`

Identifiers such as `c` and `i` that occur in parameter type lists in function prototypes are not used by the compiler. Their purpose is to provide documentation to the programmer and other readers of the code. The keyword `void` is used if a function takes no arguments. Also, the keyword `void` is used if no value is returned by the function.

"OH, NO, HAROLD. YOU'RE BECOMING A FUNCTION THAT RETURNS A VOID VALUE!"

If a function takes a variable number of arguments, then the ellipsis (...) is used. See, for example, the function prototype for printf() in the standard header file *stdio.h*.

Function prototypes allow the compiler to check the code more thoroughly. Also, values passed to functions are coerced, where necessary. For example, if the function prototype for sqrt() has been specified, the function call sqrt(4) yields the correct value. Because the compiler knows that sqrt() takes a double, the int value 4 is promoted to a double and the correct value is returned (see exercise 2 on page 163).

In traditional C, parameter type lists are not allowed in function declarations. For example, the function declaration of sqrt() is given by

```
double sqrt();          /* traditional C style */
```

With this declaration, the function call sqrt(4) does not yield the correct value. Even though ANSI C compilers accept traditional style function declarations, function prototypes are much preferred.

4.5 Top-Down Design

Imagine that we have to analyze company data that is represented by a file of integers. As we read each integer, we want to print out the count, the integer, the sum of all the integers seen up to this point, the minimum integer seen up to this point, and the maximum integer seen up to this point. In addition to this, suppose a banner must be printed at the top of the page and that all the information must be neatly printed in columns under appropriate headings. To construct this program, we use a top-down designer that can decompose the problem into the following subproblems:

Decomposing the Running Sum Program

1 Print a banner.

2 Print the headings over the columns.

3 Read the data and print it neatly in columns.

Each of these subproblems can be coded directly as functions. Then these functions can be used in main() to solve the overall problem. Note that by designing the code this way, we can add other functions to analyze the data without affecting the program structure.

```
#include <stdio.h>

void   prn_banner(void);
void   prn_headings(void);
void   read_and_prn_data(void);
int    min(int a, int b);
int    max(int a, int b);

int main(void)
{
   prn_banner();
   prn_headings();
   read_and_prn_data();
   return 0;
}
```

This illustrates, in a very simple way, the idea of top-down design. The programmer thinks of the tasks to be performed and codes each task as a function. If a particular task is complicated, then it can be subdivided into smaller tasks, each coded as a function. An additional benefit is that the program as a whole is more readable and self-documenting.

Coding the individual functions is straightforward. We put them all in the same file after `main()`. The first function contains a single `printf()` statement.

```
void prn_banner(void)
{
   printf("\n%s%s%s\n",
      "********************************************\n",
      "*   RUNNING SUMS, MINIMUMS, AND MAXIMUMS   *\n",
      "********************************************\n");
}
```

The next function writes headings over columns. The format `%5s` is used to print a string in five spaces, and the format `%12s` is used four times to print four strings, each in 12 spaces.

```
void prn_headings(void)
{
   printf("%5s%12s%12s%12s%12s\n\n",
      "Count", "Item", "Sum", "Minimum", "Maximum");
}
```

Most of the work is done in `read_and_prn_data()`. We dissect this function to show in detail how it works. In the exercises, you are asked to input data from the keyboard and see what happens when you enter invalid data (see exercise 3 on page 163).

```
void read_and_prn_data(void)
{
   int   count = 0, item, sum, smallest, biggest;

   if (scanf("%d", &item) == 1) {
      ++count;
      sum = smallest = biggest = item;
      printf("%5d%12d%12d%12d%12d\n",
         count, item, sum, smallest, biggest);
      while (scanf("%d", &item) == 1) {
         ++count;
         sum += item;
         smallest = min(item, smallest);
         biggest = max(item, biggest);
         printf("%5d%12d%12d%12d%12d\n",
            count, item, sum, smallest, biggest);
      }
   }
   else
      printf("No data was input - bye!\n\n");
}
```

Suppose this program is compiled and the executable code is put into the file named *run_sums*. If we execute the program and enter data directly from the keyboard, we get the echoing of input characters and the output of the program intermixed on the screen. To prevent this problem, we create a file called *data* containing the following integers:

```
19   23   -7   29   -11   17
```

Now we give the command

run_sums < data

This redirects the input to the program from the keyboard to the file.Here is what is printed on the screen:

```
********************************************
*   RUNNING SUMS, MINIMUMS, AND MAXIMUMS   *
********************************************

Count        Item         Sum     Minimum     Maximum

    1          19          19          19          19
    2          23          42          19          23
    3          -7          35          -7          23
    4          29          64          -7          29
    5         -11          53         -11          29
    6          17          70         -11          29
```

Dissection of the read_and_prn_data() Function

■
```
void read_and_prn_data(void)
{
   int   count = 0, item, sum, smallest, biggest;
```

The header of the function definition is the single line before the brace. Because the function does not return a value, its type is `void`. The function takes no arguments. In the body of the function definition, the local variables `count`, `item`, `sum`, `smallest`, and `biggest` are declared to be of type `int`. The variable `count` is initialized to zero. The value of the variable `item` is taken from the input stream. The values of the variables `sum`, `smallest`, and `biggest` is computed.

■
```
if (scanf("%d", &item) == 1) {
   ++count;
   sum = smallest = biggest = item;
   printf("%5d%12d%12d%12d%12d\n",
      count, item, sum, smallest, biggest);
   .....
}
else
   printf("No data was input - bye!\n\n");
```

The function `scanf()` returns the number of successful conversions made. Here `scanf()` is attempting to read characters from the standard input stream (keyboard), convert them to a decimal integer, and store the result at the address of `item`. If this conversion process is successful, the expression

```
scanf("%d", &item) == 1
```

is *true*, and the body of the `if` statement is executed. That is, `count` is incremented; the variables `sum`, `smallest`, and `biggest` is assigned the value of `item`; and these values are printed out in appropriate columns. Notice that the formats in the `printf()` statement are similar to those found in `prn_headings()`. If `scanf()` is unsuccessful in its conversion attempt, the `else` part of the `if-else` statement is executed. The conversion process can fail for two reasons. First, there might be an inappropriate character, for example a letter *x*, before any digits occur in the input stream. Because `scanf()` cannot convert the character *x* to a decimal integer, the value returned by `scanf()` is 0. Second, there may be no characters at all in the input stream, or only white space characters. Because `scanf()` skips white space, it would come to the end of the file. When the end-of-file mark is read, `scanf()` returns the value `EOF`. This value, although system-dependent, is typically -1.

■
```
while (scanf("%d", &item) == 1) {
    ++count;
    sum += item;
    smallest = min(item, smallest);
    biggest = max(item, biggest);
    printf("%5d%12d%12d%12d%12d\n",
       count, item, sum, smallest, biggest);
}
```

After the first integer has been obtained from the input stream, we use `scanf()` in this `while` loop to find others. Each time a successful conversion is made by `scanf()`, the body of this `while` loop is executed. This causes `count` to be incremented by 1, `sum` to be incremented by the current value of `item`, `smallest` to be assigned the minimum of the current values of `item` and `smallest`, `biggest` to be assigned the maximum of the current values of `item` and `biggest`, and all of these values to be printed in the appropriate columns. Eventually, `scanf()` encounters an inappropriate character in the input stream or come to the end of the file. In either case, `scanf()` returns a value different from 1, causing program control to exit from the `while` loop.

"LOOK, FRED, ANOTHER BOTTOMS UP AND YOU WON'T BE ABLE TO CODE YOUR TOP-DOWN PROJECT!"

4.6 Program Correctness: The assert() Macro

ANSI C provides the `assert()` macro in the standard header file *assert.h*. This macro can be used to ensure that the value of an expression is what the programmer expects it to be.

Suppose we are writing a critical function `f(int a, int b)` and we want to be sure the arguments passed into the function satisfy certain conditions—for example, `a` must be positive and `b` must lie in the interval [7, 11]. Suppose also that the value returned by the function must be greater than 3.

```
#include <assert.h>

double f(int a, int b)
{
   double   x;

   assert(a > 0);                          /* precondition */
   assert(b >= 7 && b <= 11);              /* precondition */
   .....
   assert(x >= 3.0);                       /* postcondition */
   return x;
}
```

If an assertion fails, the system prints out a message and abort the program. The assertion `assert(a > 0)` is called a *precondition* because it tests that the inputs are suitable for the function to work correctly. The assertion `assert(x >= 3.0)` is called a *postcondition* because it tests a relationship that must hold if the function did its work correctly.

Assertions are easy to write, add robustness to the code, and help other readers of the code understand its intent. They help guarantee that functions behave as expected. Moreover, assertions help the programmer think about correctness. This discipline is beneficial in and of itself. Assertions are not restricted in placement to the beginning and ending statements of a function, but this placement is natural. The use of assertions is good programming methodology.

Note that if the macro `NDEBUG` is defined where *assert.h* is included, then all assertions are ignored. This allows the programmer to use assertions freely during program development, and effectively discard them later by defining the macro `NDEBUG`.

4.7 Function Declarations from the Compiler's Viewpoint

To the compiler, function declarations are generated in various ways: by function invocation, by function definition, and by explicit function declarations and function prototypes. If a function call, say `f(x)`, is encountered before any declaration, definition, or prototype for it occurs, the compiler assumes a default declaration of the form

```
int f();
```

Nothing is assumed about the parameter list for the function. Now suppose the following function definition occurs first:

```
int f(x)              /* traditional C style */
double   x;
{
    .....
```

This provides both declaration and definition to the compiler. Again, however, nothing is assumed about the parameter list. It is the programmer's responsibility to pass only a single argument of type `double` as an argument to `f()`. A function call such as `f(1)` can be expected to fail because 1 is of type `int`, not `double`. Now suppose we use, instead, an ANSI C style definition.

```
int f(double x)       /* ANSI C style */
{
    .....
```

The compiler now knows about the parameter list as well. In this case a function call such as `f(1)` can be expected to work properly. When an `int` is passed as an argument, it is converted to a `double`.

A function prototype is a special case of a function declaration. A good programming style is to give either the function definition (ANSI C style) or the function prototype or both before a function is used. A major reason to include standard header files is that they contain function prototypes.

Limitations

Function definitions and prototypes have certain limitations. The function storage class specifier, if present, can be either `extern` or `static`, but not both; `auto` and `register` cannot be used (see Section 8.6, "The Storage Class `static`," on page 278). The types "array of . . ." and "function returning . . ." cannot be returned by a function. However, a pointer representing an array or a function can be returned (see Chapter 9, "Arrays and Pointers"). The only storage class specifier that can occur in the parameter type list is `register`. Parameters cannot be initialized.

4.8 Problem Solving: Random Numbers

Random numbers have many uses in computers. One use is to serve as data to test code; another use is to simulate a real-world event that involves a probability. The method of simulation is an important problem-solving technique. Programs that use random number functions to generate probabilities are called *Monte Carlo* simulations. The Monte Carlo technique can be applied to many problems that otherwise would have no possibility of solution.

A random number generator is a function that returns integers that appear to be randomly distributed in some interval 0 to *n*, where *n* is system-dependent. The function `rand()` in the standard library is provided to do this. Let us write a program that displays some random numbers generated by `rand()`. Here is the first part of the program:

```
#include <stdio.h>
#include <stdlib.h>

int    max(int a, int b);
int    min(int a, int b);
void   prn_random_numbers(int k);

int main(void)
{
   int   n;

   printf("Some random numbers will be printed.\n");
   printf("How many would you like to see?  ");
   scanf("%d", &n);
   prn_random_numbers(n);
   return 0;
}
```

Because the function prototype for `rand()` is in the standard header file *stdlib.h*, we have included it at the top of the file.

The user is asked how many random numbers are wanted. The function `scanf()` is used to convert the characters typed at the keyboard to a decimal integer and to store the value at the address of `n`. The value of `n` is passed as an argument to the function `prn_random_numbers()`.

In the remainder of the file, we write the function definitions for `max()`, `min()`, and `prn_random_numbers()`. We have already discussed `max()` and `min()`. Here is the function `prn_random_numbers()`:

```
void prn_random_numbers(int k)
{
   int   i, r, biggest, smallest;

   r = biggest = smallest = rand();
   printf("\n%7d", r);
   for (i = 1; i < k; ++i) {
      if (i % 7 == 0)
         printf("\n");
      r = rand();
      biggest = max(r, biggest);
      smallest = min(r, smallest);
      printf("%7d", r);
   }
   printf("\n\n%s%5d\n%s%5d\n%s%5d\n\n",
      "  Count: ", k,
      "Maximum: ", biggest,
      "Minimum: ", smallest);
}
```

We want to dissect this function definition, but before we do so, let us see what the output of the program looks like. Suppose we run this program and input 23 when prompted. Here is what appears on the screen:

```
Some random numbers will be printed.
How many would you like to see?  23

  16838   5758  10113  17515  31051   5627  23010
   7419  16212   4086   2749  12767   9084  12060
  32225  17543  25089  21183  25137  25566  26966
   4978  20495

  Count:    23
Maximum: 32225
Minimum:  2749
```

Dissection of the prn_random_numbers() Function

```
void prn_random_numbers(int k)
{
   int   i, r, biggest, smallest;
```

The variable k is a parameter that is declared to be an `int`. The local variables `i`, `r`, `biggest`, and `smallest` are all declared to be of type `int`.

```
r = biggest = smallest = rand();
printf("\n%7d", r);
```

The function `rand()` from the standard library is used to generate a random number. That number is assigned to the variables `r`, `biggest`, and `smallest`. The function `printf()` is used to print the value of `r` in seven spaces as a decimal integer.

```
for (i = 1; i < k; ++i) {
   if (i % 7 == 0)
      printf("\n");
   r = rand();
   .....
}
```

This `for` loop is used to print the remaining random numbers. Because one random number has already been printed, the variable `i` at the top of the loop is initialized to `1` rather than `0`. Whenever `i` is divisible by 7 (the values 7, 14, 21, . . .), the expression

```
i % 7 == 0
```

controlling the `if` statement is *true*, causing a newline character to be printed. The effect of this is to print at most seven random numbers on each line.

4.9 An Alternate Style for Function Definition Order

If we want to write a program in a single file, we usually put any `#includes` and `#defines` at the top of the file, other program elements such as enumeration types (see Chapter 7, "Enumeration Types and typedef") and structure types (see Chapter 12, "Structures and ADTs") next, and then a list of function prototypes. At the bottom of the file, we write the function definition for `main()` followed by all the other function definitions. This is the order we used in our *random* program in Section 4.8, "Problem Solving: Random Numbers," on page 139.

```
#include <stdio.h>
#include <stdlib.h>

list of function prototypes

int main(void)
{
   .....
}

int max(int a, int b)
{
   .....
}

int min(int a, int b)
{
   .....
}

void prn_random_numbers(int k)
{
   .....
}
```

Because function definitions also serve as function prototypes, an alternate style is to remove the list of function prototypes and put the function definition of any function that is called before the function definition of its caller. In particular, `main()` goes last in the file. Let us illustrate this alternate style by reordering the elements in our *random* program.

```
#include <stdio.h>
#include <stdlib.h>

int max(int a, int b)
{
   .....
}
```

```
int min(int a, int b)
{
   .....
}

void prn_random_numbers(int k)
{
   .....
}

int main(void)
{
   .....
}
```

Because `max()` and `min()` are called by `prn_random_numbers()`, they must come first, and because `prn_random_numbers()` is called by `main()`, we must put `main()` last. If we wish, we can interchange `max()` and `min()` (see exercise 11 on page 166).

Although we favor the top-down style that puts `main()` first, we occasionally use this alternate style as well.

4.10 Developing a Large Program

Typically, a large program is written in a separate directory as a collection of *.h* and *.c* files, with each *.c* file containing one or more function definitions. Each *.c* file can be recompiled as needed, saving time for both the programmer and the machine. We discuss this further in Chapter 14, "Software Tools," where we discuss libraries and the use of *make*.

Let us suppose we are developing a large program called *pgm*. At the top of each of our *.c* files we put the line

```
#include "pgm.h"
```

When the preprocessor encounters this directive, it looks first in the current directory for the file *pgm.h*. If there is such a file, it is included. If not, the preprocessor looks in other system-dependent places for the file. If the file *pgm.h* cannot be found, the preprocessor issues an error message and compilation stops.

Our header file *pgm.h* may contain `#include`s, `#define`s, declarations of enumeration types, declarations of structure types, other programming constructs, and a list of function prototypes at the bottom. Thus *pgm.h* contains program elements that are appropriate for our program as a whole. Because the header file *pgm.h* occurs at the top of each *.c* file, it acts as the "glue" that binds our program together.

Create a ***.h*** **file that is included in all the** ***.c*** **files**

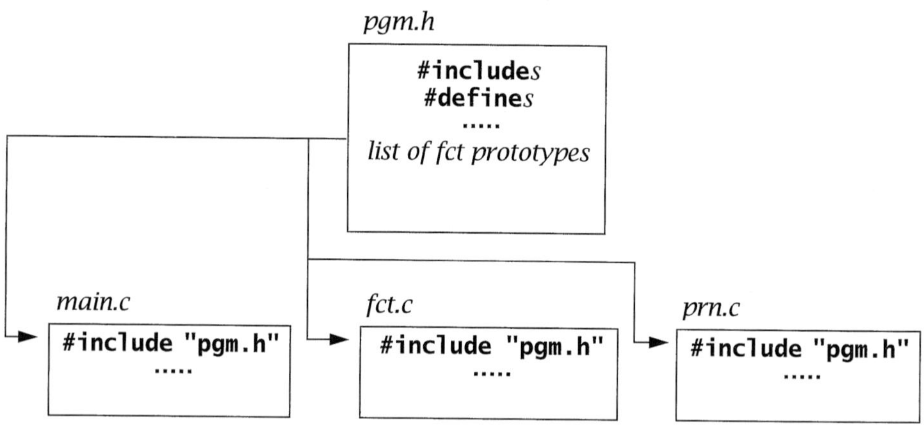

We show a very simple example of how this works. We write our program in a separate directory. It consists of a *.h* file and three *.c* files. Typically, the name of the directory and the name of the program are the same. Here is our program:

In file pgm.h:

```
#include <stdio.h>
#include <stdlib.h>

#define    N    3

void    fct1(int k);
void    fct2(void);
void    prn_info(char *);
```

In file main.c:

```
#include "pgm.h"

int main(void)
{
   char   ans;
   int    k, n = N;

   printf("\n%s",
      "This program does not do very much.\n"
      "Do you want more information?  ");
   scanf(" %c", &ans);
```

```
   putchar('\n');
   if (ans == 'y' || ans == 'Y')
      prn_info("pgm");
   for (k = 0; k < n; ++k)
      fct1(k);
   printf("Bye!\n\n");
   return 0;
}
```

In file fct.c:

```
#include "pgm.h"

void fct1(int n)
{
   int   i;

   printf("Hello from fct1()\n");
   for (i = 0; i < n; ++i)
      fct2();
}

void fct2(void)
{
   printf("Hello from fct2()\n");
}
```

In file prn.c:

```
#include "pgm.h"

void prn_info(char *pgm_name)
{
   printf("%s\n",
      "Usage:  pgm\n"
      "\n"
      "This program illustrates how one can write\n"
      "a program in more than one file.  In this\n"
      "example, we have a single .h file that is\n"
      "included at the top of our three .c files.\n"
      "Thus the .h file acts as the \"glue\"\n"
      "that binds the program together.\n"
      "\n"
      "Note that the functions fct1() and fct2()\n"
      "when called only say \"hello.\"  When writing\n"
      "a serious program, the programmer sometimes\n"
      "does this in a first working version\n"
      "of the code.\n");
}
```

Note that we used the type `char *` (pointer to `char`) in the function prototype for `prn_info()`. (We discuss pointers and strings in Chapter 10, "Strings and Pointers.") We compile the program with the command

cc –o pgm main.c fct.c prn.c

The compiler creates the executable file *pgm* along with three *.o* files which correspond to *.c* files. In MS-DOS, they are *.obj* files. The *.o* files are called object files. For further discussion about these object files and how the compiler can use them, see Section 14.2, "The C Compiler," on page 475.

In the next section we write a more interesting multifile program. For another example of a program written in many files, see Section 7.3, "An Example: The Game of Paper, Rock, Scissors," on page 246. If you have a connection to the Internet, you can use anonymous *ftp* to get more examples. Start by typing the following command:

ftp aw.com

After you have made a connection, you can log in and change directory (*cd*) to *cseng/authors*, and then *cd* to *kelley_pohl*, and then look around. A large program is much easier to investigate if you have the source code. Then you can print out whatever is of interest and, with the help of a debugger, you can step through the program if you wish to do so (see Section 14.7, "The Use of dbx," on page 486).

What Constitutes a Large Program?

For an individual, a large program might consist of just a few hundred lines of code. Which lines are counted? Usually all the lines in any READ_ME files (there should be at least one), the *.h* files, the *.c* files, and the *makefile.* (See Section 14.8, "The Use of make," on page 488.) In UNIX, the word count utility *wc* can be used to do this:

*wc READ_ME *.h *.c makefile*

In industry, programs are typically written by teams of programmers, and a large program might be considered anything over 100,000 lines.

The style of writing a program in its own directory as a collection of *.h* and *.c* files works well for any serious program, whether it is large or small, and all experienced programmers follow this style. To become proficient in the style, the programmer has to learn how to use *make* or some similar tool (see Section 14.8, "The Use of make," on page 488).

4.11 A Simulation: The Game of Heads or Tails

To provide another example of the use of functions, we implement a computer game that simulates the children's game of calling heads or tails. In this game the first child tosses a coin, and the second child calls heads or tails. If the second child guesses the outcome correctly, he wins; otherwise he loses. The game can be played repeatedly, with a count kept of the number of wins and losses.

The machine uses `rand()` to simulate tossing a coin. This is a simple form of Monte Carlo simulation. If the integer returned by `rand()` is even, it is considered heads, and if it is odd, it is considered tails. The program begins by printing instructions to the player. These instructions contain some of the design considerations for the program. After each toss of the coin, a report of the outcome is printed. At the conclusion of the program, a final report is printed.

We write our program in its own directory. The program consists of a *.h* file and five *.c* files. Top-down design reveals the need for a number of functions. Each function is short, making the overall program easy to read.

In file heads_or_tails.h:

```
#include <stdio.h>
#include <stdlib.h>

#define   MAXWORD   100

int    get_call_from_user(void);
void   play(int how_many);
void   prn_final_report(int win, int lose, int how_many);
void   prn_instructions(void);
void   report_a_win(int coin);
void   report_a_loss(int coin);
int    toss(void);
```

In file main.c:

```
#include "heads_or_tails.h"

int main(void)
{
   char   ans;
   int    no_of_plays;

   printf("\n"
      "THE GAME OF HEADS OR TAILS\n"
      "\n"
      "Do you want instructions?  ");
   scanf(" %c", &ans);
   putchar('\n');
   if (ans == 'y' || ans == 'Y')
      prn_instructions();
   printf("How many times do you want to play?  ");
   scanf("%d", & no_of_plays);
   putchar('\n');
   play( no_of_plays);
   return 0;
}
```

In file get.c:

```
#include "heads_or_tails.h"

int get_call_from_user(void)
{
   int   guess;                     /* 0 = heads, 1 = tails */

   do {
      printf("Call it:  ");
      if (scanf("%d", &guess) != 1) {
         printf("\nSORRY: Severe input error - bye!\n\n");
         exit(1);
      }
      if (guess != 0 && guess != 1) {
         printf("\n%s\n\n",
            "ERROR: Type 0 for heads, 1 for tails.");
      }
   } while (guess != 0 && guess != 1);
   return guess;
}
```

In file play.c:

```
#include "heads_or_tails.h"

void play(int how_many)      /* machine tosses, user calls */
{
   int   coin, i, lose = 0, win = 0;

   for (i = 0; i < how_many; ++i) {
      coin = toss();
      if (get_call_from_user() == coin) {
         ++win;
         report_a_win(coin);
      }
      else {
         ++lose;
         report_a_loss(coin);
      }
   }
   prn_final_report(win, lose, how_many);
}

int toss(void)
{
   return (rand() % 2);      /* 0 = heads, 1 = tails */
}
```

In file prn.c:

```
#include "heads_or_tails.h"

void prn_instructions(void)
{
   printf("%s\n",
      "This is the game of calling heads or tails.\n"
      "I will flip a coin; you call it.  If you\n"
      "call it correctly, you win; otherwise,\n"
      "I win.\n"
      "\n"
      "As I toss the (simulated) coin, I will\n"
      "tell you to \"call it.\"  To call heads,\n"
      "type 0; to call tails, type 1.\n"
      "\n");
}
```

```
void prn_final_report(int win, int lose, int how_many)
{
   printf("\n%s\n%s%3d\n%s%3d\n%s%3d\n\n",
      "FINAL REPORT:",
      "    Number of games that you won:  ", win,
      "    Number of games that you lost: ", lose,
      "    Total number of games:         ", how_many);
}
```

There are only a few new ideas in this program. In the function definition for `prn_instructions()`, the format `%s` is used in the `printf()` statement to print a string argument that consists of a number of constant strings separated by white space. These constant strings are concatenated by the compiler into a single string. Notice that `\"call it\"` is part of the string argument. When a double quote is contained as a character within a string, it must be preceded by the escape character `\` to prevent the string from ending prematurely. In the next chapter we see other examples of the escape mechanism.

The body of the function `toss()` consists of a single statement. The value being returned is the value of the expression

```
rand() % 2
```

Recall that a modulus expression of the form `a % b` has the value of the remainder after `b` is divided into `a`. For example, `4 % 2` has the value 0, and `5 % 2` has the value 1. Thus `rand() % 2` has the value 0 if the integer returned by `rand()` is even and 1 if the integer returned by `rand()` is odd.

The user of this program has to type 0 for heads and 1 for tails. A better strategy would be to type the letter *h* for heads and *t* for tails, but we need the ideas presented in Chapter 5, "Character Processing," to do this (see exercise 11 on page 166).

4.12 Invocation and Call-by-Value

A function is invoked by writing its name and an appropriate list of arguments within parentheses. Typically, these arguments match in number and type the parameters in the parameter list in the function definition. All arguments are passed call-by-value. This means that each argument is evaluated, and its value is used locally in place of the corresponding formal parameter. Thus if a variable is passed to a function, the stored value of that variable in the calling environment is not changed.

Let us write an elementary program that clearly illustrates the concept of call-by-value.

```
#include <stdio.h>

int   compute_sum(int n);

int main(void)
{
   int   n = 3, sum;

   printf("%d\n", n);                    /* 3 is printed */
   sum = compute_sum(n);
   printf("%d\n", n);                    /* 3 is printed */
   printf("%d\n", sum);                  /* 6 is printed */
   return 0;
}

int compute_sum(int n)           /* sum ints from 1 to n */
{
   int   sum = 0;

   for ( ; n > 0; --n)   /* in main(), n is unchanged */
      sum += n;
   printf("%d\n", n);                    /* 0 is printed */
   return sum;
}
```

Even though n is passed to compute_sum(), and the value of n in the body of that function is changed, the value of n in the calling environment remains unchanged.

In Chapter 8, "Functions, Pointers, and Storage Classes," we explain how to accomplish the effect of call-by-reference. It is a way to pass addresses (references) of variables to a function that then allows the body of the function to make changes to the values of variables in the calling environment.

4.13 Recursion

Computation that is done repeatedly, such as the prn_message() function presented at the beginning of this chapter, is usually implemented with an iterative statement. An alternative flow-of-control scheme that C functions support is *recursion*. Recursion is the ability of a function to call itself, either directly or indirectly. Here is a program that illustrates the use of recursion:

```
#include <stdio.h>

void   r_prn_message(int k);

int main(void)
{
   int   how_many;

   printf("%s",
      "There is a message for you.\n"
      "How many times do you want to see it?  ");
   scanf("%d", &how_many);
   printf("Here is the message:\n");
   r_prn_message(how_many);
   return 0;
}

void r_prn_message(int k)
{
   if (k > 0) {
      printf("   Have a nice day!\n");
      r_prn_message(k - 1);       /* recursive fct call */
   }
}
```

The function `r_prn_message()` is recursive because it calls itself. In both recursion and iteration, a computation is repeated until a terminating condition occurs.

"I'M SO PROUD OF YOU, HAROLD. YOU ARE ALMOST RECURSING WITHOUT HAVING TO CURSE IN THE FIRST PLACE!"

In the preceding program, the terminating condition is `k <= 0`. If the integer argument `k` to the function `r_prn_message()` is positive, a line is printed and the function is called recursively with the argument `k - 1`. Because the argument goes down by 1 with each function call, the recursion is guaranteed to terminate.

The beginning programmer can easily make mistakes using recursion, and we illustrate one type of error in Section 4.15, "Common Programming Errors," on page 155.

For a discussion of indirect recursion, see exercise 7 on page 164. Recursion is an important concept in more advanced programs. See Chapter 11, "Recursion," for further discussion.

4.14 Style

Breaking a problem into small subproblems that are then coded as functions is critical to good programming style. To be easily readable, a function should be at most a page of code. Where the purpose of a function is not transparent from the choice of identifier names, functions should be commented. Each parameter should also be an identifier that clearly indicates its own purpose, or else a comment is needed.

The order in which function definitions occur in a file is not important. It is usually a matter of taste whether one writes `main()` followed by the other function definitions, or vice versa. If a function is invoked and its definition occurs in another file, or later in the same file, then its function prototype should occur before the function invocation. If one is doing a top-down development, however, it is natural to start with `main()`. Of course, for large projects a good deal of program organization might be done on paper first, so even in a top-down development effort, the coding of the functions can occur first.

It is considered good programming style to have only a few `return` statements in a given function. If there are many `return` statements, the logic of the code may be difficult to follow.

The names `read`, `write`, and `print` are commonly used as parts of names for system functions. For example, `printf()` uses `print` in its name. To clearly distinguish our names from system names, we often use `prn` and `wrt` as parts of names. We could write a function named `print()`, but it would be confusing.

Whenever something is being counted inside a loop, it is a good idea to count it as soon as it is possible to do so. This rule is followed in the incrementing of `count` in the function definition for `read_and_prn_data()`.

4.15 Common Programming Errors

A common error is to assume that a function is changing the value of a variable. Because the function mechanism in C is strictly call-by-value, it is not possible to change the value of a variable in the calling environment by invoking a function with the variable as an argument. If `f()` is a function and `v` is a variable, then the statement

```
f(v);
```

cannot change the value of `v` in the calling environment. However, if `f()` returns a value, then the statement

```
v = f(v);
```

can change the value of `v`.

In ANSI C, `main()` is supposed to return an integer value to the host environment, or operating system. Typically, the programmer writes

```
int main(void)
{
    .....
    return 0;
}
```

Some compilers accept the use of `void` as the function type, along with the omission of a `return` statement.

```
void main(void)          /* non ANSI C style */
{
    .....                /* no return statement */
}
```

Although a particular compiler may be happy with this, it is technically wrong, and this style is not acceptable to other ANSI C compilers.

In `main()`, the programmer causes an integer value to be returned to the host environment by writing either

```
    return expr;      or      exit( expr );
```

These two statements are equivalent in `main()`, but in any other function their effects are different. A call to `exit()` from within any function causes the program to terminate and a value to be returned to the host environment. The value returned is called the *exit status* or *program status.* By convention, a zero exit status indicates successful program termination, whereas a nonzero exit status indicates an abnormal or unusual situation (see Section A.13, "Leaving the Program," on page 551).

The lack of function prototypes can cause run-time errors that are hard to detect. Traditional C was considered unsuitable for novice programmers because the function parameter mechanism did not provide the safety of type checking. Consider the following program:

```
/* Print a table of square roots. */

#include <math.h>
#include <stdio.h>

double   sqrt();              /* traditional C style */

int main()
{
   int   i;

   for (i = 1; i < 20; ++i)
      printf("%5d:%7.3f\n", i, sqrt(i));
   return 0;
}
```

What is printed is compiler-dependent. Some compilers output the following:

```
 1:  0.000
 2:  0.000
 3:  0.000
.....
20:  0.000
```

In this example, when the `int` value `i` is passed to the `sqrt()` function, it is not converted to a `double`, which is what the function expects. This causes incorrect values to be printed. In ANSI C, the function prototype for `sqrt()` is provided in *math.h* as

```
double   sqrt(double);
```

If we use this prototype in place of the traditional C declaration, the value of any integer expression passed as an argument to `sqrt()` is converted to a `double`, and the program output is more meaningful. Many C practitioners consider this improvement in the type-safety of the parameter-passing mechanism to be the single most important advantage of ANSI C over traditional C.

It is easy to incorrectly write the terminating condition for a recursive function. This type of error often leads to an infinite recursion. When this happens, the user can usually (but not always) kill the program by typing a control-c. Here is an example of a simple program that does not terminate properly. *Caution:* On some MS-DOS systems, if you execute this program, you may have to reboot the system to stop the program.

```
#include <stdio.h>

int main(void)
{
   int   count = 0;

   if (++count < 77) {
      printf("   The universe is ever expaning!   ");
      main();
   }
   return 0;
}
```

With each recursive call to `main()`, a new local variable `count` is initialized to zero; hence the stopping condition `++count >= 7` is never reached. One way to correct the problem is to use the declaration

```
static int   count = 0;
```

A `static` variable is not reinitialized when the function is called again, and the variable keeps its value from one function invocation to the next (see Section 8.6, "The Storage Class static," on page 278).

4.16 System Considerations

A call to `rand()` produces a value in the interval [0, RAND_MAX], where RAND_MAX is a symbolic constant given in *stdlib.h*. Because RAND_MAX typically has the relatively small value 32767, the function `rand()` is not useful for many scientific applications. Most C systems on UNIX machines provide the programmer with the `rand48` family of random number generators, so-called because 48-bit arithmetic is used to generate the numbers. The function `drand48()`, for example, can be used to produce randomly distributed doubles in the range [0, 1], and `lrand48()` can be used to produce randomly distributed integers in the range [0, 2^{31} - 1]. Typically, the function prototypes for this family of functions are in *stdlib.h*. To find out more about pseudo random number generators, consult the book *Numerical Recipes in C* by William Press et al. (Cambridge, England: Cambridge University Press, 1992), pages 274–328.

It is important to configure your compiler so that all warnings are turned on. Suppose we are using the command line version of Borland C in an MS-DOS environment. When we give the command

bcc -w pgm.c

the option *-w* turns on all warnings. In particular, if *pgm.c* is missing one or more function prototypes, the compiler tells us. We can configure *bcc* so that it is invoked automatically with the *-w* option by placing *-w* in the file *turboc.cfg* in the directory where *bcc.exe* exists. Similarly, the integrated environment for Borland C can be configured so that all warnings are automatically turned on. (See the Borland C manuals.) To understand the value of having warnings, try the following program:

```
#include <stdio.h>

int main(void)
{
   printf("%d\n", f(2));          /* 7 is printed */
   printf("%d\n", f(2.0));        /* 1 is printed */
   return 0;
}

int f(int n)
{
   return (3 * n + 1);
}
```

What is printed by this program is system-dependent. We have shown what is printed on our Borland C system.

ANSI C is compatible with traditional C. Because traditional C does not have function prototyping, if we write a program without prototypes on an ANSI C system, actual arguments are passed into functions "as is," which means without type checking or conversion. In the preceding program, when the constant `2.0`, which is a `double`, is passed to `f()`, no conversion takes place. This causes an error because an `int` is expected inside `f()`. If we place the function prototype

```
int   f(int);
```

just above `main()`, the compiler converts the value of any arithmetic expression passed to `f()` to an `int`.

The type-safety feature of function prototyping in ANSI C is very powerful, but the programmer must consistently use prototypes to reap the benefits.

4.17 Moving to C++

C++ adds a large number of ideas and constructs that extend the usefulness and efficiency of functions. We discuss three such ideas: inline functions, default arguments, and function overloading.

A function can be modified by placing the keyword `inline` in front of the function return type. If possible, such a function is compiled inline, thus avoiding function call and function return overhead. This is similar to C's use of the preprocessor for `#define` macros with arguments (see Section B.2, "The Use of #define," on page 566). Here is a simple macro:

```
#define  CUBE(x)  ((x) * (x) * (x))     /* C style macro */
```

After this macro has been defined, we can use it the same way we use a function:

```
double   x, y = 2;

x = CUBE(y);          /* x has value 8 */
```

In modern programming methodology, the use of macros with arguments is considered nonrobust and therefore should be avoided or at least minimized. (See Appendix B, "The Preprocessor," for more on this topic.) In contrast, the use of inline functions in C++ is considered good programming practice. Here is how the `cube()` function would be written as an inline function:

```
inline double cube(double x) { return x * x * x; }
```

Short inline functions are typically written on one line, as we have done here. There are several reasons to prefer inline functions to macros. In general, inlining is safer because type and scope rules are enforced by the compiler. Macros, on the other hand, are implemented by using text substitution via the preprocessor, and the preprocessor does not "know" C.

In C++, functions can have default arguments. This effect is achieved by assigning a default value to a formal parameter in a function prototype. However, if this is done, any other parameters to the right must also be given default values. A default value is usually an appropriate constant that occurs frequently when the function is called. The following program illustrates the mechanism:

```
// Illustrate default values for a function.

#include <iostream.h>

int   sum(int a, int b = 2, int c = 3);  // default values

int main(void)
{
   cout << "sum(3)        = " << sum(3)        << "\n"
           "sum(3, 5)     = " << sum(3, 5)     << "\n"
           "sum(3, 5, 7)  = " << sum(3, 5, 7)  << "\n";
}

int sum(int a, int b, int c)
{
   return a + b + c;
}
```

When `sum(3)` is invoked, control passes to the function with the parameter a having value 3 and the parameters `b` and `c` having their default values of 2 and 3, respectively. Thus the value 8 is returned and printed. Similarly, when `sum(3, 5)` is invoked, a has value 3, `b` has value 5, and `c` has its default value of 3, causing the value 11 to be returned and printed.

If we wish, we can rewrite this program so the function definition serves as the function prototype.

```
// Illustrate default arguments for a function.

#include <iostream.h>

int sum(int a = 1, int b = 2, int c = 3)   // fct def
{
   return a + b + c;
}

int main(void)
{
   cout << "sum()         = " << sum()         << "\n"
           "sum(3)        = " << sum(3)        << "\n"
           "sum(3, 5)     = " << sum(3, 5)     << "\n"
           "sum(3, 5, 7)  = " << sum(3, 5, 7)  << "\n";
}
```

If a parameter in a function prototype is assigned a default value, then all the remaining parameters in the list must also be assigned default values. The parameter itself need not be present. Some examples are

```
int     f(int a = 1, int b = 2, char c = 'A');    // ok
char    g(char, float = 0.0, double d = 3.14);    // ok
float   h(int i, int j, float, float, int = 0);   // ok
float   k(int = 0, int, int, float f = 3.579);    // wrong
```

In C++, two or more functions or operators can have the same name. When this occurs, the function or operator is said to be *overloaded.* We discuss function overloading here and leave our discussion of operator overloading to Section 15.3, "Overloading," on page 508. In the following program we overload the function `max()`:

In file find_max.h:

```
#include <iostream.h>

int      max(int a, int b);
double   max(double x, double y);
```

In file main.c:

```
#include "find_max.h"

int main(void)
{
   int      a, b;
   double   x, y;

   cout << "Enter two integers a and b:  ";
   cin >> a >> b;
   cout << "Enter two doubles x and y:  ";
   cin >> x >> y;
   cout << "max(a, b) = " << max(a, b) << ", an int\n";
   cout << "max(x, y) = " << max(x, y) << ", a double\n";
}
```

In file max.c:

```
#include "find_max.h"

int   max(int a, int b)              // int version
{
   return ((a > b) ? a : b);
}

double   max(double x, double y)    // double version
{
   return ((x > y) ? x : y);
}
```

By *signature* we mean the number and types of arguments that are passed to a function. The compiler uses the function name and signature to choose one of the overloaded functions; thus, for example, because the signature for the function call `max(a, b)` matches the function definition for

```
int   max(int, int);
```

that is the function that is invoked.

Function Prototypes in C++

In C++, function prototypes are required, and the use of `void` in the parameter type list in both function prototypes and function definitions is optional. Thus, for example, in C++

`int f()` is equivalent to `int f(void)`

Note carefully that this idea is in conflict with the construct as used in either traditional C and ANSI C. In both traditional C and ANSI C, a function declaration such as

```
int f();
```

means that `f()` takes an unknown number of arguments. In traditional C, `void` is not a keyword and cannot be used as a type in a parameter list in a function declaration or definition. In ANSI C, the programmer is advised to use function prototypes.

Summary

- Structured programming is a problem solving strategy and a programming methodology that strives for simple flow of control and uses top-down design.
- Top-down design, also referred to as stepwise refinement, consists of repeatedly decomposing a problem into smaller problems.
- A long program should be written as a collection of functions, each one being no longer than, say, a page. Each function should capture some small task of the overall problem.

- In the body of a function, the compiler recognizes a name followed by parentheses, such as `prn_message()` or `min(x, y)`, as a call to a function.

- A programmer creates a function by writing a function definition, which consists of a header and a body. The header consists of the type returned by the function, the function name, and a comma-separated list of declarations of parameters enclosed by parentheses. The body consists of declarations and statements enclosed by braces.

- When a function is called, program control is passed to the function. When a `return` statement is executed, or the end of the function is reached, control is passed back to the calling environment. If a `return` statement contains an expression, the value of the expression is passed back to the calling environment as well.

- A function prototype mechanism exists in ANSI C but not in traditional C. A function prototype has the following general form:

  type function_name (*parameter type list*) ;

  The *type* is the type returned by the function. The *parameter type list* is typically a comma-separated list of types. If a function has no parameters, the keyword `void` is used. A function prototype allows the compiler to enforce type compatibility when the function is called.

- In a function prototype an identifier may follow each of the types in the parameter type list. For example, the two function prototypes

  `int f(int a, float b);`   and   `int f(int, float);`

  are equivalent. The compiler does not need the parameter identifiers, only the types of the parameters. However, the parameters themselves may provide further documentation for the human reader.

- In C, all arguments are passed call-by-value. This means that when a variable is passed as an argument to a function, its value remains unchanged in the calling environment.

- Although all C systems provide the function `rand()`, for serious work, other random number generators may be more appropriate.

- All functions in C can be used recursively. That is, any function can call itself, either directly or indirectly.

Exercises

1 Rewrite the *message* program so that its output is

```
Message for you:  Have a nice day!
                  Have a nice day!
                  Have a nice day!
                  .....
```

2 Write a function `square()` that takes an integer and return its square, and a function `cube()` that takes an integer and return its cube. Use your `square()` and `cube()` functions to write the functions `quartic()` and `quintic()`, which return the fourth and fifth powers of an integer, respectively. Use your functions to write a program that prints a table of powers of integers from 1 to 25. The output of your program should look like this:

```
A TABLE OF POWERS
-----------------

Integer      Square      Cube     Quartic     Quintic
-------      ------      ----     -------     -------
      1           1         1           1           1
      2           4         8          16          32
      3           9        27          81         243
.....
```

3 Execute the program *run_sums* and enter data directly from the keyboard. When you are finished entering data, type an end-of-file signal (see Section 1.11, "Typing an End-of-File Signal," on page 29). What happens if you enter a letter instead of a number?

4 The program *prn_rand* does not work correctly if the user types in 0 when asked for the number of random numbers desired. Correct the program so that it works correctly for this case.

5 Consider the `for` loop in the function `prn_random_numbers()` that begins

```
for (i = 1; i < k; ++i) {
   if (i % 7 == 0)
      printf("\n");
      .....
```

Suppose we rewrite the first line as follows:

```
for (i = 2; i <= k; ++i) {
```

Are the same number of random numbers printed? This modification causes the format of the output to change. Try it and see. Make a further program modification in the body of the `for` loop to have the output formatted correctly.

6 Run the *prn_rand* program three times to print out, say, 100 randomly distributed integers. Observe that the same list of numbers is printed each time. For many applications, this is not desirable. Modify the *prn_rand* program by using `srand()` to seed the random number generator. The first few lines of your program should look like this:

```
#include <stdio.h>
#include <stdlib.h>
#include <time.h>

int main(void)
{
   int   i, n, seed;

   seed = time(NULL);
   srand(seed);
   printf("\n%s",
      "Some randomly distributed "
      "integers will be printed.\n"
      "How many do you want to see?  ");
   .....
```

The function call `time(NULL)` returns the number of elapsed seconds since 1 January 1970 (see Appendix A, "The Standard Library"). We store this value in the variable `seed`, and then we use the function call `srand(seed)` to seed the random number generator. Repeated calls to `rand()` eventually generate all the integers in the interval [0, RAND_MAX], but in a mixed-up order. The value used to seed the random number generator determines at what point in the mixed-up order the function `rand()` starts to generate numbers. If we use the value produced by `time()` as a seed, then whenever we run the program, the seed is different, causing a different set of numbers to be produced. Run this program repeatedly. You should see a different set of numbers printed each time. Do you?

7 In the previous exercise, we suggested the code

```
seed = time(NULL);
srand(seed);
```

In place of these two lines, most programmers would write

```
srand(time(NULL));
```

Make this change to your program, then compile and execute it to see if it behaves the same as before. (It should.)

8 Investigate how to write your own random number generator. There are many ways to do it. If you are not concerned with statistical reliability, then the task is easy (but you have to look it up). Understanding the theory of a random number generator can be much more difficult than writing the code for it.

9 In Section 4.3, "The `return` Statement," on page 128, we wrote an interactive program that computes the minimum of two integers. Rewrite the code to work with type `double`. After you have tested your program and are satisfied that it works correctly, modify it to find the minimum and maximum of four numbers.

10 Let n_0 be a given positive integer. For $i = 0, 1, 2, \ldots$ define

if n_i is even, then $n_{i+1} = n_i / 2$

if n_i is odd, then $n_{i+1} = 3n_i + 1$

if n_i is 1, the sequence ends

Numbers that are generated this way are called *hailstones*. Write a program that generates some hailstones. Your program should use the function

```
void   hailstones(int n);
```

to compute and print the sequence generated by *n*. The output of your program might look as follows:

```
Hailstones generated by 77:

      77        232        116         58         29         88
      44         22         11         34         17         52
      26         13         40         20         10          5
      16          8          4          2          1

Number of hailstones generated:  23
```

You might find that all the sequences you generate are finite. Whether this is true in general is still an open question. *Hint:* Use variables of type `long` instead of `int` if the program misbehaves. (See Chapter 6, "The Fundamental Data Types.")

11 If you write a program in a single file with `main()` first, a list of function prototypes can occur in the file just before `main()`. If you write a program in more than one file, a list of function prototypes can occur at the bottom of the *.h* file. Function prototypes, provided they are consistent, can be repeated. Add the following list of function prototypes to the program you wrote in the previous exercise:

```
void   hailstones(int);
void   hailstones(int k);
void   hailstones(int n);
void   hailstones(int nn);
```

Your compiler should be happy. Is it?

12 Write a program that prints out the first *n* primes, where *n* is input by the user. When you execute your program, here is an example of what you should see printed on the screen:

```
PRIMES WILL BE PRINTED.

How many do you want to see?  3000

    1:      2
    2:      3
    3:      5
    4:      7
    5:     11
  .....
   25:     97
   26:    101
  .....
 2998:  27431
 2999:  27437
 3000:  27449
```

Write your program in its own directory in three files: *primes.h*, *main.c*, and *is_prime.c*. Here is some of the program:

In file primes.h:

```
#include <stdio.h>
#include <stdlib.h>

int   is_prime(int n);
```

In file is_prime.c:

```
#include "primes.h"

int is_prime(int n)
{
   int   k, limit;

   if (n == 2)
      return 1;
   if (n % 2 == 0)
      return 0;
   limit = n / 2;
   for (k = 3; k <= limit; k += 2)
      if (n % k == 0)
         return 0;
   return 1;
}
```

Explain how `is_prime()` works. *Hint:* Do some examples by hand. Complete the program by writing `main()` in *main.c*. There are 168 primes that are less than 1000. Does your program confirm this? How many primes are there that are less than 10,000?

13 Write a variation of the program you wrote in the previous exercise by having the user input both the number of primes to be printed and the starting index. The output of your program should look like this:

```
PRIMES WILL BE PRINTED.

How many do you want to see?  33

Beginning at what index?  700

   700:   5279
   701:   5281
   702:   5297
   .....
   731:   5527
   732:   5531
```

14 (Advanced) In 1792, the German mathematician and astronomer Karl Friedrich Gauss, at the age of 15, conjectured what is now known as the *Prime Number Theorem*: Let $\pi(x)$ represent the number of primes less than or equal to x. Then $\pi(x)$ is asymptotic to $x/\log(x)$; that is, the limit of the quotient $\pi(x)/(x/\log(x))$ goes to 1 as x goes to infinity. Modify the program you wrote in exercise 12 of this chapter, to investigate this limit. The output from your program might look like this:

```
PRIME NUMBER THEOREM:

   lim     (pi(x) / (x / log(x)) = 1
   x -> inf

where pi(x) is the number of primes
less than or equal to x.

How many primes do you want to consider?  3000

     x        pi(x)     pi(x) / (x / log(x))
   -----      -----     --------------------
   1000        168        1.160502886868999
   2000        303        1.151536722620625
   3000        430        1.147579351363202
  .....
  27000       2961        1.118993938566849
  27449       3000        1.116989873919079
```

You can observe that the convergence is very slow. For that reason you should let *x* step by 500 or 1000 instead of by 1, except on the last line, where you should let *x* have the value that corresponds to the number of primes requested.

15 In 1742, Goldbach made the following conjecture: Every even integer greater than 6 is the sum of two odd primes. So far, this conjecture has been neither proved nor disproved. Computers have been used extensively to test the conjecture, but no counterexample has ever been found. Write a program that proves that the conjecture is true for all the even integers between the symbolic constants BEGIN and END. For example, if you write

```
#define   BEGIN   700
#define   END     1100
```

then the output of your program might look like this:

```
GOLDBACH'S CONJECTURE:
Every even number n > 6 is the sum of two odd primes:

    700 = 17 +  683
    702 = 11 +  691
    704 =  3 +  701
   .....
   1098 =  5 + 1093
   1100 =  3 + 1097
```

Hint: Use the function `is_prime()` given in exercise 12 of this chapter.

16 In this exercise we want to modify a program that uses the random number generator `rand()` to simulate tossing a coin repeatedly. Here is the program:

```
#include <stdio.h>
#include <stdlib.h>
#include <time.h>          /* for time() */

int main(void)
{
   int   count_heads = 0, count_tails = 0, i, n, val;

   srand(time(NULL));  /* seed the rand. no. generator */
   printf("\n%s",
      "SIMULATED COIN TOSSING:\n"
      "How many times?  ");
   if (scanf("%d", &n) != 1) {
      printf("INPUT ERROR: Bye!\n\n");
      exit(1);
   }

if (n < 1) {
      printf("Bye!\n\n");
      exit(1);
   }


   for (i = 0; i < n; ++i) {
      val = rand() % 2;
      (val == 1) ? ++count_heads : ++count_tails;
      if (i % 10 == 0)
         putchar('\n');
      printf("%7s", (val == 1) ? "heads" : "tails");
   }
   printf("\n\n%s%d\n%s%d\n\n",
      "Number of heads: ", count_heads,
      "Number of tails: ", count_tails);
   return 0;
}
```

Note the use of the conditional operator `?:` (see Section 3.19, "The Conditional Operator," on page 105). Also, note that the format `%7s` is used to print a string in a field of seven characters. What happens if you change the format to `%15s`? Without the call to `srand()`, the program produces the same output every time you run it. What happens if you move the call to `srand()` so it is the first statement in the body of the `for` loop? Explain why the behavior of the program is so strikingly different. (Were you surprised?) The correct programming practice is to seed the random number generator only once in a program.

17 In the following program, `main()` is recursive because `main()` calls `f()`, `f()` calls `g()`, and `g()` calls `main()`.

```
#include <stdio.h>

void   f(void);
void   g(void);

int main(void)
{
   static int   count = 0;

   printf("Hello from main()\n");
   if (++count <= 2)
      f();
   return 0;
}

void f(void)
{
   printf("Hello from f()\n");
   g();
}

void g(void)
{
   printf("Hello from g()\n");
   main();
}
```

This is an example of indirect recursion. First write down what you think is printed, then execute the program to check. Next, change the `if` statement in `main()` to the following:

```
if (++count <= 2) {
   f();
   g();
}
```

Again, first write down what you think is printed, then execute the program to check. *Caution:* Even though the change to the program was very minor, it is now much more difficult to see what is printed.

18 C++: Rewrite the programs in the previous exercise using `cout` instead of `printf()`. When executed, the programs should behave as they did before.

19 C++: Write a set of overloaded `print()` functions that print values with a nice message. Here is an example:

```
void print(double x)
{
   cout << "double x = " << x << endl;
}
```

Do this for at least three types and test that they work.

20 Java: In Java, all functions are also known as methods. They must reside in a class. In C functions are global or external, residing in a file. In C, compilation works by compiling the contents of files. In Java, compilation works by compiling classes (of course, the classes are inside files as well). C functions are somewhat akin to Java static methods.

```
// Message2.java: method parameter use - Java by Dissection
page 98.
class Message2 {
  public static void main(String[] args) {
    System.out.println("HELLO DEBRA!");
    printMessage(5); //actual argument is 5
    System.out.println("Goodbye.");
  }
  static void printMessage(int howManyTimes) {
  //formal parameter  is howManyTimes
    System.out.println("A message for you:  ");
      for (int i = 0; i < howManyTimes; i++)
        System.out.println("Have a nice day!\n");
  }
}
```

Rewrite this program in C. Change the code to accept as input the number of times the message should be printed. If you know how, also change the program so it asks for the name to be printed out, and test it by inputting "LAURA".

21 Java: Here is a simple recursion in Java. What function is being computed? Convert it to a C function that is recursive. Convert it to a C function that is iterative. Which runs more efficiently on your machine—the recursion or the iteration?

```
class RecursionExercise {
  public static void main(String[] args) {
    for (int i = 0; i < 10; i++)
      System.out.println(recurse(i));
  }
  static long recurse(long n) {
    if (n <= 0)
      return 1;
    else
      return 2 * recurse(n - 1);
  }
}
```

Notice that C and Java both have a `long` type for extra large integers. On your machine, is the range of `long` for C and Java the same? Remember, C has system-dependent representations for its basic types.

Chapter 5

Character Processing

In this chapter we introduce some of the basic ideas involved in character processing. We want to discuss how characters are stored and manipulated in a machine, how characters can be treated as small integers, and how use is made of certain standard header files. To illustrate these ideas, we present simple character-processing programs that accomplish useful work. These example programs use the character input/output macros `getchar()` and `putchar()`. For anyone trying to master a new language, getting data into and out of a machine is a skill that has to be developed early.

A number of important concepts are covered in this chapter. The use of the symbolic constant `EOF` is explained. When `getchar()` detects an end-of-file mark, it returns the value `EOF`, which makes it possible for the programmer to detect when the end of a file has been reached. The use of the header file *ctype.h* is explained in detail; this file provides the programmer with a set of macros that can be used to process character data. Programmers use macros in the same manner as functions. The use of system header files such as *ctype.h* lets the programmer write portable code. The programs, such as *caps*, presented in this chapter are quite simple but can explain the essential ideas of character processing.

5.1 The Data Type char

The type `char` is one of the fundamental types of the C language. Constants and variables of this type are used to represent characters. Each character is stored in a machine in one byte. We assume throughout that a byte is composed of eight bits and is capable of storing 2^8, or 256, distinct values.

When a character is stored in a byte, the contents of that byte can be thought of as either a character or as a small integer. Although 256 distinct values can be stored in a byte, only a subset of these values represent actual printing characters. These include the lowercase letters, uppercase letters, digits, punctuation, and special characters such as +, *, and %. The character set also includes the white space characters: blank, tab, and newline. Examples of nonprinting characters are newline and the alert character, or bell. We illustrate the use of the bell in this chapter.

A character constant is written between single quotes, as in `'a'`, `'b'`, or `'c'`. A typical declaration for a variable of type `char` is

```
char   c;
```

Character variables can be initialized, as in the example

```
char   c1 = 'A', c2 = 'B', c3 = '*';
```

A character is stored in memory in one byte according to a specific encoding. Most machines use either ASCII or EBCDIC character codes. In the discussion that follows we use the ASCII code. For any other code, the numbers are different, but the ideas are analogous. A table of the ASCII code appears in Appendix E, "ASCII Character Codes."

In C, a character is considered to have the integer value corresponding to its ASCII encoding. Some examples are given in the following table.

Some character constants and their integer ASCII values					
lowercase	'a'	'b'	'c'	...	'z'
ASCII value	97	98	99	...	112
uppercase	'A'	'B'	'C'	...	'Z'
ASCII value	65	66	67	...	90
digit	'0'	'1'	'2'	...	'9'
ASCII value	48	49	50	...	57
other	'&'	'*'	'+'	...	
ASCII value	38	42	43	...	

Observe that there is no particular relationship between the value of the character constant representing a digit and the digit's intrinsic integer value. That is, the value of `'7'` is *not* 7. The fact that the values of `'a'`, `'b'`, `'c'`, and so forth occur in order is an important property that facilitates the sorting of characters, words, lines, and more, into lexicographical order.

In the functions `printf()` and `scanf()`, a %c is used to designate the character format. For example, the statement

```
printf("%c", 'a');                  /* a is printed */
```

causes the character constant `'a'` to be printed in character format. Similarly,

```
printf("%c%c%c", 'A', 'B', 'C');    /* ABC is printed */
```

causes ABC to be printed.

Constants and variables of type `char` can be treated as small integers. The statement

```
printf("%d", 'a');                  /* 97 is printed */
```

causes the value of the character constant `'a'` to be printed in the format of a decimal integer. Thus 97 is printed. On the other hand, the statement

```
printf("%c", 97);                   /* a is printed */
```

causes the value of the decimal integer constant 97 to be printed in the format of a character. Thus a is printed.

"I SEE THAT YOU ARE OF A GOOD CHARACTER. AND FOR FIVE EXTRA DOLLARS, I CAN GIVE YOU ITS ASCII CODE."

Some nonprinting and hard-to-print characters require an *escape sequence.* For example, the newline character is written as `'\n'` in a program, and even though it is being described by the two characters \ and n, it represents a single

ASCII character. The backslash character \ is also called the *escape character* and it is used to "escape" the usual meaning of the character that follows it. The following table contains some nonprinting and hard-to-print characters.

Nonprinting and hard-to-print characters		
Name of character	**Written in C**	**Integer value**
alert	`\a`	7
backslash	`\\`	92
backspace	`\b`	8
carriage return	`\r`	13
double quote	`\"`	34
formfeed	`\f`	12
horizontal tab	`\t`	9
newline	`\n`	10
null character	`\0`	0
single quote	`\'`	39
vertical tab	`\v`	11

The double quote character " has to be escaped if it is used as a character in a string. Otherwise it would prematurely terminate the string. An example is

```
printf("\"ABC\"");        /* "ABC" is printed */
```

However, inside single quotes one could write `'"'`, although `'\"'` is also accepted. In general, escaping an ordinary character has no effect.

Inside a string, the single quote is just an ordinary character:

```
printf("'ABC'");          /* 'ABC' is printed */
```

Another way to write a character constant is by means of a one-, two-, or three-octal-digit escape sequence, as in `'\007'`. This is the alert character `\a`, or the audible bell. It can be written also as `'\07'` or `'\7'`, but not as `'7'`.

5.2 The Use of getchar() and putchar()

The system provides `getchar()` and `putchar()` for the input and output of characters. These are macros defined in *stdio.h*. To read a character from the keyboard, `getchar()` is used; to write a character to the screen, `putchar()` is used. For example, a program that prints the line

```
She sells sea shells by the seashore.
```

on the screen can be written as follows:

```
#include <stdio.h>

int main(void)
{
   putchar('S');
   putchar('h');
   putchar('e');
   putchar(' ');
   .....
   putchar('e');
   putchar('.');
   putchar('\n');
   return 0;
}
```

Of course, this is a tedious way to accomplish the task; using a `printf()` statement would be much easier.

In the next program, `getchar()` gets a character from the input stream (keyboard) and assigns it to the variable `c`. Then `putchar()` is used to print the character twice on the screen.

```
#include <stdio.h>

int main(void)
{
   char   c;

   while (1) {
      c = getchar();
      putchar(c);
      putchar(c);
   }
   return 0;
}
```

Note that the variable c is of type char. In the next version of this program, we change this. Also, because 1 is nonzero, as an expression it is always *true*. Thus the construct

```
while (1) {
   .....
}
```

is an infinite loop. The only way to stop this program is with an interrupt, which on our system is effected by typing a control-c.

For a number of reasons, the preceding program is not really acceptable. Let us rewrite it and call the new version *dbl_out*.

```
#include <stdio.h>

int main(void)
{
   int   c;

   while ((c = getchar()) != EOF) {
      putchar(c);
      putchar(c);
   }
   return 0;
}
```

Dissection of the dbl_out Program

■ `#include <stdio.h>`

Lines that begin with a # are preprocessing directives. These lines communicate with the preprocessor. A preprocessing directive of the form

`#include` *<filename>*

causes the preprocessor to include a copy of the named file into the source code at that point before passing the code to the compiler. The angle brackets around `stdio.h` tell the system to look for this file in the "usual place," which is system-dependent. The file *stdio.h* is a standard header file supplied with C systems and is typically included in functions that use certain standard input/output constructs. One line of this header file is

```
#define    EOF    (-1)
```

The identifier `EOF` is mnemonic for "end-of-file." What is actually used to signal an end-of-file mark is system-dependent. Although the `int` value -1 is often used, different systems can have different values. By including the file *stdio.h* and using the symbolic constant `EOF`, we have made the program portable: The source file can be moved to a different system and run with no changes.

■ `int    c;`

The variable `c` has been declared in the program as an `int` rather than a `char`. Whatever is used to signal the end of a file, it cannot be a value that represents a character. Because `c` is an `int`, it can hold all possible character values, as well as the special value `EOF`. Although one usually thinks of a `char` as a very short `int` type, one can also think of an `int` as a very long `char` type.

■ `while ((c = getchar()) != EOF) {`

The expression

```
(c = getchar()) != EOF
```

is composed of two parts. The subexpression

```
c = getchar()
```

gets a value from the keyboard and assigns it to the variable `c`, and the value of the subexpression takes on that value as well. The symbol `!=` represents the "not equal to" operator. As long as the value of the subexpression `c = getchar()` is not equal to `EOF`, the body of the `while` loop is executed. To exit the loop, we have to enter an end-of-file signal at the keyboard. Then the operating system tells `getchar()` that the end of the file has been reached, which in turn causes `getchar()` to return `EOF`. How an end-of-file value is entered at the keyboard is system-dependent. In UNIX, it is usually entered by typing a carriage return followed by a control-d. In MS-DOS, the user types a control-z instead.

■ `(c = getchar()) != EOF`

The parentheses around the subexpression `c = getchar()` are necessary. Suppose we had typed

```
c = getchar() != EOF
```

Because of operator precedence, this is equivalent to

```
c = (getchar() != EOF)
```

This gets a character from the input stream, tests to see if it is equal to `EOF`, and assigns the result of the test (either 0 or 1) to the variable `c` (see exercise 10 on page 200).

This program can also be written as a simple recursion. In most cases, elementary `while` loops are easily replaced by simple recursion, where the `while` loops test is used to terminate the recursion.

```
#include <stdio.h>

void dbl_out(int c)
{
   if ((c != EOF) {
      putchar(c);
      putchar(c);
      dbl_out(getchar())
   }
}
```

```
int main(void)
{
   dbl_out(getchar());
   return 0;
}
```

5.3 An Example: Capitalize

Characters have an underlying integer-valued representation that on most C systems is the numeric value of their 7-bit ASCII representation. For example, the character constant `'a'` has value 97. If one thinks of characters as small integers, then arithmetic on characters makes sense. Because the values of the letters in both the lower- and uppercase alphabet occur in order, the expression `'a' + 1` has the value `'b'`, `'b' + 1` has the value `'c'`, and `'Z' - 'A'` has the value 25. Moreover, `'A' - 'a'` has a value that is the same as `'B' - 'b'`, which is the same as `'C' - 'c'`, and so on. Because of this, if the variable `c` has the value of a lowercase letter, then the expression `c + 'A' - 'a'` has the value of the corresponding uppercase letter. These ideas are incorporated into the next program, which capitalizes all lowercase letters and doubles the newline characters.

```
/* Capitalize lowercase letters and double space. */

#include <stdio.h>

int main(void)
{
   int   c;

   while ((c = getchar()) != EOF)
      if ('a' <= c && c <= 'z')
         putchar(c + 'A' - 'a');
      else if (c == '\n') {
         putchar('\n');
         putchar('\n');
      }
      else
         putchar(c);
   return 0;
}
```

Dissection of the caps Program

```
■ while ((c = getchar()) != EOF)
```

The macro `getchar()` gets a character and assigns it to the variable `c`. As long as the value of `c` is not `EOF`, the body of the `while` loop is executed.

```
■ if ('a' <= c && c <= 'z')
     putchar(c + 'A' - 'a');
```

Because of operator precedence, the expressions

`'a' <= c && c <= 'z'` and `('a' <= c) && (c <= 'z')`

are equivalent. The symbols <= represent the operator "less than or equal to." The subexpression `'a' <= c` tests to see if the value `'a'` is less than or equal to the value of `c`. The subexpression `c <= 'z'` tests to see if the value of `c` is less than or equal to the value `'z'`. The symbols && represent the "logical and" operator. If both subexpressions are *true*, then the expression

```
'a' <= c && c <= 'z'
```

is *true*; otherwise it is *false*. Thus the expression as a whole is *true* if and only if `c` is a lowercase letter. If the expression is *true*, then the statement

```
putchar(c + 'A' - 'a');
```

is executed, causing the corresponding uppercase letter to be printed.

```
■ else if (c == '\n') {
     putchar('\n');
     putchar('\n');
  }
```

The symbols == represent the "is equal to" operator. If `c` is not a lowercase letter, a test is made to see if it is equal to a newline character. If it is, two newline characters are printed.

```
■ else
     putchar(c);
```

If the value of `c` is not a lowercase letter and it is not a newline character, then the character corresponding to the value of `c` is printed. An `else` is always associated with the immediately preceding `if`.

Although the *caps* program is portable to any ASCII machine, it does not work as expected on an EBCDIC machine. The reason for this is that the uppercase letters are not all contiguous in the EBCDIC code. Here is a version of the *caps* program that can be expected to work on all machines:

```
/* Capitalize lowercase letters and double space. */

#include <stdio.h>
#include <ctype.h>

int main(void)
{
   int   c;

   while ((c = getchar()) != EOF)
      if (islower(c))
       putchar(toupper(c));
      else if (c == '\n') {
         putchar('\n');
         putchar('\n');
      }
      else
         putchar(c);
   return 0;
}
```

Dissection of the Portable caps Program

■
```
#include <stdio.h>
#include <ctype.h>
```

The file *ctype.h*, along with *stdio.h*, is a standard header file provided with the C system. This file contains the macros and prototypes of functions that are often used when processing characters. A macro is code that is expanded by the preprocessor. In Appendix B, "The Preprocessor," we explain in detail how macros work. For the purposes of this chapter, we treat the macros in *ctype.h* as if they were functions. Although there are technical differences between a macro and a function, they are used in a similar fashion. The program *caps* uses `islower()` and `toupper()`. Because *ctype.h* contains the macro definition for `islower()` and the function prototype for `toupper()`, this header file is included.

■
```
while ((c = getchar()) != EOF)
   if (islower(c))
    putchar(toupper(c));
```

A character is read from the input stream and assigned to `c`. As long as the value of `c` is not `EOF`, the body of the `while` loop is executed. The macro `islower()` is defined in *ctype.h*. If `c` is a lowercase letter, then `islower(c)` has a nonzero value; otherwise it has the value 0. The function prototype for `toupper()` is given in *ctype.h*. The function itself is provided by the standard library. If `c` is a lowercase letter, then `toupper(c)` has the value of the corresponding uppercase letter. Therefore, the `if` statement has the effect of testing to see whether `c` has the value of a lowercase letter. If it does, the corresponding uppercase letter is written on the screen. Note carefully that the stored value of `c` itself is not changed by invoking `isupper(c)` or `toupper(c)`.

A novice C programmer need not know exactly how the macros in *ctype.h* are implemented. Along with functions in the standard library such as `printf()` and `scanf()`, these macros can be treated as a system-supplied resource. The important point to remember is that by using these functions and macros, you are writing portable code that runs in any ANSI-conforming environment.

Why learn about a construct such as `c + 'A' - 'a'` at all? Well, a lot of C code is written just for an ASCII environment, and even though the construct is not considered good programming practice, one commonly sees it. Because a programmer must learn to read code as well as write it, this particular construct should be mastered. In order to avoid nonportable code, it is good programming practice to use the macros in *ctype.h* wherever appropriate.

5.4 The Macros in *ctype.h*

The system provides a standard header file *ctype.h*, which contains a set of macros that are used to test characters and a set of function prototypes that are used to convert characters. They are made accessible by the preprocessing directive

```
#include <ctype.h>
```

The macros in the following table are used to test characters. These macros all take an argument of type `int`, and they return an `int` value that is either nonzero (*true*) or zero (*false*).

Character macros	
Macro	**Nonzero (true) is returned if**
`isalpha(c)`	c is a letter
`isupper(c)`	c is an uppercase letter
`islower(c)`	c is a lowercase letter
`isdigit(c)`	c is a digit
`isalnum(c)`	c is a letter or digit
`isxdigit(c)`	c is a hexadecimal digit
`isspace(c)`	c is a white space character
`ispunct(c)`	c is a punctuation character
`isprint(c)`	c is a printable character
`isgraph(c)`	c is printable, but not a space
`iscntrl(c)`	c is a control character
`isascii(c)`	c is an ASCII code

In the next table we list the functions `toupper()` and `tolower()`, which are in the standard library, and the macro `toascii()`. The macro and the prototypes for the two functions are in *ctype.h*. The functions and the macro each take an `int` and return an `int`. Note carefully that the value of `c` stored in memory is not changed.

Character macros and functions	
Function or macro	**Effect**
`toupper(c)`	Changes `c` from lowercase to uppercase
`tolower(c)`	Changes `c` from uppercase to lowercase
`toascii(c)`	Changes `c` to ASCII code

5.5 Problem Solving: Repeating Characters

The use of a function with proper parameterization is a very powerful problem-solving idea. It is an aspect of *generalization*. Frequently, one can solve a particular problem in a simple special case. An example might be a need to print the letter *C* three times.

```
printf("%c%c%c", 'C', 'C', 'C');
```

Now, if we need to print four *C*s or six *b*s, then we need a different solution. By parameterizing both the character to be printed and the number of times to print it, we solve a far more general problem. We write a function to do this:

```
void   repeat(char c, int  how_many);
```

Once our function is written and the code is correct, we may reuse the function for many purposes. Indeed, many of the standard library functions were developed as useful general operations that commonly occur.

In the program *dbl_out*, on page 178, we showed how every character read in can be printed out twice. Here we want to generalize that simple idea by writing a function that prints out a given character *how_many* times.

```
void repeat(char c, int how_many)
{
   int   i;

   for (i = 0; i < how_many; ++i)
      putchar(c);
}
```

Notice that the variable c is declared as a char, not an int. Because a test for EOF is not made in this function, there is no need to declare c an int. Suppose we invoke the function with the statement

```
repeat('B' - 1, 2);
```

The arguments of this function call are 'B' - 1 and 2. The respective values of these arguments are passed and associated with the formal parameters of the function. The effect of the function call is to print the letter A two times. Here is a main() function that can be used to test repeat():

```
#include <ctype.h>
#include <stdio.h>

void repeat(char, int);

int main(void)
{
   int          i;
   const char   alert = '\a', c = 'A';

   repeat('B' - 1, 2);
   putchar(' ');
   for (i = 0; i < 10; ++i) {
      repeat(c + i, i);
      putchar(' ');
   }
   repeat(alert, 100);
   putchar('\n');
   return 0;
}
```

Note that we have used the type specifier `const` to indicate that the variables `alert` and `c` cannot be changed. When we compile the program and run it, here is what we see on the screen:

```
AA  B CC DDD EEEE FFFFF GGGGGG HHHHHHH IIIIIIII JJJJJJJJJ
```

The function `repeat()` can be used to draw simple figures on the screen. In exercise 8 on page 199, we show how to use `repeat()` to draw a triangle and leave as an exercise the problem of drawing a diamond.

5.6 Problem Solving: Counting Words

Many computations are repetitive, and sometimes the repetition is based on counting. An example would be a recipe that says, "Stir for 40 seconds." Here we count up to 40. Sometimes the repetition waits for some condition to change. An example would be a recipe that says, "Stir until browned." In problem solving, looking for a special characteristic that logically ends the computation is an important method. In character processing, we often look for the end-of-file condition.

Suppose we want to count the number of words being input at the keyboard. Again, top-down design leads us to break the problem into small pieces. To do this, we need to know the definition of a word, and we need to know when to end our task. For our purposes, we assume that words are separated by white space. Thus any word is a contiguous string of non-white space characters. As usual, we end the processing of characters when we encounter the end-of-file sentinel. The heart of our program is a function, `found_next_word()`, that detects a word. We explain this function in some detail.

```
#include <stdio.h>
#include <ctype.h>

int found_next_word(void);

int main(void)
{
   int   word_count = 0;

   while (found_next_word() == 1)
      ++word_count;
   printf("Number of words = %d\n\n", word_count);
   return 0;
}
```

```
int found_next_word(void)
{
   int   c;

   while (isspace(c = getchar()))
      ;                     /* skip white space */
   if (c != EOF) {          /* found a word */
      while ((c = getchar()) != EOF && !isspace(c))
       ;     /* skip all except EOF and white space */
      return 1;
   }
   return 0;
}
```

Dissection of the word_count Program

■ `int   word_count = 0;`

The `int` variable `word_count` is initialized to zero.

■
```
while (found_next_word() == 1)
   ++word_count;
```

As long as the function `found_next_word()` returns the value 1, the body of the `while` loop is executed, causing `word_count` to be indexed.

■ `printf("Number of words = %d\n\n", word_count);`

Just before exiting the program, we print out the number of words found.

■
```
int found_next_word()
{
   int   c;
```

This is the beginning of the function definition for `found_next_word()`. The function has no parameters in its parameter list. In the body of the function, the `int` variable `c` is declared. Although we are going to use `c` to take on character values, we declare `c` as an `int`, not a `char`. Eventually, `c` holds the special value `EOF`, and on some systems that value may not fit in a `char`.

■
```
while (isspace(c = getchar()))
    ;                      /* skip white space */
```

A character is read from the input stream and assigned to `c`. The value of the subexpression `c = getchar()` takes on this value as well. As long as this value is not a white space character, the body of the `while` loop is executed. However, the body of the `while` loop is just the empty statement. Thus the effect of the `while` loop is to skip white space. Notice that the empty statement is clearly displayed on a line by itself. Good programming practice requires this. If we had written

```
while (isspace(c = getchar()));
```

the visibility of the empty statement would be reduced.

■
```
if (c != EOF) {        /* found a word */
    while ((c = getchar()) != EOF && !isspace(c))
        ;     /* skip all except EOF and white space */
    return 1;
}
```

After white space has been skipped, the value of `c` is either `EOF` or the first "letter" of a word. If the value of `c` is not `EOF`, then a word has been found. The test expression in the `while` loop consists of three parts. First, a character is read from the input stream and assigned to `c`, and the subexpression `c = getchar()` takes on the value of `c` as well. A test is then made to see if that value is `EOF`. If it is, the body of the `while` loop is not executed, and control passes to the next statement. If the value is not `EOF`, a test is made to see if the value is a white space character. If it is, the body of the `while` loop is not executed, and control passes to the next statement. If the value is not a white space character, the body of the `while` loop is executed. However, the body is just the empty statement. Thus the effect of this `while` loop is to skip everything except `EOF` and white space characters; that is, the word that has been found has now been skipped.

■
```
return 1;
```

After a word has been found and skipped, the value 1 is returned.

■
```
return 0;
```

If a word was not found, then the value 0 is returned.

5.7 Style

Simple character variables are often given the identifier `c`, or identifiers starting with `c`, such as `c1`, `c2`, and `c3`. Professional C programmers tend to be terse. It is often clearer to use `ch`, `chr`, or even `ch_var` as an identifier for a `char` variable. Functions and macros that do character manipulation frequently have `char` as part of their name, or the name ends with the letter `c`. Examples are `getchar()` and `putchar()`, and, as we shall see in Chapter 13, "Input/Output and Files," `getc()` and `putc()`. The choice of identifiers for the macros in *ctype.h* is instructive. Those macros that answer a true/false question, such as `isalpha()` and `isupper()`, all have names that start with `is`. Those functions with prototypes in *ctype.h* that change a character value, such as `toupper()`, all have names that start with `to`. The proper choice of identifier names is crucial to readability and documentation.

For character-processing tasks, we can use either `getchar()` or `scanf()` to read characters. Similarly, we can use either `putchar()` or `printf()` to write characters. In many instances the choice is a matter of personal taste. However, if a great deal of character processing is being done, then the use of `getchar()` and `putchar()`, along with the standard header file *stdio.h*, can result in faster code because `getchar()` and `putchar()` are implemented as macros in *stdio.h*. As we shall see in Appendix B, "The Preprocessor," macros are a code-substitution mechanism that can be used to avoid a function call.

One difference between `putchar()` and `printf()` is that `putchar()` returns the value of the character written to the output stream as an `int`, whereas `printf()` returns the number of characters printed. This may dictate the use of `putchar()`.

A common C programming practice is to perform both an assignment and a test in the expression that controls a `while` or `for` loop; one most often sees this done in code used to process characters. For example, the code

```
while ((c = getchar()) != EOF) {
    .....
}
```

uses this idiom. In contrast to this, we could write

```
c = getchar();
while (c != EOF) {
    .....
    c = getchar();
}
```

but now, if the body of the loop is long, the last statement, which affects the control of the loop, is a long way from the test expression. On the other hand, a construct such as

```
while (isspace(c = getchar()))
   ;      /* skip white space */
```

can just as well be written

```
c = getchar();
while (isspace(c))
   c = getchar();
```

Here the body of the loop is very short—so short, in fact, that if we put all the control at the top, the body of the loop is empty. Which form you see is largely a matter of taste.

5.8 Common Programming Errors

We have already explained that if a program uses a variable to read in characters and to test for the value EOF, the variable should be an `int`, not a `char`. This is, in part, a portability consideration. Some C systems cannot detect EOF as an end-of-file signal if the value is assigned to a variable of type `char` instead of `int`. Try the following code:

```
char   c;                          /* wrong */

while ((c = getchar()) != EOF)
   putchar(c);
```

This may or may not work on your system. Even if it does, do not use a `char` when testing for EOF. You may not be porting your code today, but if you keep programming, you are likely do so in the future.

Suppose we have text files that are double- or triple-spaced, and our task is to copy the files, except that multiple occurrences of newlines are to be reduced to a single newline. For example, we want to be able to change a double-spaced file into one that is single-spaced. Here is a program that does this:

```
/* Copy stdin to stdout, except single space only. */

#include <stdio.h>

int main(void)
{
   int   c, last_c = '\0';

   while ((c = getchar()) != EOF) {
      if (c == '\n') {
         if (last_c != '\n')
            putchar('\n');
      }
      else
         putchar(c);
      last_c = c;
   }
   return 0;
}
```

At the start of this program, the variable `last_c` is initialized to the null character, but thereafter that variable holds the last character read from the input stream (keyboard). There is nothing special about the use of the null character here. We just need to initialize `last_c` with some character other than a newline character. Two common errors can be made in this program. Suppose we had typed

```
if (c = '\n') {
```

using = instead of ==. Because the expression `c = '\n'` is always *true*, the `else` part is never executed, and the program fails badly. Another error would have occurred if we had typed

```
if (c == '\n')
   if (last_c != '\n')
      putchar(c);
else
   putchar(c);
```

The indentation shows the logic we want, but not what we are actually getting. Because an `else` statement always attaches to the nearest preceding `if`, the preceding code is equivalent to

```
if (c == '\n')
   if (last_c != '\n')
      putchar(c);
   else
      putchar(c);
```

and this is clearly in error. The programmer must always remember that the compiler sees only a stream of characters.

5.9 System Considerations

We have discussed redirecting the standard input and output (see Section 1.11, "Redirection of the Input and the Output," on page 30). You should review that material and try redirection with the *caps* program. Create a file called *input* and put some text in it. Then try the following commands:

```
caps
caps < input
caps > output
caps < input > output
```

Most operating systems have a command that copies one file to another. In MS-DOS, the command is *copy*; in UNIX, it is *cp*. The following program can be considered a simple version of such a command:

```
#include <stdio.h>

int main(void)
{
   int   c;

   while ((c = getchar()) != EOF)
      putchar(c);
   return 0;
}
```

If we compile this program and put the executable code in *my_copy*, then the command

```
my_copy < infile > outfile
```

copies the contents of *infile* to *outfile*.

If `c` has the value of a lowercase letter, then `toupper(c)` returns the value of the corresponding uppercase letter. The ANSI C standard states that if `c` does not have the value of a lowercase letter, then `toupper(c)` should return as its value the value of the argument unchanged. Thus, to change all lowercase letters to uppercase, we could use the code

```
while ((c = getchar()) != EOF)
   putchar(toupper(c));
```

However, in many older C systems, toupper() is implemented as a macro, and the preceding code fails badly. On those systems an explicit test of c must be made:

```
while ((c = getchar()) != EOF)      /* traditional C code */
   if (islower(c))
      putchar(toupper(c));
   else
      putchar(c);
```

Similar remarks hold for tolower().

Many C systems provide the macros _toupper() and _tolower() for more efficient character processing. These macros, if they exist, are provided in *ctype.h*. Here is an example of their use:

```
while ((c = getchar()) != EOF)
   if (_islower(c))
      putchar(_toupper(c));
   else
      putchar(c);
```

Note, however, that many C systems, both traditional and ANSI, do not support _toupper() and _tolower(). *Warning:* If you are trying to write portable code, use toupper() and tolower() cautiously. Some organizations use traditional C, some use ANSI C, and some are somewhere in between.

All compilers treat a char as a small integer. On most systems, but not all, the default range of values for a char is from -128 to 127. Many compilers provide an option to change the range of values to go from 0 to 255 instead. This option could be useful for minimizing the amount of disk space required to store a lot of data. If all your numbers are in the range 0 to 255, a program compiled with this option can manipulate the data and store it as chars instead of ints. As we see in Chapter 6, "The Fundamental Data Types," a char is stored in less space than an int.

5.10 Moving to C++

C++ output is inserted into an object of type ostream, declared in the header file *iostream.h*. An operator << is overloaded in this class to perform output conversions from standard types. The overloaded left-shift operator is called the *insertion* or *put to* operator. The operator is left-associative and returns a value of type ostream&. The standard output ostream corresponding to stdout is cout, and the standard output ostream corresponding to stderr is cerr.

The effect of executing a simple output statement such as

```
cout << "x = " << x << '\n';
```

is to first print to the screen a string of four characters, followed by an appropriate representation for the output of x, followed by a new line. The representation depends on which overloaded version of << is invoked.

The class ostream contains public members, such as

```
ostream& operator<<(int i);
ostream& operator<<(long i);
ostream& operator<<(double x);
ostream& operator<<(char c);
ostream& operator<<(const char* s);
ostream& put(char c);
ostream& write(const char* p, int n);
ostream& flush();
```

The member function put outputs the character representation of c; write outputs the string of length n pointed at by p; flush forces the stream to be written. Because these are member functions, they can be used as follows:

```
cout.put('A');                  //output A

char*  str = "ABCDEFGHI";
cout.write(str + 2, 3);         //output CDE
cout.flush();                   //write contents of buffered stream
```

The put to operator << produces by default the minimum number of characters needed to represent the output. As a consequence, output can be confusing, as seen in the following example:

```
int  i = 8, j = 9;
cout << i << j ;                //confused: prints 89
cout << i << "   " << j;        //better: prints 8   9
cout << "i= " << i << " j= " << j;  //best: i= 8 j= 9
```

Two schemes that we have used to properly space output are (1) to have strings separating output values and (2) to use \n and \t to create newline characters and tabbing. We can also use manipulators in the stream output to control output formatting.

A manipulator is a value or function that has a special effect on the stream it operates on. A simple example of a manipulator is endl defined in *iostream.h*. It outputs a newline and flushes the ostream.

```
x = 1;
cout << "x = " << x << endl;
```

This immediately prints the line

```
x = 1
```

Another manipulator, `flush`, flushes the ostream, as in

```
cout << "x = " << x << flush;
```

This has almost the same effect as the previous example, but does not advance to a newline.

The manipulators dec, hex, and oct can be used to change integer bases. The default is base ten. The conversion base remains set until explicitly changed

```
//Using different bases in integer I/O.
#include  <iostream.h>

int main(void)
{
   int  i = 10, j = 16, k = 24;

   cout << i << '\t' << j << '\t' << k << endl;
   cout << oct << i << '\t' << j << '\t' << k << endl;
   cout << hex << i << '\t' << j << '\t' << k << endl;
   cout << "Enter 3 integers, e.g. 11 11 12a" << endl;
   cin >> i >> hex >> j >> k;
   cout << dec << i << '\t' << j << '\t' << k << endl;
}
```

The resulting output is

```
10      16      24
12      20      30
a       10      18
Enter 3 integers, e.g. 11 11 12a
11      17      298
```

The reason the final line of output is 11 followed by 17 is that the second 11 in the input was interpreted as a hexadecimal, 16 + 1.

The preceding manipulators are found in *iostream.h*. Other manipulators are found in *iomanip.h*. For example, `setw(int width)` is a manipulator that changes the default field width for the next formatted I/O operation to the value of its argument. This value reverts back to the default. The following table briefly lists the standard manipulators, the function of each, and where each is defined.

C++ I/O manipulators		
Manipulator	**Function**	**File**
`endl`	output newline and flush	*iostream.h*
`ends`	output null in string	*iostream.h*
`flush`	flush the output	*iostream.h*
`dec`	use decimal	*iostream.h*
`hex`	use hexadecimal	*iostream.h*
`oct`	use octal	*iostream.h*
`ws`	skip white space on input	*iostream.h*
`setw(int)`	set field width	*iomanip.h*
`setfill(int)`	set fill character	*iomanip.h*
`setbase(int)`	set base format	*iomanip.h*
`setprecision(int)`	set floating-point precision	*iomanip.h*
`setiosflags(long)`	set format bits	*iomanip.h*
`resetiosflags(long)`	reset format bits	*iomanip.h*

Summary

- A `char` is stored in one byte according to its ASCII encoding, and is considered to have the corresponding integer value. For example, the value of the character constant `'a'` is 97.

- There are nonprinting characters. Examples are the alert character, or audible bell, `'\a'`, and the newline character `'\n'`. The newline character is used extensively to format output.

- Basic input/output for characters is accomplished readily with the macros `getchar()` and `putchar()`. These macros are defined in the standard header file *stdio.h* and, in most respects, may be treated as functions.

- When using certain input/output constructs, the system header file *stdio.h* should be included. This is done with the preprocessing directive

```
#include <stdio.h>
```

- When doing character input, it is frequently necessary to test for the end-of-file mark. This is accomplished by using the symbolic constant `EOF` in a program. The symbolic constant `EOF` is defined in the system header file *stdio.h*. On most systems, the value of `EOF` is -1.

- A number of system-supplied macros and functions test or convert character values. The macros and the prototypes of these functions are made available by including the system header file *ctype.h*.

Exercises

1 Write a program using `putchar()` and `getchar()` that reads characters from the keyboard and writes to the screen. Every letter that is read should be written three times and followed by a newline. Any newline that is read should be disregarded. All other characters should just be copied to the screen.

2 Write a program using `getchar()` that reads characters from the standard input stream (keyboard) until the sentinel character # is encountered. The program should count the number of occurrences of the letters *a*, *b*, and *c*.

3 Change the program in the previous exercise so that characters are read until `EOF` is encountered. Use redirection to test the program.

4 Write a program that reads characters from the keyboard and writes to the screen. Write all vowels as uppercase letters and all nonvowels as lowercase letters. *Hint:* Write a function `isvowel()` that tests whether or not a character is a vowel. You can reuse your code in exercise 12 on page 200.

5 Of the characters backspace, newline, space, and tab, which are considered printable? Take as the authority in this matter the macro `isprint()` in *ctype.h*.

6 Write a program that formats text files so that most lines contain approximately *N* characters. Start with the preprocessing directive

```
#define    N    30
```

Count the characters as they are written. As long as the count is less than *N*, change any newline character to a space. When the count is *N* or more, write any white space character as a newline and change the count to zero. If we assume that most words contain fewer than 10 characters, then the effect of the program is to write lines containing between *N* and *N* + 10 characters. Typists usually follow such an algorithm. Compile your program and put the executable output in the file *reformat*. Use redirection to test the program by giving the command

reformat < text

Of course, you can get different length lines by changing the value of the symbolic constant N.

7 Write a program that indents all the lines in a text file. Each line should be preceded by N blank spaces, where N is a symbolic constant.

8 The function repeat() can be used to draw simple figures on your screen. For example, the following program draws a triangle:

```
#include <ctype.h>
#include <stdio.h>

#define   N   33

void repeat(char, int);

int main(void)
{
   char   c = 'X';
   int    i;

   for (i = 1; i < N; i += 2) {
      repeat(c, i);
      putchar('\n');
   }
   return 0;
}
```

Compile and run this program so that you understand its effects. Write a similar program that prints a diamond in the middle of your screen.

9 One difference between putchar() and printf() is that putchar() returns the value of the character written to the output stream as an int, whereas printf() returns the number of characters printed. What is printed by the following code?

```
for (putchar('0'); putchar('1'); putchar('2'))
   putchar('3');
```

Does the following make sense? Explain.

```
printf("%c%c%c\n", putchar('A'), putchar('B'),
       putchar('C'));
```

10 To copy the standard input file to the standard output file, a programmer can use the following loop:

```
while ((c = getchar()) != EOF)
   putchar(c);
```

Suppose that, by mistake, the inner parentheses are left out, causing the loop to be written instead as

```
while (c = getchar() != EOF)
   putchar(c);
```

Write a test program to see what the effect is. If the input file has *n* characters, are *n* characters written to the output file? Explain.

11 The game of calling heads or tails requires the user to input 0 for heads and 1 for tails (see Section 4.11, "A Simulation: The Game of Heads or Tails," on page 147). Rewrite the program so that the user must input *h* for heads and *t* for tails. *Hint:* You can use `%c` with `scanf()` to read in characters typed by the user, but you have to deal with white space characters, too, because the user always types in *h* or *t* followed by a newline.

12 The ancient Egyptians wrote in hieroglyphics, in which vowel sounds are not represented, only consonants. Is written English generally understandable without vowels? To experiment, write a function `isvowel()` that tests whether or not a character is a vowel. Use your function in a program that reads the standard input file and writes to the standard output file, deleting all vowels. Use redirection on a file containing some English text to test your program.

13 Most operating systems provide data compression utilities that reduce the size of text files so that they take up less room on the disk. These utilities work both ways; compressed files can be uncompressed later. Write a *crunch* program that reduces the size of C source files by removing all extraneous white space, including newline characters. Test your program as follows:

```
crunch < pgm.c > try_me.c
```

The code in *try_me.c* should compile and execute with the same effects as *pgm.c*. Does it? Try your program on a number of your *.c* files. On average, what is the reduction in space achieved by *crunch*, expressed as a percent? To answer this question, write a simple routine that counts the number of characters in a file.

14 Most systems have "pretty printing" utilities that take crunched or poorly laid out C programs and transform them into a more readable format. Such a utility, when applied to the crunched C code that you produced in the previous exercise, would print it with nice spacing. Write your own version of a "pretty printing" utility. Given a C program as input, it should add white space and newline characters to make the program more readable. Test your "pretty printer" by running it on previously crunched C code.

15 We presented the output from our program *repeat* (see Section 5.5, "Problem Solving: Repeating Characters," on page 187). Here it is again:

```
AAAAA  B CC DDD EEEE FFFFF GGGGGG HHHHHHH IIIIIIII JJJJJJJJJ
```

Note that there are two blanks just before the `B`, whereas thereafter all the blanks occur singly. Explain why.

16 C++: Rewrite the *caps* program (see Section 5.3, "An Example: Capitalize," on page 181) in C++ and if possible use a recursion to replace the `while` loop.

17 C++: Using the `hex` manipulator write a program that prints all the characters with their hexadecimal representations.

18 Java: Here is a simple Java program that reads ten characters from the keyboard. Convert the program to C.

```
import tio.*;
import java.io.IOException;

public class TestChar {
    public static void main (String args[]) throws
IOException
    {
        System.out.println("Read a Char:");
        for(int i = 0; i < 10; i++) {
            int c = Console.in.readChar();
            System.out.println(c + " in char " + (char)c);
        }
    }
}
```

In Java, `char` is represented as a 2-byte type capable of storing 16 bits. This can be used to represent all the major international alphabets. C uses 1-byte ASCII code to represent only the standard American alphabet and keyboard characters.

The Fundamental Data Types

Chapter 6

We begin this chapter with a brief discussion of declarations and expressions. Then we give a detailed explanation for each of the fundamental data types, paying particular attention to how C treats characters as small integers. In expressions with operands of different types, certain implicit conversions occur. We explain the rules for conversion and we discuss the cast operator, which forces explicit conversion.

6.1 Declarations and Expressions

Variables and constants are the objects a program manipulates. In C, all variables must be declared before they can be used. Declarations serve two purposes. First, they tell the compiler to set aside an appropriate amount of space in memory to hold values associated with variables, and second, they enable the compiler to instruct the machine to perform specified operations correctly. In the expression `a + b`, the operator + is being applied to two variables. The addition the machine does as a result of applying the + operator to variables of type `int` is different from the addition that results from applying the + operator to variables of type `float`. Of course, the programmer need not be concerned that the two + operations are mechanically different, but the C compiler has to recognize the difference and give the appropriate machine instructions.

Expressions are meaningful combinations of constants, variables, and function calls. Like variables, most expressions have both a *value* and a *type*. In many situations, what happens depends on the type of the expression, which in turn depends on the types of the constants, variables, and function calls making up the expression. In the following sections we discuss issues related to the concept of type.

6.2 The Fundamental Data Types

C provides several fundamental types, many of which we have already seen. For all of them, we need to discuss limitations on what can be stored.

Fundamental data types: long form		
`char`	`signed char`	`unsigned char`
`signed short int`	`signed int`	`signed long int`
`unsigned short int`	`unsigned int`	`unsigned long int`
`float`	`double`	`long double`

The types shown in the table are all keywords; they may not be used as names of variables. Other data types, such as arrays and pointers, are derived from the fundamental types (see Chapter 9, "Arrays and Pointers").

Usually, the keyword `signed` is not used. For example, `signed int` is equivalent to `int`, and because shorter names are easier to type, `int` is typically used. The type `char`, however, is special in this regard (see the next section). Also, the keywords `short int`, `long int`, and `unsigned int` may be, and usually are, shortened to just `short`, `long`, and `unsigned`, respectively. The keyword `signed` by itself is equivalent to `int`, but it is seldom used in this context. All these conventions give us a new list of fundamental data types.

Fundamental data types		
`char`	`signed char`	`unsigned char`
`short`	`int`	`long`
`unsigned short`	`unsigned`	`unsigned long`
`float`	`double`	`long double`

The fundamental types can be grouped according to functionality. The integral types are those types that can be used to hold integer values; the floating types are those that can be used to hold real values. They are all arithmetic types.

Fundamental types grouped by functionality			
Integral types	`char`	`signed char`	`unsigned char`
	`short`	`int`	`long`
	`unsigned short`	`unsigned`	`unsigned long`
Floating types	`float`	`double`	`long double`
Arithmetic types	*Integral types + Floating types*		

These collective names are a convenience. For example, in Chapter 9, "Arrays and Pointers," when we discuss arrays, we explain that only integral expressions are allowed as subscripts, meaning that expressions involving integral types are allowed.

6.3 Characters and the Data Type char

In C, variables of any integral type can be used to represent characters. In particular, both `char` and `int` variables are used for this purpose. As we saw in Chapter 5, "Character Processing," when a variable is used to read in characters and a test must be made for `EOF`, the variable should be of type `int`, not `char`. Constants such as `'a'` and `'+'` that we think of as characters are of type `int`, not of type `char`. There are no constants of type `char`.

Recall that characters are treated as small integers and, conversely, small integers are treated as characters. In particular, any integral expression can be printed either in the format of a character or an integer.

```
char   c = 'a';             /* 'a' has ASCII encoding 97 */
int    i = 65;              /* 65 is ASCII encoding for 'A' */
printf("%c", c + 1);        /*  b is printed */
printf("%d", c + 2);        /* 99 is printed */
printf("%c", i + 3);        /*  D is printed */
```

In C, each `char` is stored in one byte of memory. On almost all machines, a byte is composed of eight bits. Let us see how a `char` is stored in memory at the bit level. Consider the declaration

```
char   c = 'a';
```

We can think of `c` stored in one byte of memory as

0	1	1	0	0	0	0	1
7	6	5	4	3	2	1	

Here, each box represents a bit, and the bits are numbered beginning with the least significant bit. The bits making up a byte are either on or off, and these states are represented by 1 and 0, respectively. This leads us to think of each byte in memory as a string of eight binary digits. Strings of binary digits are also called *bit strings.* We can think of the variable `c` stored in memory as the bit string

```
01100001
```

More generally, each machine word can be thought of as a string of binary digits grouped into bytes.

A string of binary digits is interpreted as a binary number. Before we describe how this is done, recall how strings of decimal digits are interpreted as decimal numbers. Consider, for example, the decimal number 10,753. Its value is given by

$$1 \times 10^4 + 0 \times 10^3 + 7 \times 10^2 + 5 \times 10^1 + 3 \times 10^0$$

More generally, a decimal positional number is written in the form

$$d_n d_{n-1} \cdots\cdots d_2 d_1 d_0$$

where each d_i is a decimal digit. It has the value

$$d_n \times 10^n + d_{n-1} \times 10^{n-1} + \cdots\cdots + d_2 \times 10^2 + d_1 \times 10^1 + d_0 \times 10^0$$

A binary, or base two, positional number is written in the form

$$b_n b_{n-1} \cdots\cdots b_2 b_1 b_0$$

where each b_i is a binary digit, either 0 or 1. It has the value

$$b_n \times 2^n + b_{n-1} \times 2^{n-1} + \cdots\cdots + b_2 \times 2^2 + b_1 \times 2^1 + b_0 \times 2^0$$

Now let us consider the value for `c` again. It was stored in a byte as 01100001. This binary number has the value

$$1 \times 1^6 + 1 \times 2^5 + 0 \times 2^4 + 0 \times 2^3 + 0 \times 2^2 + 0 \times 2^1 + 1 \times 2^1$$

which is 64 + 32 + 1, or 97 in decimal notation.

ANSI C provides the three types `char`, `signed char`, and `unsigned char`. Typically, the type `char` is equivalent to either `signed char` or `unsigned char`, depending on the compiler. Each of the three `char` types is stored in one byte, which can hold 256 distinct values. For a `signed char`, the values go from -128 to 127. For an `unsigned char`, the values go from 0 to 255.

6.4 The Data Type `int`

The data type `int` is the principal working type of the C language. This type, along with the other integral types, such as `char`, `short`, and `long`, is designed for working with the integer values that can be represented on a machine.

In mathematics the natural numbers are 0, 1, 2, 3, . . ., and these numbers, along with their negatives, comprise the integers. On a machine, only a finite portion of these integers is representable for a given integral type.

Typically, an `int` is stored in a machine word. Some computers use a machine word of two bytes (16 bits); others use a machine word of four bytes (32 bits). There are other possibilities, but many machines fall within these two classes. Personal computers, for example, use 2-byte words; 4-byte words are used by high-end personal computers and workstations made by Apollo, Hewlett-Packard, Next, Silicon Graphics, Sun, and others. Also, many kinds of mainframes have 4-byte machine words. Because the word size varies from one machine to another, the number of distinct values an `int` can hold is machine-dependent. Suppose we are working on a computer that has 4-byte words. This implies that an `int`, because it is stored in a word with 32 bits, can take on 2^{32} distinct states. Half of these states are used to represent negative integers, and half are used to represent nonnegative integers:

$$-2^{31},\ -2^{31}+1,\ \cdots\cdots,\ -3,\ -2,\ -1,\ 0,\ 1,\ 2,\ 3,\ \cdots\cdots,\ 2^{31}-1$$

If, on the other hand, we are using computer that has 2-byte words, then an `int` can take on only 2^{16} distinct states. Again, half of these states are used to represent negative integers, and half are used to represent nonnegative integers:

$$-2^{15},\ -2^{15}+1,\ \cdots\cdots,\ -3,\ -3,\ -1,\ 0,\ 1,\ 2,\ 3,\ \cdots\cdots,\ 2^{15}-1$$

Let N_{min_int} represent the smallest integer that can be stored in an `int`, and let N_{max_int} represent the largest integer that can be stored in an `int`. If `i` is a variable of type `int`, the range of values that `i` can take on is given by

$$N_{min\_int} \le i \le N_{max\_int}$$

with the end points of the range being machine-dependent. The typical situation is as follows:

On machines with 4-byte words:

$$N_{min\_int} = -2^{31} = -2147483648 \approx -2 \textit{ billion}$$
$$N_{max\_int} = +2^{31} - 1 = +2147483647 \approx +2 \textit{ billion}$$

On machines with 2-byte words:

$$N_{min\_int} = -2^{15} = -32768 \approx -32 \textit{ thousand}$$
$$N_{max\_int} = +2^{15} - 1 = +32767 \approx +32 \textit{ thousand}$$

On any machine the following code is syntactically correct:

```
#define   BIG   2000000000       /* 2 billion */

int main(void)
{
   int   a, b = BIG, c = BIG;

   a = b + c;      /* out of range? */
   .....
```

However, at run-time the variable a may be assigned an incorrect value. The logical value of the expression b + c is 4 billion, which probably is greater than N_{max_int}. If it is, the addition causes what is called an *integer overflow*. Typically, when an integer overflow occurs, the program continues to run, but with logically incorrect results. For this reason, the programmer must strive at all times to keep the values of integer expressions within the proper range.

In addition to decimal integer constants, there are hexadecimal integer constants, such as 0x1a, and octal integer constants, such as 0377. Many C programmers have no particular need for hexadecimal and octal numbers, but all programmers have to know that integers that begin with a leading zero are not decimal integers. For example, 11 and 011 do not have the same value.

6.5 The Integral Types short, long, and unsigned

In C, the data type int is considered the "natural" or "usual" type for working with integers. The other integral types, such as char, short, and long, are intended for more specialized use. The data type short, for example, might be used when storage is a concern. The compiler may provide less storage for a short than for an int although it is not required to do so. In a similar fashion, the type long might be used when large integer values are needed. The compiler may provide more storage for a long than for an int, although it is not required to do so. Typically, a short is stored in two bytes, and a long is stored in four bytes. Thus on machines with 4-byte words, the size of an int is the same as the size of a long, and on machines with 2-byte words, the size of an int is the same as the size of a short. If small is a variable of type short, then the range of values that small can take on is given by

$$N_{min\_short} \leq small \leq N_{max\_short}$$

where typically

$$N_{min\_short} = -2^{15} = -32768 \approx -32 \text{ thousand}$$
$$N_{max\_short} = +2^{15} - 1 = +32767 \approx +32 \text{ thousand}$$

If `big` is a variable of type `long`, then the range of values that `big` can take on is given by

$$N_{min\_long} \leq big \leq N_{max\_long}$$

where typically

$$N_{min\_long} = -2^{31} = -2147483648 \approx -2 \text{ billion}$$
$$N_{max\_long} = +2^{31} - 1 = +2147483647 \approx +2 \text{ billion}$$

A variable of type `unsigned` is stored in the same number of bytes as an `int`. However, as the name implies, the integer values stored have no sign. Typically, variables of type `int` and `unsigned` are stored in a machine word. If `u` is a variable of type `unsigned`, then the range of values `u` can take on is given by

$$0 \leq u \leq 2^{wordsize} - 1$$

The typical situation is as follows: On machines with 4-byte words

$$N_{max\_unsigned} = 2^{32} - 1 = +4294967295 \approx +4 \text{ billion}$$

On machines with 2-byte words:

$$N_{max\_unsigned} = 2^{32} - 1 = +65535 \approx +65 \text{ thousand}$$

Arithmetic on unsigned variables is performed modulo $2^{wordsize}$ (see exercise 17 on page 236).

Suffixes can be appended to an integer constant to specify its type. The type of an unsuffixed integer constant is either `int`, `long`, or `unsigned long`. The system chooses the first of these types that can represent the value. For example, on machines with 2-byte words, the constant `32000` is of type `int`, but `33000` is of type `long`.

Combining long and unsigned		
Suffix	**Type**	**Example**
u or U	unsigned	37U
l or L	long	37L
ul or UL	unsigned long	37UL

6.6 The Floating Types

ANSI C provides the three floating types: `float`, `double`, and `long double`. Variables of this type can hold real values such as 0.001, 2.0, and 3.14159. A suffix can be appended to a floating constant to specify its type. Any unsuffixed floating constant is of type `double`. Unlike other languages, the working floating type in C is `double`, not `float`.

Combining float and unsigned		
Suffix	**Type**	**Example**
`f` or `F`	`float`	`3.7F`
`l` or `L`	`long double`	`3.7L`

Integers are representable as floating constants, but they must be written with a decimal point. For example, the constants `1.0` and `2.0` are both of type `double`, whereas the constant 3 is an `int`.

In addition to the ordinary decimal notation for floating constants, there is an exponential notation, as in the example `1.234567e5`. This corresponds to the scientific notation 1.234567×10^5. Recall that

$$1.234567 \times 10^5 = 1.234567 \times 10 \times 10 \times 10 \times 10 \times 10$$
$$= 1.234567 \times 100000$$
$$= 123456.7 \qquad \textit{(decimal point shifted five places)}$$

In a similar fashion, the number `1.234567e-3` calls for shifting the decimal point three places to the left to obtain the equivalent constant 0.001234567.

Now we want to carefully describe the exponential notation. After we give the precise rules, we show some examples. A floating constant such as `333.77777e-22` may not contain any embedded blanks or special characters. Each part of the constant is given a name.

Floating-point constant parts for `333.7777e-22`		
Integer	**Fraction**	**Exponent**
333	77777	e-22

A floating constant may contain an integer part, a decimal point, a fractional part, and an exponential part. A floating constant *must* contain either a decimal point or an exponential part or both. If a decimal point is present, either an integer part or fractional part or both *must* be present. If no decimal point is present, then there must be an integer part along with an exponential part. Some examples of floating constants are

```
3.14159
 314.159e-2F    /* of type float */
 0e0            /* equivalent to 0.0 */
 1.             /* equivalent to 1.0, but harder to read */
```

but not

```
 3.14,159       /* comma not allowed */
 314159         /* decimal point or exponent part needed */
 .e0            /* integer or fractional part needed */
 -3.14159       /* this is floating constant expression */
```

Typically, a C compiler provides more storage for a variable of type `double` than for one of type `float`, although it is not required to do so. On most machines a `float` is stored in four bytes, and a `double` is stored in eight bytes. The effect of this is that a `float` stores about six decimal places of accuracy, and a `double` stores about 15 decimal places of accuracy. An ANSI C compiler may provide more storage for a variable of type `long double` than for one of type `double` though it is not required to do so. Many compilers implement a `long double` as a `double` (see exercise 16 on page 236).

The possible values that a floating type can be assigned are described in terms of attributes called *precision* and *range*. The precision describes the number of significant decimal places that a floating value carries. The range describes the limits of the largest and smallest positive floating values that can be represented in a variable of that type. A `float` on many machines has an approximate precision of six significant figures and an approximate range of 10^{-38} to 10^{+38}. This means that a positive `float` value is represented in the machine in the form

$$0.d_1d_2d_3d_4d_5d_6 \times 10^n$$

where each d_i is a decimal digit; the first digit, d_1, is positive; and $-38 \leq n \leq +38$. The representation of a `float` value in a machine is actually in base two, not base ten, but the ideas as presented give the correct flavor.

A `double` on many machines has an approximate precision of 15 significant figures and approximate range of 10^{-308} to 10^{+308}. This means that a positive `double` value is represented in the machine in the following form (approximately):

$$0.d_1d_2 \cdots\cdots d_{15} \times 10^n$$

where each d_i is a decimal digit; the first digit, d_1 is positive; and $-308 \leq n \leq +308$. Suppose `x` is a variable of type `double`. Then the statement

```
x = 123.45123451234512345;      /* 20 significant digits */
```

results in x being assigned a value that is stored in the form (approximately):

$0.123451234512345 \times 10^{+3}$ (15 significant digits)

The main points you must be aware of are (1) not all real numbers are representable, and (2) floating arithmetic operations, unlike the integer arithmetic operations, need not be exact. For small computations this is usually of no concern. For very large computations, such as numerically solving a large system of ordinary differential equations, a good understanding of rounding effects, scaling, and so on may be necessary. This is the domain of numerical analysis.

6.7 The `sizeof` Operator

C provides the unary operator `sizeof` to find the number of bytes needed to store an object. It has the same precedence and associativity as all the other unary operators. An expression of the form

`sizeof(`*object*`)`

returns an integer that represents the number of bytes needed to store the object in memory. An object can be a type such as `int` or `float`, or it can be an expression such as `a + b`, or it can be an array or structure type. The following program uses this operator. On a given machine, it provides precise information about the storage requirements for the fundamental types.

```
/* Compute the size of some fundamental types. */

#include <stdio.h>

int main(void)
{
   printf("Size of some fundamental types computed.\n\n");
   printf("       char:%3d byte \n", sizeof(char));
   printf("      short:%3d bytes\n", sizeof(short));
   printf("        int:%3d bytes\n", sizeof(int));
   printf("       long:%3d bytes\n", sizeof(long));
   printf("   unsigned:%3d bytes\n", sizeof(unsigned));
   printf("      float:%3d bytes\n", sizeof(float));
   printf("     double:%3d bytes\n", sizeof(double));
   printf("long double:%3d bytes\n", sizeof(long double));
   return 0;
}
```

Because the C language is flexible in its storage requirements for the fundamental types, the situation can vary from one machine to another. However, it is guaranteed that

```
sizeof(char)  =  1
sizeof(short) ≤ sizeof(int) ≤ sizeof(long)
sizeof(signed) = sizeof(unsigned) = sizeof(int)
sizeof(float) ≤ sizeof(double) ≤ sizeof(long double)
```

Moreover, all the signed and unsigned versions of each of the integral types are guaranteed to have the same size.

Notice that we wrote `sizeof( · · · · · )` as if it were a function. However, this is not so—it is an operator. If `sizeof` is being applied to a type, then parentheses are required; otherwise they are optional. For example,

`sizeof(a + b + 7.7)` and `sizeof a + b + 7.7`

are equivalent expressions. The type of the value returned by the operator is typically `unsigned`. This is system-dependent.

6.8 Mathematical Functions

There are no built-in mathematical functions in C. Functions such as

`sqrt()` `pow()` `exp()` `log()` `sin()` `cos()` `tan()`

are available in the mathematics library, which is conceptually part of the standard library. In traditional C systems, the mathematics library is often considered to be separate. On such systems the *-lm* option or some other option may be needed to compile a program that uses mathematical functions (see Section 6.13, "System Considerations," on page 228).

All of the preceding functions except the power function, `pow()`, take a single argument of type `double` and return a value of type `double`. The power function takes two arguments of type `double` and returns a value of type `double`. Our next program illustrates the use of `sqrt()` and `pow()`. The program asks the user to input a value for *x*, and then prints it out, along with the square root of *x* and the value of *x* raised to the *x* power.

```
#include <stdio.h>
#include <math.h>

int main(void)
{
   double   x;

   printf("\n%s\n%s\n%s\n\n",
      "The square root of x and x raised",
      "to the x power will be computed.",
      "---");

   while (1) {                        /* do it forever */
      printf("Input x:  ");
      scanf("%lf", &x);
      if (x >= 0.0)
         printf("\n%15s%22.15e\n%15s%22.15e\n%15s%22.15e\n\n",
            "x = ", x,
            "sqrt(x) = ", sqrt(x),
            "pow(x, x) = ", pow(x, x));
      else
         printf("\nSorry, number must be nonnegative.\n\n");
   }
   return 0;
}
```

If we execute the program and enter 2 when prompted, here is what appears on the screen:

```
The square root of x and x raised
to the x power will be computed.
---

Input x:  2

           x = 2.000000000000000e+000
     sqrt(x) = 1.414213562373095e+000
   pow(x, x) = 4.000000000000000e+000

Input x:
```

Dissection of the sqrt_pow Program

■
```
#include <stdio.h>
#include <math.h>
```

These header files contain function prototypes. In particular, *math.h* contains the prototypes for the functions in the mathematics library. As an alternative to including *math.h*, we can supply our own function prototypes:

```
double   sqrt(double), pow(double, double);
```

This declaration can be placed in the file above `main()` or in the body of `main()` itself.

■
```
while (1) {                    /* do it forever */
    .....
```

Because any nonzero value is considered to be *true*, the expression `1` creates an infinite `while` loop. The user is expected to input values repeatedly and to interrupt the program when finished.

■
```
scanf("%lf", &x);
```

The format `%lf` is used in the control string because `x` is a `double`. A common error is to use `%f` instead of `%lf`. Notice that we typed `2` to illustrate the use of this program. We could have typed `2.0`, `2e0`, or `0.2e1`; the function call `scanf("%lf", &x)` would have converted each of these to the same `double`. In C, source code `2` and `2.0` are different. The first is of type `int`, and the second is of type `double`. The input stream that is read by `scanf()` is *not* source code, so the rules for source code do not apply. When `scanf()` reads in a `double`, the number 2 is just as good as the number `2.0` (see Section 13.2, "Conversion Specifications," on page 436).

■
```
if (x >= 0.0)
    .....
```

Because the square root function is defined only for nonnegative numbers, a test is made to ensure that the value of `x` is nonnegative. A call such as `sqrt(-1.0)` causes a run-time error (see exercise 19 on page 236).

```
■ printf("\n%15s%22.15e\n%15s%22.15e\n%15s%22.15e\n\n",
      "x = ", x,
      "sqrt(x) = ", sqrt(x),
      "pow(x, x) = ", pow(x, x));
```

Notice that we are printing `double` values in the format `%22.15e`. This results in one place to the left of the decimal point and 15 places to the right, 16 significant places in all. On our machine, only *n* places are valid, where *n* is between 15 and 16. *n* is variable because of the conversion from binary to decimal. You can ask for lots of decimal places to be printed, but you should not believe all that you read.

6.9 Conversions and Casts

An arithmetic expression such as `x + y` has both a value and a type. For example, if both `x` and `y` have type `int`, then the expression `x + y` also has type `int`. But if both `x` and `y` have type `short`, then `x + y` is of type `int`, not `short`. This is because in any expression, a `short` is always promoted, or converted, to an `int`. In this section we want to give the precise rules for conversions.

The Integral Promotions

A `char` or `short`, either `signed` or `unsigned`, or an enumeration type can be used in any expression where an `int` or `unsigned int` may be used (see Chapter 7, "Enumeration Types and typedef"). If all the values of the original type can be represented by an `int`, the value is converted to an `int`; otherwise it is converted to an `unsigned int`. This is called an *integral promotion*. Here is an example:

```
char   c = 'A';

printf("%c\n", c);
```

The `char` variable `c` occurs by itself as an argument to `printf()`. However, because an integral promotion takes place, the type of the expression `c` is `int`, not `char`.

The Usual Arithmetic Conversions

Arithmetic conversions can occur when the operands of a binary operator are evaluated. Suppose that `i` is an `int` and `f` is a `float`. In the expression `i + f`, the operand `i` is promoted to a `float` and the expression `i + f` as a whole has type `float`. The rules governing this are called the *usual arithmetic conversions.*

Usual Arithmetic Conversions

1 If either operand is of type `long double`, the other operand is converted to `long double`.

2 Otherwise, if either operand is of type `double`, the other operand is converted to `double`.

3 Otherwise, if either operand is of type `float`, the other operand is converted to `float`.

4 Otherwise, the integral promotions are performed on both operands, and the following rules are applied:

A If either operand is of type `unsigned long`, the other operand is converted to `unsigned long`.

B Otherwise, if one operand has type `long` and the other has type `unsigned`, then one of two possibilities occurs:

If a `long` can represent all the values of an `unsigned`, then the operand of type `unsigned` is converted to `long`.

If a `long` cannot represent all the values of an `unsigned`, then both of the operands are converted to `unsigned long`.

C Otherwise, if either operand has type `long`, the other operand is converted to `long`.

D Otherwise, if either operand has type `unsigned`, the other operand is converted to `unsigned`.

E Otherwise, both operands have type `int`.

This process goes under various names: automatic conversion, implicit conversion, coercion, promotion, or widening.

The idea of automatic conversions is shown in the following declarations and mixed expressions, with their corresponding types.

Declarations			

`char c;`
`unsigned u;`
`double d;`
	`short s;`
	`unsigned long ul;`
	`long double ld;`
		`int i;`
		`float f;`	

Expression	**Type**	**Expression**	**Type**
`c - s / i`	`int`	`u * 7 - i`	`unsigned`
`u * 2.0 - i`	`double`	`f * 7 - i`	`float`
`c + 3`	`int`	`7 * s * ul`	`unsigned long`
`c + 5.0`	`double`	`ld + c`	`long double`
`d + s`	`double`	`u - ul`	`unsigned long`
`2 * i / l`	`long`	`u - l`	*system-dependent*

In addition to automatic conversions in mixed expressions, an automatic conversion can occur across an assignment. For example,

```
d = i
```

causes the value of `i`, which is an `int`, to be converted to a `double` and then assigned to `d`; `double` is the type of the expression as a whole. A promotion or widening such as `d = i` is usually well behaved, but a narrowing or demotion such as `i = d` can lose information. Here, the fractional part of `d` is discarded. Precisely what happens in each case is system-dependent.

Casts

In addition to implicit conversions, which can occur across assignments and in mixed expressions, there are explicit conversions called *casts*. If `i` is an `int`, then

```
(double) i
```

casts the value of `i` so the expression has type `double`. The variable `i` itself remains unchanged. Casts can be applied to expressions. Some examples are

```
(long) ('A' + 1.0)
x = (float) ((int) y + 1)
(double) (x = 77)
```

but not

```
(double) x = 77      /* equivalent to      ((double) x) = 77, error */
```

The cast operator (*type*) is a unary operator having the same precedence and right-to-left associativity as other unary operators. Thus the expression

`(float) i + 3` is equivalent to `((float) i) + 3`

because the cast operator (*type*) has higher precedence than +.

"YOU THOUGHT THAT 'A' WAS THE SAME AS 97 OR 97.0? NO, ALL THREE ARE DIFFERENT, BUT YOU CAN USE CASTS TO CONVERT FROM ONE TYPE TO ANOTHER."

6.10 Problem Solving: Computing Interest

Everyone is familiar with putting money into a savings account to earn interest. In the business world many transactions and agreements involve the borrowing and lending of money with interest. To illustrate some of the ideas presented in this chapter, we show how to compute interest that is compounded yearly. In exercise 12 on page 234, we indicate how to compute interest compounded quarterly and daily.

Suppose that we put P dollars into a savings account that pays 7 percent interest compounded yearly. At the end of the first year we have P, our original principal, plus 7 percent of P, the earned interest. Because 7 percent of P is $0.07 \times P$, we have in our savings account

$P + 0.07 \times P$ or equivalently $1.07 \times P$

At the end of every year, to find the amount in our savings account, we take the amount that we started with at the beginning of the year and multiply it by 1.07. Thus we have

at the end of the first year	$1.07 \times P$		
at the end of the second year	$1.07 \times (1.07 \times P)$	or	$1.07^2 \times P$
at the end of the third year	$1.07 \times (1.07^{2} \times P)$	or	$1.07^3 \times P$
. . . . .			
at the end of the nth year	$1.07 \times (1.07^{n-1} \times P)$	or	$1.07^n \times P$

We want to use these ideas to write an interactive program to compute interest that is compounded yearly. Values corresponding to principal, interest rate, and number of years are supplied by the user. Our top-down design of this program is to print instructions, read in values, compute the interest, and print out the results. Following this structured design, we write the program to consist of `main()` and the three functions `prn_instructions()`, `compute()`, and `prn_results()`. Let us suppose these functions are all in the file *interest.c.* At the top of the file we put our `#include` line, the function prototypes, and `main()`.

```
/* Compute interest compounded yearly. */

#include <stdio.h>

double   compute(double p, double r, int n);
void     prn_instructions(void);
void     prn_results(double a, double p, double r, int n);

int main(void)
{
   double   amount;        /* principal + interest */
   double   principal;     /* beginning amount in dollars */
   double   rate;          /* example: 7% corresponds to 0.07 */
   int      nyears;        /* number of years */

   prn_instructions();
   for ( ; ; ) {
      printf("Input three items:  ");
      scanf("%lf%lf%d", &principal, &rate, &nyears);
      amount = compute(principal, rate, nyears);
      prn_results(amount, principal, rate, nyears);
   }
   return 0;
}
```

Notice that we wrote the function prototypes near the top of the file outside of `main()`. Although we could have written them inside `main()`, they are typically written outside, or in an included *.h* file. The remaining function definitions follow `main()` in this same file.

```
void prn_instructions(void)
{
   printf("%s",
     "This program computes interest compounded yearly.\n"
     "Input principal, interest, and no. of years.\n"
     "For $1000 at 5.5% for 17 years here is example:\n\n"
     "Example input:  1000  5.5  17\n\n");
}
```

Before we show the code for the rest of the program, it is helpful to see what the program does. Suppose we execute the program and input `1000.00`, `7.7`, and `20` when prompted. Here is what appears on the screen:

```
This program computes interest compounded yearly.
Input principal, interest, and no. of years.
For $1000 at 5.5% for 17 years here is example:

Example input:  1000  5.5  17

Input three items:  1000.00  7  20

Interest rate:  7%
  Time period:  20 years

Beginning principal:  1000.00
   Interest accrued:  2869.68
       Total amount:  3869.68
```

In `main()`, the value returned by the function call `compute()` is assigned to the variable `amount`. This value represents the principal and interest at the end of the period. The computation of this value is at the heart of the program.

```
double compute(double principal, double rate, int nyears)
{
   int       i;
   double    amount = principal;

   rate *= 0.01;          /* example: convert 7% to 0.07 */
   for (i = 0; i < nyears; ++i)
      amount *= 1.0 + rate;
   return amount;
}
```

Dissection of the compute() Function

- ```
  double compute(double principal, double rate, int nyears)
  {
     int       i;
     double    amount = principal;
  ```

The first `double` tells the compiler that this function returns a value of that type. The parameter list contains three identifiers: two `double`s and an `int`. In the body of the function we initialize `amount` to `principal`, the amount of money with which we began the computation.

- ```
  rate *= 0.01;          /* example: convert 7% to 0.07 */
  ```

Of the three values entered by the user, the middle one, 7, indicates that 7 percent is to be used in the calculation. This value is stored as a `double` in the variable `rate` in `main()`, and then `rate` is passed as an argument to `compute()`. This statement converts the value of `rate` to 0.07, which is what we need in our algorithm. Note that `rate` in `main()` is not changed by this statement. It is only a copy of `rate` that is used in `compute()`.

- ```
  for (i = 0; i < nyears; ++i)
     amount *= 1.0 + rate;
  ```

If `rate` has value 0.07, then `1.0 + rate` has value 1.07, and every time through the loop, `amount` is multiplied by 1.07. Because `amount` was initialized to `principal`, the first time through the loop, `amount` has the value 1.07 times the value of `principal`; the second time through the loop, its value is 1.07^2 times the value of `principal`; and so forth. At the end of the loop its value is 1.07^{nyears} times the value of `principal`.

- ```
  return amount;
  ```

The value of the variable `amount` is returned to the calling environment.

Finally, back in `main()`, we want to print the results of our computation on the screen. We pass the relevant variables as arguments to the `prn_results()` function and call it.

```
void prn_results(double a, double p, double r, int n)
{
   double   interest = a - p;      /* amount - principal */

   printf("\n%s%g%c\n%s%d%s\n\n",
      "Interest rate:  ", r, '%',
      "  Time period:  ", n, " years");
   printf("%s%9.2f\n%s%9.2f\n%s%9.2f\n\n",
      "Beginning principal:", p,
      "   Interest accrued:", interest,
      "       Total amount:", a);
}
```

Notice that we used the format %g to suppress the printing of extraneous zeros, and %9.2f to align numbers on the screen.

Next, we want to show how to simplify our program by making use of pow() in the mathematical library. This function takes as arguments two expressions of type double and returns a value of type double. A function call such as pow(x, y) computes the value of x raised to the y power. Here is how we modify our program. Because pow() takes the place of compute(), we discard the code making up the function definition for compute(), as well as its function prototype near the top of the file. To get the function prototype for pow(), we can add the line

```
#include <math.h>
```

Alternatively, we can supply the function prototype ourselves.

```
double   pow(double, double);
```

Finally, we replace the statement

```
amount = compute(principal, rate, nyears);
```

with the statements

```
rate *= 0.01;
amount = pow(1.0 + rate, (double) nyears) * principal;
```

Notice that nyears has been cast to a double. With the use of function prototyping, this cast is not necessary; any int value passed to pow() is automatically converted to a double. If, however, we are using a traditional C compiler in which function prototyping is not available, then the cast is essential.

"THE BANK SAID THEY COULDN'T FLOAT OUR LOAN BECAUSE WE ARE LONG ON DEBT, SHORT OF FUNDS, OUR APPLICATION WAS UNSIGNED, SO THE WHOLE DEAL WAS VOID. CAN YOU BELIEVE IT? THE BANK REJECTED US IN C-SPEAK!"

6.11 Style

A common programming style is to use the identifiers `i`, `j`, `k`, `m`, and `n` as variables of type `int`, and to use identifiers such as `x`, `y`, and `z` as floating variables. This naming convention is loosely applied in mathematics, and historically, some early programming languages assumed that a variable name beginning with `i` through `n` was an integer type by default. This style is still acceptable in simple situations, such as using `i` as a counter in a `for` or `while` loop. In more complicated situations, however, you should use variable names that describe their use or purpose.

Some programmers dislike the deliberate use of infinite loops. However, if a program is meant to be used only interactively, the practice is acceptable. In our program that computes accrued interest in Section 6.10, "Problem Solving: Computing Interest," on page 221, we used the following construct:

```
for ( ; ; ) {
   printf("Input three items:  ");
   scanf("%lf%lf%d", &principal, &rate, &nyears);
   .....
```

The intent here is for the user to input data interactively. The user does this repeatedly until he or she is finished, at which time an interrupt signal must be typed (control-c on our system). Advantages of this coding style are that it is simple, and the reader of the code sees immediately that something is being done repeatedly until an interrupt occurs. A disadvantage of this style is that on some systems, redirecting the input to the program does not work (see exercise 10 on page 234). It is easy to adopt another, more conservative style. Here we can write instead

```
printf("Input three items:  ");
while (scanf("%lf%lf%d", &principal,
        &rate, &nyears) == 3) {
   .....
   printf("Input three items:  ");
}
```

Now the interactive user can either interrupt the program as before or end the program by typing an end-of-file signal at the keyboard (control-d on our system). In addition, the program now works with redirection.

Another stylistic issue concerns the use of floating constants in floating expressions. Suppose `x` is a floating variable. Because of automatic conversion, the value of an expression such as

`x >= 0.0` is equivalent to `x >= 0`

Nonetheless, the use of the first expression is considered good programming practice. The use of the floating constant `0.0` reminds the reader that `x` is a floating type. Similarly, the expression

`1.0 / 3.0` is preferable to `1 / 3.0`

Again, due to automatic conversion, the values of both expressions are the same. However, because in the first expression both the numerator and denominator are of type `double`, the reader is more likely to recognize immediately that the expression as a whole is of type `double`.

6.12 Common Programming Errors

On machines with 2-byte words, the problem of integer overflow can occur easily. It is the responsibility of the programmer to keep values within proper bounds. The type `long` should be used for integer values larger than 32,000.

In a `printf()` or `scanf()` statement, a format such as %d, which is appropriate for an `int`, may cause unexpected results when used with a `long`. If it does, the format `%ld` should be used. In this context the modifier `l` preceding the conversion character d stands for *long*. Similarly, when using a `short`, the format %hd should be used. In this context the modifier h preceding the conversion character stands for *short*.

Let us show a specific example that illustrates what can go wrong. We assume that we are on a machine with 2-byte words.

```
int   a = 1, b = 1776, c = 32000;

printf("%d\n", a + b + c);   /* error: -31759 is printed */
```

The expression `a + b + c` is of type `int`, and on machines with 2-byte words the logical value 33,777 is too large to be stored in an `int`. One way to fix this code is to write

```
int   a = 1, b = 1776, c = 32000;

printf("%ld\n", (long) a + b + c);   /* 33777 is printed */
```

Because of operator precedence, the two expressions

`(long) a + b + c`   and   `(((long) a) + b) + c`

are equivalent. First, a is cast to type `long`. This causes the other summands to be promoted to type `long` and causes the expression

```
(long) a + b + c
```

as a whole to be of type `long`. Finally, the `%ld` format is used to print the value of the expression. Note carefully that using the %d format would have caused a wrong value to be printed. In a similar fashion, when using `scanf()` to read values into a `long`, the format `%ld` should be used.

With `printf()`, the programmer can use the format `%f` to output either a `float` or a `double`. However, with `scanf()`, the format `%f` must be used to input a `float`, and the format `%lf` must be used to input a `double`. This dichotomy is confusing to beginning programmers. If the wrong format is used, unexpected results occur. Typically, a C system provides no indication of the error (see exercise 2 on page 231).

Using integer constants in what is meant to be a floating expression can produce unintended results. Although the expressions `1/2` and `1.0/2.0` look similar, the first is an `int` having value zero, whereas the second is a `double` having value 0.5. To minimize the chance of using the first expression in a situation in which the second is correct, get into the habit of coding floating constants in floating expressions. If, for example, the variable x is a `float`, and you want to assign zero as its value, it is better to code `x = 0.0` rather than `x = 0`.

Another common programming error is to pass an argument of the wrong type to a function. Consider, for example, the function call `sqrt(4)`. If the programmer has provided a prototype for the `sqrt()` function, the compiler automatically converts the `int` value 4 to a `double`, and the function call causes no difficulty. If the programmer has not provided a function prototype, the program runs but with logically incorrect results. Traditional C systems do not have the function prototype mechanism. On these systems, the programmer should write

```
sqrt(4.0)      or      sqrt((double) 4)
```

A good programming style is to provide prototypes for all functions. This helps the compiler to guard against the error of invoking a function with inappropriate arguments.

On machines with 2-byte words, a cast is sometimes needed to make a constant expression behave properly. Here is an example:

```
long   product = (long) 2 * 3 *5 * 7 * 11 * 13 * 17;
```

Without the cast, this initialization has unexpected behavior.

6.13 System Considerations

Throughout this chapter we have explained what normally happens on machines with 2- and 4-byte words. However, the notion of a machine having either 2- or 4-byte words is somewhat difficult to pin down. Intel produces a Pentium chip that is commonly used as the CPU in personal computers. These computers are often called "Pentium machines." In any case, the chip has a 4-byte word; however, if the operating system on the machine is MS-DOS, it may act as if it has a 2-byte word. If this happens, then the operating system is not using the full power of the CPU. The same machine with the UNIX operating system on it acts as a 4-byte machine.

The computing world has been slowly coming to agreement on how floating values should be represented in machines. In this regard, the ANSI C committee suggests that the recommendations in the document *IEEE Standard for Binary Floating-Point Arithmetic* (ANSI/IEEE Std 754-1985) be followed. On most machines that use this standard, a `double` has an approximate precision of 15 significant figures and an approximate range of 10^{-308} to 10^{+308}. Another effect of this standard is that division by zero, or trying to deal with numbers outside the range of a `double`, does not necessarily result in a run-time error. Instead, a value called *not a number* is produced (see exercise 24 on page 238).

If you check the size of the fundamental types on a Cray supercomputer, you find that the size of a `char` is 1 and that the size of everything else is 8, except for a `long double`, which is 16. This means that a Cray can handle some very large integer values.

Some C systems still treat the mathematics library as separate from the standard library. On these systems, the loader may not be able to find the object code corresponding to a mathematical function such as `sqrt()` unless you tell it where to look. On many older UNIX systems, the option *-lm* is needed. For example,

cc pgm.c -lm

Note the unusual placement of the option. This is because it is for the loader, not the compiler. Recall that the *cc* command invokes first the preprocessor, then the compiler, and finally the loader.

On all C systems, the types `short`, `int`, and `long` are equivalent to `signed short`, `signed int`, and `signed long`, respectively. With respect to the type `char`, however, the situation is system-dependent. A `char` can be equivalent to either a `signed` or `unsigned char`.

The type `long double` is a new addition to the C language. Some C systems treat it as a `double`; others provide extended precision. In Turbo C, a `long double` is stored in ten bytes. On a Sun workstation, a `long double` is stored in 16 bytes, providing approximately 33 significant digits of precision.

The absolute value function `abs()` is provided in the standard library. However, it takes an `int` argument and returns an `int` value. This means it is *not* the function that corresponds to the usual mathematical operation of taking the absolute value of a real number. The correct function for this use is `fabs()`, the floating-point absolute value function. It is in the standard library, and its function prototype is in *math.h*.

C is a general-purpose language, but it is also suited for writing operating system code. System programmers frequently have to deal with the explicit representation of values stored in a byte or a word. Because hexadecimal and octal integers are useful for these purposes, they were included as part of the C language. However, we do not make explicit use of them in this text.

6.14 Moving to C++

C++ allows user-defined types to be used as if they were native types. A good illustration of this is the type `complex` provided by *complex.h*:

```
//Roots of quadratic equations.
#include <iostream.h>
#include <complex.h>
```

```
int main(void)
{
   complex z1, z2;
   double  a, b, c, discriminant;

   cout << "ENTER A B C from Ax*x + Bx + C :";
   cin >> a >> b >> c;
   discriminant = b * b - 4* a * c;
   if (discriminant > 0.0) {
      z1 = (b + sqrt(discriminant)) / (2 * a);
      z2 = (b - sqrt(discriminant)) / (2 * a);
   }
   else if (discriminant == 0.0) {
      z1 = z2 = b / ( 2 * a);
   }
   else {
      z1 = (b + sqrt(-discriminant)) / (2 * a);
      z2 = (b - sqrt(-discriminant)) / (2 * a);
   }
   cout << "ROOTS in complex terms are :" << z1 << " "
        << z2 << endl;
}
```

In this program `complex` and `double` variables are mixed seamlessly. Such mixing allows C programming to be readily extended into many new domains without burdening the general programming community with learning or using all the additional types.

Summary

- The compiler needs to know the type and value of constants, variables, and expressions; this information allows it to set aside the right amount of space in memory to hold values and to issue the correct kind of instructions to the machine to carry out specified operations.
- The fundamental data types are `char`, `short`, `int`, `long`, unsigned versions of these, and three floating types. The type `char` is a 1-byte integral type mostly used for representing characters.
- The type `int` is designed to be the "natural" or "working" integral type. The other integral types such as `short`, `long`, and `unsigned` are provided for more specialized situations.

- Three floating types—`float`, `double`, and `long double`—are provided to represent real numbers. Typically, a `float` is stored in four bytes and a `double` in eight. Unlike integer arithmetic, floating arithmetic is not always exact. The type `double`, not `float`, is the "working" type.

- The type `long double` is available in ANSI C but not in traditional C. On some C systems, a `long double` is implemented as a `double`; on other systems, a `long double` provides more precision than a `double`.

- The unary operator `sizeof` can be used to find the number of bytes needed to store a type or the value of an expression. The expression `sizeof(int)` has the value 2 on machines with 2-byte words and has the value 4 on machines with 4-byte words.

- In ANSI C, the mathematical library is conceptually part of the standard library. It contains the usual mathematical functions, such as `sin()`, `cos()`, and `tan()`. The header file *math.h* is supplied by the system. It contains the function prototypes for the mathematical functions.

- Most of the functions in the mathematical library take a single argument of type `double` and return a value of type `double`. The function `pow()` is an exception. It takes two arguments of type `double` and returns a value of type `double`.

- Automatic conversions occur in mixed expressions and across an equal sign. Casts can be used to force explicit conversions.

- Integer constants beginning with `0x` and `0` designate hexadecimal and octal integers, respectively.

- Suffixes can be used to explicitly specify the type of a constant. For example, `3U` is of type `unsigned` and `7.0F` is of type `float`.

Exercises

1 Not all real numbers are machine-representable; there are too many of them. Thus the numbers that are available on a machine have a "graininess" to them. As an example of this, the code

```
double   x = 123.45123451234512345;
double   y = 123.45123451234512300;
                         /* last two digits different */

printf("%.17f  %.17f\n", x, y);
```

causes two identical numbers to be printed. How many zeros must be at the end of the initializer for y to have different numbers printed? Explain your answer.

2 If the number 3.777 is truncated to two decimal places, it becomes 3.77, but if it is rounded to two places, it becomes 3.78. Write a test program to find out whether printf() truncates or rounds when printing a float or double with a fractional part.

3 If you use a library function and do not declare it, the compiler assumes that the function returns an int value by default. (This idea was discussed in Chapter 4, "Functions and Structured Programming.") Consider the following code:

```
double   cos(double), x, y;      /* sin() not declared */

while (1) {
   printf("Input a number:  ");
   scanf("%lf", &x);
   y = sin(x) * sin(x) + cos(x) * cos(x);
   printf("\n%s%.15g\n%s%.15e\n\n",
      "x = ", x,
      "sin(x) * sin(x) + cos(x) * cos(x) = ", y);
}
```

This code, when correctly written, illustrates the mathematical fact that

$$\sin^2(x) + \cos^2(x) = 1 \qquad \text{for all } x \text{ real}$$

Note that the function prototype for sin() is missing. Execute the code with the correct declaration so you understand its proper effects. Then experiment to see what the effect is when the sin() function is not declared. Does your compiler complain? It should.

4 Using the %f format with scanf() to read in a double is a common programming error. Try the following code on your system. Note that your compiler does not complain. The only thing that happens is that logically incorrect results are printed.

```
double   x;

printf("Input a number:  ");
scanf("%f", &x);                    /* error: wrong format */
printf("\nHere it is:  %f\n", x);
```

5 Write a program that prints a table of trigonometric values for sin(), cos(), and tan(). The angles in your table should go from zero to π in 20 steps.

6 If your machine stores an int in two bytes, run the following program and explain its output. If your machine stores an int in four bytes, change the value of the symbolic constant BIG to 2000000000 before running the program.

```
#define   BIG   32000      /* 32 thousand is big? */

int main(void)
{
   int          i = BIG + BIG;
   unsigned     u = BIG + BIG;

   printf("\n%s%d\n%s%d\n%s%u\n%s%u\n\n",
      "i with %d format is ", i,
      "u with %d format is ", u,
      "i with %u format is ", i,
      "u with %u format is ", u);
   return 0;
}
```

7 The following table shows how many bytes are required on most machines to store some of the fundamental types. What are the appropriate values for your machine? Execute the program presented in Section 6.7, "The sizeof Operator," on page 212, and complete the table.

Fundamental type	Memory required on machines with 4-byte words	Memory required on machines with 2-byte words	Memory required on your machine
`char`	1 byte	1 byte	
`short`	2 bytes	2 bytes	
`int`	4 bytes	2 bytes	
`unsigned`	4 bytes	2 bytes	
`long`	4 bytes	4 bytes	
`float`	4 bytes	4 bytes	
`double`	8 bytes	8 bytes	

8 Before the age of computers, it was common to make tables of square roots, sines, cosines, and so forth. Write a program that makes a table of square roots and fourth roots of the integers from 1 to 100. Your table should look like this:

```
Integer             Square root              Fourth root
-----------------------------------------------------

      1         1.000000000e+00         1.000000000e+00
      2         1.414213562e+00         1.189207115e+00
      3         1.732050808e+00         1.316074013e+00
      4         2.000000000e+00         1.414213562e+00
  .....
```

Hint: The fourth root of a number is just the square root of its square root.

9 The program in this exercise needs to be studied carefully.

```
#include <stdio.h>

int main(void)      /* mystery? */
{
   printf("Why is 21 + 31 equal to %d?\n", 21 + 31);
   return 0;
}
```

Here is the output from the program:

```
Why is 21 + 31 equal to 5?
```

Can you deduce the moral?

10 A program with an infinite loop may not work as expected with redirection. Put some real numbers into a file called *data*, and try the command

```
sq_roots < data
```

Now modify the *sq_roots* program so that the `for` loop is replaced by a `while` loop of the form

```
while (scanf("%lf", &x) == 1) {
    .....
}
```

After you get the program to work properly in an interactive mode, try redirection again.

11 Rewrite the *interest* program (in Section 6.10, "Problem Solving: Computing Interest," on page 220) making use of the function `pow()` in the mathematical library. Does the modified program yield the same results as before? What happens if, in the call to `pow()`, the variable `nyears` is not cast as a `double`?

12 Suppose Constance B. DeMogul has a million dollars to invest. She is thinking of investing the money at 9 percent compounded yearly, or 8.75 percent compounded quarterly, or 8.7 percent compounded daily, for a period of either 10 or 20 years. For each of these investment strategies and periods, what interest will she earn? Write a program that helps you to advise her. *Hint:* Suppose that *P* dollars is invested at 8.75 percent compounded quarterly. The amount of principal and interest is given by

$(1 + 0.875/4)^4 \times P$	at the end of the first year
$(1 + 0.875/4)^{4\times 2} \times P$	at the end of the second year
$(1 + 0.875/4)^{4\times 3} \times P$	at the end of the third year
.....	

For *P* dollars invested at 8.7 percent compounded daily, the formulas are similar, except that 0.0875 is replaced by 0.087, and 4 is replaced by 365. These computations can be carried out by writing a function such as

```
double find_accrued_interest(
   double   principal,
   double   rate,           /* interest rate */
   double   c_rate,         /* compounding rate: example:
                               with daily compounding,
                               c_rate = 365.0 */
   double   period          /* in years */
)
{
   .....
```

13 Try the following code:

```
unsigned long    a = -1;

printf("The biggest integer: %lu\n", a);
```

What is printed and explain why? It should match one or more of the numbers in the standard header file *limits.h* on your system. Does it?

14 Occasionally, a programmer needs a power function for integers. Because such a function is so easy to write, it is not usually found in a mathematics library. Write the function definition for `power()` so that if `m` and `n` are integers and `n` is nonnegative, the call `power(m, n)` returns `m` raised to the `n`th power. *Hint:* Use the following code:

```
product = 1;
for (i = 1; i ≤ n; ++i)
   product *= m;
```

15 A variable of type `char` can be used to store small integer values. What happens if a large value is assigned to a `char` variable? Consider the following code:

```
char   c = 256;              /* too big! */

printf("c = %d\n", c);
```

Some compilers warn you that the number is too big; others do not. What happens on your machine? Can you guess what is printed?

16 Consider the following code:

```
char    a = 1, b = 2, c = 3;

printf("sizeof(c)             = %d\n", sizeof(c));
printf("sizeof('a')           = %d\n", sizeof('a'));
printf("sizeof(c = 'a')       = %d\n", sizeof(c = 'a'));
printf("sizeof(a + b + 7.7)   = %d\n", sizeof(a + b + 7.7));
```

First, write down what you think is printed; then execute the code to check your answer.

17 On a 24-hour clock, the zero hour is midnight and the 23rd hour is 11 P.M., one hour before midnight. On such a clock, when 1 is added to 23, we do not get 24; instead, we get 0. There is no 24. In a similar fashion, 22 + 5 yields 3 because 22 + 2 = 0, and 3 more is 3. This is an example of modular arithmetic, or, more precisely, of arithmetic modulo 24. Most machines do modular arithmetic on all the integral types. This is most easily illustrated with the unsigned types. Run the following program and explain what is printed:

```
#include <stdio.h>
#include <limits.h>       /* for UINT_MAX */

int main(void)
{
   int         i;
   unsigned    u = UINT_MAX;

   printf("The largest unsigned int is %u\n\n", u);
   for (i = 0; i < 10; ++i)
      printf("%u + %d = %u\n", u, i, u + i);
   for (i = 0; i < 10; ++i)
      printf("%u * %d = %u\n", u, i, u * i);
   return 0;
}
```

18 Let $N_{min\_u\_long}$ and $N_{max\_u\_long}$ represent the minimum and maximum values that can be stored in an `unsigned long` on your system. What are those values? *Hint:* Read the standard header file *limits.h*.

19 The function call `sqrt(-1.0)` causes a run-time error. Most compilers provide adequate diagnostics for this error. What diagnostics does your compiler provide?

20 When the value of x is too large, the function call pow(x, x) either causes a run-time error or exhibits some other peculiar behavior. What is the least integer value for x that makes this happen on your system? Write an interactive program that gets x from the user and then prints x and pow(x, x) on the screen.

21 What is the largest double available on your machine? What happens when you go beyond this value? Experiment by running the following program:

```
#include <stdio.h>
#include <float.h>

int main(void)
{
   double   x = 1.0, y = -1.0, z = 0.0;

   printf("The largest double: %.3e\n", DBL_MAX);
   printf("  Add a little bit: %.3e\n", DBL_MAX + 1.0);
   printf("          Add a lot: %.3e\n",
          DBL_MAX + DBL_MAX);
   printf("  Division by zero: %.3e  %.3e\n",
         x / z, y / z);
   return 0;
}
```

Modify the program so that it also prints out the largest float available on your machine. Is it a lot smaller than the largest double? *Hint:* Read the header file *float.h* on your system.

22 This problem is for those readers who are familiar with hexadecimal and octal numbers. In a program, an integer written with a leading 0 is an octal number, and an integer written with a leading 0x or 0X is a hexadecimal number. For example,

```
int   i = 077, j = 0x77, k = 0xcbd;

printf("Some numbers:%7d%7d%7d\n", i, j, k);
```

causes the line

```
Some numbers:     63    119   3261
```

to be printed. Just as the conversion character d is used in a format in printf() to print a decimal integer, the conversion character x is used to print hexadecimal numbers, and the conversion character o is used to print octal numbers. Define a symbolic constant LIMIT and print a table of values containing corresponding decimal, hexadecimal, and octal integers from 1 to LIMIT. *Hint:* Print an appropriate heading and then use

```
for (i = 0; i <= LIMIT; ++i)
   printf("%12d%12x%12o\n", i, i, i);
```

23 In mathematics, the numbers e and π are well known; e is the base of the natural logarithms, and π is the ratio of the diameter of a circle to its circumference. Which is larger, e^{π} or π^{e}? This is a standard problem for students in an honors calculus course. However, even if you have never heard of e and π and know nothing about calculus, you should be able to answer this question. *Hint:*

$$e \approx 2.71828182845904524 \quad \text{and} \quad \pi \approx 3.14159265358979324$$

24 In Section 6.13, "System Considerations," on page 227, we discussed an IEEE recommendation for floating-point arithmetic. Does your machine follow this standard? Try executing the following code:

```
double   x = 1e+308;                    /* on the edge */

printf("x * x = %e\n", x * x);         /* too big? */
```

If `Inf` or `NaN` is printed, you can think of the value as "infinity" or "not a number." If this happens, it is an indication (but not a proof) that floating-point arithmetic on your machine follows the IEEE recommendations.

25 C++: Convert the following root finder program to a C++ function:

```
void roots(double a,           //a*x*x +
           double b,           //b*x +
           double c,           //c
           complex r1,         //root one
           complex r2          //root two
);
```

26 C++: Add an `assert` to the end of `roots()` that checks that the calculation was done correctly. Remember that floating-point arithmetic has roundoff.

27 Java: Java allows only a subset of the conversions that C allows. Java is considered safer because it does not allow automatic narrowing conversions. In Java, if `n` is an `int` and `x` is a `double`, then

```
n = x; //okay in Java and C
x = n; //okay in C but illegal in Java
x = (double)n; //okay in both C and Java
```

Can you list the allowable automatic C conversions and indicate which are allowed in Java?

28 Java: Java has a `Math` class that is a library of standard functions, much like *math.h* in C. This library includes a pseudorandom number generator for numbers in the range (0.0 - 1.0). Convert the following Java program to C:

```
//RandomPrint.java: Print Random numbers  in the
//    range (0.0 - 1.0).  Java by Dissection page 107.
class RandomPrint {
  public static void main(String[] args) {
    int n = 10;

    System.out.println("We will print " + n +
       " random numbers");
    printRandomNumbers(n);
  }
  static void printRandomNumbers(int k) {
    for (int i = 0; i < k; i++)
      System.out.println(Math.random());
  }
}
```

Chapter 7

Enumeration Types and typedef

In this chapter we first discuss the enumeration types. These are user-defined types that allow the programmer to name a finite set together with its elements, which are called *enumerators*. These types are defined and used by the programmer as the need arises. Next, we discuss the `typedef` facility, which allows you to give a new name to a type. A common use of this facility is to provide shorter names for enumeration and structure types.

7.1 Enumeration Types

The keyword `enum` is used to declare enumeration types. It allows you to name a finite set and to declare identifiers, called *enumerators*, elements of the set. Consider, for example, the declaration

```
enum day {sun, mon, tue, wed, thu, fri, sat};
```

This creates the user-defined type `enum day`. The keyword `enum` is followed by the tag name `day`. The enumerators are the identifiers `sun`, `mon`, . . ., `sat`. They are constants of type `int`. By default, the first one is given the value 0, and each succeeding one has the next integer value. This declaration is an example of a type specifier. No variables of type `enum day` have been declared yet. To declare them, we can write

```
enum day   d1, d2;
```

This declares `d1` and `d2` to be of type `enum day`. They can take on as values only the elements (enumerators) in the set. Thus

```
d1 = fri;
```

assigns the value `fri` to `d1`, and

```
if (d1 == d2)
    .....             /* do something */
```

tests whether d1 is equal to d2. Note carefully that the type is enum day; the keyword enum by itself is not a type.

The enumerators can be initialized. Also, we can declare variables directly after the enumerator declaration, if we wish. Here is an example:

```
enum suit {clubs = 1, diamonds, hearts, spades}   a, b, c;
```

Because clubs has been initialized to 1, diamonds, hearts, and spades have the values 2, 3, and 4, respectively. This declaration consists of two parts:

The type specifier:
`enum suit {clubs = 1, diamonds, hearts, spades}`

Variables of this type:
`a, b, c;`

Here is another example of initialization:

```
enum fruit {apple = 7, pear, orange = 3, lemon}   frt;
```

Because the enumerator apple has been initialized to 7, pear has value 8. Similarly, because orange has value 3, lemon has value 4. Multiple values are allowed, but the identifiers themselves must be unique.

```
enum veg {beet = 17, corn = 17}   vege1, vege2;
```

The tag name need not be present. Consider, for example,

```
enum {fir, pine}   tree;
```

Because there is no tag name, no other variables of type enum {fir, pine} can be declared.

In general, one should treat enumerators as programmer-specified constants and use them to aid program clarity. If necessary, the underlying value of an enumerator can be obtained by using a cast. The variables and enumerators in a function must all have distinct identifiers.

7.2 The Use of typedef

C provides the typedef facility so that an identifier can be associated with a specific type. A simple example is

```
typedef   int   color;
```

This makes `color` a type that is synonymous with `int`, and it can be used in declarations, just as other types are used. For example,

```
color   red, blue, green;
```

The `typedef` facility allows the programmer to use type names that are appropriate for a specific application. Also, the facility helps to control complexity when programmers are building complicated or lengthy user-defined types, such as enumeration types and structure types (see Chapter 12, "Structures and ADTs").

We illustrate the use of the enumeration type by writing a function that computes the next day. As is commonly done, we `typedef` our enumeration type.

```
/* Compute the next day. */

enum day {sun, mon, tue, wed, thu, fri, sat};

typedef   enum day   day;

day find_next_day(day d)
{
   day   next_day;

   switch (d) {
   case sun:
      next_day = mon;
      break;
   case mon:
      next_day = tue;
      break;
   .....
   case sat:
      next_day = sun;
      break;
   }
   return next_day;
}
```

Dissection of the `find_next_day()` Function

■ `enum day {sun, mon, tue, wed, thu, fri, sat};`

This declaration is an example of a type specifier. It tells the compiler that `enum day` is the name of a type and that `sun`, `mon`, . . ., `sat` are the allowable values for variables of this type. No variables of this type have been declared yet. It provides a type that can be used later on in the program.

■ `typedef enum day day;`

We use the `typedef` facility to create a new name for our type. As is commonly done, we choose for the name of our type the tag name. In ANSI C, the name space for tags is separate from other names. Thus the compiler understands the difference between the tag name `day` and the type `day`. If we remove this `typedef` from our program, then throughout the remainder of the code, wherever we used the identifier `day`, we must use `enum day` instead.

■
```
day find_next_day(day d)
{
   day   next_day;
```

The header of the function definition for `find_next_day()` tells the compiler that this function takes a single argument of type `day` and returns a value of type `day` to the calling environment. There is a single declaration in the body of the function definition. It tells the compiler that `next_day` is a variable of type `day`.

■
```
switch (d) {
case sun:
   next_day = mon;
   break;
```

Recall that only a constant integral expression can be used in a `case` label. Because enumerators are constants, they can be used in this context. Note that the value assigned to `next_day` is an enumerator.

■ `return next_day;`

The value `next_day`, which is of type `day`, is returned to the calling environment.

The following is another version of this function, which uses a cast to accomplish the same ends:

```
/* Compute the next day with a cast. */

enum day {sun, mon, tue, wed, thu, fri, sat};

typedef   enum day   day;

day find_next_day(day d)
{
   return ((day) (((int) d + 1) % 7));
}
```

Enumeration types can be used in ordinary expressions as long as type compatibility is maintained. However, if one uses them as a form of integer type and constantly accesses their implicit representation, it is better just to use integer variables instead. The importance of enumeration types is their self-documenting character, where the enumerators are themselves mnemonic. Furthermore, they force the compiler to provide programmer-defined type checking so that one does not inadvertently mix apples and diamonds.

"HAROLD, YOU CAN'T FOOL ME BY JUST PROGRAMMING IN EXTRA WEEKEND DAYS!"

7.3 An Example: The Game of Paper, Rock, Scissors

We illustrate the use of enumeration types by writing a program to play the traditional children's game, *paper, rock, scissors.* In this game each child uses her or his hand to represent one of the three objects. A flat hand held in a horizontal position represents paper, a fist represents rock, and two extended fingers represents scissors. The children face each other and, at the count of three, display their choices. If the choices are the same, the game is a tie. Otherwise, a win is determined by the rules.

Rules of Paper, Rock, Scissors

- Paper covers the rock.
- Rock breaks the scissors.
- Scissors cut the paper.

We write this as a multifile program in its own directory, as was discussed in Section 4.11, "A Simulation: The Game of Heads or Tails," on page 147. The program consists of one *.h* file and a number of *.c* files. Each of the *.c* files includes the header file at the top. In the header file we put `#include` directives, declarations for our enumeration types, type definitions, and function prototypes.

In file p_r_s.h:

```
/* The game of paper, rock, scissors. */

#include <ctype.h>          /* for isspace() */
#include <stdio.h>          /* for printf(), etc */
#include <stdlib.h>         /* for rand() and srand() */
#include <time.h>           /* for time() */

enum p_r_s {paper, rock, scissors,
            game, help, instructions, quit};


enum outcome {win, lose, tie, error};

typedef   enum p_r_s     p_r_s;
typedef   enum outcome   outcome;

outcome   compare(p_r_s player_choice, p_r_s machine_choice);
void      prn_final_status(int win_cnt, int lose_cnt);
void      prn_game_status(int win_cnt,
                          int lose_cnt, int tie_cnt);

void      prn_help(void);
void      prn_instructions(void);
void      report(outcome result, int *win_cnt_ptr,
                 int *lose_cnt_ptr, int *tie_cnt_ptr);
p_r_s     selection_by_machine(void);
p_r_s     selection_by_player(void);
```

We do not usually add a comment to our `#include` lines, but here we are trying to provide a cross-reference for the novice programmer.

In file main.c:

```
#include "p_r_s.h"

int main(void)
{
   int         win_cnt = 0, lose_cnt = 0, tie_cnt = 0;
   outcome     result;
   p_r_s       player_choice, machine_choice;

   srand(time(NULL));    /* seed the random number generator */
   prn_instructions();

   while ((player_choice = selection_by_player()) != quit)
      switch (player_choice) {
      case paper:
      case rock:
      case scissors:
         machine_choice = selection_by_machine();
         result = compare(player_choice, machine_choice);
         report(result, &win_cnt, &lose_cnt, &tie_cnt);
         break;
      case game:
         prn_game_status(win_cnt, lose_cnt, tie_cnt);
         break;
      case instructions:
         prn_instructions();
         break;
      case help:
         prn_help();
         break;
      default:
         printf("PROGRAMMER ERROR: Cannot get to here!\n\n");
         exit(1);
      }
   prn_game_status(win_cnt, lose_cnt, tie_cnt);
   prn_final_status(win_cnt, lose_cnt);
   return 0;
}
```

The first executable statement in `main()` is

```
srand(time(NULL));
```

This seeds the random number generator `rand()`, causing it to produce a different sequence of integers each time the program is executed. More explicitly, passing `srand()` an integer value determines where `rand()` starts. The function call `time(NULL)` returns a count of the number of seconds that have elapsed because 1 January 1970 (the approximate birthday of UNIX). Both `srand()` and `time()` are provided in the standard C library. The function prototype for `srand()` is in *stdlib.h*, and the function prototype for `time()` is in *time.h*. Both of these header files are provided by the system. Note that we included them in *p_r_s.h*.

The next executable statement in `main()` calls `prn_instructions()`. This provides instructions to the user. Embedded in the instructions are some of the design considerations for programming this game. We wrote this function, along with other printing functions, in *prn.c*.

In file prn.c:

```
#include "p_r_s.h"

void prn_final_status(int win_cnt, int lose_cnt)
{
   if (win_cnt > lose_cnt)
      printf("CONGRATULATIONS - You won!\n\n");
   else if (win_cnt == lose_cnt)
      printf("A DRAW - You tied!\n\n");
   else
      printf("SORRY - You lost!\n\n");
}


void prn_game_status(int win_cnt, int lose_cnt, int tie_cnt)
{
   printf("\n%s\n%s%4d\n%s%4d\n%s%4d\n%s%4d\n\n",
      "GAME STATUS:",
      "    Win:    ", win_cnt,
      "    Lose:   ", lose_cnt,
      "    Tie:    ", tie_cnt,
      "    Total: ", win_cnt + lose_cnt + tie_cnt);
}

void prn_help(void)
{
   printf("\n%s\n",
      "The following characters can be used for input:\n"
      "    p   for paper\n"
      "    r   for rock\n"
      "    s   for scissors\n"
      "    g   print the game status\n"
      "    h   help, print this list\n"
      "    i   reprint the instructions\n"
      "    q   quit this game\n");
}
```

```
void prn_instructions(void)
{
   printf("\n%s\n",
      "PAPER, ROCK, SCISSORS:\n"
      "\n"
      "In this game\n"
      "\n"
      "   p is for \"paper\"\n"
      "   r is for \"rock\"\n"
      "   s is for \"scissors\"\n"
      "\n"
      "Both the player and the machine will choose one\n"
      "of p, r, or s.  If the two choices are the same,\n"
      "then the game is a tie.  Otherwise:\n"
      "\n"
      "   \"paper covers the rock\"      (a win for paper)\n"
      "   \"rock breaks the scissors\"   (a win for rock)\n"
      "   \"scissors cut the paper\"     (a win for scissors)\n"
      "\n"
      "There are other allowable inputs:\n"
      "\n"
      "   g  for game status    (print number of wins)\n"
      "   h  for help           (print short instructions)\n"
      "   i  for instructions   (print these instructions)\n"
      "   q  for quit           (quit the game)\n"
      "\n"
      "This game is played repeatedly until q is entered.\n"
      "\n"
      "Good luck!\n");
}
```

To play the game, both the machine and the player (user) must make selections from among paper, rock, scissors. We write these routines in *select.c*.

In file select.c:

```
#include "p_r_s.h"

p_r_s selection_by_machine(void)
{
   return ((p_r_s) (rand() % 3));
}
```

```
p_r_s selection_by_player(void)
{
   char    c;
   p_r_s   player_choice;

   printf("Input p, r, or s:  ");
   scanf(" %c", &c);
   switch (c) {
   case 'p':
      player_choice = paper;
      break;
   case 'r':
      player_choice = rock;
      break;
   case 's':
      player_choice = scissors;
      break;
   case 'g':
      player_choice = game;
      break;
   case 'i':
      player_choice = instructions;
      break;
   case 'q':
      player_choice = quit;
      break;
   default:
      player_choice = help;
      break;
   }
   return player_choice;
}
```

The machine's selection is computed by the using the expression `rand() % 3` to produce a randomly distributed integer between 0 and 2. Because the type of the function is `p_r_s`, the value returned is converted to this type, if necessary. We provided an explicit cast to make the code more self-documenting. In `selection_by_player()`, we used

```
scanf(" %c", &c);
```

to pick up a character from the input stream and place it at the address of `c`. The blank character before the % sign is significant; it causes `scanf()` to match optional white space. The effect of this is to skip any white space (see Section 13.2, "White Space Characters," on page 436). Observe that all non-white space characters input at the keyboard are processed, most of them through the `default` case of the `switch` statement.

The value returned by selection_by_player() depends on what the player types. For example, if the player types the character *g*, then the enumerator game is returned to the calling environment in main(), which causes prn_game_status() to be invoked. In selection_by_player(), if any character other than white space or *p*, *r*, *s*, *g*, *i*, or *q* is typed, the enumerator help is returned to the calling environment in main(), which then invokes prn_help().

Once the player and the machine have made a selection, we need to compare the two selections to determine the outcome of the game. The following function does this:

In file compare.c:

```
#include "p_r_s.h"

outcome compare(p_r_s player_choice, p_r_s machine_choice)
{
   outcome   result;

   if (player_choice == machine_choice)
      return tie;
   switch (player_choice) {
   case paper:
      result = (machine_choice == rock) ? win : lose;
      break;
   case rock:
      result = (machine_choice == scissors) ? win : lose;
      break;
   case scissors:
      result = (machine_choice == paper) ? win : lose;
      break;
   default:
      printf("PROGRAMMER ERROR: Unexpected choice!\n\n");
      exit(1);
   }
   return result;
}
```

The value returned by compare() in main() is passed to the function report(), which reports to the user the result of a round of play and increments as appropriate the number of wins, losses, and ties.

In file report.c:

```
#include "p_r_s.h"

void report(outcome result, int *win_cnt_ptr,
            int *lose_cnt_ptr, int *tie_cnt_ptr)
{
   switch (result) {
   case win:
      ++*win_cnt_ptr;
      printf("%27sYou win.\n", "");
      break;
   case lose:
      ++*lose_cnt_ptr;
      printf("%27sYou lose.\n", "");
      break;
   case tie:
      ++*tie_cnt_ptr;
      printf("%27sA tie.\n", "");
      break;
   default:
      printf("PROGRAMMER ERROR: Unexpected result!\n\n");
      exit(1);
   }
}
```

We are now ready to compile our program. We can do this with either of the following commands:

cc -o p_r_s main.c compare.c prn.c report.c select.c
*cc -o p_r_s *.c*

The second command works only if we are in a directory that contains only the *.c* files pertaining to this program. Later, after we have learned about the *make* utility in Section 14.8, "The Use of make," on page 488, we can facilitate program development by using an appropriate makefile.

7.4 Style

Because enumerators can be mnemonic, their use tends to be self-documenting. Thus the use of enumeration types is considered good programming style.

Rather than using 0 and 1 to distinguish between alternate choices, the programmer can easily use an enumeration type. Some typical examples are

```
enum bool   {false, true};
enum off_on {off, on};
enum no_yes {no, yes};
enum speed  {slow, fast};
```

The use of such constructs makes the code more readable. A declaration such as

```
enum no_yes {no, yes};
```

tells the compiler that `enum no_yes` is a user-defined type. It is considered good programming style to put such declarations in header files. (Constructs that allocate space in memory do not belong in a header file.)

Because tag names have their own name space, we can reuse a tag name as a variable or as an enumerator. For example,

```
enum veg {beet, carrot, corn}   veg;              /* poor style */
```

Although this is legal, it is not considered good programming practice. On the other hand, it is considered a good programming style to use a tag name as a type definition (in C++, this is done automatically). An example is

```
typedef   enum veg {beet, carrot, corn}   veg;  /* good style */
```

This tells the compiler that `veg` is a user-defined type. To declare variables of this type, we can write

```
veg   v1, v2;
```

This practice reduces clutter, especially if there are a lot of enumeration types.

When using a `typedef` to create a new name for an enumeration type, there are several ways to proceed. We can write the declaration and then the `typedef`:

```
enum lo_hi {lo, hi};
typedef   enum lo_hi   lo_hi;
```

Or, we can do both steps at the same time.

```
typedef   enum lo_hi {lo, hi}   lo_hi;
```

Finally, if we do not plan to refer to the type via its tag name, we can dispense with the tag name and write

```
typedef   enum {lo, hi}   lo_hi;
```

Each of these coding styles is acceptable. Which one is used is a matter of personal taste.

7.5 Common Programming Errors

The same type definition cannot occur more than once in a file. Suppose the following line occurs in your *.c* file and also in your header file:

```
typedef   enum {off, on}   off_on;
```

If you include the header file at the top of your *.c* file, the compiler complains. In this regard, a `typedef` is not like a `#define`. The same `#define` can occur more than once in a file.

The order in which you define enumerators in an enumeration type can lead to logical errors. Consider the following code:

```
#include <stdio.h>

typedef   enum {yes, no}   yes_no;      /* poor */

yes_no   is_good(void);

int main(void)
{
   .....
   if (is_good())
      printf("Hooray!  A good condition exists.\n");
   else
      printf("Rats!  Another bummer.\n");
   .....
```

The idea here is that the `is_good()` function checks something and returns either `yes` or `no`, depending on the situation. Let us suppose in the preceding code that `yes` is returned. Because `yes` has the `int` value 0 (*false*), the string

```
Rats!  Another bummer.
```

is printed, and it is not what we intended to happen. We can guard against this kind of error by explicitly checking the value returned.

```
if (is_good() == yes)
   .....                     /* do something */
```

As an additional safeguard, it is better to rewrite the `typedef` as

```
typedef   enum {no, yes}   no_yes;
```

Now the enumerator `no` has value 0 (*false*) and `yes` has value 1 (*true*), which is a more logical state of affairs.

7.6 System Considerations

System programmers make extensive use of enumeration types. Here is a simple example that comes from a system header file on a Sun machine:

```
enum fp_precision_type {      /* extended precision */
   fp_extended    = 0,
   fp_single      = 1,
   fp_double      = 2,
   fp_precision_3 = 3
};
```

Note that the initialization of the enumerators is superfluous, but it makes the code more readable.

In C, enumeration types and `int`s can be freely mixed, but it is not considered good programming style. Here is an example:

```
#include <stdio.h>

typedef   enum {no, yes}   no_yes;

int main(void)
{
   int      i;
   no_yes   val = yes;

   i = val;          /* acceptable programming style */
   val = 777;        /* poor programming style */
   .....
```

In C++, assigning an `int` to an enumeration type is not supposed to be allowed, although many compilers merely issue a warning. If we change the assignment to `val` to read

```
val = (no_yes) 777;      /* use a cast */
```

the compiler is happy. Although the value assigned to `val` does not correspond to either `no` or `yes`, this is not considered an error.

7.7 Moving to C++

Enumeration types in C++ are more strongly typed than those in C. Each type is distinct. Assignment to an enumeration type by some other value is an error (although some compilers treat this only as a warning). Without appropriate casts, a program may not compile.

Enumeration tag names in C++ are automatically types, so there is less need for `typedef` in C++. Let us write a simple program that illustrates this idea.

```
#include <iostream.h>

enum color {black, red, blue, green, white, other};

int main(void)
{
   color   val = blue;

   if (val == red)
      cout << "Value of red = " << red << "\n";
   else if (val == blue)
      cout << "Value of blue = " << blue << "\n";
   else
      cout << "The color is neither red nor blue.\n";
  }
```

Summary

- The keyword `enum` allows the programmer to define enumeration types. Consider the declaration

  ```
  enum no_yes {no, yes};
  ```

  This tells the compiler that `enum no_yes` is a user-defined type. The word `enum` by itself is not a type. A declaration such as

  ```
  enum no_yes   answer;
  ```

  defines the variable `answer` to be of type `enum no_yes`. It can take as values members of the set `{no, yes}`. The members are called *enumerators*. They are constants and have `int` values. By default, the compiler assigns 0 to the first enumerator, 1 to the second, and so forth.

- Enumerators are distinct identifiers chosen for their mnemonic significance. Their use provides a type-checking constraint for the programmer, and self-documentation for the program.

- When mixing enumerators or variables of enumeration type with integers in an expression, casts can be used to resolve type conflicts.

- Because enumerators are constants of type `int`, they can be used in `case` labels in a `switch`.

- One type definition can be used in another (see exercise 8 on page 259). As we shall see in later chapters, this is an important idea.

- Systems programmers routinely use enumeration types. In some instances this can interfere with application programs (see exercise 7 on page 259, and exercise 9 on page 260).

- In C++, the tag name of an enumeration type is automatically available as an alternative name for the type.

- In C++, the type `bool` with the literals `false` and `true` is built into the system.

Exercises

1 Write a function called `previous_month()` that returns the previous month. Start with the code

```
enum month {jan = 1, feb, ....., dec};

typedef   enum month   month;
```

If `dec` is passed as an argument to the function, `jan` should be returned. Write another function that prints the name of a month. More explicitly, if the enumerator `jan` is passed as an argument, `January` should be printed. Write `main()` so that it calls your functions and produces a table of all twelve months, each one listed next to its predecessor month. *Caution:* When `printf()` is used, a variable of an enumeration type is printed as its implicit integer value. That is,

```
printf("%d\n", jan);
```

prints the value 1, not `jan`.

2 Write a next-day program for a particular year. The program should take as input two integers—say, 17 and 5, which represent 17 May—and it should print as output `18 May`, which is the next day. Use enumeration types in the program. Pay particular attention to the problem of crossing from one month to the next.

3 Write a roulette program. The roulette machine selects a number between 0 and 35 at random. The player can place an odd/even bet or a bet on a particular number. A winning odd/even bet is paid off at 2 to 1, except that all odd/even bets lose if the roulette machine selects 0. If the player places a bet on a particular number and the roulette machine selects it, the player is paid off at 35 to 1. If you play this game and make $1 bets, how long can you play before you lose $10?

4 Use enumeration types to define five basic food groups in a balanced meal program: fish, fruits, grains, meats, and vegetables. For example,

```
enum fish {bass, salmon, shrimp, trout};
enum fruit {apple, peach, pear};
.....
```

Use a random number generator to select an item from each food group. Write a function `meal()` that picks an item from each of the groups and prints out a menu. Print 20 randomly generated menus. How many different menus are available?

5 In the game of paper, rock, scissors, an outcome that is not a tie is conveyed to the player by printing

`You win.` or `You lose.`

Rewrite the program so that messages like the following are printed:

```
You chose paper and I chose rock.  You win.
```

6 Boolean types are automatically available in Pascal, whereas in C, the programmer must explicitly provide them. Here are two ways to do it:

```
typedef   enum {true, false}   boolean;
typedef   enum {false, true}   boolean;
```

Which of these two `typedef`s is preferable? Explain.

7 Some identifiers can cause unexpected difficulties. Consider the following simple program that uses the enumerator `sun`:

```
#include <stdio.h>

enum day {sun, mon, tue, wed, thu, fri, sat};

typedef   enum day   day;

int main(void)
{
   day   val = sun;

   if (val == sun)
      printf("Today is Sunday.\n");
   else
      printf("Today is a working day.\n");
   return 0;
}
```

Some C systems on Sun machines automatically define `sun` as a symbolic constant via a mechanism that is equivalent to using a `#define` preprocessing directive. This interferes with the use of `sun` as an identifier in the program. If you can, try this program on both a Sun machine and on some other machine to see what happens. If the program does not compile, you can observe that the error messages are not helpful at all. To circumvent the difficulty, you can use the following preprocessing directive at the top of the file:

```
#undef sun
```

Modify the program by putting this line at the top of the file. If you are on a Sun machine, this line may solve your problem. If you are not on a Sun machine, this preprocessing directive should not affect the program.

8 One type definition can be used in another (in Chapter 11, "Recursion," we see that this is an important idea). Here is a simple program that illustrates this concept:

```
#include <stdio.h>

typedef   enum no_yes {no, yes, maybe}   no_yes;
typedef   no_yes                         chk_it_out;
```

```
int main(void)
{
   char        c;
   chk_it_out  ans;

   printf("Do you like vegetables?  ");
   scanf(" %c", &c);
   if (c == 'n' || c == 'N')
      ans = no;
   else if (c == 'y' || c == 'Y')
      ans = yes;
   else
      ans = maybe;
   switch (ans) {
   case yes:
      printf("The answer was yes.\n");
   case no:
      printf("The answer was no.\n");
   case maybe:
      printf("You probably typed a nonsense reply.\n");
   default:
      printf("Impossible to get here.\n");
   }
   return 0;
}
```

Compile and execute this program on your system. Your compiler should not complain, but when you run the program, you may be surprised at what happens. Modify the program so that it behaves in a more appropriate manner. Also, pay attention to the control string `%c` in the `scanf()` function call. The blank before the percent sign causes optional white space to be matched. After you have modified the program, execute it repeatedly, typing various amounts of white space before answering yes or no. Do this repeatedly until you understand the effects of the program. Then modify the control string by removing the blank. Does the program act differently?

9 In the previous exercise, enumerators were used in the `case` labels in the body of the `switch`. Because the expression in a `case` label must be a constant integral expression, what can you conclude about enumerators? Could you use a statement such as

```
no = yes = 3;
```

in the body of `main()`? Explain.

10 C++: Rewrite the paper, rock, scissors program in C++. If your system has type-safe casts, use them. If your system has the enumeration type `bool` built in, use it.

11 C++: Implement a ternary logic evaluator that uses the following:

```
enum ternary_logic {false, maybe, true};

ternary_logic tern_not(ternary_logic v);
```

The function should return `false` when `v` is `true`, `true` when `v` is `false`, and `maybe` when `v` is `maybe`. The idea is to mimic ordinary conversation where the meaning of "Maybe it will rain today" and "Maybe it will not rain today" are logically equivalent. Code `tern_and()`, `tern_or()`, and `tern_not()` in a consistent manner.

12 The following Java program simulates coin tossing. Convert the program to C. You can use an enumeration type to simulate the Java `boolean` type. Java does not have either `typedef` or an `enum` type. Java uses classes to build types and does not need `typedef`. Some Java programmers would like Java to be extended to include an enumeration type.

```
//CoinToss.java - Compute the approximate probability
//    of n heads in a row by simulating coin tosses. Java by
Dissection pages 110-111.

class CoinToss {
  public static void main(String[] args) {
    //Input the number of tosses in a row to try for.
    int numTosses = 4;       //Just use 4 for testing

    //Input the number of trials to run.
    int numTrials = 10000;  //Use 10000 for testing

    //Perform the specified number of trials
    int numSuccesses =  performTrials(numTosses,numTrials);

    //Print the results
    double probability =   numSuccesses / (double)numTrials;
    System.out.println("Probability found in "
          + numTrials + " is  " + probability);
  }
```

```
// return true if numTosses heads are tossed
// before a tail
  static boolean isAllHeads(int numTosses) {
    double outcome;
    for (int numHeads = 0; numHeads < numTosses;
          numHeads++) {
      outcome = Math.random();    // toss the coin
      if ( outcome < 0.5)
        return false;             // tossed a tail
    }
    return true;                  // tossed all heads
   }

// perform numTrials simulated coin tosses
// and return the number of successes
   static int performTrials(int numTosses,
                            int numTrials) {
    System.out.println("Monte Carlo " + numTosses +
                      " in a row heads");
    int numSuccesses = 0;
    for (int trials= 0 ; trials < numTrials; trials++)
      // perform one trial
      if ( isAllHeads(numTosses))
        numSuccesses++;          // trial was a success
    return numSuccesses;
  }
}
```

Functions, Pointers, and Storage Classes

Chapter 8

When an expression is passed as an argument to a function, a copy of the value of the expression is made, and it is the copy, not the original, that is passed to the function. This mechanism is known as *call-by-value*, and it is strictly adhered to in C. Suppose `v` is a variable and `f()` is a function. If we write `v = f(v)`, then a value returned by the function can change `v` in the calling environment. Apart from this, the function call `f(v)` by itself cannot change `v`. This is because only a copy of the value of `v` is passed to `f()`. In other programming languages, however, a function call by itself *can* change the value of `v` in the calling environment. The mechanism that accomplishes this is known as *call-by-reference.*

It is often convenient to have functions modify the values of the variables referred to in the argument list. To get the effect of call-by-reference in C, we must use pointers in the parameter list in the function definition and pass addresses of variables as arguments in the function call. Before we explain this in detail, however, we need to understand how pointers work.

In C, pointers have many uses. In this chapter we explain how they are used as arguments to functions. In the two chapters that follow, we explain their use with arrays and strings. In Chapter 12, "Structures and ADTs," we show how pointers are used with structures, and in Chapter 13, "Input/Output and Files," we see how pointers are used with files.

In this chapter we also discuss scope rules and storage classes. Global variables are known throughout the program unless they are masked by a redeclaration in a function or a block.

8.1 Pointer Declaration and Assignment

Pointers are used in programs to access memory and manipulate addresses. We have already seen the use of addresses as arguments to `scanf()`. A function call such as `scanf("%d", &v)` causes an appropriate value to be stored at a particular address in memory.

If v is a variable, then &v is the address, or location, in memory of its stored value. The address operator & is unary and has the same precedence and right-to-left associativity as the other unary operators. Pointer variables can be declared in programs and then used to take addresses as values. The declaration

```
int   i, *p;
```

declares i to be of type int and p to be of type "pointer to int." The legal range of values for any pointer always includes the special address 0 and a set of positive integers that are interpreted as machine addresses on a particular C system. Typically, the symbolic constant NULL is defined as zero in *stdio.h*. Some examples of assignment to the pointer p are

```
p = &i;
p = 0;
p = NULL;              /* equivalent to  p = 0; */
p = (int *) 1307;      /* an absolute address in memory */
```

In the first example we think of p as "referring to i," or "pointing to i," or "containing the address of i." The compiler decides what address to use to store the value of the variable i. This varies from machine to machine and may even be different for different executions on the same machine. The second and third examples show assignments of the special value zero to the pointer p. In the last example the cast (int *) is necessary to avoid a compiler error. The type in the cast is "pointer to int." The last example is unusual because programmers ordinarily do not assign absolute addresses to pointers, except for the special value zero. This special value does not need to be cast.

8.2 Addressing and Dereferencing

We want to examine some elementary code and show some diagrams to illustrate what is happening in memory. Let us start with the declarations

```
int   a, b;
int *p;
```

The first declaration is read as "a is an int variable, and b is an int variable." The second declaration is read as "p is a pointer to int variable." Anytime one declares a pointer variable, it has an underlying type such as int that it can reference. The declaration of a and b causes the compiler to allocate memory space for two ints. The declaration of p causes the compiler to allocate memory space for a pointer to int. At this point, the contents of the variables are garbage because no values have been assigned.

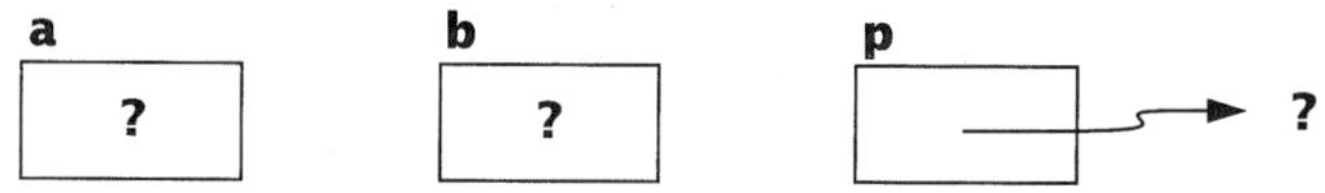

We used question marks in the diagram because we do not know what values are stored in the three variables. After the assignment statements

```
a = b = 7;
p = &a;
```

have been executed, we have

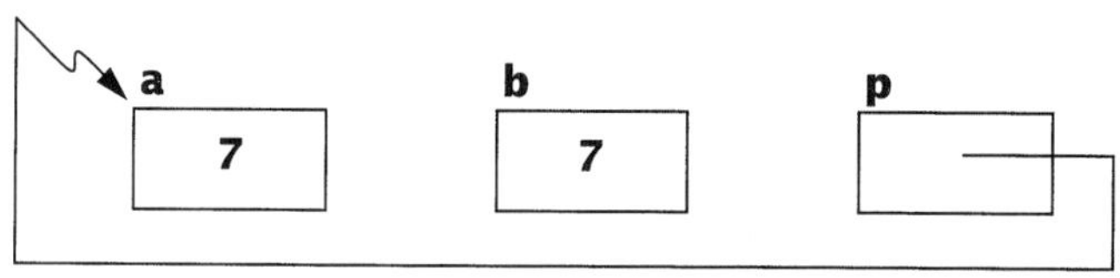

Now we can use the pointer p to access the value stored in a. This is done through the *dereference*, or *indirection*, operator *. This operator is unary, and it has the same precedence and right-to-left associativity as the other unary operators. Because p is a pointer, the expression *p has the value of the variable to which p points. The pointer p is said to have an address of the int variable a. The term *indirection* is taken from machine-language programming. The direct value of p is a memory location, whereas *p is the indirect value of p—namely, the value at the memory location stored in p. Consider the statement

```
printf("*p = %d\n", *p);          /* 7 is printed */
```

Because p points to a, and a has value 7, the dereferenced value of p is 7, and that is what is printed. Now consider

```
*p = 3;
printf("a = %d\n", a);            /* 3 is printed */
```

The first statement is read, "The object pointed to by p is assigned the value 3." Because p points to a, the stored value of a in memory is overwritten with the value 3. Thus, when we print out the value of a, 3 is printed. At this point, this is what we have in memory:

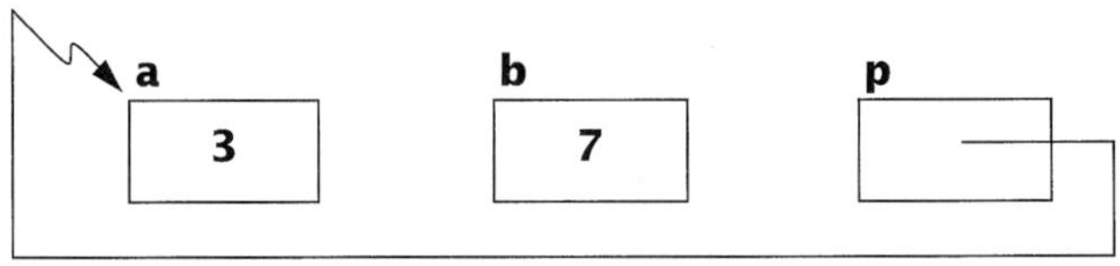

Our next statement causes p to point at b.

```
p = &b;
```

This time, we draw our diagram differently to show what is happening in memory.

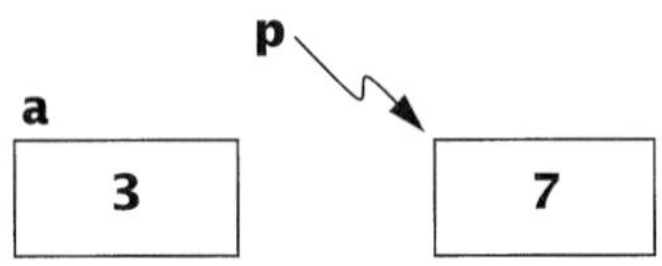

We do not really care about the place in memory where p is stored; our only concern is the object to which p is pointing. Now consider the code

```
*p = 2 * *p - a;
printf("b = %d\n", b);        /* 11 is printed */
```

We read the first statement as "The object pointed to by p is assigned the value 2 times what p is pointing to minus a." Note that the expression *p on the right side of the assignment is evaluated first. This is because the dereference operator * has higher precedence than the binary arithmetic operators.

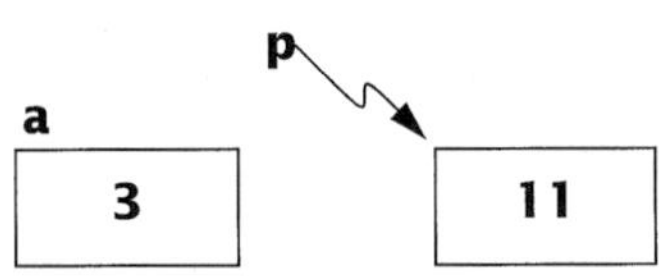

Now let us suppose we want to read in a value for a from the keyboard. Although there is no advantage in doing so, we can use the pointer p to accomplish this.

```
p = &a;
printf("Input an integer:  ");
scanf("%d", p);              /* put it at the address of a */
```

When `scanf()` is invoked, the characters typed at the keyboard are converted to a decimal integer value, and that value is placed at the address `p`. We can think of a pointer as an address and an address as a pointer. If we type 77 when prompted, this is what we have in memory:

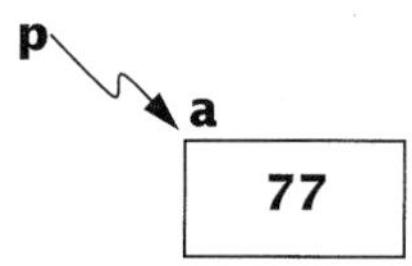

In simple terms, the dereference operator * is the inverse of the address operator &. Consider the following code:

```
double   x, y, *p;

p = &x;
y = *p;
```

First `p` is assigned the address of `x`. Then `y` is assigned the value of the object pointed to by `p`. The two statements are equivalent to

```
y = *&x;
```

which in turn is equivalent to

```
y = x;
```

A pointer variable can be initialized in a declaration, but the notation is confusing to the beginning programmer. Here is an example:

```
int   a, *p = &a;
```

This declaration tells the compiler that `p` is a pointer to `int` and that the initial value of `p` is `&a`. *Caution:* Do *not* read this as "The object pointed to by `p` is initialized to the address of `a`." Also note that

```
int   *p = &a, a;          /* wrong */
```

does not work. The compiler must allocate space in memory for `a` before `p` can be initialized with its address. The compiler is not allowed to look ahead.

In the following function definition, the parameter `p` is a pointer to `int`. We can use it to initialize variables in a declaration.

```
void f(int *p)
{
   int   a = *p, *q = p;

   .....
}
```

This declares a to be an int and initializes it to the object p is pointing to; it also declares q to be a pointer to int and initializes it to p.

The following table illustrates how some pointer expressions are evaluated. Be careful to read the pointer initializations correctly.

Declarations and initializations		
`int i = 3, j = 5, *p = &i, *q = &j, *r;` `double x;`		
Expression	**Equivalent expression**	**Value**
`p == & i`	`p == (& i)`	1
`p = i + 7`	`p = (i + 7)`	*illegal*
`* * & p`	`* (* (& p))`	3
`r = & x`	`r = (& x)`	*illegal*
`7 * * p / * q + 7`	`(((7 * (* p))) / (* q)) + 7`	11
`* (r = & j) *= * p`	`(* (r = (& j))) *= (* p)`	15

In ANSI C, the only integer value that can be assigned to a pointer is the special value zero. To assign any other value, a cast must be used. In contrast to this, pointers and integers may be freely mixed in traditional C.

In the preceding table we attempted to assign r the value &x. Because r is a pointer to int, and the expression &x is of type pointer to double, this is illegal. Also note that we used the expression

```
7 * * p / * q + 7
```

If instead we had written

```
7 * * p /* q + 7                /* trouble? */
```

we would have found that the compiler treats /* as the start of a comment. This can result in a difficult bug.

Let us write a short program that illustrates the distinction between a pointer value and its dereferenced value. Also, we illustrate how the %p format can be used to print pointer values, or addresses.

```
#include <stdio.h>

int main(void)
{
   int   i = 777, *p = &i;

   printf("  Value of i: %d\n", *p);
   printf("Address of i: %u or %p\n", p, p);
   return 0;
}
```

Here is the output of this program on our system:

```
  Value of i: 777
Address of i: 234880252 or dfffcfc
```

The actual location of a variable in memory is system-dependent. The operator * takes the value of p to be a memory location and returns the value stored at this location, appropriately interpreted according to the type declaration of p. We used the %u format to print the address of i as an unsigned decimal integer and %p to print the address of i in a way natural for the system. On our system this is a hexadecimal integer. The %p format is not available in some traditional C systems. In MS-DOS, the %u format does not always work (see exercise 13 on page 298).

"YOU'RE RIGHT, ASHLEY, C IS NOT DIFFICULT. BUT AS A KID, I WAS TAUGHT THAT ALL POINTERS WERE V-E-R-Y IMPOLITE!"

8.3 Pointers to void

In traditional C, pointers of different types are considered to be *assignment-compatible.* In ANSI C, however, one pointer can be assigned to another only when they both have the same type, or when one of them is of type pointer to `void`. Thus we can think of `void *` as a generic pointer type. The following table shows examples of both legal and illegal pointer assignments.

Declarations	

`int *p;`
`double *q;`
`void *v;`	

Legal assignments	**Illegal assignments**
`p = 0;`	`p = 1;`
`p = (int *) 1;`	`v = 1;`
`p = v = q;`	`p = q;`
`p = (int *) q;`	

In Section 9.9, "Dynamic Memory Allocation," on page 320, we discuss the standard library functions `calloc()` and `malloc()`, which provide dynamic storage allocation for arrays and structures. Because they return a pointer to `void`, we can write

```
int   *a;

a = calloc(·····);
```

In traditional C, we would need to use a cast.

```
a = (int *) calloc(·····);          /* traditional C */
```

In traditional C, the type `char *` is used as a (sort of) generic pointer type, but this requires the use of casts. The type `void *` does not exist in traditional C.

8.4 Call-by-Reference

Whenever variables are passed as arguments to a function, their values are copied to the corresponding function parameters, and the variables themselves are not changed in the calling environment. This call-by-value mechanism is strictly adhered to in C. In this section we describe how the *addresses* of variables can be used as arguments to functions so as to achieve the effect of call-by-reference.

For a function to effect call-by-reference, pointers must be used in the parameter list in the function definition. Then, when the function is called, addresses of variables must be passed as arguments. The function swap() in the following program illustrates these ideas.

```
#include <stdio.h>

void   swap(int *, int *);

int main(void)
{
   int   a = 3, b = 7;

   printf("%d  %d\n", a, b);     /* 3  7 is printed */
   swap(&a, &b);
   printf("%d  %d\n", a, b);     /* 7  3 is printed */
   return 0;
}
```

Because the addresses of a and b are passed as arguments to swap(), the function is able to interchange the values of a and b in the calling environment.

```
void swap(int *p, int *q)
{
   int   tmp;

   tmp = *p;
   *p = *q;
   *q = tmp;
}
```

Dissection of the swap() Function

■
```
void swap(int *p, int *q)
{
   int   tmp;
```

The type of the function is void, which means that no value is returned. The two parameters p and q are of type pointer to int. The variable tmp is local to this function. We think of it as temporary storage. When we call this function in main() with &a and &b as arguments, this is what we have in memory at this point:

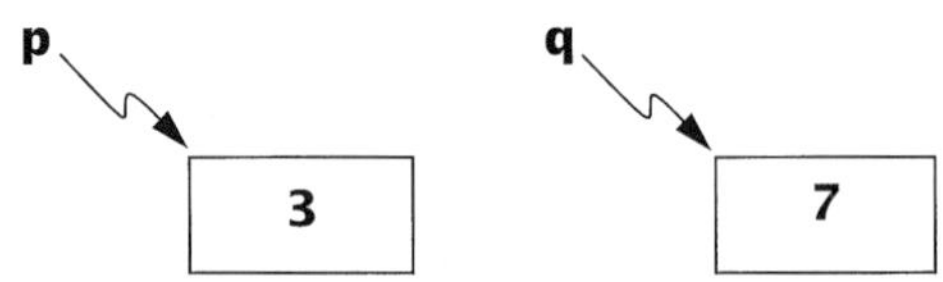

■
```
tmp = *p;
*p = *q;
*q = tmp;
```

We read this as follows:

> The variable tmp is assigned the value of the object pointed to by p.
>
> The object pointed to by p is assigned the value of the object pointed to by q.
>
> The object pointed to by q is assigned the value tmp.

After these three statements have been executed, here is what we have in memory:

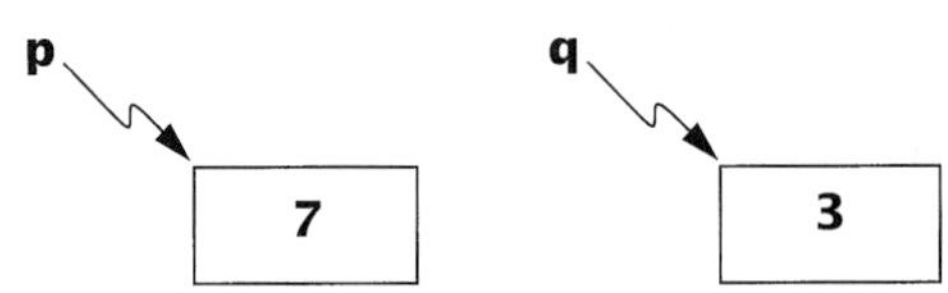

If pointers are new to you, you should draw a diagram of what is in memory after each statement has been executed (see exercise 2 on page 296).

The Effect of Call-by-Reference Is Accomplished by

1 Declaring a function parameter to be a pointer

2 Using the dereferenced pointer in the function body

3 Passing an address as an argument when the function is called

8.5 Scope Rules

The *scope* of an identifier is the part of the program text in which the identifier is known or accessible. This concept depends on the notion of a *block*, which is a compound statement with declarations.

The basic rule of scoping is that identifiers are accessible only within the block in which they are declared. They are unknown outside the boundaries of that block. This would be an easy rule to follow, except that programmers, for a variety of reasons, choose to use the same identifier in different declarations. We then have the question of which object the identifier refers to. Let us give a simple example of this state of affairs.

```
/* The Block Scope program. */
#include <stdio.h>

int main(void)
{
   int a = 2;                /* outer block a */
   int *p = &a;
   printf("%d\n", a);        /* 2 is printed */
   {
      int a = 7;             /* inner block a */
      printf("%d\n", a);     /* 7 is printed */
      printf("%d\n", *p);    /* 2 is printed*/
   }                         /* back to the outer block */
   printf("%d\n", ++a);      /* 3 is printed */
   return 0;
}
```

Dissection of the Block Scope Program

- ```
  {
     int a = 2;               /* outer block a */
     int *p = &a;
  ```

  A function is a block. If you get confused by the reuse of identifier a in different blocks, consider rewriting this code as
  ```

```
{
   int a_outer = 2;
   int *p = &a_outer;
   printf("%d\n", a_outer);
```

So it should be clear that 2 is printed and that p is pointing at the variable a_outer.

■
```
{
         int a = 7;               /* inner block a */
         printf("%d\n", a);       /* 7 is printed */
         printf("%d\n", *p);      /* 2 is printed*/
}                                 /* back to the outer block */
```

The open brace introduces an inner block. The identifier a is now declaring an inner block a that is distinct and hides the outer block a. We can better understand this if we rewrite the code as

```
{
   int a_inner = 7;
   printf("%d\n", a_inner);
   printf("%d\n", *p);  /* 2 is printed*/
```

The pointer variable p is pointing at the variable a_outer. Therefore 2 is printed by the second printf().

Each block introduces its own nomenclature. An outer block name is valid unless an inner block redefines it. If redefined, the outer block name is hidden, or masked, from the inner block. Inner blocks may be nested to arbitrary depths that are determined by system limitations.

8.6 Storage Classes

Every variable and function in C has two attributes: *type* and *storage class*. The four storage classes are automatic, external, register, and static, with the corresponding keywords

```
auto      extern      register      static
```

By far the most common storage class for variables is automatic. However, the programmer needs to know about all the storage classes. They all have important uses.

The Storage Class auto

Variables declared within function bodies are by default automatic. Thus automatic is the most common of the four storage classes. If a compound statement starts with variable declarations, then these variables can be acted on within the scope of the enclosing compound statement. A compound statement with declarations is called a *block* to distinguish it from one that does not begin with declarations.

Declarations of variables within blocks are implicitly of storage class automatic. The keyword auto can be used to explicitly specify the storage class. An example is

```
auto int     a, b, c;
auto double   f;
```

Because the storage class is automatic by default, the keyword auto is seldom used.

When a block is entered, the system allocates memory for the automatic variables. Within that block, these variables are defined and are considered local to the block. When the block is exited, the system releases the memory that was set aside for the automatic variables. Thus the values of these variables are lost. If the block is reentered, the system once again allocates memory, but previous values are unknown. The body of a function definition constitutes a block if it contains declarations. If it does, then each invocation of the function sets up a new environment.

The Storage Class extern

One method of transmitting information across blocks and functions is to use external variables. When a variable is declared outside a function, storage is permanently assigned to it, and its storage class is extern. A declaration for an external variable can look identical to a declaration for a variable that occurs inside a function or block. Such a variable is considered to be global to all functions declared after it, and upon exit from the block or function, the external variable remains in existence. The following program illustrates these ideas:

```
#include <stdio.h>

int   a = 1, b = 2, c = 3;          /* global variables */
int   f(void);                      /* function prototype */
```

```
int main(void)
{
   printf("%3d\n", f());                 /* 12 is printed */
   printf("%3d%3d%3d\n", a, b, c);      /* 4  2  3 printed */
   return 0;
}

int f(void)
{
   int   b, c;                  /* b and c are local */
                                /* global b, c are masked */
   a = b = c = 4;
   return (a + b + c);
}
```

Note that we could have written

```
extern int   a = 1, b = 2, c = 3;    /* global variables */
```

This use of `extern` causes some traditional C compilers to complain. Although this use of `extern` is allowable in ANSI C, it is not required. Variables defined outside of a function have external storage class even if the keyword `extern` is not used. Such variables cannot have automatic or register storage class. The keyword `static` can be used, but its use is special, as explained in Section 8.7, "Static External Variables," on page 279.

The keyword `extern` is used to tell the compiler, "Look for it elsewhere, either in this file or in some other file." Let us rewrite the last program to illustrate a typical use of the keyword `extern`.

```
#include <stdio.h>

int   a = 1, b = 2, c = 3;       /* external variables */
int   f(void);

int main(void)
{
   printf("%3d\n", f());
   printf("%3d%3d%3d\n", a, b, c);
   return 0;
}
```

In file file2.c:

```
int f(void)
{
   extern int a;                /* look for it elsewhere */
   int        b, c;

   a = b = c = 4;
   return (a + b + c);
}
```

The two files can be compiled separately. The use of `extern` in the second file tells the compiler that the variable a is defined elsewhere, either in this file or in another. The ability to compile files separately is important when writing large programs.

External variables never disappear. Because they exist throughout the execution life of the program, they can be used to transmit values across functions. They may, however, be hidden if the identifier is redefined. Another way to conceive of external variables is to think of them as being declared in a block that encompasses the whole program.

Information can be passed into a function in two ways: (1) by the use of external variables and (2) by the use of the parameter mechanism. Although there are exceptions, the use of the parameter mechanism is the preferred method. It tends to improve the modularity of the code and reduces the possibility of undesirable side effects.

One side effect occurs when a function changes a global variable from within its body rather than through its parameter list. Such a construction is error prone. Correct practice is to effect changes to global variables through the parameter and return mechanisms. Adhering to this practice improves modularity and readability, and because changes are localized, programs are typically easier to write and maintain.

All functions have external storage class. This means we can use the keyword `extern` in function definitions and function prototypes. For example,

```
extern double   sin(double);
```

is a valid function prototype for the `sin()` function, and for its function definition we can write

```
extern double sin(double x)
{
   .....
```

The Storage Class `register`

The storage class `register` tells the compiler that the associated variables should be stored in high-speed memory registers, provided it is physically and semantically possible. Because resource limitations and semantic constraints sometimes make this impossible, this storage class defaults to automatic whenever the compiler cannot allocate an appropriate physical register. Typically, the compiler has only a few such registers available; many are required for system use and cannot be allocated otherwise.

Basically, the use of storage class `register` is an attempt to improve execution speed. When speed is a concern, the programmer may choose a few variables that are most frequently accessed and declare them to be of storage class `register`. Common candidates for such treatment include loop variables and function parameters. Here is an example:

```
{
    register int   i;

    for (i = 0; i < LIMIT; ++i) {
        .....
    }
}           /* block exit will free the register */
```

The declaration

`register i;` is equivalent to `register int i;`

If a storage class is specified in a declaration and the type is absent, then the type is `int` by default.

Note that in our example the register variable `i` was declared as close to its place of use as possible. This is to allow maximum availability of the physical registers, using them only when needed. Always remember that a register declaration is taken only as *advice* to the compiler.

The Storage Class `static`

Static declarations have two important and distinct uses. The more elementary use is to allow a local variable to retain its previous value when the block is reentered. This is in contrast to ordinary automatic variables, which lose their value upon block exit and must be reinitialized. The second and more subtle use is in connection with external declarations. This is discussed in the next section.

As an example of the value retention use of `static`, we write the outline of a function that behaves differently, depending on how many times it has been called.

```
void f(void)
{
   static int   cnt = 0;

   ++cnt;
   if (cnt % 2 == 0)
      .....                 /* do something */
   else
      .....                 /* do something different */
}
```

The first time the function is invoked, the variable `cnt` is initialized to zero. On function exit, the value of `cnt` is preserved in memory. Whenever the function is invoked again, `cnt` is not reinitialized. Instead, it retains its previous value from the last time the function was called. The declaration of `cnt` as a `static int` inside of `f()` keeps it private to `f()`. If it were declared outside of the function, then other functions could access it, too.

8.7 Static External Variables

The second and more subtle use of `static` is in connection with external declarations. With external constructs, it provides a *privacy* mechanism that is very important for program modularity. By privacy, we mean visibility or scope restrictions on otherwise accessible variables or functions.

At first glance, static external variables seem unnecessary. External variables already retain their values across block and function exit. The difference is that static external variables are scope-restricted external variables. The scope is the remainder of the source file in which they are declared. Thus they are unavailable to functions defined earlier in the file or to functions defined in other files, even if these functions attempt to use the `extern` storage class keyword.

```
void f(void)
{
   .....                    /* v is not available here */
}

static int   v;             /* static external variable */

void g(void)
{
   .....                    /* v can be used here */
}
```

Let us use this facility to provide a variable that is global to a family of functions but at the same time is private to the file. We write two pseudorandom number generators, both of which use the same seed. (The algorithm is based on linear congruential methods; see *The Art of Computer Programming*, 2nd ed., vol. 2, *Seminumerical Algorithms*, by Donald Ervin Knuth, published by Addison-Wesley in 1981.)

```
/* A family of pseudo random number generators. */

#define   INITIAL_SEED       17
#define   MULTIPLIER         25173
#define   INCREMENT          13849
#define   MODULUS            65536
#define   FLOATING_MODULUS   65536.0

static unsigned   seed = INITIAL_SEED;    /* external, but
                                        private to this file */
unsigned random(void)
{
   seed = (MULTIPLIER * seed + INCREMENT) % MODULUS;
   return seed;
}

double probability(void)
{
   seed = (MULTIPLIER * seed + INCREMENT) % MODULUS;
   return (seed / FLOATING_MODULUS);
}
```

The function `random()` produces an apparently random sequence of integer values between zero and `MODULUS`. The function `probability()` produces an apparently random sequence of floating values between zero and one.

Notice that a call to `random()` or `probability()` produces a new value of the variable `seed` that depends on its old value. Because `seed` is a static external variable, it is private to this file and its value is preserved between function calls. We can now create functions in other files that invoke these random number generators without worrying about side effects.

A last use of `static` is as a storage class specifier for function definitions and prototypes. This causes the scope of the function to be restricted. Static functions are visible only within the file in which they are defined. Unlike ordinary functions, which can be accessed from other files, a `static` function is available throughout its own file, but no other. Again, this facility is useful in developing private modules of function definitions.

```
void f(int a)
{
   .....   /* g() available here, but not in other files */
}
```

```
static int g(void)
{
   .....
}
```

8.8 Default Initialization

In C, both external variables and static variables that are not explicitly initialized by the programmer are initialized to zero by the system. This includes arrays, strings, pointers, structures, and unions. For arrays and strings, this means that each element is initialized to zero; for structures and unions, it means that each member is initialized to zero. In contrast to this, automatic and register variables usually are not initialized by the system. This means they start with garbage values. Although some C systems do initialize automatic variables to zero, this feature should not be relied on, as it makes the code nonportable.

8.9 An Example: Processing Characters

A function that uses a `return` statement can pass back to the calling environment a single value. If more than one value is needed in the calling environment, addresses must be passed as arguments to the function. To illustrate this idea, let us write a program that processes characters in a particular way. Here is what we want to accomplish.

Character-Processing Goals

- Read characters from the input stream until `EOF` is encountered.
- Change any lowercase letter to an uppercase letter.
- Print three words to a line, with a single space between each word.
- Count the number of characters and the number of letters printed.

In this program we consider a word to be a sequence of non-white space characters of maximal length. Here is `main()`:

```
#include <stdio.h>
#include <ctype.h>

#define   NWORDS   3          /* number of words per line */

int   process(int *, int *, int *);
```

```
int main(void)
{
   int   c, nchars = 0, nletters = 0;

   while ((c = getchar()) != EOF)
      if (process(&c, &nchars, &nletters) == 1)
         putchar(c);
      printf("\n%s%5d\n%s%5d\n\n",
             "Number of characters:", nchars,
             "Number of letters:    ", nletters);
   return 0;
}
```

The processing of each character takes place in the function `process()`. Because the values of the variables `c`, `nchars`, and `nletters` are to be changed in the calling environment, addresses of these variables are passed as arguments to `process()`. Notice that `c` is an `int` rather than a `char`. This is because `c` must eventually take on the special value `EOF`, which is not a character. Notice also that a character is written to the screen only if `process()` returns the value 1. In this context we think of 1 as signaling that the character has been appropriately processed and is ready to print. We use the value 0 to signal that the character is not to be printed. This case occurs when contiguous white space characters occur. Let us see how `process()` does its work.

```
int process(int *p, int *nchars_ptr, int *nletters_ptr)
{
   static int   cnt = 0, last_char = ' ';

   if (isspace(last_char) && isspace(*p))
      return 0;

   if (isalpha(*p)) {
      ++*nletters_ptr;
      if (islower(*p))
         *p = toupper(*p);
   }

   else if (isspace(*p))
      if (++cnt % NWORDS == 0)
         *p = '\n';
      else
         *p = ' ';
   ++*nchars_ptr;
   last_char = *p;
   return 1;
}
```

Before we dissect this function, we want to show some output from the program. First we compile the program and put the executable code in the file *process.* Then we create a file called *data* with the following lines in it:

```
    she sells sea shells
by       the      seashore
```

Notice that we have deliberately put contiguous blanks into the file. Now, if we give the command

process < data

here is what appears on the screen:

```
SHE SELLS SEA
SHELLS BY THE
SEASHORE
Number of characters:   37
Number of letters:      30
```

Dissection of the process() Function

- ```
  int process(int *p, int *nchars_ptr, int *nletters_ptr)
  {
     static int   cnt = 0, last_char = ' ';
  ```

The type of the function is `int`, which means that it returns an `int` value. The parameters of the function are three pointers to `int`. Although we think of `p` as a pointer to a character, its declaration here should be consistent with its use in `main()`. The local variables `cnt` and `last_char` are of the storage class `static`. Thus they are initialized only once, and their values are retained between function calls. If these variables were of storage class `auto`, they would be reinitialized every time the function is called.

- ```
  isspace(last_char)
  ```

The macro `isspace()` is defined in *ctype.h.* It returns a nonzero value (*true*) if its argument is a blank, tab, or newline.

■
```
if (isspace(last_char) && isspace(*p))
   return 0;
```

If the last character seen was a white space character, and the character pointed to by p is also a white space character, the value 0 is returned to the calling environment. Back in the calling environment—that is, back in main()—when this value is received, the current character is not printed.

■
```
if (isalpha(*p)) {
   ++*nletters_ptr;
   if (islower(*p))
      *p = toupper(*p);
}
```

If the character pointed to by p is a letter, then we increment the value of the object pointed to by nletters_ptr. If, moreover, the value of the object pointed to by p is a lowercase letter, then the object pointed to by p is assigned the corresponding uppercase letter.

```
++*nletters_ptr;
```

Let us consider this statement in some detail. The increment operator ++ and the indirection operator * are both unary and associate from right to left. Thus

```
++(*nletters_ptr);
```

is equivalent to it. What is being incremented is the dereferenced value in the calling environment. Note carefully that the expression

`++*nletters_ptr` is not equivalent to `*nletters_ptr++`

The latter expression is equivalent to

```
*(nletters_ptr++)
```

which causes the current pointer value to be dereferenced and the pointer itself to be incremented. This is an instance of pointer arithmetic.

■
```
else if (isspace(*p))
   if (++cnt % NWORDS == 0)
      *p = '\n';
   else
      *p = ' ';
```

If the character pointed to by p is a white space character, then last_char cannot also be a white space character; we have already handled that case. No matter what this character is, we want to print a newline or a blank, depending on the incremented value of cnt. Because the symbolic constant NWORDS has the value 3, we print a newline every third time, and the other two times we print a blank. The effect of this is to print at most three words to a line, with a single blank between them.

■
```
++*nchars_ptr;
last_char = *p;
return 1;
```

First we increment the value of the object pointed to by nchars_ptr. Then we assign to last_char the value of the object pointed to by p. Finally, we return the value 1 to the calling environment to indicate that a character is to be printed.

8.10 Function Declarations and Definitions

To the compiler, function declarations are generated in various ways: by function invocation, by function definition, and by explicit declarations and prototypes. If a function call such as f(x) is encountered before any declaration, definition, or prototype for the function occurs, then the compiler assumes a default declaration of the form

```
int   f();
```

Nothing is assumed about the parameter list for the function. Now suppose the following function definition occurs first:

```
int f(x)          /* traditional C style */
double x;
{
    .....
```

This provides both declaration and definition to the compiler. Again, nothing is assumed about the parameter list. It is the programmer's responsibility to pass only a single argument of type double. A function call such as f(1) can be expected to fail. Suppose that, instead, we use the following new style definition:

```
int f(double x)     /* ANSI C style */
{
    .....
```

The compiler now knows about the parameter list. In this case, if an `int` is passed as an argument, it is converted appropriately to a `double`.

A function prototype is a special case of a function declaration. A good programming style is to give either the function definition (new style), the function prototype, or both before a function is used. A major reason for including standard header files is that they contain function prototypes.

Certain limitations exist for function definitions and prototypes. The function storage class specifier, if present, can be either `extern` or `static`, but not both; `auto` and `register` cannot be used. The types "array of . . ." and "function returning . . ." cannot be returned by a function. However, a pointer representing an array or a function can be returned. The only storage class specifier that can occur in the parameter type list is `register`. The parameters cannot be initialized.

8.11 The Type Qualifiers const and volatile

The ANSI committee has added the keywords `const` and `volatile` to the C language. They are not available in traditional C. Because they are used in declarations to tell the compiler how identifiers can be used, they are called *type qualifiers*.

Let us first discuss how `const` is used. Typically, in a declaration, `const` comes after the storage class, if any, but before the type. Consider the declaration

```
static const int   k = 3;
```

We read this as "k is a constant `int` with static storage class." Because the type for k has been qualified by `const`, we can initialize k, but thereafter k cannot be assigned to, incremented, or decremented. Even though a variable has been qualified with `const`, it still cannot be used to specify an array size in another declaration.

```
const int   n = 3;
int         v[n];         /* the compiler will complain */
```

Thus a `const` qualified variable is not equivalent to a symbolic constant.

An unqualified pointer should not be assigned the address of a `const` qualified variable. The following code causes the compiler to complain:

```
const int   a = 7;
int         *p = &a;      /* the compiler will complain */
```

The reason for this is that, because p is an ordinary pointer to `int`, we could use it later in an expression such as ++*p. However, that would change the stored value of a, violating the concept that a is constant. If, on the other hand, we write

```
const int   a = 7;
const int   *p = &a;
```

then the compiler is happy. The last declaration is read "p is a pointer to a constant `int` and its initial value is the address of a." Note that p itself is not a constant. We can assign to it some other address. We may not, however, assign a value to *p. The object pointed to by p should not be modified.

Suppose we want p itself to be constant, but not a. This is achieved with the declarations

```
int           a;
int * const   p = &a;
```

We read the last declaration as "p is a constant pointer to `int`, and its initial value is the address of a." Thereafter, we may not assign a value to p, but we may assign a value to *p. Now consider

```
const int             a = 7;
const int * const     p = &a;
```

The last declaration tells the compiler that p is a constant pointer to a constant `int`. Neither p nor *p can be assigned to, incremented, or decremented.

In contrast to `const`, the type qualifier `volatile` is seldom used. A `volatile` object is one that can be modified in some unspecified way by the hardware. Consider the declaration

```
extern const volatile int   real_time_clock;
```

The `extern` means "Look for it elsewhere, either in this file or in some other file." The qualifier `volatile` indicates that the object may be acted on by the hardware. Because `const` is also a qualifier, the object may not be assigned to, incremented, or decremented within the program.

8.12 Style

One often finds p, q, and r used as identifiers for pointer variables in a program. This is a natural convention, with p standing for *pointer*, and q and r being the next letters in the alphabet. In a similar fashion p1, p2, . . . are also used as identifiers for pointer variables. Other common ways to designate that an identifier is a pointer is to prepend `p_` to a name, as in `p_hi` and `p_lo`, or to append `_ptr`, as in `nchars_ptr`.

An alternative declaration style for a pointer is

`char*   p;`   which is equivalent to   `char   p;`

Some programmers prefer this style because the * is now more closely associated with the type being pointed to. One must be careful, however, because

`char*  p, q, r;`   is not equivalent to   `char  *p, *q, *r;`

Instead, it is equivalent to

```
char   *p, q, r;
```

Our next concern deals with functions that have *side effects.* Side effects occur when a function call changes the stored value in memory of a variable in the calling environment. A good programming style is to effect such changes by using the `return` or parameter mechanism. To illustrate, let us rewrite our *swap* program.

```
#include <stdio.h>

int    a = 3, b = 7;                  /* global variables */
void   swap(void);                    /* function prototype */

int main(void)
{
   printf("%d  %d\n", a, b);          /* 3  7 is printed */
   swap();
   printf("%d  %d\n", a, b);          /* 7  3 is printed */
   return 0;
}
```

We have moved the declaration of a and b outside of `main()`, making these variables global. Now we rewrite the `swap()` function.

```
void swap(void)              /* very bad programming style */
{
   extern int   a, b;
   int          tmp;

   tmp = a;
   a = b;
   b = tmp;
}
```

The modification of the global variables a and b is a side effect of the function call `swap()`. With this programming style, large programs can be very difficult to read and maintain. Ideally, one writes code that is locally intelligible.

8.13 Common Programming Errors

Beginning programmers often make conceptual mistakes when learning to use pointers. A typical example of this is

```
int   *p = 3;
```

Here an attempt is being made to initialize the value of the object pointed to by p. But this is an initialization of p itself, which is most likely not what was intended. Suppose we try to fix this by writing

```
int   *p = &i, i = 3;
```

Now there is a more subtle error. C does not provide look-ahead capability. At the point where p is initialized to the address of i, space for the variable i has not yet been allocated. To correct this, we can write

```
int   i = 3, *p = &i;
```

First space for i is allocated, and i is initialized to 3; then space for p is allocated and p is initialized to the address of i.

When dealing with pointers, the programmer must learn to distinguish carefully between a pointer p and its dereferenced value *p. To minimize any chance of confusion, one should use names for pointer variables that indicate pointer usage. Here is an example of what *not* to do. Suppose v1 and v2 are floating variables and we want to interchange their values in the calling environment by the function call swap(&v1, &v2). To code swap(), one could write

```
void swap(double *v1, double *v2)            /* poor style */
{
   .....
```

But now there is confusion. In main(), the identifiers v1 and v2 are used as names of variables of type double, but in swap(), the same identifiers are used as names of variables of type pointer to double. It would be much better to use p_v1 and p_v2. Using names that clearly indicate pointer usage helps the programmer minimize mistakes and helps others who read the code to understand its intent.

Of course, not every value is stored in an accessible memory location. It is useful to keep in mind the following prohibitions.

Constructs not to be pointed at		
Do not point at constants	&3	*illegal*
Do not point at ordinary expressions	&(k + 99)	*illegal*
Do not point at register variables	register v; &v	*illegal*

The address operator can be applied to variables and array elements. If a is an array, then expressions such as &a[0] and &a[i+j+7] make sense (see Chapter 9, "Arrays and Pointers").

One common use of a block is for debugging purposes. Imagine we are in a section of code where a variable, v, is misbehaving. By inserting a block temporarily into the code, we can use local variables that do not interfere with the rest of the program.

```
{                               /* debugging starts here */
   static int   cnt = 0;

   printf("*** debug: cnt = %d   v = %d\n", ++cnt, v);
}
```

The variable cnt is local to the block. It does not interfere with another variable of the same name in an outer block. Because its storage class is static, it retains its old value when the block is reentered. Here, it is being used to count the number of times the block is executed (perhaps we are inside a for loop). We are assuming that the variable v has been declared in an outer block and is therefore known in this block. We are printing its value for debugging purposes. Later, after we have fixed our code, this block becomes extraneous, and we remove it.

8.14 System Considerations

In traditional C, integer values can be assigned to a pointer, but in ANSI C, only the special value zero can be assigned to a pointer regardless of the pointer type. Some compilers issue an error message if a nonzero value is assigned to a pointer; other compilers issue only a warning. They are all supposed to issue an error message, but many ANSI C compilers are used in an environment where both old and new C code must be compiled.

Programs that make explicit use of absolute addresses are frequently nonportable. Different systems have different address spaces, and they may use their address spaces in noncompatible ways. If you must write programs with absolute addresses, it is best to use the #define facility to localize any possible system-dependent code.

Pointer expressions should not be of mixed type. As an example, suppose p is of type pointer to char and q is of type pointer to int. Then the assignment expression p = q has mixed pointer type. Although such expressions are considered illegal in ANSI C, many compilers only issue a warning. In Turbo C, for example, we get

```
Suspicious pointer conversion in .....
```

The proper style is to use casts. For example, we could write

```
p = (char *) q;
```

When writing portable code, the programmer must heed all compiler warnings because what is a warning on one system may be prohibited on another.

In ANSI C, the %p format can be used in a printf() statement to print pointer values. Typically, these are hexadecimal numbers. This format is not available in some traditional C compilers.

The preferred placement of function prototypes is either in a header file that is included or at the top of the file but after the #includes, #defines, and typedefs. This gives the function prototypes file visibility. In ANSI C, function prototypes placed in a block (in the body of a function, for example) are supposed to have just the scope of that block. In traditional C, function declarations were often given file visibility no matter where they were placed in the file. Some ANSI C compilers continue to do this with respect to both function prototypes and function declarations although it is technically wrong to do so. In some instances this can cause porting difficulties.

8.15 Moving to C++

Reference declarations are a new feature of C++. They declare the identifier to be an alternative name, or *alias,* for an object specified in an initialization of the reference, and they allow a simpler form of call-by-reference parameters. Examples are

```
int      n;
int&     nn = n          //nn is alternative name for n
double   a[10];
double&  last = a[9];    //last is an alias for a[9]
```

Declarations of references that are definitions must be initialized, usually to simple variables. The initializer is an lvalue expression, which gives the variable's location in memory. In these examples, the names n and nn are aliases for each other; that is, they refer to the same object. Modifying nn is equivalent to modifying n and vice versa. The name `last` is an alternative to the single array element `a[9]`. These names, once initialized, cannot be changed.

When a variable `i` is declared, it has an address and memory associated with it. When a pointer variable p is declared and initialized to `&i`, it has an identity separate from `i`. When a reference variable r is declared and initialized to `i`, it is identical to `i`. It does not have a separate identity from the other names for the same object.

The following definitions demonstrate the use of pointers, dereferencing, and aliasing. They assume that memory at location 1004 is used for integer variable `a`, and memory at location 1008 is used for pointer variable p.

```
int    a = 5;        //declaration of a
int*   p = &a;       //p points to a
int&   ref_a = a;    //alias for a
*p = 7;              //lvalue in effect a is assigned 7
a = *p + 1;          //rvalue 7 added to 1 and a assigned 8
```

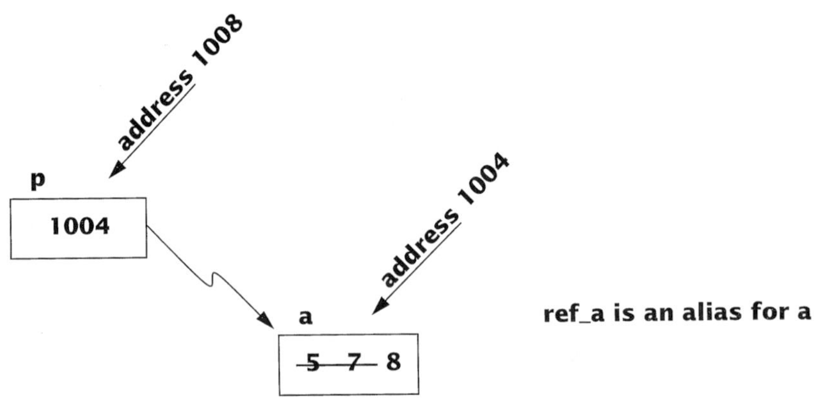

Notice in the preceding figure that any change to the value of a is equivalent to changing `ref_a`. Such a change affects the dereferenced value of p. The pointer p can be assigned another address and lose its association with a. However, a and `ref_a` are aliases and, within the scope, must refer to the same object.

These declarations can be used for call-by-reference arguments, which allows C++ to have call-by-reference arguments directly. This feature is not available in C; it is similar to Pascal var parameters.

Using this mechanism, the function `order()` is recoded as

```
void order(int& p, int& q)
{
   int  temp;

   if (p > q) {
      temp = p;
      p = q;
      q = temp;
   }
}
```

It would be prototyped and invoked in `main()` as follows:

```
void  order(int&, int&);
int main(void)
{
   int  i, j;
   .....
   order(i, j);
   .....
}
```

Let us use this mechanism to write a function `greater()`, which exchanges two values if the first is greater than the second.

```
int greater(int& a, int& b)
{
   if (a > b) {         //exchange
      int  temp = a;
      a = b;
      b = temp;
      return 1;
   }
   else
      return 0;
}
```

Now, if `i` and `j` are two `int` variables,

```
greater(i, j)
```

uses the reference to `i` and the reference to `j` to exchange, if necessary, their two values.

Summary

- A pointer variable usually takes as values either NULL or addresses of other variables.

- The address operator & and the indirection, or dereferencing, operator * are unary operators with the same precedence and right-to-left associativity as the other unary operators. If v is a variable, then the expression

  *&v   is equivalent to   v

  Remember, however, that if v has storage class register, then the operation &v is not allowed.

- In C, the call-by-value mechanism is strictly adhered to. This means that when an expression occurs as an argument to a function, a copy of the value of the expression is made, and it is this copy that is passed to the function. Thus a function call such as f(v) by itself cannot change the stored value of v in the calling environment.

- The effect of call-by-reference can be achieved by using pointers, the address operator &, and the dereferencing operator *.

- To achieve the effect of call-by-reference, the programmer must use a pointer as a formal parameter in the header of the function definition. Then the assignment of a value to the dereferenced pointer in the body of the function can change the value of a variable in the calling environment. When such a function is called, an address is passed as an actual argument.

- The four storage classes are auto, extern, register, and static; auto is the most common. Automatic variables appear and disappear with block entry and exit. They can be hidden when an inner block redeclares an outer block identifier.

- The keyword extern means "Look for it elsewhere, either in this file or in some other."

- All variables declared outside of functions have external storage class; the keyword extern does not have to be added. These variables may be used throughout the program. They can be hidden by redeclaration, but their values cannot be destroyed.

- All functions have external storage class. The type specifier of a function is `int` unless explicitly declared otherwise. The type of the expression in the `return` statement must be compatible with the type of the function.

- The storage class `register` can be used to try to improve execution speed. It is semantically equivalent to automatic.

- The storage class `static` is used to preserve exit values of variables. It is also used to restrict the scope of external identifiers.

- Scope rules are the visibility constraints associated with identifiers. The keyword `static` used with external identifiers provides a form of privacy that is very important for program modularity. Consider the following code:

```
static void f(int k)
{
    .....
}

static int   a, b, c;
    .....
```

  The function `f()` is known throughout this file but in no other. The variables `a`, `b`, and `c` are known only in this file and only below the place where they are declared.

- External and static variables that are not explicitly initialized by the programmer are initialized to zero by the system.

Exercises

1 What is printed by the following code?

```
int   i = 5, *p = &i;

printf("%p %d %d %d %d\n",
        p, *p + 2, **&p, 3**p, **&  p+4);
```

Note that we used the `%p` format to print a pointer value. All ANSI C compilers understand this format. What happens if you change the `%p` to `%d`? In UNIX, it probably works, but in MS-DOS, it probably fails. If MS-DOS is available to you, try the `%u` format as well.

2 Consider the following code:

```
char    c1 = 'A', c2 = 'B', tmp;
char    *p = &c1, *q = &c2;

tmp = *p;
*p = *q;
*q = tmp;
```

Draw a diagram of what is in memory after each of the declarations and statements has been executed.

3 Consider the code

```
double    *p, *q;

p = 3;
q = 7 - 5 - 2;
```

Your compiler should complain about one of these lines but not the other. Explain why. If you use pointers to `int` rather than pointers to `double`, is your compiler any happier?

4 If `i` and `j` are `int`s, and `p` and `q` are pointers to `int`, which of the following assignment expressions are illegal?

```
p = &i        p = &*&i        i = (int) p        q = &p
*q = &j       i = (*&)j       i = *&*&j      i = (*p)++ + *q
```

5 Write a program with the declaration

```
char    a, b, c, *p, *q, *r;
```

that prints out the locations assigned to all these variables by your compiler. From the values that are printed out, can you tell how many bytes are allocated for each of the variables?

6 Write a function that shifts the stored value of five character variables in a circular fashion. Your function should work in the following way. Suppose that `c1`, `c2`, . . ., `c5` are variables of type `char`, and suppose that the values of these variables are `'A'`, `'B'`, . . ., `'E'`, respectively. The function call `shift(&c1, &c2, &c3, &c4, &c5)` should cause the variables `c1`, `c2`, . . ., `c5` to have the values `'B'`, `'C'`, `'D'`, `'E'`, `'A'`, respectively. Your function definition should start as follows:

```
void shift(char *p1, char *p2, char *p3, char *p4, char *p5)
{
   .....
```

Test your function by calling it five times and printing out, in turn, BCDEA, CDEAB, DEABC, EABCD, and ABCDE.

7 Write a function that orders the stored values of three characters. Suppose, for example, that `c1`, `c2`, and `c3` are character variables having the values `'C'`, `'B'`, and `'D'`, respectively. Then the function call `order_chars(&c1, &c2, &c3)` should cause the stored values of `c1`, `c2`, and `c3` to be `'B'`, `'C'`, and `'D'`, respectively. Write a program that tests your function.

8 The program we wrote to process characters in Section 8.9, "An Example: Processing Characters," on page 281, is short enough that one could do away with the function `process()` and write all the code in `main()`. Of course, we did the work in `process()` to illustrate how pointers can be used. Rewrite the program using no pointers.

9 In Section C.4, "Packing and Unpacking," on page 589, we wrote the function `unpack()`. It can unpack one byte at a time from an `int`. Rewrite the function so it unpacks all the bytes at once. On a machine with 4-byte words, begin your function as follows:

```
/* Unpack the packed int p into 4 characters. */

void unpack(int p, char *pa, char *pb, char *pc,
            char *pd)
{
   unsigned   mask = 255;    /* turn on low-order byte */
   .....
```

Write a program to check your function. Your program should use the `bit_print()` function (see Section C.3, "Printing an int Bitwise," on page 586).

10 How many bytes are used by your C system to store pointer variables? Does it take less space to store a pointer to `char` than a pointer to `long double`? Use the `sizeof` operator to find out. Write a program that prints a table of values that shows the number of bytes needed to store a pointer to each of the fundamental types.

11 Because the symbol * represents both the indirection operator and the multiplication operator, it is not always immediately clear what is intended. Consider the following code:

```
int   i = 2, j = 4, k = 6;
int   *p = &i, *q = &j, *r = &k;

printf("%d\n",  *  p  *  *  q  *  *  r);
printf("%d\n",  ++  *  p  *  --  *  q  *  ++  *  r);
```

What is printed? Write down your answers; then execute the code to check them. Rewrite the expressions in the `printf()` statements in two ways. First, remove all the blanks in the two expressions. Does your compiler get confused when you do this? Second, leave a blank around each binary operator, but remove the blanks between any unary operator and whatever it is operating on. Does your compiler produce the same answers as before? If you think formatting is for wimps, change all the multiplication operators to division and redo this exercise. It may give you a surprise!

12 The following program has a conceptual mistake; see if you can spot it.

```
#include <stdio.h>

#define   LUCKY_NUMBER   777

int main(void)
{
   int   *p = LUCKY_NUMBER;

   printf("Is this my lucky number?  %d\n", *p);
   return 0;
}
```

On our system the program produces the following output:

```
Is this my lucky number?  24864
```

Can you explain this output?

13 Just as there are pointers to `int`, there are pointers to pointers to `int`. Write a test program with the declaration

```
int   v = 7, *p = &v, **q = &p;
```

The identifier `q` is a pointer to pointer to `int`, and its initial value is the address of `p`. To test this concept, use the statement

```
printf("%d\n%d\n%d\n", q, *q, **q);
```

to print some values. Does an expression such as `q == &p` make sense? Include this expression in your test program. *Caution:* If you are using the MS-DOS operating system, you must be careful when printing pointer values. The `%p` format can be expected to work, and of course it works in UNIX as well. The `%u` format works in the small memory model but not in the larger memory models. Try the following code:

```
printf("%p\n%p\n%d\n", q, *q, **q);
printf("---\n");
printf("%u\n%u\n%u\n", q, *q, **q);
```

When you examine your output, you can tell if something is wrong.

14 In this exercise we continue with the ideas discussed in the previous exercise. Consider the code

```
int   v = 7, *p = &v, **q = &p;

printf("%d\n%d\n%d\n%d\n%d\n%d\n%d\n%d\n%d\n",
   &v, *&v, &p, *&p, **&p, &q, *&q, **&q, ***&q);
```

The output has an interesting pattern. Can you explain why some of the numbers repeat? Notice that we have used the combination `*&` but not `&*`. Are there situations in which `&*` is semantically correct? *Caution:* In MS-DOS, try replacing all the `%d` formats with `%u`. If that does not seem right, replace all the `%d` formats with `%p`, except for the second, fifth, and last.

15 Extend the ideas presented in the previous exercise by writing a test program where `r` is declared to be a pointer to pointer to pointer to `int`.

16 In ANSI C, at most one storage class can be specified in a declaration. What happens when you try the following code on your system?

```
#include <stdio.h>

static extern int   a = 1;

int main(void)
{
   printf("a = %d\n", a);
   return 0;
}
```

The point of this exercise is that you want to use a static external variable, but the compiler does not let you declare one. What should you do?

17 If you use `const` in a declaration and then try to perform an inappropriate initialization or assignment, your compiler complains. Whether it is an error or a warning is system-dependent. Try the following code on your system:

```
const double   x = 7.7;
double         *p = &x;   /* compiler error or warning? */

printf("x = %g\n", *p);
```

Rewrite the code keeping `const`, but at the same time make the compiler happy.

18 C++: Redo exercise 6, the circular shift, using reference declarations.

19 C++: Redo the random number generator in Section 8.7, "Static External Variables," on page 280, as an inline C++ function and compare the time it takes to generate 100,000 random numbers in C as an ordinary function versus in C++ as an inline function. In light of these results, it is often claimed that C++ in many cases is actually more efficient than C.

20 C++: Write a `mem_swap(void* x, void* y, size_t n)` generic routine. The routine swaps `n` bytes starting at memory address `x` with `n` bytes starting at memory address `y`. The function should assert that `n` is a suitable value and that the swap does not occur with an overlap.

21 Java: To call one method from another method in the same class in Java, we write the name of the called method and an appropriate list of arguments within parentheses. These arguments must *match in number and type* the parameters in the parameter list in the method definition. The arguments are passed *call-by-value.* That is, each argument is evaluated, and its *value* is used within the called method to initialize the corresponding formal parameter. Thus, if a variable is passed to a method, the stored value of that variable in the calling environment won't be changed. In the following example, we attempt to swap the values of two local variables using a method similar to that in Section 8.4, "Call-by-Reference," on page 271.

```
//FailedSwap.java - Call-By-Value test   Java by Dissection
page 113.
class FailedSwap {
  public static void main(String[] args) {
    int numOne = 1, numTwo = 2;
    swap(numOne, numTwo);
    System.out.println("numOne = " + numOne);
    System.out.println("numTwo = " + numTwo);
  }
```

```
    static void swap(int x, int y) {
      int temp;
      System.out.println("x = " + x);
      System.out.println("y = " + y);
      temp = x;
      x = y;
      y = temp;
      System.out.println("x = " + x);
      System.out.println("y = " + y);
    }
  }
```

The output of this program is

```
x = 1
y = 2
x = 2
y = 1
numOne = 1
numTwo = 2
```

Note that, although we successfully swapped the values of the formal parameters, `x` and `y`, doing so had no effect on the actual arguments, `numOne` and `numTwo`. The formal parameters are effectively local variables in the method `swap()` that have their values initialized with the values of the corresponding actual arguments. Five memory locations are identified in this program for storing integers: `numOne`, `numTwo`, `x`, `y`, and `temp`.

In Java we can't write a method `swap()` similar to the one presented that actually swaps the values of two primitive type variables passed as parameters. If `swap()` had actually caused the values in `main()` to change, then we would have said that it achieved its result by causing a *side effect* instead of returning a value. The side effect would have been the changes in the two actual arguments. Any method with a return type of `void` must cause some side effect or else be completely useless. Write a C program that fails in the same way as this Java program.

Arrays and Pointers

Chapter 9

An array is a sequence of data items that are of the same type, that can be indexed, and that are stored contiguously. Typically, arrays are a data type that is used to represent a large number of homogeneous values. The elements of an array are accessed by the use of subscripts. Arrays of all types are possible, including arrays of arrays. Strings are just arrays of characters, but they are sufficiently important to be treated separately in the next chapter.

A typical array declaration allocates memory starting from a base address. The array name is in effect a pointer constant to this base address. This chapter carefully explains this relationship of array to address. Another key point covered is how to pass arrays as parameters to functions. A number of carefully worked examples illustrate these concepts.

9.1 One-Dimensional Arrays

Programs often use homogeneous data. For example, if we want to manipulate some grades, we might declare

```
int   grade0, grade1, grade2;
```

However, if the number of grades is large, it is cumbersome to represent and manipulate the data by means of unique identifiers. Instead, we can use an array, which is a derived type. Individual elements of the array are accessed using a subscript, also called an *index*. The brackets `[ ]` are used to contain the subscripts of an array. To use `grade[0]`, `grade[1]`, and `grade[2]` in a program, we declare

```
int   grade[3];
```

where the integer 3 in the declaration represents the size of the array, or the number of elements in the array. The indexing of array elements always starts at `0`. This is a characteristic feature of the C language.

A one-dimensional array declaration is a type followed by an identifier with a bracketed constant integral expression. The value of the constant expression, which must be positive, is the size of the array; it specifies the number of elements in the array. To store the elements of the array, the compiler assigns an appropriate amount of memory, starting from a base address.

To illustrate some of these ideas, let us write a small program that fills an array, prints out values, and sums the elements of the array.

```
/*Fill and Print an array. */
#include <stdio.h>

#define   N   5

int main(void)
{
   int   a[N];        /* allocate space for a[0] to a[4] */
   int   i, sum = 0;

   for (i = 0; i < N; ++i)                /* fill the array */
      a[i] = 7 + i * i;
   for (i = 0; i < N; ++i)                /* print the array */
      printf("a[%d] = %d    ", i, a[i]);
   for (i = 0; i < N; ++i)                /* sum the elements */
      sum += a[i];
   printf("\nsum = %d\n", sum);           /* print the sum */
   return 0;
}
```

The output of this program is

```
a[0] = 7    a[1] = 8    a[2] = 11    a[3] = 16    a[4] = 23
sum = 65
```

The array a requires space in memory to store four integer values. Let us suppose our machine stores an `int` in four bytes. If `a[0]` is stored at location 1000, then the remaining array elements are stored successively at locations 1004, 1008, 1012, and 1016.

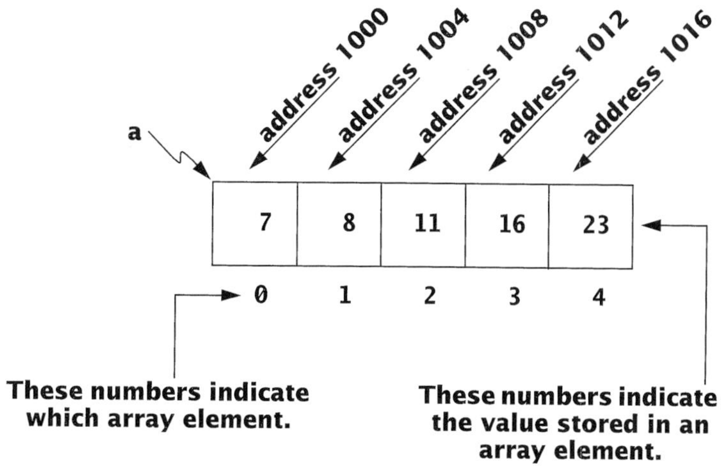

Dissection of Fill_and_Print Program

- ```
  #define   N   5

  int main(void)
  {
     int   a[N];        /* allocate space for a[0] to a[4] */
     int   i, sum = 0;
  ```

It is considered good programming practice to define the size of an array as a symbolic constant. Because much of the code may depend on this value, it is convenient to be able to change a single `#define` line to process arrays of different sizes. Notice how `a[N]` allocates memory for 5 `int` elements. The variable `i` is typically used for an int variable that indexes an array.

- ```
     for (i = 0; i < N; ++i)           /* fill the array */
        a[i] = 7 + i * i;
  ```

This is the critical idiom for processing all the array elements. The index variable starts with element `0` and proceeds to index value `N-1`. Note it would be wrong to use `i <= N`. This would lead to accessing a[5], an element that is one past the end of the array.

```
■     for (i = 0; i < N; ++i)              /* print the array */
         printf("a[%d] = %d    ", i, a[i]);
      for (i = 0; i < N; ++i)              /* sum the elements */
         sum += a[i];
```

Again we have the `for` loop idiom for processing each element in turn.

Initialization

Arrays may be of storage class automatic, external, static, or constant but not register. As with simple variables, arrays can be initialized within a declaration. An *array initializer* is a sequence of initializing values written as a brace-enclosed, comma-separated list. An example is

```
float   x[7] = {-1.1, 0.2, 33.0, 4.4, 5.05, 0.0, 7.7};
```

This initializes `x[0]` to `-1.1`, `x[1]` to `0.2`, and so forth. When a list of initializers is shorter than the number of array elements to be initialized, the remaining elements are initialized to zero. If an external or static array is not initialized, then the system initializes all elements to zero automatically. Uninitialized automatic and constant arrays start with garbage values—that is, with arbitrary values that happen to be in memory when the array is allocated. In traditional C, only external and static arrays could be initialized using an array initializer. ANSI C allows automatic and constant arrays to be initialized as well.

If an array is declared without a size and is initialized to a series of values, it is implicitly given the size of the number of initializers. Thus the following declarations are equivalent:

```
int a[] = {3, 4, 5, 6};      and      int a[4] = {3, 4, 5, 6};
```

Subscripting

Assume that a declaration of the form

```
int   i, a[size];
```

has been made. Then we can write `a[i]` to access an element of the array. More generally, we may write `a[`*expr*`]`, where *expr* is an integral expression, to access an element of the array. We call *expr* a *subscript*, or *index*, of `a`. The value of a subscript must lie in the range 0 to *size* - 1. An array subscript value outside this range causes a run-time error. This is a common programming error called *overrunning the bounds of the array* or *subscript out of bounds*. The effect of the error is system-dependent and can be quite confusing. One frequent result is that the value of some unrelated variable is returned or modified. Thus the programmer must ensure that all subscripts stay within bounds.

"GEE, MISS FEENEY, IF I HAVE THE SAME TYPE OF SPELLING ERROR ON EACH PAGE, DOES THAT MAKE IT A LEGAL C-ARRAY OF SPELLING ERRORS?"

9.2 An Example: Counting Each Letter Separately

In previous chapters we showed how to count digits, letters, and so on. By using an array, we can easily count the occurrence of each uppercase letter. Here is a program that does this:

```
/* Count each uppercase letter separately. */

#include <stdio.h>
#include <ctype.h>
```

```
int main(void)
{
   int   c, i, letter[26];

   for (i = 0; i < 26; ++i)          /* init array to zero*/
      letter[i] = 0;
   while ((c = getchar()) != EOF)    /* count the letters */
      if (isupper(c))
         ++letter[c - 'A'];
   for (i = 0; i < 26; ++i) {        /* print the results */
      if (i % 6 == 0)
         printf("\n");
      printf("%4c:%3d", 'A' + i, letter[i]);
   }
   printf("\n\n");
   return 0;
}
```

Among our files is one that contains the current version of this chapter. If we compile the program into *cnt_abc* and then give the command

cnt_abc < chapter9

the following appears on the screen:

```
A: 75   B: 52   C:219   D: 14   E:121   F: 13
G:  9   H: 13   I:121   J:  1   K:  1   L: 39
M: 25   N: 44   O: 38   P:243   Q:  1   R: 37
S: 73   T: 96   U:  7   V:  3   W: 17   X:  9
Y: 11   Z: 27
```

Dissection of the cnt_abc Program

■ `int   c, i, letter[26];`

The count for each of the 26 capital letters is stored in the array `letter`. Remember, the elements of the array are `letter[0]`, `letter[1]`, . . . , `letter[25]`. Forgetting that array subscripting starts at 0 causes many errors. The variable `i` is used as a subscript.

■
```
for (i = 0; i < 26; ++i)              /* init array to zero*/
   letter[i] = 0;
```

Automatic arrays must be explicitly initialized. This `for` loop follows a standard pattern for processing all the elements of an array. It is a C programming cliché. The subscripting variable is initialized to 0. The termination test is to see if the upper bound is exceeded.

■
```
while ((c = getchar()) != EOF)     /* count the letters */
   if (isupper(c))
      ++letter[c - 'A'];
```

The library function `getchar()` is used repeatedly to read a character in the input stream and assign its value to `c`. The `while` loop is exited when the end-of-file sentinel is detected. The macro `isupper()` from `<ctype.h>` is used to test whether `c` is an uppercase letter. If it is, then an appropriate element of the array `letter` is incremented.

■
```
++letter[c - 'A'];
```

This line of code is system-dependent. On ASCII machines the expression `c - 'A'` has the value 0 if `c` has the value `'A'`, 1 if `c` has the value `'B'`, and so forth. Thus the uppercase letter value of `c` is mapped into the range of values 0 to 25. Because brackets have higher precedence than ++, an equivalent statement is

```
++(letter[c - 'A']);
```

Thus we see that `letter[0]` is incremented if `c` has the value `'A'`, `letter[1]` is incremented if `c` has the value `'B'`, and so forth.

■
```
for (i = 0; i < 26; ++i) {          /* print the results */
   if (i % 6 == 0)
      printf("\n");
   printf("%4c:%3d", 'A' + i, letter[i]);
}
```

The same `for` loop cliché is used to process the array `letter`. Every sixth time through the loop, a newline is printed. As `i` runs from 0 to 25, the expression `'A' + i` is used to print A through Z, with the letter followed by a colon and count.

9.3 The Relationship between Arrays and Pointers

An array name by itself is an address, or pointer value, and pointers and arrays are almost identical in terms of how they are used to access memory. However, there are differences, and these differences are subtle and important. A pointer is a variable that takes addresses as values. An array name is a particular fixed address that can be thought of as a constant pointer. When an array is declared, the compiler must allocate a base address and a sufficient amount of storage to contain all the elements of the array. The base address of the array is the initial location in memory where the array is stored; it is the address of the first element (index 0) of the array. Suppose we write the declaration

```
#define   N   100

int   a[N], *p;
```

and the system causes memory bytes numbered 300, 304, 308, . . . , 696 to be the addresses of `a[0], a[1], a[2], ... , a[99]`, respectively, with location 300 being the base address of a. The two statements

```
    p = a;        and        p = &a[0];
```

are equivalent and would assign 300 to p. Pointer arithmetic provides an alternative to array indexing. The two statements

```
    p = a + 1;        and        p = &a[1];
```

are equivalent and would assign 304 to p. Assuming that the elements of a have been assigned values, we can use the following code to sum the array.

```
sum = 0;
for (p = a; p < &a[N]; ++p)
   sum += *p;
```

In this loop the pointer variable p is initialized to the base address of the array a. Then the successive values of p are equivalent to `&a[0]`, `&a[1]`, . . ., `&a[N-1]`. In general, if `i` is a variable of type `int`, then `p + i` is the *i*th offset from the address p. In a similar manner, `a + i` is the *i*th offset from the base address of the array a. Here is another way to sum the array:

```
sum = 0;
for (i = 0; i < N; ++i)
   sum += *(a + i);
```

Just as the expression `*(a + i)` is equivalent to `a[i]`, so the expression `*(p + i)` is equivalent to `p[i]`. Here is a third way to sum the array:

```
p = a;
sum = 0;
for (i = 0; i < N; ++i)
    sum += p[i];
```

Although in many ways arrays and pointers can be treated alike, there is one essential difference. Because the array a is a constant pointer and not a variable, expressions such as

```
a = p        ++a        a += 2
```

are illegal. We cannot change the address of a.

9.4 Pointer Arithmetic and Element Size

Pointer arithmetic is one of the powerful features of C. If the variable p is a pointer to a particular type, then the expression `p + 1` yields the correct machine address for storing or accessing the next variable of that type. In a similar fashion, pointer expressions such as `p + i` and `++p` and `p += i` all make sense. If p and q are both pointing to elements of an array, then `p - q` yields the `int` value representing the number of array elements between p and q. Even though pointer expressions and arithmetic expressions have a similar appearance, there is a critical difference in interpretation between the two types of expressions. The following code illustrates the difference:.

```
#include <sdtio.h>

int main(void)
{
    double   a[2], *p, *q;

    p = &a[0];                  /* points at base of array   */
    q = p + 1;                  /* equivalent to q = &a[1]; */

    printf("%d\n", q - p);                 /* 1 is printed */
    printf("%d\n", (int) q - (int) p);     /* 8 is printed */
    return 0;
}
```

What is printed by the last statement is system-dependent. On many systems a `double` is stored in eight bytes. Hence, the difference between the two machine addresses interpreted as integers is 8.

9.5 Passing Arrays to Functions

In a function definition, a formal parameter that is declared as an array is actually a pointer. When an array is being passed, its base address is passed call-by-value. The array elements themselves are not copied. As a notational convenience, the compiler allows array bracket notation to be used in declaring pointers as parameters. To illustrate this, we write a function that sums the elements of an array of type `int`.

```
int sum(int a[], int n)    /* n is the size of the array */
{
   int   i, s = 0;

   for (i = 0; i < n; ++i)
      s += a[i];
   return s;
}
```

As part of the header of a function definition, the declaration

`int a[];`   is equivalent to   `int *a;`

On the other hand, as declarations within the body of a function, these are *not* equivalent. The first creates a constant pointer (and no storage), whereas the second creates a pointer variable.

Suppose `v` has been declared to be an array with 100 elements of type `int`. After the elements have been assigned values, we can use the preceding function `sum()` to add various elements of `v`. The following table illustrates some of the possibilities.

Various ways that sum() might be called	
Invocation	**What gets computed and returned**
`sum(v, 100)`	`v[0] + v[1] + ····· + v[99]`
`sum(v, 88)`	`v[0] + v[1] + ····· + v[87]`
`sum(&v[7], k - 7)`	`v[7] + v[8] + ····· + v[k - 1]`
`sum(v + 7, 2 * k)`	`v[7] + v[8] + ····· + v[2 * k + 6]`

The last function call illustrates again the use of pointer arithmetic. The base address of `v` is offset by 7, and `sum()` initializes the local pointer variable `a` to this address. This causes all address calculations inside the function call to be similarly offset.

9.6 A Sorting Algorithm: Bubble Sort

Algorithms that order information are critical to searching large databases. Think of the dictionary or the telephone book. In both cases it is relatively easy and convenient to look up information because the information is sorted in alphabetic, or lexicographic, order. Sorting is a very useful problem-solving technique. Moreover, the question of how to sort efficiently is an important area of study in its own right.

Efficient sorting algorithms typically require on the order of $n \log n$ comparisons to sort an array with n elements. A bubble sort is inefficient because it requires n^2 comparisons; nonetheless, for small arrays, its performance is usually acceptable. After we present the code for `bubble()`, we illustrate in detail how the function works on a particular array of integers. We use the function `swap()`, written in Section 8.4, "Call-by-Reference," on page 271.

```
void  swap(int *, int *);

void bubble(int a[], int n)      /* n is the size of a[] */
{
   int   i, j;

   for (i = 0; i < n - 1; ++i)
      for (j = n - 1; i < j; --j)
       if (a[j-1] > a[j])
          swap(&a[j-1], &a[j]);
}
```

Suppose we declare

```
int   a[] = {7, 3, 66, 3, -5, 22, -77, 2};
```

and then invoke `bubble(a, 8)`. The following table shows the elements of the array `a[]` after each pass of the outer loop.

Elements of array a[] after each pass								
Unordered data	7	3	66	3	-5	22	-77	2
First pass	-77	7	3	66	3	-5	22	2
Second pass	-77	-5	7	3	66	3	2	22
Third pass	-77	-5	2	7	3	66	3	22
Fourth pass	-77	-5	2	3	7	3	66	22
Fifth pass	-77	-5	2	3	3	7	22	66
Sixth pass	-77	-5	2	3	3	7	22	66
Seventh pass	-77	-5	2	3	3	7	22	66

At the start of the first pass, `a[6]` is compared with `a[7]`. Because the values are in order, they are not exchanged. Then `a[5]` is compared with `a[6]`, and because these values are out of order, they are exchanged. Then `a[4]` is compared with `a[5]`, and so forth. Adjacent out-of-order values are exchanged. The effect of the first pass is to "bubble" the smallest value in the array into the element `a[0]`. In the second pass, `a[0]` is not examined and is therefore left unchanged, while `a[6]` is compared first with `a[7]`, and so forth. After the second pass, the next to the smallest value is in `a[1]`. Because each pass bubbles the next smallest element to its appropriate array position, the algorithm, after `n - 1` passes, has put all the elements in order. Notice that in this example all the elements have been ordered after the fifth pass. It is possible to modify the algorithm to terminate earlier by adding a variable that detects if no exchanges are made in a given pass (see exercise 7 on page 331).

9.7 Two-Dimensional Arrays

The C language allows arrays of any type, including arrays of arrays. With two bracket pairs, we obtain a two-dimensional array. To obtain arrays of higher dimension, we simply continue to add brackets. With each bracket pair, we add another array dimension.

Array dimensions	
Declarations of arrays	**Remarks**
`int a[100];`	a one-dimensional array
`int b[2][7];`	a two-dimensional array
`int c[5][3][2];`	a three-dimensional array

A *k*-dimensional array has a size for each of its *k* dimensions. If we let s*i* represent the size of the array's *i*th dimension, then the declaration of the array allocates space for $s_1 \times s_2 \times \cdots\cdots \times s_k$ elements. In the preceding table, b has 2×7 elements, and c has $5 \times 3 \times 2$ elements. Starting at the base address of the array, all the array elements are stored contiguously in memory.

Even though array elements are stored contiguously one after the other, it is often convenient to think of a two-dimensional array as a rectangular collection of elements with rows and columns. For example, if we declare

```
int   a[3][5];
```

then we can think of the array elements arranged as follows:

	col 1	col 2	col 3	col 4	col 5
row 1	a[0][0]	a[0][1]	a[0][2]	a[0][3]	a[0][4]
row 2	a[1][0]	a[1][1]	a[1][2]	a[1][3]	a[1][4]
row 3	a[2][0]	a[2][1]	a[2][2]	a[2][3]	a[2][4]

To illustrate these ideas, let us write a program that fills a two-dimensional array, prints out values, and sums the elements of the array.

```
#include <stdio.h>

#define   M   3      /* number of rows */
#define   N   4      /* number of columns */
```

```
int main(void)
{
   int   a[M][N], i, j, sum = 0;

   for (i = 0; i < M; ++i)           /* fill the array */
      for (j = 0; j < N; ++j)
         a[i][j] = i + j;
   for (i = 0; i < M; ++i) {         /* print array values */
      for (j = 0; j < N; ++j)
         printf("a[%d][%d] = %d      ", i, j, a[i][j]);
      printf("\n");
   }
   for (i = 0; i < M; ++i)           /* sum the array */
      for (j = 0; j < N; ++j)
         sum += a[i][j];
   printf("\nsum = %d\n\n", sum);
   return 0;
}
```

The output of this program is

```
a[0][0] = 0     a[0][1] = 1     a[0][2] = 2     a[0][3] = 3
a[1][0] = 1     a[1][1] = 2     a[1][2] = 3     a[1][3] = 4
a[2][0] = 2     a[2][1] = 3     a[2][2] = 4     a[2][3] = 5

sum = 30
```

In processing every element of a multidimensional array, each dimension requires a single `for` loop.

Because of the relationship between arrays and pointers, there are numerous ways to access elements of a two-dimensional array.

Expressions equivalent to `a[i][j]`
`*(a[i] + j)`
`(*(a + i))[j]`
`*((*(a + i)) + j)`
`*(&a[0][0] + 5*i + j)`

The parentheses are necessary because the brackets `[ ]` have higher precedence than the indirection operator `*`. We can think of `a[i]` as the *i*th row of `a` (counting from 0), and we can think of `a[i][j]` as the element in the *i*th row, *j*th column of the array (counting from 0). The array name `a` by itself is equivalent to `&a[0]`; it is a pointer to an array of five `int`s. The base address of the array is `&a[0][0]`, not `a`. Starting at the base address of the array, the compiler allocates contiguous space for 15 `int`s. For any array, the mapping between pointer values and array indices is called the *storage mapping function.* For the array `a`, the storage mapping function is specified by noting that

```
a[i][j]        is equivalent to        *(&a[0][0] + 5*i + j)
```

When a multidimensional array is a formal parameter in a function definition, all sizes except the first must be specified, so that the compiler can determine the correct storage mapping function. After the elements of the array a just given have been assigned values, the following function can be used to sum the elements of the array. Note carefully that the column size must be specified.

```
int sum(int a[][5])
{
   int   i, j, sum = 0;

   for (i = 0; i < 3; ++i)
      for (j = 0; j < 5; ++j)
         sum += a[i][j];
   return sum;
}
```

In the header of the function definition, the following parameter declarations are equivalent:

```
int a[][5]      int (*a)[5]      int a[3][5]
```

Because of operator precedence, the parentheses are necessary. The constant 3 acts as a reminder to human readers of the code, but the compiler disregards it.

There are a number of ways to initialize a two-dimensional array. The following three initializations are equivalent:

```
int   a[2][3] = {1, 2, 3, 4, 5, 6};
int   a[2][3] = {{1, 2, 3}, {4, 5, 6}};
int   a[ ][3] = {{1, 2, 3}, {4, 5, 6}};
```

If there are no inner braces, then each of the array elements `a[0][0]`, `a[0][1]`, . . ., `a[1][2]` is initialized in turn. Note that the indexing is by rows. If there are fewer initializers than elements in the array, then the remaining elements are initialized to zero. If the first bracket pair is empty, then the compiler takes the size from the number of inner brace pairs. All sizes except the first must be given explicitly. A classic use of two-dimensional arrays is a matrix of *n* by *n* elements.

A chessboard can be easily represented as a two-dimensional array. The pieces could be named using typedefs.

This data structure is an important scientific abstract data type and is central to all of linear algebra.We show how to `typedef` this type and perform the basic computation of multiplying two matrices in Section 12.7, "The Use of `typedef`," on page 405.

9.8 Multidimensional Arrays

Arrays of dimension higher than two work in a similar fashion. Let us describe how three-dimensional arrays work. If we declare

```
int   a[7][9][2];
```

the compiler allocates space for $7 \times 9 \times 2$ contiguous `int`s. The base address of the array is `&a[0][0][0]`, and the storage mapping function is specified by noting that

`a[i][j][k]`   is equivalent to   `*(&a[0][0][0] + 9*2*i + 2*j + k)`

If an expression such as `a[i][j][k]` is used in a program, the compiler uses the storage mapping function to generate object code to access the correct array element in memory. Although normally it is not necessary to do so, the programmer can use of storage mapping function directly. Here is a function that sums the elements of the array `a`:

```
int sum(int a[][9][2])
{
   int   i, j, k, sum = 0;

   for (i = 0; i < 7; ++i)
      for (j = 0; j < 9; ++j)
         for (k = 0; k < 2; ++k)
            sum += a[i][j][k];
   return sum;
}
```

In the header of the function definition, the following parameter declarations are equivalent:

```
int a[][9][2]        int a[7][9][2]       int (*a)[9][2]
```

The constant 7 acts as a reminder to human readers of the code, but the compiler disregards it. The other two constants are needed by the compiler to generate the correct storage mapping function.

There are a number of ways to initialize a multidimensional array. Consider the initialization

```
int   a[2][2][3] = {
         {{1, 1, 0}, {2, 0, 0}},
         {{3, 0, 0}, {4, 4, 0}}
      };
```

An equivalent initialization is given by

```
int   a[][2][3] = {{{1, 1}, {2}}, {{3}, {4, 4}}};
```

If the initializers are fully and consistently braced, then wherever there is an insufficient number of initializers listed, the remaining elements are initialized to zero.

In general, if an array of storage class automatic is not explicitly initialized, then array elements start with garbage values. Static and external arrays, however, are initialized to zero by default. Here is a simple way to initialize all array elements to zero:

```
int   a[2][2][3] = {0};
```

9.9 Dynamic Memory Allocation

C provides `calloc()` ("contiguous allocation") and `malloc()` ("memory allocation") in the standard library for dynamic memory allocation. The function prototypes are in *stdlib.h*. Rather than having an array size given by a specific constant in a program, it may be desirable to allow the user to input the array size or to obtain the array size in a computation. A function call of the form

`calloc( n, object_size )`

returns a pointer to enough space in memory to store *n* objects, each of *object_size* bytes. Both *n* and *object_size* should be positive. If the system is unable to allocate the requested memory, the pointer value `NULL` is returned.

In ANSI C, the type `size_t` is given by a `typedef` in *stdlib.h*. Typically, the type is *unsigned*, but it can vary from one system to another. This type definition is used in the function prototypes for `calloc()` and `malloc()`:

```
void    *calloc(size_t, size_t);
void    *malloc(size_t);
```

Because the return pointer has type `void *`, it can be assigned to other pointers without casting. The storage set aside by `calloc()` is automatically initialized to zero, whereas the storage set aside by `malloc()` is not initialized and therefore starts with garbage values. To illustrate the use of `calloc()`, let us write a small program that prompts the user to input an array size interactively.

```
#include <stdio.h>
#include <stdlib.h>

int main(void)
{
   int   *a, i, n, sum = 0;
   printf("\n%s",
      "An array will be created dynamically.\n\n"
      "Input an array size n followed by n integers:  ");
   scanf("%d", &n);
   a = calloc(n, sizeof(int));   /* get space for n ints */
   for (i = 0; i < n; ++i)
      scanf("%d", &a[i]);
   for (i = 0; i < n; ++i)
      sum += a[i];
   free(a);                      /* free the space */
   printf("\n%s%7d\n%s%7d\n\n",
      " Number of elements:", n,
      "Sum of the elements:", sum);
   return 0;
}
```

Notice that we invoked `free(a)` to release the space allocated by `calloc()` back to the system. In this small program, this is not necessary; the space is released when the program exits. The function prototype for `free()` is given in *stdlib.h* as

```
void    free(void *ptr);
```

Space allocated by `calloc()` and `malloc()` remains in use for the duration of the program unless it is explicitly released by the programmer. Space is *not* released on function exit.

In the preceding program, we allocated space dynamically for the array `a` by using `calloc()`. Here is the line we typed:

```
a = calloc(n, sizeof(int));   /* get space for n ints */
```

Instead of using `calloc()`, we could have used `malloc()`. To do so we would write

```
a = malloc(n * sizeof(int));   /* get space for n ints */
```

The only difference is that `malloc()` does not initialize the allocated space to zero. Because our program did not require the array to be initialized, we could just as well have used `malloc()`. For arrays, however, we tend to use `calloc()`.

9.10 Style

As the examples in this chapter have shown, it is often desirable to use a symbolic constant to define the size of an array. This constant allows the programmer to make a single modification if code is needed to process an array of a different size.

A `for` loop that is to be used to do ten things repetitively can be written

```
for (i = 1; i <= 10; ++i)
   .....
```

or it can be written

```
for (i = 0; i < 10; ++i)
   .....
```

Which form is used depends on just what is in the body of the loop. However, in some cases either form can be used. C programmers generally favor the second form because, when dealing with arrays, the second form is the correct programming idiom. Because arrays are used extensively in programming tasks, most experienced C programmers begin counting from 0 rather than 1.

A generally important style consideration is to structure a program so that each elementary task is accomplished by its own function. This approach is at the heart of structured programming. However, this can lead to inefficient code when processing arrays. Let us look at a specific example.

```
/* Compute various statistics. */

#include <stdio.h>

#define   N   10                          /* size of the array */

double   average(double *, int);
double   maximum(double *, int);
double   sum(double *, int);

int main(void)
{
   int      i;
   double   a[N];

   printf("Input %d numbers:  ", N);
   for (i = 0; i < N; ++i)
      scanf("%lf", &a[i]);
   printf("\n%s%5d\n%s%7.1f\n%s%7.1f\n%s%7.1f\n\n",
      "      Array size:", N,
      "Maximum element:", maximum(a, N),
      "         Average:", average(a, N),
      "             Sum:", sum(a, N));
   return 0;
}
```

We have written main() so that it calls three other functions, each one computing a desired value. Let us write these functions next.

```
double maximum(double a[], int n)
{
   int      i;
   double   max = a[0];

   for (i = 0; i < n; ++i)
      if (max < a[i])
         max = a[i];
   return max;
}

double average(double a[], int n)
{
   return (sum(a, n) / (double) n);
}
```

```
double sum(double a[], int n)
{
   int      i;
   double   s = 0.0;

   for (i = 0; i < n; ++i)
      s += a[i];
   return s;
}
```

Two of these three functions use a `for` loop to process the elements of an array, and `average()` calls `sum()` to do its work. For the sake of efficiency, we could restructure our program as follows. First we rewrite `main()`.

```
/* Compute various statistics more efficiently. */

#include <stdio.h>

#define   N   10

void   stats(double *, int, double *, double *, double *);

int main(void)
{
   int      i;
   double   a[N], average, max, sum;

   printf("Input %d numbers:  ", N);
   for (i = 0; i < N; ++i)
      scanf("%lf", &a[i]);
   stats(a, N, &average, &max, &sum);
   printf("\n%s%5d\n%s%7.1f\n%s%7.1f\n%s%7.1f\n\n",
      "      Array size:", N,
      "Maximum element:", max,
      "         Average:", average,
      "             Sum:", sum);
   return 0;
}
```

Now we write the function `stats()`, using a single `for` loop to compute all the desired values.

```
void stats(double a[], int n,
           double *p_average,
           double *p_max,
           double *p_sum)
{
   int   i;

   *p_max = *p_sum = a[0];
   for (i = 1; i < n; ++i) {
      *p_sum += a[i];
      if (*p_max < a[i])
         *p_max = a[i];
   }
   *p_average = *p_sum / (double) n;
}
```

The second version avoids repeated function call overhead. It calls `stats()` once in place of the 3 × N function calls of the first version. This example is so small that efficiency is not really an issue, but, when code is to be used in a serious working environment, the ideas that we have presented are often relevant. In general, along with clarity and correctness, efficiency is an important consideration in programming.

9.11 Common Programming Errors

The most common programming error with arrays is using a subscript value that is out of bounds. Suppose `10` is the size of an array `a[]` of integers. If we were to write

```
sum = 0;
for (i = 1; i <= 10; ++i)
   sum += a[i];
```

we would get an error. The value at the address corresponding to `a[10]` would be used, but the value in memory at this address would be unpredictable.

In many programming languages, when an array of size n is declared, the corresponding subscript range is from 1 to n. It is very important to remember that C uses zero as a lower bound and $n - 1$ as an upper bound. Bounds checking is an important programming skill to cultivate. It is often useful to manually simulate programs on small arrays before processing very large arrays.

When the programmer uses dynamic memory allocation, a common programming error is to forget to release space. In small programs this usually is not a problem. If, however, we are in a loop and we repeatedly allocate space, use it, and then forget to release it, the program can fail unexpectedly because no more space is available.

9.12 System Considerations

If efficiency is an issue, programmers prefer

```
malloc(n * sizeof(something))
```

instead of

```
calloc(n, sizeof(something))
```

unless the allocated space must be initialized to zero. For most programs, the difference in execution time is not noticeable.

Space in memory is a limited resource. When `calloc()` or `malloc()` is invoked to allocate space dynamically, the programmer should check that the call succeeded. The following code shows how this can be done with `calloc()`:

```
int   *a, n;

 .....                            /* get n from somewhere */
if ((a = calloc(n, sizeof(int))) == NULL) {
   printf("\nERROR: calloc() failed - bye!\n\n");
   exit(1);
}
```

If we are writing a lot of code and need to call `calloc()` and `malloc()` repeatedly, then we write graceful versions of these functions. Here is a graceful version of `calloc()`:

```
/* graceful function */
void *gcalloc(size_t n, size_t sizeof_something)
{
   void   *p;

   if ((p = calloc(n, sizeof_something)) == NULL) {
      printf("\nERROR: calloc() failed - bye!\n\n");
      exit(1);
   }
   return p;
}
```

In any serious coding effort, graceful functions are essential. We see this idea again in Section 13.7, "Using Temporary Files and Graceful Functions," on page 450.

9.13 Moving to C++

In C++, `malloc()` and `free()` are replaced by `new` and `delete`. These are operators that are in the language. They are type-safe and convenient. The unary operators `new` and `delete` are available to manipulate *free store*. Free store is a system-provided memory pool for objects whose lifetime is directly managed by the programmer. The programmer creates the object by using `new` and destroys the object by using `delete`. This is important for dynamic data structures such as lists and trees.

In C++, operator `new` is used in the following forms:

`new` *type-name*
`new` *type-name initializer*
`new` (*type-name*)

In each case there are at least two effects. First, an appropriate amount of store is allocated from free store to contain the named type. Second, the base address of the object is returned as the value of the `new` expression. The expression is of type `void*` and can be assigned to any pointer type variable. The operator `new` returns the value 0 when memory is unavailable.

The following example uses `new`:

```
int*  ptr_i;
ptr_i = new int(5);    //allocation and initialization
```

In this code, the pointer to `int` variable `ptr_i` is assigned the address of the store obtained in allocating an object of type `int`. The location pointed at by `ptr_i` is initialized to the value 5. This use is not usual for a simple type such as `int`, in that it is far more convenient and natural to automatically allocate an integer variable on the stack or globally.

The operator `delete` destroys an object created by `new`, in effect returning its allocated storage to free store for reuse. The operator `delete` is used in the following forms:

`delete` *expression*
`delete [ ]` *expression*

The first form is used when the corresponding `new` expression did not allocate an array. The second form has empty brackets indicating that the original allocation was an array of objects. The operator `delete` does not return a value; one can say its return type is `void`.

The following example uses these constructs to dynamically allocate an array:

```
//Use of new to dynamically allocate an array.
#include  <iostream.h>

int main(void)
{
   int*  data;
   int   size;

   cout << "\nEnter array size: ";
   cin >> size;
   data = new int[size];      //allocate an array of ints

   for (int j = 0; j < size; ++j)
      cout << (data[j] = j) << '\t';

   cout << "\n\n";
   delete[] data;             //deallocate an array
   data = new int[size];
   for (j = 0; j < size; ++j)
      cout << data[j] << '\t';
   return 0;
}
```

Dissection of the dyn_array Program

- ```
  int*  data;
  int   size;

  cout << "\nEnter array size: ";
  cin >> size;
  data = new int[size];      //allocate an array of ints
  ```

The pointer variable `data` is used as the base address of a dynamically allocated array whose number of elements is the value of `size`. The user is prompted for the integer-valued `size`. The `new` operator is used to allocate storage from free store capable of storing an object of type `int[size]`. On a system where integers take two bytes, this would allocate 2 × `size` bytes. At this point, `data` is assigned the base address of this store.

- ```
  for (int j = 0; j < size; ++j)
     cout << (data[j] = j) << '\t';
  ```

This statement initializes the values of the `data` array and prints them.

■
```
delete[] data;              //deallocate an array
```

The operator `delete` returns the storage associated with the pointer variable `data` to free store. This can be done only with objects allocated by `new`. The bracket form is used because the corresponding allocation was of an array.

■
```
data = new int[size];
for (j = 0; j < size; ++j)
   cout << data[j] << '\t';
```

We access free store again, but this time we do not initialize the `data` array. On a typical system, the same memory just returned to free store is used, with the old values reappearing. However, there are no guarantees on what values appear in objects allocated from free store. Test this on your system. The programmer is responsible for properly initializing such objects.

Summary

- An array is a sequence of data items that are of the same type, that can be indexed, and that are stored contiguously. Arrays can be used to deal with a large number of homogeneous values. A declaration such as

  ```
  int   a[100];
  ```

  makes `a` an array of `int`s. The compiler allocates contiguous space in memory for 100 `int`s and numbers the elements of `a` from 0 to 99.

- Elements of the array are accessed by expressions such as `a[i]`. More generally, we can use `a[`*expr*`]`, where the subscript, or index, *expr* is an integral expression having a nonnegative value that does not overrun the upper bound of `a`. It is the programmer's responsibility to make sure that an array index stays within bounds.

- When an array name is passed as an argument to a function, only a copy of the base address of the array is actually passed. In the header to a function definition, the declaration

  `int   a[];`   is equivalent to   `int   *a;`

  In the header to a function definition, the declaration of a multidimensional array must have all sizes specified except the first (see exercise 9 on page 331).

- An array can be initialized by assigning an appropriate-length list of values within braces. If an external or static array is declared but not initialized, all the elements of the array are automatically initialized to zero. Automatic arrays that are not initialized start with garbage values.

- Arrays of any type can be created, including arrays of arrays. For example,

```
double   a[30][50];
```

declares a to be an array of "array of 50 doubles." The elements of a are accessed by expressions such as a[i][j].

Exercises

1 Explain the following terms:

(a) lower bound
(b) subscript
(c) out of bounds

2 The following array declarations have several errors. Identify each of them.

```
#define   SIZE   4

int main(void)
{
   int   a[SIZE] = {0, 2, 2, 3, 4};
   int   b[SIZE - 5];
   int   c[3.0];
```

3 Write a function that separately sums the even indexed elements and odd indexed elements of an array of doubles. Each element of the array contributes to one of the two sums, depending on whether the index of the element is even or odd. Your function definition should look something like this:

```
void sum(double a[],
         int    n,              /* n is the size of a[] */
         double *even_index_sum_ptr,
         double *odd_index_sum_ptr)
{
   .....
```

4 Write a function that computes two sums from the elements of an array of integers. Each element of the array contributes to one of the two sums, depending on whether the element itself is even or odd. Your function definition should look something like this:

```
void sum(int a[],
         int n,
         int *even_element_sum_ptr,
         int *odd_element_sum_ptr)
{
   .....
```

5 Modify the *cnt_abc* program in Section 9.2, "An Example: Counting Each Letter Separately," on page 307, to also count each lowercase letter separately.

6 This exercise is designed to test your understanding of pointer arithmetic. Suppose SIZE is a symbolic constant with value 100. If the declaration is

```
char   a[SIZE], *p = a;
int    i;
```

the compiler allocates 100 bytes of contiguous storage in memory, with the array name a pointing to the base address of this storage. We are deliberately using an array of chars because each char is stored in one byte. The pointer p is initialized to have the same value as a. Now we want to fill the array in a very simple way.

```
for (i = 0; i < SIZE; ++i)
   a[i] = i;
```

The elements of the array have been assigned consecutive integer values from 0 to 99. Now consider

```
printf("%d\n", *(p + 3));
printf("%d\n", *(char *)((int *) p + 3));
printf("%d\n", *(char *)((double *) p + 3));
```

What is printed? The answer to this question is system-dependent. Explain why this is so, and explain what would be printed on a machine different from your own. *Hint:* Consider the expression

```
(int *) p + 3
```

Of the two operators that are acting, which has the higher precedence? Use this information to determine which element of the array this pointer expression is pointing to. Now consider

```
(char *) pointer_expression
```

This casts the pointer expression as a pointer to `char`. Now consider

```
*(char *) pointer_expression
```

How do the two acting unary operators associate?

7 Write a program that uses the `bubble()` function to sort an array of integers. Write another version of your program, modifying `bubble()` so that it terminates after the first pass in which no two elements are interchanged. Time the two versions of your program. Which version is faster?

8 Write a program that finds the maximum and minimum elements of a two-dimensional array. Do all of this within `main()`.

9 Rewrite the program from the previous exercise, using a function that has a two-dimensional array in its parameter list. *Hint:* When a multidimensional array occurs as a parameter in a header to a function definition, the size for each dimension, except the first, must be specified. The effect of this is to hardwire the function so that it can be used only for certain arrays. Consider

```
double sum(double a[][5], int m)
                             /* m is the number of rows */
{
    .....
```

In this example we specified `5` as the column size of `a`. This information is needed by the compiler to handle expressions of the form `a[i][j]` within the function. We can invoke this function by writing `sum(a, 3)` if `a` is a 3-by-5 array in the calling environment, or `sum(a, 7)` if `a` is a 7-by-5 array. In general, we can pass to `sum()` any *n*-by-5 array. From all of this, you may gather that C does not handle multidimensional arrays gracefully, but that is not true. There is more to the story but, because it involves a more sophisticated use of pointers, we cannot tell the rest of the story here.

10 Write a program that keeps sales data for ten years by month. The array should have a month index of size 12. Given this data, compute by sorted order the months of the year for which sales are best.

11 There are many known sorting methods. Here is the heart of a simple transposition sort:

```
for (i = 0; i < SIZE; ++i)
   for (j = i + 1; j < SIZE; ++j)
      if (a[i] > a[j])
         swap(&a[i], &a[j]);
```

Write a program that implements this sort. After your program is working, modify it so that all the elements of the array are printed after each pass of the outer loop. Suppose, for example, that the size of your array is 8 and its starting values are

```
7   3   66   3   -5   22   -77   2
```

Your program should print the following on the screen:

```
Unordered data:    7    3   66    3   -5   22  -77    2
  After pass 1:  -77    7   66    3    3   22   -5    2
  After pass 2:  -77   -5   66    7    3   22    3    2
.....
```

12 The output of the program you wrote for the previous exercise illustrated the effects of a particular sorting method acting on a particular array. In this exercise we want to dig a little deeper. Modify the program you wrote for the previous exercise so that every time two elements are interchanged, the array is written out with the interchanges underlined. With the array of size 8 previously suggested, your program should print the following on the screen:

```
     3      7     66      3     -5     22    -77      2
    --     --

    -5      7     66      3      3     22    -77      2
    --                          --

 .....
```

13 Write a program that reads *n* integers into an array, then prints on a separate line the value of each distinct element along with the number of times it occurs. The values should be printed in descending order. Suppose, for example, that you input the values

```
-7  3  3  -7  5  5  3
```

as the elements of your array. Then your program should print

```
 5 occurs 2 times
 3 occurs 3 times
-7 occurs 2 times
```

Use your program to investigate the output of `rand()`. First use `rand()` to create a file—say, *rand_out*—containing 100 random numbers in the range 1 to 10. Recall that this can be done with a `for` loop of the form

```
for (i = 1; i <= 100; ++i) {
   printf("%7d", rand() % 10 + 1);
   if (i % 10 == 0)
      printf("\n");
}
```

Because we have not yet explained how one writes to a file, see Chapter 13, "Input/Output and Files." Write a small program, call it *cr_rand* (for "create random"), and then give the following command to redirect the output:

cr_rand > rand_out

14 Rewrite the previous program to make use of `calloc()`. Suppose the file *rand_out* has as its first entry the number of random numbers contained in that file. Write your program to read that first entry into a variable named `size`. Suppose the variable `rand_array` has been declared as a pointer to `int`. You can dynamically allocate storage by making use of `calloc()` as follows:

```
rand_array = calloc(size, sizeof(int));
```

The pointer `rand_array` can be treated as an array after space has been allocated. For example, to fill the array, you can write

```
for (i = 0; i < size; ++i)
   scanf("%d", &rand_array[i]);
```

15 Recall that the semantics of the assignment operator += is specified by the rule that

variable op= expression

is equivalent to

variable = *variable op* (*expression*)

with the exception that if *variable* is itself an expression, it is evaluated only once. This means, for example, that

`a[expr] += 2` as compared to `a[expr] = a[expr] + 2`

need not have the same effects. This is an important technical point. Try the following code:

```
int   a[] = {3, 3, 3}, i = 0;
int   b[] = {3, 3, 3}, j = 0;

a[++i] += 2;                    /* perfectly acceptable */
b[++j] = b[++j] + 2;            /* legal, but unacceptable */
for (i = 0; i < 3; ++i)
   printf("a[%d] = %d      b[%d] = %d\n",
          i, a[i], i, b[i]);
```

On most systems, the arrays a[] and b[] end up with different values. What is printed on your system?

16 C++: Write a program that performs string reversal using storage allocated with new.

```
char* strrev(char*& s1, const char* s2);
//s1 ends up with the reverse of the string s2
//use new to allocate s1 adequate store strlen(s2) + 1
```

17 C++: Write a program that allocates a single dimensional array from free store with user-provided lower and upper bounds. The program should check that the upper bound exceeds the lower bound. If it does not, perform an error exit using the *assert.h* package as follows:

```
#include  <assert.h>
 .....//input lower bound and upper bound
assert(ub - lb > 0);
 .....
```

18 C++: The size of this array is (*upper bound* – *lower bound* + 1) elements. Given a standard C++ array of this many elements, write a function that uses the standard array to initialize the dynamic array. Test this by writing out both arrays before and after initialization in a nicely formatted style.

19 Java: Let's say that we want to find the prime numbers between 2 and 100. To do so, we write code based on the *sieve of Eratosthenes*. We allocate a boolean array isPrime of 100 elements. We set each element to true. Starting with element isPrime[2], we use its index value 2 and proceed through the remaining array elements isPrime[4], isPrime[6], . . . , isPrime[98], setting each value to false. Then we go to isPrime[3] and set each element in every third

space to false. We do this until we reach 10 because 10 is the square root of 100 and is sufficient for checking primality in the range 2 through 100. When we have finished, only those entries that remain true are primes.

```
//Primes.java-Sieve of Eratosthenes for Primes up to 100.
// see Java by Dissection page 160
class Primes {
  public static void main(String[] args) {
    boolean[] sieve = new boolean[100];
    int i;
    System.out.println(" Table of primes to 100.");
    for (i = 0; i < 100; i++)
      sieve[i] = true;
    for (int j = 2; j < Math.sqrt(100); j++)
      if (sieve[j])
         crossOut(sieve, j, j + j);
    for (i = 0; i < 100; i++) //print primes
      if (sieve[i])
         System.out.print(" " + i);
  }

  public static void crossOut(boolean[] s,
                              int interval, int start)
  {
   for (int i = start; i < s.length; i += interval)
      s[i] = false;
  }
}
```

We can readily generalize this program to an arbitrarily large *n*. The key is to replace the hard-coded value 100 with a variable *n*. Convert the preceding program to C using `typedef` to create a `boolean` type and generalize it to *n*. Print out a table of the primes up to 300.

20 Java: Rewrite as C code the following Java program, which uses a two-dimensional array:

```
// TwoD.java - simple example of two-dimensional array
//Java by Dissection page 164.
class TwoD {
  public static void main(String[] args) {
    int[][] data = new int[3][5];
    for (int i = 0; i < data.length; i++) {
      System.out.print("Row " + i + ":   ");
      for (int j = 0; j < data[i].length; j++) {
        data[i][j] = i * j;
        System.out.print(data[i][j] + ", ");
      }
      System.out.println();
    }
  }
}
```

Java uses new for allocation where C uses `calloc()` or `malloc()`. Also, Java automatically tracks the size of the dimensions by using the member `length`. These make Java easier and safer to use than C.

Chapter 10

Strings and Pointers

In C, a *string* is a one-dimensional array of type char. A character in a string can be accessed either as an element in an array or by making use of a pointer to char. The flexibility this provides makes C especially useful in writing string-processing programs. The standard library provides many useful string-handling functions.

Although string processing can be viewed as a special case of array processing, it has characteristics that give it a unique flavor. Important to this is the use of the character value \0 to terminate a string. This chapter includes a number of example programs that illustrate string- processing ideas. Again, as in Chapter 9, "Arrays and Pointers," we see that arrays and pointers are closely related. The type pointer to char is conceptually a string. Our examples illustrate the pointer arithmetic and dereferencing needed to properly process string data.

"OH, C'MON, MITTENS, HOW SMART CAN HUMANS BE IF THEY THINK THAT STRINGS ARE DIFFICULT?"

10.1 The End-of-String Sentinel \0

By convention, a string is terminated by the *end-of-string* sentinel \0, or null character. A constant string such as "abc" is stored in memory as four characters, the last one being \0. Thus the length of the string "abc" is 3, but the size of the string is 4. To allocate storage in memory for a string, we could write

```
#define   MAXWORD   100

int main(void)
{
   char   w[MAXWORD];
   .....
```

After storage has been allocated, there are a number of ways to get character values into the string w. First, we could do it character by character, as follows:

```
w[0] = 'A';
w[1] = 'B';
w[2] = 'C';
w[3] = '\0';
```

Notice that we ended the string with the null character.

Another way to get character values into w is to make use of scanf(). The format %s is used to read in a string. The process can be thought of as having three distinct steps. The statement

```
scanf("%s", w);
```

first positions the input stream to an initial non-white space character. Second, non-white space characters are read in and placed in memory beginning at the base address of w. Finally, the process stops when a white space character or EOF is encountered. At that point, a null character is placed in memory to end the string. Because an array name is a pointer to the base address of the array, the expression w is equivalent to &w[0]. Because the size of w is 100, we can enter up to 99 characters on the keyboard and still have the string sentinel \0 stored. If more are entered, we overrun the bounds of w.

The sentinel \0 is also called a *delimiter*. It allows a simple test to detect the end of a string. It is useful to think of strings as having a variable length delimited by the null character but with a maximum length determined by the size of the string. The size of a string must include the storage needed for the null character. As with all arrays, the programmer must make sure that string bounds are not overrun.

Note carefully that 'a' and "a" are very different. The first is a character constant, and the second is a string constant. The string "a" is an array of characters with two elements, the first with value 'a' and the second with value '\0'.

10.2 Initialization of Strings

Recall that arrays, including character arrays, can be initialized.

```
char   s[] = {'a', 'b', 'c', '\0'};
```

This declares and stores in a 4-element `char` array `s` the string `abc`. There is a second equivalent syntax for initializing character arrays.

```
char   s[] = "abc";
```

This is exactly identical in meaning to the first example but is terser and is the preference of most C programmers. In both cases the array is one more than the string length. Thus in this example the size is 4.

A pointer to `char` can also be initialized with a constant string, but the interpretation is different. Here is an example:

```
char   *p = "abc";
```

Recall that an array name by itself is treated as a pointer to the base of the array in memory. A string constant, like all other constants, is stored in memory by the compiler. (The programmer does not provide space for constants.) Thus `"abc"` is stored in memory by the compiler. The variable `p` is being initialized with this pointer value.

Thus the difference between initializing an array with a constant string and initializing a pointer with a constant string is that the array contains the individual characters followed by the null character, whereas the pointer is assigned the address of the constant string in memory.

10.3 An Example: Have a Nice Day

Because a string is an array of characters, one way to process a string is to use array notation with subscripts. We want to write an interactive program to illustrate this. Our program reads a line of characters typed by the user into a string, print the string in reverse order, and then sum the letters in the string.

```
/* Have a nice day! */

#include   <stdio.h>
#include   <ctype.h>

#define   MAXSTRING   100
```

```
int main(void)
{
   char   c, name[MAXSTRING];
   int    i, sum = 0;

   printf("\nHi!  What is your name?  ");
   for (i = 0; (c = getchar()) != '\n'; ++i) {
      name[i] = c;
      if (isalpha(c))                    /* sum the letters */
         sum += c;
   }
   name[i] = '\0';
   printf("\n%s%s%s\n%s",
      "Nice to meet you ", name, ".",
      "Your name spelled backward is ");
   for (--i; i >= 0; --i)
      putchar(name[i]);
   printf("\n%s%d%s\n\n%s\n",
      "and the letters in your name sum to ", sum, ".",
      "Have a nice day!");
   return 0;
}
```

Suppose we execute this program and enter "C. B. Diligent" when prompted. Here is what appears on the screen:

```
Hi!  What is your name?  C. B. Diligent

Nice to meet you C. B. Diligent.
Your name spelled backward is tnegiliD .B .C
and the letters in your name sum to 949.

Have a nice day!
```

Dissection of the nice_day Program

■
```
#include   <stdio.h>
#include   <ctype.h>
```

The standard header file *stdio.h* contains the function prototype for `printf()`. It also contains the macro definitions for `getchar()` and `putchar()`. The standard header file *ctype.h* contains the macro definition for `isalpha()`.

■
```
#define    MAXSTRING    100
```

The symbolic constant MAXSTRING is used to set the size of the character array name. We are making the assumption that the user of this program does not type in more than 100 characters.

■
```
char    c, name[MAXSTRING];
int     i, sum = 0;
```

The variable c is of type char. The identifier name is of type "array of char," and its size is MAXSTRING. In C, all array subscripts start at 0. Thus name[0], name[1], . . . , name[MAXSTRING - 1] are the elements of the array. The variables i and sum are of type int; sum is initialized to 0.

■
```
printf("\nHi!  What is your name?  ");
```

This is a prompt to the user. The program now expects a name to be typed in followed by a carriage return.

■
```
(c = getchar()) != '\n'
```

This expression consists of two parts. On the left we have

```
(c = getchar())
```

Unlike other languages, assignment in C is an operator (see Section 2.10, "Assignment Operators," on page 55). Here, getchar() is being used to read a character from the keyboard and assign it to c. The value of the expression as a whole is the value of whatever is assigned to c. Parentheses are necessary because the order of precedence of the = operator is less than that of the != operator. Thus

c = getchar() != '\n' is equivalent to c = (getchar() != '\n')

which is syntactically correct, but not what we want.

■
```
for (i = 0; (c = getchar()) != '\n'; ++i) {
   name[i] = c;
   if (isalpha(c))              /* sum the letters */
      sum += c;
}
```

The variable i is initially assigned the value 0. Then getchar() gets a character from the keyboard, assigns it to c, and tests to see if it is a newline character. If it is not, the body of the for loop is executed. First, the value of c is assigned to the array element name[i].

Next, the macro `isalpha()` is used to determine whether `c` is a lower- or uppercase letter. If it is a letter, `sum` is incremented by the value of `c`. As we saw in Chapter 5, "Character Processing," a character in C has the integer value corresponding to its ASCII encoding. For example, `'a'` has value 97, `'b'` has value 98, and so forth. Finally, the variable `i` is incremented at the end of the `for` loop. The `for` loop is executed repeatedly until a newline character is received.

■ `name[i] = '\0';`

After the `for` loop is finished, the null character `\0` is assigned to the element `name[i]`. By convention, all strings end with a null character. Functions that process strings, such as `printf()`, use the null character `\0` as an end-of-string sentinel. We now can think of the array `name` in memory as

C	.		B	.		D	i	l	i	g	e	n	t	\0	*	...	*
0	1	2	3	4	5	6	7	8	9	10	11	12	13	1	15		99

Notice that * has been used to indicate that the contents of all the characters beyond `\0` in the array are not known.

■
```
printf("\n%s%s%s\n%s",
   "Nice to meet you ", name, ".",
   "Your name spelled backward is ");
```

The format `%s` is used to print a string. Here, the array `name` is one of four string arguments being printed. The elements of the array are printed one after another until the end-of-string sentinel `\0` is encountered. The effect of this statement is to print on the screen

```
Nice to meet you C. B. Diligent.
Your name spelled backward is
```

■
```
for (--i; i >= 0; --i)
   putchar(name[i]);
```

If we assume that "C. B. Diligent" followed by a carriage return was typed in, then `i` has value 14 at the beginning of this `for` loop. (Do not forget to count from 0, not 1.) After `i` has been decremented, the subscript corresponds to the last character of the name that was typed in. Thus the effect of this `for` loop is to print the name on the screen backward.

■
```
printf("\n%s%d%s\n\n%s\n",
    "and the letters in your name sum to ", sum, ".",
    "Have a nice day!");
```

We print the sum of the letters in the name typed in by the user, and then we print a final message.

10.4 Using Pointers to Process a String

In the last section we illustrated string processing with the use of subscripts. In this section we want to use pointers to process a string. Also, we want to show how strings can be used as arguments to functions.

Let us write a small interactive program that reads into a string a line of characters input by the user. Then the program creates a new string and print it.

```
/* Character processing: change a line. */

#include <stdio.h>

#define   MAXLINE   100
void   read_in(char *);

int main(void)
{
   char   line[MAXLINE], *change(char *);

   printf("\nWhat is your favorite line?  ");
   read_in(line);
   printf("\n%s\n\n%s\n\n",
      "Here it is after being changed:", change(line));
   return 0;
}
```

After prompting the user, this program uses `read_in()` to put characters into `line`. Then `line` is passed as an argument to `change()`, which returns a pointer to `char`. The returned pointer value is printed by `printf()` in the format of a string. Here is the function `read_in()`:

```
void read_in(char s[])
{
   int    c, i = 0;

   while ((c = getchar()) != EOF && c != '\n')
      s[i++] = c;
   s[i] = '\0';
}
```

The parameter s is of type pointer to char. We could just as well have written

```
void read_in(char *s)
{
   .....
```

In the while loop, successive characters are taken from the input stream and placed one after another into the array with base address s. When a newline character is received, the loop is exited and a null character is put into the array to act as the end-of-string sentinel. Notice that this function allocates no space. In main(), space is allocated with the declaration of line. We are making the assumption that the user types in fewer than MAXLINE characters. Checking this with an assertion is left as an exercise (see exercise 6 on page 355). When line is passed as an argument to read_in(), a copy of the base address of the array is made, and this value is taken on by the parameter s. The array elements themselves are not copied, but they are accessible in read_in() via this base address.

```
char *change(const char *s)
{
   static char    new_string[MAXLINE];
   char           *p = new_string;

   *p++ = '\t';
   for ( ; *s != '\0'; ++s)
      if (*s == 'e')
         *p++ = 'E';
      else if (*s == ' ') {
         *p++ = '\n';
         *p++ = '\t';
      }

      else
         *p++ = *s;
   *p = '\0';
   return new_string;
}
```

This function takes a string and copies it, changing every e to E and replacing every blank with a newline and a tab. Suppose we run the program and type in the line

```
she sells sea shells
```

after receiving the prompt. Here is what appears on the screen:

```
What is your favorite line?  she sells sea shells
```

Here it is after being changed:

```
shE
sElls
sEa
shElls
```

We want to explain in some detail how the function `change()` works.

Dissection of the change() Function

- ```
  char *change(const char *s)
  {
     static char   new_string[MAXLINE];
     char          *p = new_string;
  ```

The first `char *` is the return type of the function and tells the compiler that `change()` returns a value of type pointer to `char`. The parameter `s` and the local variable `p` are both declared to be of type pointer to `char`. Because `s` is a parameter in a function header, we could just as well have written

```
char *change(const char s[])
{
   .....
```

However, because `p` is a local variable and not a parameter, a similar declaration for `p` would be wrong. The array `new_string` is declared to have static storage class, and space is allocated for `MAXLINE` characters. The reason for static rather than automatic is explained following this dissection. The pointer `p` is initialized to the base address of `new_string`.

- `*p++ = '\t';`

This one line of code is equivalent to

```
*p = '\t';
++p;
```

The situation is analyzed as follows. Because the operators * and ++ are both unary and associate from right to left, the expression `*p++` is equivalent to `*(p++)`. Thus the `++` operator causes `p` to be incremented. In contrast, the expression `(*p)++` would cause the value of what is pointed to by `p` to be incremented, which is something quite different.
```

Because the ++ operator occurs on the right side of p rather than the left, p is incremented after the total expression *p++ = '\t' has been evaluated. Assignment is part of the evaluation process, and this causes a tab character to be assigned to what is pointed to by p. Because p points to the base address of new_string, a tab character is assigned to new_string[0]. After p is incremented, p points to new_string[1].

■
```
for ( ; *s != '\0'; ++s)
```

Each time through the for loop, a test is made to see if the value of what is pointed to by s is the end-of-string sentinel. If it is not, then the body of the for loop is executed and s is incremented. The effect of incrementing a pointer to char is to cause it to point at the next character in the string.

■
```
if (*s == 'e')
  *p++ = 'E';
```

In the body of the for loop, a test is made to see if s is pointing to the character e. If it is, then the character E is assigned to the object p is pointing to, and p is incremented.

■
```
else if (*s == ' ') {
  *p++ = '\n';
  *p++ = '\t';
}
```

Otherwise, a test is made to see if s is pointing to a blank character. If it is, a newline character is assigned to the object p is pointing to, then p is incremented. Then a tab character is assigned to the object p is pointing to, and then p is incremented again.

■
```
else
  *p++ = *s;
```

Finally, if the character to which s is pointing is neither an e nor a blank, then the object p is pointing to is assigned the value of the object s is pointing to, and then p is incremented. The effect of this for loop is to copy the string passed as an argument to change() into the string with base address &new_string[1], except that each e is replaced by an E, and each blank is replaced by a newline and a tab.

■
```
*p = '\0';
```

When the for loop is exited, the object pointed to by p is assigned an end-of-string sentinel.

■ `return new_string;`

The array name `new_string` is returned. An array name by itself is treated as a pointer to the base of the array in memory. Because `new_string` is of storage class static, it is preserved in memory on function exit.

If `new_string` were automatic instead of static, the memory allocated to it would not be preserved on function exit. On many systems, this leads to an error that is hard to diagnose. One possibility is that the memory is overwritten and the final `printf()` statement in `main()` does not work properly.

10.5 Problem Solving: Counting Words

The example in the last section illustrated the use of pointers and pointer arithmetic to process a string. In this section we want to give another illustration of this. We write a function that counts the number of words in a string. For the purposes of this function, a sequence of non-white space characters constitute a word.

```
/* Count the number of words in a string. */

#include <ctype.h>

int word_cnt(const char *s)
{
   int   cnt = 0;

   while (*s != '\0') {
      while (isspace(*s))              /* skip white space */
         ++s;
      if (*s != '\0') {                /* found a word */
         ++cnt;
       while (!isspace(*s) && *s != '\0')  /* skip word */
          ++s;
      }
   }
   return cnt;
}
```

This is a typical string-processing function. Pointer arithmetic and dereferencing are used to search for various patterns or characters.

10.6 Passing Arguments to main()

C provides for arrays of any type, including arrays of pointers. Although this is an advanced topic that we do not wish to treat in detail, we need to use arrays of pointers to char to write programs that use command line arguments. Two arguments, conventionally called argc and argv, can be used with main() to communicate with the operating system. Here is a program that prints its command line arguments:

```
/* Echo the command line arguments. */

#include <stdio.h>

int main(int argc, char *argv[])
{
   int   i;

   printf("argc = %d\n", argc);
   for (i = 0; i < argc; ++i)
      printf("argv[%d] = %s\n", i, argv[i]);
   return 0;
}
```

The variable argc provides a count of the command line arguments. The array argv is an array of pointers to char and can be thought of as an array of strings. Because the element argv[0] always contains the name of the command itself, the value of argc is always 1 or more. Suppose we compile the preceding program and put the executable code in the file *my_echo*. If we give the command

my_echo

the following is printed on the screen:

```
argc = 1
argv[0] = my_echo
```

Now suppose we give the command

my_echo try this

Here is what appears on the screen:

```
argc = 3
argv[0] = my_echo
argv[1] = try
argv[2] = this
```

The parameter argv could just as well have been declared as follows:

```
char   **argv;
```

It is a pointer to pointer to char that can be thought of as an array of pointers to char, which in turn can be thought of as an array of strings. Notice that we have not allocated any space for the strings on the command line. The system does this for us and passes information to main() via the two arguments argc and argv.

10.7 String-Handling Functions in the Standard Library

The standard library contains many useful string-handling functions. They all require that strings passed as arguments be null-terminated, and they all return either an integer value or a pointer to char. The following list describes some of the functions. (All the string-handling functions are described in Appendix A, "The Standard Library.") The function prototypes are given in the header file *string.h*. This file should be included when using these string-handling functions.

Some String-handling functions in the Standard Library

- `char *strcat(char *s1, const char *s2);`

  This function takes two strings as arguments, concatenates them, and puts the result in s1. The programmer must ensure that s1 points to enough space to hold the result. The string s1 is returned.

- `int strcmp(const char *s1, const char *s2);`

  Two strings are passed as arguments. An integer is returned that is less than, equal to, or greater than zero, depending on whether s1 is lexicographically less than, equal to, or greater than s2.

- `char *strcpy(char *s1, const char *s2);`

  The string s2 is copied into s1 until \0 is moved. Whatever exists in s1 is overwritten. It is assumed that s1 has enough space to hold the result. The value s1 is returned.

- `unsigned strlen(const char *s);`

  A count of the number of characters before \0 is returned.

There is nothing special about these functions. They are written in C and are all quite short. Variables in them are often declared to have storage class register for faster execution. Here is one way the function strlen() could be written:

```
unsigned strlen(const char *s)
{
   register int   n = 0;

   for ( ; *s != '\0'; ++s)
      ++n;
   return n;
}
```

String-handling functions are illustrated in the next table. Note carefully that it is the programmer's responsibility to allocate sufficient space for strings that are passed as arguments to functions. Overrunning the bounds of a string is a common programming error.

Declarations and initializations	
`char s1[] = "beautiful big sky country",` `     s2[] = "how now brown cow";`	
Expression	**Value**
`strlen(s1)`	25
`strlen(s2 + 8)`	9
`strcmp(s1, s2)`	*negative integer*
Statements	**What is printed**
`printf("%s", s1 + 10);`	`big sky country`
`strcpy(s1 + 10, s2 + 8);`	
`strcat(s1, "s!");`	
`printf("%s", s1);`	`beautiful brown cows!`

Before using any string functions in the standard library, you must provide the function prototypes. Typically, you write the line

```
#include <string.h>
```

to include the header file *string.h*. This header file contains all the prototypes of the string-handling functions in the standard library.

10.8 Style

Two styles of programming can be used to process strings: array notation with subscripts or pointers and pointer arithmetic. Although both styles are common, there is a tendency for experienced programmers to favor the use of pointers.

Because the null character is always used to delimit a string, it is common programming style to explicitly test for `\0` when processing a string. However, it is not necessary to do so. The alternative is to use the length of the string. As an example of this we could write

```
n = strlen(s);
for (i = 0; i <= n; ++i)
   if (islower(s[i]))
      s[i] = toupper(s[i]);
```

to capitalize all the letters in the string `s`. This style of string processing is certainly acceptable. Notice, however, that a `for` loop of the form

```
for (i = 0; i <= strlen(s); ++i)
   .....
```

is inefficient. This code causes the length of `s` to be recomputed every time through the loop.

It is sometimes convenient to use a pointer to `char` to point at a constant string. As an example of this, consider

```
char   *p;

p = "RICH";
printf("C. B. DeMogul is %s %s %s!\n", p, p, p);
```

which is an alternative to

```
printf("C. B. DeMogul is %s %s %s!\n",
       "RICH", "RICH", "RICH");
```

In this example the repetitive use of `p` saves a little space. Compilers allocate separate storage for each constant string, even if one is the same as another.

Where possible, the programmer should use a function in the standard library rather than code an equivalent routine, even when the specially coded routine would give a marginal gain in efficiency. The functions in the standard library are designed to be portable across systems.

Although it is considered poor programming practice to do so, a pointer to a constant string can change the contents of the string on most systems (see exercise 9 on page 356).

10.9 Common Programming Errors

A common programming error is overrunning the bounds of a string. As with other arrays, it is the programmer's responsibility to make sure enough space is allocated for a string. Consider

```
char   s[17], *strcpy();

strcpy(s, "Have a nice day!\n");
```

Here the programmer made a careful count of the characters in the string to be copied into `s` but forgot to allocate space for the null character. Overrunning the bounds of a string can easily occur with a function call such as `strcat(s1, s2)`. The concatenation of the two strings must fit within the space allocated for `s1`.

Another common programming error is to forget to terminate a string with the null character. On most systems this type of error cannot be caught by the compiler. The effect of the error can be sporadic; sometimes the program runs correctly and other times it won't. This kind of error can be very difficult to find.

Another common error is writing `'a'` for `"a"`, and vice versa. Usually the compiler finds this kind of mistake. Using a function call such as `scanf("%s", &w)` to read a string into the character array `w` is also an error. Because `w` is itself a pointer, the correct function call is `scanf("%s", w)`.

10.10 System Considerations

In ANSI C, string constants that are separated by zero or more white space characters are concatenated by the compiler into one long string. Traditional C compilers do not support this feature. Here is an example:

```
char   *long_string;

long_string = "A list of words:\n"
              "\n"
              "   1  abacus\n"
              "   2  bracelet\n"
              "   3  cafeteria\n";
```

In this example the advantage is that the string embodies the look it has when it is printed. Traditional C compilers do not support this feature.

The standard library contains 17 string-handling functions (see Appendix A, "The Standard Library"). It is considered good programming practice to use these functions rather than write your own. They enhance portability to other systems although not all the string-handling functions are supported by older compilers. The new ANSI C standard has added many functions.

10.11 Moving to C++

C++ can also use null-terminated character sequences as strings. But it is increasingly using the data type string found in the C++ Standard Template Library (STL). The string type is readily convertible to char*. In modern C++, the C libraries have names prefixed by *c*, so *cstring* is the same as the C library *string.h*. The new string type is defined by including file *string*.

The type string has an extensive collection of functions and operations. Here are some examples:

```
string a, b("ABC"), c("DEF"); // a is empty , b is "ABC",
                              // c is "DEF"
b + c  // + stands for concatenation
b == c // == is an equality test
a = b  // = is assignment
a.to_lower()  //changes a's value to lowercase
```

Summary

- Strings are one-dimensional arrays of type char. The null character \0 is used to delimit a string. System functions such as printf() work properly only on null-terminated strings.

- A function call such as scanf("%s", w) can be used to read a sequence of non-white space characters into the string w. After all the characters have been read in, scanf() automatically ends the string with the null character.

- Strings may be initialized. An initialization of the form

  ```
  char   *s[] = "cbd";
  ```

  is taken by the compiler to be equivalent to

  ```
  char   *s[] = {'c', 'b', 'd', '\0'};
  ```

- String processing can be done by using array notation with subscripts and by using pointers and pointer arithmetic. Because of this flexibility, C is used extensively for string processing.

- C provides access to the command line arguments by using the two parameters argc and argv in the function definition of main(). The parameter argc is an int; its value is the number of command line arguments. The parameter argv is an array of pointers to char; it can be thought of as an array of strings. The system places the command line arguments in memory as strings and causes the elements of the array argv to point to them. The value of argc is always 1 or more, and the string pointed to by argv[0] is always the name of the command.

- The standard library contains many useful string-handling functions. For example, a function call such as strcmp(s1, s2) can be used to lexicographically compare the strings s1 and s2.

Exercises

1 Rewrite the *nice_day* program in Section 10.3, "An Example: Have a Nice Day," on page 339, using pointers and pointer arithmetic throughout.

2 Rewrite the function word_cnt() in Section 10.5, "Problem Solving: Counting Words," on page 347, using array notation with subscripts. Write an interactive program that reads in lines typed by the user, then reports the number of words in the line. Your program should allow for long lines. Experiment to see what happens when you type in a line that is so long it runs off the screen.

3 Write a function search() that searches the alphabetic characters in a string. From among the letters that occur in the string, the function is to find the letter that occurs least often, but at least once, and the letter that occurs most often. Report this information back to the calling environment along with the count of the occurrences of the two letters. Your function definition should start as follows:

```
void search(char s[], char *p_least, char *p_most,
            int *p_least_cnt, int *p_most_cnt)
{
   .....
```

Treat lower- and uppercase letters separately. Make sure you handle gracefully the case when there are no letters in the string. Write a program to test your function.

4 Write a function that when invoked as bubble_string(s) causes the characters in the string s to be bubble-sorted. If s contains the string "xylophone", then the following statement should cause ehlnoopxy to be printed.

```
printf("%s\n", bubble_string(s));
```

5 Modify the *my_echo* program in Section 10.6, "Passing Arguments to main()," on page 348, so that it has the following effect. If the command line

my_echo pacific sea

is typed, the following should be printed:

```
pacific
sea
```

Further modify it so that if the option *-c* is present, the arguments are printed in capital letters. Do not print out the argument that contains the option.

6 Make `void read_in(char s[])` in Section 10.4, "Using Pointers to Process a String," on page 343, more robust by adding an `assert()` that checks that `MAXLINE` characters are not exceeded.

7 Write your own version of the library function `strncmp()`. The function prototype and a description of how the function behaves are given in Appendix A, "The Standard Library."

8 In this exercise we use a multidimensional array of pointers to `char`. Complete the following table.

Declarations and initializations		
`char *p[2][3] = { "abc", "defg", "hi", "jklmno", "pqrstuvw", "xyz" };`		
Expression	**Equivalent expression**	**Value**
`***p`	`p[0][0][0]`	`'a'`
`**p[1]`		
`**(p[1] + 2)`		
`*(*(p + 1) + 1)[7]`		*error*
`(*(*(p + 1) + 1))[7]`		
`*(p[1][2] + 2)`		

9 On many systems, the value of constant strings can be altered. This is a very bad coding practice. Here is an example of what *not* to do. Explain what is printed and why.

```
#include <stdio.h>

int main(void)
{
   char   *p, *q;

   p = q = " RICH";
   printf("C. B. DeMogul is%s%s%s!\n", p, p, p);
   *++q = 'p';
   *++q = 'o';
   *++q = 'o';
   *++q = 'r';
   printf("C. B. DeMogul is%s%s%s!\n", p, p, p);
   return 0;
}
```

Note: On some systems this form of constant string alteration is detected and prohibited.

10 Write an interactive program that uses `scanf()` to read in seven strings input by the user. The program should print the seven strings as a list, then sort them alphabetically and print a new list. Use the function `strcmp()` to assist in the sorting of the strings. Also, use the preprocessing directive

```
#define   N_STRINGS   7
```

to write your program in such a way that it can sort a different number of strings by changing only this line.

11 (Advanced) Write a program similar to the one you wrote in the previous exercise that sorts and prints command line arguments.

12 C++: Using `string` as found in *cstring*, write a program that counts the number of occurrences of the string `"in"` found in an input file *test.txt*.

13 Java: In the following Java program, we have an array of Java strings.

```
// StringArray.java - uses a string array initializer
// Java by Dissection page 176.
class StringArray {
  public static void main(String[] args) {
    String[] myStringArray = { "zero", "one", "two",
        "three", "four", "five", "six", "seven",
        "eight", "nine"};
    for (int i = 0; i < myStringArray.length; i++)
      System.out.println(myStringArray[i]);
  }
}
```

Rewrite this as a C program. Java programmers are accustomed to Java handling the storage management issues, so this is more complex in C. In C, you need an array whose elements are pointers to `char`.

14 Java: In Java, we have both `String` and `StringBuffer` as forms of unmodifiable and modifiable string types. Rewrite the following as C code:

```
// StringTest.java - demo some String methods
// Java by Dissection pages 193-194
public class StringTest {
  public static void main(String[] args) {
     String str1 = "aBcD", str2 = "abcd", str3;
     System.out.println(str1.equals(str2));
     System.out.println(str1.length());
     System.out.println(str1.charAt(1));
     System.out.println(str1.compareTo("aBcE"));
     System.out.println(str1.compareTo("aBcC"));
     System.out.println(str1.compareTo("aBcD"));
     System.out.println(str1.indexOf('D'));
     System.out.println(str1.indexOf("Bc"));
     System.out.println(str1.indexOf("zz"));
     System.out.println(str1.concat("efg"));

     str3 = str1.toLowerCase();
     System.out.println(str3);
     str3 = str1.toUpperCase();
     System.out.println(str3);
     System.out.println(str1);
     str3 = String.valueOf(123);
     System.out.println(str3.equals("123"));
  }
}
```

This test program prints

```
false
4
B
-1
1
0
3
1
-1
aBcDefg
abcd
ABCD
aBcD
true
```

Remember that in Java, the method `equals()` is used to compare two strings; the calls to method `compareTo()` returns -1 if `str1` is lexicographically before the parameter; the method `indexOf()` is overloaded to accept either a `String` or a `char` as a parameter. When the parameter is a `char`, the method returns the index of the first position in the string where the character appears. When the parameter is a `String`, the method returns the index of the position in the `String` operated upon (`str1` in our example) where the parameter `String` appears. If the parameter `String` isn't a substring of the `String` operated upon, the method returns `-1`. It is best to think of `str1 + "efg"` as shorthand for `str1.concat("efg")`. Remember that the `String str1` is unaffected by the calls to `toLowerCase()` and `toUpper-Case()`. These calls return new `String` objects that contain the appropriate characters. The method `valueOf()` is an example of a class method; it isn't an instance method nor does it operate on a `String` object. It is related to the `String` class because it can be used to create `String` objects and thus is defined in the `String` class. The method `valueOf()` is overloaded to accept parameters of any primitive type. In each case, the method returns the `String` representation of the primitive value.

Chapter 11

Recursion

Recursion is a function invoking itself, either directly or indirectly. Some programming tasks are naturally solved with the use of recursion, which can be considered an advanced form of flow of control. Recursion is an alternative to iteration.

Recursion is explained using some simple example programs. One particularly nice example is a function that draws patterns on the screen. Another example is the recursive calculation of string length. Recursion is a programming technique that naturally implements the divide-and-conquer problem-solving methodology, a powerful strategy that is explained along with an example of sorting algorithms.

11.1 Recursive Problem Solving

A function is said to be *recursive* if it calls itself, either directly or indirectly. In C, all functions can be used recursively. In its simplest form the idea of recursion is straightforward.

```
#include <stdio.h>

void   count_down(int n);

int main(void)
{
   count_down(10);
   return 0;
}
```

```
void count_down(int n)
{
   if (n) {
      printf("%d !  ", n);
      count_down(n - 1);
   }
   else
      printf("\nBLAST OFF\n");
}
```

This program prints

```
10 !  9 !  8 !  7 !  6 !  5 !  4 !  3 !  2 !  1 !
BLAST OFF
```

This could have been accomplished by using an iterative statement enclosing the `printf()`. What is new here is that `count_down()` invokes itself.

Another simple example of a recursive function is the following, which computes the sum of the first *n* positive integers:

```
int sum(int n)
{
   if (n <= 1)
      return n;
   else
      return (n + sum(n - 1));
}
```

The recursive function `sum()` is analyzed as illustrated in the following table. First, the base case is considered; then, working out from the base case, the other cases are considered.

What sum() returns			
Function call	**Value returned**		
sum(1)	1		
sum(2)	2 + sum(1)	or	2 + 1
sum(3)	3 + sum(2)	or	3 + 2 + 1
sum(4)	4 + sum(3)	or	4 + 3 + 2 + 1

Simple recursive routines follow a standard pattern. Typically, there is a base case that is tested for on entry to the function. Then there is a general recursive case in which one of the variables, often an integer, is passed as an argument in such a way as to ultimately lead to the base case. In `sum()`, the variable `n` was reduced by one each time until the base case with `n` equal to 1 was reached.

Recursion is a very powerful problem-solving technique. The key is to identify a general case. A pitfall is to forget to reach the base case, which terminates the recursion.

When an integer *n* is passed to `sum()`, the recursion activates *n* nested copies of the function before returning, level by level, to the original call. This means that *n* function calls are used in the computation. Most simple recursive functions can be rewritten in an equivalent iterative form. Because function calls usually require more computation than iteration, why use recursion at all? If the code is easier to write and maintain using recursion, and run-time efficiency is not critical, then the use of recursion is justified.

"THIS IS THE THIRTEENTH TIME SHE'S TURNED ME DOWN. BUT I CAN'T DECIDE IF IT'S AN ITERATIVE OR A RECURSIVE THING."

In the remainder of this chapter we present examples that illustrate the ideas and power of recursion. The following program first prompts the user to type in a line; then, by means of a recursive function, reprints the line backward:

```
/* Write a line backward. */

#include <stdio.h>

void  prn_it(void);

int main(void)
{
   printf("Input a line:  ");
   prn_it();
   printf("\n\n");
   return 0;
}
```

```
void prn_it(void)
{
   char   c;

   if ((c = getchar()) != '\n')
      prn_it();
   putchar(c);
}
```

If the user types in the line `sing a song of sixpence` when prompted, then the following appears on the screen:

```
Input a line:  sing a song of sixpence

ecnepxis fo gnos a gnis
```

Dissection of the wrt_bkwd Program

- ```
  printf("Input a line:  ");
  prn_it();
  ```

The invocation of the recursive function `prn_it()` occurs after a prompt to the user. The user writes a line and terminates it by hitting a carriage return, which is the character `\n`.

- ```
  if ((c = getchar()) != '\n')
     prn_it();
  ```

As each character is read in, it initiates a new call to `prn_it()`. Each call has its own local storage for the variable `c`, in which the individual characters of the input line are stored. Each call is stacked until the newline character is read.

- ```
  putchar(c);
  ```

Only after the newline character is read does anything get written. Each invocation of `prn_it()` now prints the value stored in its local variable `c`. First the newline character is output, then the character just before it, and so on until the first character is output. Thus the input line is reversed.

An interesting variation on this theme is to read in a line of words and print the line back out with the order of the words reversed. Here is a program that does this:
  ```

```
#include <ctype.h>
#include <stdio.h>

#define   MAXWORD   100

void   prn_it_by_word(void);
void   get_word(char *);

int main(void)
{
   printf("Input a line:  ");
   prn_it_by_word();
   printf("\n\n");
   return 0;
}

void prn_it_by_word(void)
{
   char   w[MAXWORD];

   get_word(w);
   if (w[0] != '\n')
      prn_it_by_word();
   printf("%s ", w);
}

void get_word(char *s)
{
   static char   c = '\0';

   if (c == '\n')
      *s++ = c;
   else
      while (!isspace(c = getchar()))
       *s++ = c;
   *s = '\0';
}
```

If the user types `deep in the heart of texas` when prompted, the following appears on the screen:

```
Input a line:  deep in the heart of texas

 texas of heart the in deep
```

Notice that the variable `c` has storage class `static`, so that when a newline character is read in and assigned to `c`, that sentinel value is not be lost on function exit. The initialization of `c` occurs only when the function `get_word()` is invoked for the first time. This is because the storage class of `c` is `static`. On subsequent function calls, the value of c is whatever was there when the previous call exited. Because static storage is guaranteed to be initialized to zero, the explicit initialization of c is not really necessary. Nonetheless, it reminds the reader that the initial value of the variable c is the null character.

The next example illustrates a recursive function that manipulates characters in a string. It can easily be rewritten as an equivalent iterative function.

```
/* Recursively reverse characters from s[j] to s[k]. */

#include <stdio.h>

void   reverse(char *s, int j, int k);
void   swap(char *, char *);

int main(void)
{
   char   phrase[] = "by the sea, by the beautiful sea";

   reverse(phrase, 3, 17);
   printf("%s\n", phrase);
   return 0;
}

void reverse(char *s, int j, int k)
{
   if (j < k) {
      swap(&s[j], &s[k]);
      reverse(s, ++j, --k);
   }
}

void swap(char *p, char *q)
{
   char   tmp;

   tmp = *p;
   *p = *q;
   *q = tmp;
}
```

Here is the output of our program:

```
by eht yb ,aes eht beautiful sea
```

Notice that the characters from position 3 to position 17 have been reversed, counting from zero.

11.2 An Example: Drawing Patterns on the Screen

Elaborate patterns can be drawn on the screen with the use of recursive functions. We illustrate this with a simple example.

```
#include <stdio.h>

#define   SYMBOL   '*'
#define   OFFSET   0
#define   LENGTH   19

void  display(char, int, int);
void  draw(char, int);

int main(void)
{
   display(SYMBOL, OFFSET, LENGTH);
   return 0;
}

void display(char c, int m, int n)
{
   if (n > 0) {
      draw(' ', m);
      draw(c, n);
      putchar('\n');
      display(c, m + 2, n - 4);
   }
}

void draw(char c, int k)
{
   if (k > 0) {
      putchar(c);
      draw(c, k - 1);
   }
}
```

The function main() calls display(), which in turn calls draw() and display(). Thus display() is recursive. The function draw() prints k copies of a character c. We have written this function to be recursive as well. Here is what appears on the screen when we execute this program:

```
*******************
  ***************
    ***********
      *******
        ***
```

11.3 String Handling Using Recursion

A string consists of contiguous characters in memory, ending with the null character \0. Conceptually, we can think of a string as either the null string, consisting of just the null character, or as a character followed by a string. This definition of a string describes it as a recursive data structure. We can use this to code some basic string-handling functions recursively.

In Chapter 10, "Strings and Pointers," we showed how the standard library function strlen() could be coded as an iteration. Here we show how it can be coded recursively.

```
/* Recursive string length. */
int r_strlen(const char *s)
{
   if (*s == '\0')
      return 0;
   else
      return (1 + r_strlen(s + 1));
}
```

The base case tests for the empty string and returns if it is found. The recursion is invoked as r_strlen(s + 1), where s + 1 is a pointer expression. The expression points one character further down the string.

The elegance of this recursive formulation is paid for in a loss of run-time efficiency. If a string is length k, computing it requires $k + 1$ function calls of r_strlen(). An optimizing compiler could avoid this penalty.

String comparison is somewhat more complicated. Here we write a recursive version of the standard library function strncmp(). It lexicographically compares at most the first n characters of two strings.

```
/* Recursive string n compare. */

int r_strncmp(const char *s1, const char *s2, int n)
{
   if (*s1 != *s2 || *s1 == '\0' || n == 1)
      return (*s1 - *s2);
   else
      return (r_strncmp(++s1, ++s2, --n));
}
```

This function looks at the first character of the two strings pointed at by s1 and s2. If the two characters are different, or if they are both the null character, or the value of n is 1, then the value returned is the difference between the two characters. Otherwise, the function recurs, incrementing both string pointers and decrementing n. The recursion terminates at the first position where the two strings differ, or where both of the characters are null, or after at most n - 1 recursions.

11.4 The Divide-and-Conquer Methodology

A typical place where recursion is used is in coding a divide-and-conquer algorithm. Such an algorithm divides the problem into smaller pieces, solves each piece either directly or by recursion, and recombines the solution of the parts into the solution of the whole.

Let us use the divide-and-conquer method to find both the maximum and minimum element in an array of integers. In 1972 in the article "A Sorting Problem and Its Complexity" (*Communications of the ACM*, 15, no. 6), one of the authors, Ira Pohl, published the best possible algorithm for this problem. The criterion for "best" is the least number of comparisons needed. For simplicity, we treat here only the case in which the number of elements in the array is a power of 2. In exercise 11 on page 387, we continue our discussion of the algorithm and modify it to remove the power-of-2 restriction.

```
/*  best possible minmax algorithm - Pohl, 1972 */

/*  size of the array a is n; it must be a power of 2. */
/*  code can be rewritten to remove this restriction.  */

void minmax(int a[], int n, int *min_ptr, int *max_ptr)
{
   int   min1, max1, min2, max2;

   if (n == 2)
      if (a[0] < a[1]) {
         *min_ptr = a[0];
         *max_ptr = a[1];
      }
      else {
         *min_ptr = a[1];
         *max_ptr = a[0];
      }

   else {
      minmax(a, n/2, &min1, &max1);
      minmax(a + n/2, n/2, &min2, &max2);
      if (min1 < min2)
         *min_ptr = min1;
      else
         *min_ptr = min2;
      if (max1 < max2)
         *max_ptr = max2;
      else
         *max_ptr = max1;
   }
}
```

Dissection of the minmax() Function

■
```
if (n == 2)
   if (a[0] < a[1]) {
      *min_ptr = a[0];
      *max_ptr = a[1];
   }
   else {
      *min_ptr = a[1];
      *max_ptr = a[0];
   }
```

This is the base case. The smaller of the two elements a[0] and a[1] is assigned to the value pointed to by min_ptr, and the larger of the two elements is assigned to the value pointed to by max_ptr.

■
```
else {
   minmax(a, n/2, &min1, &max1);
   minmax(a + n/2, n/2, &min2, &max2);
```

This is the divide-and-conquer step. The array a is divided into two halves. The first invocation finds the minimum and the maximum among the elements a[0], . . ., a[n/2 - 1]. The second invocation looks for the minimum and maximum among the second half of the elements a[n/2], . . . , a[n - 1]. Note that a is a pointer expression having the value &a[0] and that a + n/2 is a pointer expression having the value &a[n/2].

■
```
if (min1 < min2)
   *min_ptr = min1;
else
   *min_ptr = min2;
```

The minimum values from the two halves are compared; the smaller of the two is assigned to the object pointed to by min_ptr, the overall minimum.

■
```
if (max1 < max2)
   *max_ptr = max2;
else
   *max_ptr = max1;
```

Similarly, the overall maximum value is assigned to the object pointed to by max_ptr.

This algorithm has theoretical, as well as practical, implications. Further ideas are discussed in exercise 10 on page 386. Exercise 11 on page 387 concerns the removal of the power-of-2 restriction on the size of the array a[].

Many algorithms for sorting use the divide-and-conquer technique. An especially important one is the sorting algorithm "quicksort"; see *A Book on C* by Al Kelley and Ira Pohl (Reading, Mass.: Addison-Wesley, 1998).

11.5 An Example: The Towers of Hanoi

In the game called *Towers of Hanoi*, there are three towers labeled A, B, and C. The game starts with *n* disks on tower A. For simplicity, suppose *n* is 3. The disks are numbered from 1 to 3, and without loss of generality we may assume that the diameter of each disk is the same as its number. That is, disk 1 has diameter 1 (in some unit of measure), disk 2 has diameter 2, and disk 3 has diameter 3. All three disks start on tower A in the order 1, 2, 3. The object of the game is to move all the disks on tower A to tower C. Only one disk may be moved at a time. Any of the towers A, B, or C may be used for the intermediate placement of disks. After each move, the disks on each of the towers must be in order. That is, at no time can a larger disk be placed on a smaller disk.

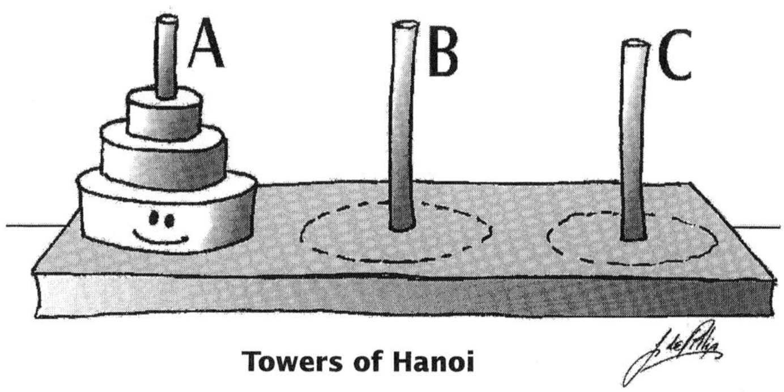

Towers of Hanoi

We write a program that uses recursion to produce a list of moves that shows how to accomplish the task of transferring the *n* disks from tower A to tower C. In addition, at each step we print the configuration of the disks on each tower. Here is the header file for the program:

In file hanoi.h

```
#include <assert.h>
#include <stdio.h>
#include <stdlib.h>

extern int   cnt;                                    /* # of moves */

enum no_yes {no, yes};
```

```
// The towers will be tagged with 'A', 'B', and 'C'.
typedef   char          tower_tag;
typedef   int           disk;
typedef   int *         tower;
typedef   const char    cchr;
typedef   enum no_yes   no_yes;

void     chk(tower a, tower b, tower c, int sz);
void     error_exit_cannot_get_here(cchr* place);
void     error_exit_wrong_order(tower a, int sz);
int      get_n_from_user(void);
no_yes   is_out_of_order(tower a, int sz);

void     move(int n, tower a, tower b, tower c, int sz);
int      ndisks(tower a, int sz);
int      top_index(tower a, int sz);
void     wrt(tower a, tower b, tower c, disk d, int sz);
void     wrt_tower(tower a, int sz);
```

The global variable `cnt` is used to keep track of the number of moves. Note that we used the type definition facility to create the types `tower_tag`, `disk`, `tower`, and so on. A variable of type `tower` is a pointer to `int`, and after space has been allocated, it can be treated as an array.

In file main.c

```
#include "hanoi.h"

int   cnt = 0;                               /* # of moves */

int main(void)
{
   int     i;
   int     n;                                /* number of disks */
   int     sz;                               /* size of the arrays */
   tower   a, b, c;                          /* the towers of Hanoi */

   n = get_n_from_user();
   assert(n > 0);
   sz = n + 1;

   // Create space for towers a, b, and c.
   // Each tower has space for a tag and n disks.
   a = calloc(sz, sizeof(int));
   b = calloc(sz, sizeof(int));
   c = calloc(sz, sizeof(int));
```

```
    // Tag towers a, b, and c with 'A', 'B', and 'C', respectively.
    a[0] = 'A';
    b[0] = 'B';
    c[0] = 'C';

    // Start with n disks on tower a.
    for (i = 1; i < sz; ++i)
       a[i] = i;
    // Write the starting picture on the screen.
    wrt(a, b, c, 0, sz);

    // Move n disks from tower A to tower C,
    // using tower B as an intermediate tower.
    move(n, a, b, c, sz);                       /* recur*/
    return 0;
}
```

In `main()`, we first get `n` from the user. Suppose `n` has value 3. Then the arrays `a[]`, `b[]`, and `c[]` have size 4, and `a[]` contain `'A'`, 1, 2, 3. Because `calloc()` assigns all its elements value zero, in `b[]` we have `'B'`, 0, 0, 0, and in `c[]` we have `'C'`, 0, 0, 0. All the work gets done in the recursive function call

```
move(n, a, b, c, sz)
```

We read this as "move *n* disks from tower A to tower C, using tower B as an intermediate tower." Alternatively, we can think of this as "move *n* disks from tower A through tower B to tower C." We want to explain in detail how the function `move()` works, but before we do so, here is the output of the program if we enter 4 when prompted:

```
TOWERS OF HANOI:

There are three towers: A, B, and C.

The disks on tower A must be moved to tower C.  Only one
disk can be moved at a time, and the order on each tower
must be preserved at each step.  Any of the towers A, B,
or C can be used for intermediate placement of a disk.

The problem starts with n disks on Tower A.

Input n: 4
```

```
 0: Start:                       1 2 3 4
 1: Move disk 1 from A to B:       2 3 4         1
 2: Move disk 2 from A to C:         3 4         1          2
 3: Move disk 1 from B to C:         3 4                  1 2
 4: Move disk 3 from A to B:           4         3        1 2
 5: Move disk 1 from C to A:         1 4         3          2
 6: Move disk 2 from C to B:         1 4       2 3
 7: Move disk 1 from A to B:           4     1 2 3
 8: Move disk 4 from A to C:                 1 2 3          4
 9: Move disk 1 from B to C:                   2 3        1 4
10: Move disk 2 from B to A:           2         3        1 4
11: Move disk 1 from C to A:         1 2         3          4
12: Move disk 3 from B to C:         1 2                  3 4
13: Move disk 1 from A to B:           2         1        3 4
14: Move disk 2 from A to C:                     1      2 3 4
15: Move disk 1 from B to C:                          1 2 3 4
```

To save space, the disks on each tower are written from left to right instead of vertically. From this output, we can tell at a glance that a larger disk is never placed on a smaller one. Notice the symmetry in the output, which shows that the last half of the moves can be deduced from the first half. Symmetry, if it exists, can sometimes be used to improve program execution time. Fortunately, this is not of concern in the "towers of Hanoi" problem.

Let us look at some of the other functions in this program.

In file get.c

```
#include "hanoi.h"

int get_n_from_user(void)
{
   int   n;

   printf("%s",
      "TOWERS OF HANOI:\n\n"
      "There are three towers: A, B, and C.\n\"
      "The disks on tower A must be moved to tower C.  Only one\n"
      "disk can be moved at a time, and the order on each tower\n"
      "must be preserved at each step.  Any of the towers A, B,\n"
      "or C can be used for intermediate placement of a disk.\n"
      "\n"
      "The problem starts with n disks on Tower A.\n\n"
      "Input n: ");
   if (scanf("%d", &n) != 1 || n < 1) {
      printf("\nERROR: Positive integer not found - bye!\n\n");
      exit(1);
   }
   printf("\n");
   return n;
}
```

In file move.c

```
/*
// Move n disks from tower a to tower c,
// using tower b for temporary storage.//
// CAUTION:
//    The tags for the towers a, b, and c
//    need not be A, B, and C, respectively.
*/

#include "hanoi.h"

void move(int n, tower a, tower b, tower c, int sz)
{
   int    i;
   int    j;
   disk   d;

   chk(a, b, c, sz);
   if (n == 1) {
      ++cnt;
      i = top_index(a, sz);
      j = top_index(c, sz);
      assert(i >= 1 && i <= sz - 1);
      assert(j >= 2 && j <= sz);
      d = a[i];
      a[i] = 0;
      c[j - 1] = d;
      wrt(a, b, c, d, sz);
   }
   else {
      move(n - 1, a, c, b, sz);
      move(1, a, b, c, sz);
      move (n - 1, b, a, c, sz);
   }
}
```

Dissection of the Recursive Function move()

■ `void move(int n, tower a, tower b, tower c, int sz)`

This is the header to the function definition for `move()`. Recall that in the header file we created the type `tower` to be synonymous with "pointer to `int`." Thus we can treat the towers `a`, `b`, and `c` as arrays of type `int`. In `main()`, where we first call `move()`, the tags in the towers a, b, and c are `'A'`, `'B'`, and `'C'`, respectively. Note, however, that when `move()` calls itself within the body of `move()`, this association need not hold.

■ `disk d;`

In the header file we used the `typedef` facility to make the type `disk` synonymous with the type `int`. Here, we want to think of `d` as a disk on a tower.

■ `chk(a, b, c, sz);`

This function provides help to the programmer during program construction. It checks that the disks on each of the towers are in order; that is, no big disk sits on top of a smaller disk. If an error is found, a message to the user gets printed on the screen and the program exits.

■
```
if (n == 1) {
    ++cnt;
    i = top_index(a, sz);
    j = top_index(c, sz);
    assert(i >= 1 && i <= sz - 1);
    assert(j >= 2 && j <= sz);
```

If the number of disks to be moved is 1, we increment the counter, find the top index for `a[]` and `c[]`, and use `assert()` to make sure that the indices are in the expected range. Suppose that `sz` has value 5 and that we have the following values in `a[]` and `c[]`:

```
in a[]: 'C'  0  0  1  2
in c[]: 'A'  0  0  0  4
```

To find the top index, we disregard the tag and find the index of the first nonzero element in the array. (Remember to count from zero.) Thus the top index for `a[]` is 3, and the top index for `c[]` is 4. These index, or subscript, values get used to move the disk.

■
```
    d = a[i];
    a[i] = 0;
    c[j - 1] = d;
    wrt(a, b, c, d, sz);
}
```

We assign the value of the top disk in tower `a[]` to `d`, remove the disk from the tower by assigning `0` to `a[i]`, put the disk on tower `c[]` by assigning `d` to `c[j - 1]`, and write a line on the screen that illustrates what we have done.

■
```
else {
    move(n - 1, a, c, b, sz);
    move(1, a, b, c, sz);
    move (n - 1, b, a, c, sz);
}
```

> This is the recursive part of the algorithm. If `n` is greater than 1, we first move `n - 1` of the disks from `a` through `c` to `b`, then move one disk from `a` through `b` to `c`, and finally move the `n - 1` disks that we previously had moved to `b` from `b` through `a` to `c`. The net effect of these three moves is to move `n` disks from `a` through `b` to `c`.

Moving a bunch of disks comes down to moving just one disk repeatedly. Once we get the base case of moving just one disk correct, recursion takes care of the rest.

Here are the rest of the functions.

In file error.c

```
#include "hanoi.h"

void error_exit_cannot_get_here(cchr* place)
{
   printf("%s%s%s\n",
      "---\n"
      "PROGRAMMER ERROR: Cannot get here:\n"
      "\n"
      "   In ", place, ":\n"
      "\n"
      "Bye!\n");
   exit(1);
}

void error_exit_wrong_order(tower a, int sz)
{
   printf("%s%c%s\n",
      "---\n"
      "ERROR: Tower ", a[0], " is out of order:\n");
   wrt_tower(a, sz);
   printf("\n\n");
   exit(1);
}
```

In file fct.c

```
#include "hanoi.h"

void chk(tower a, tower b, tower c, int sz)
{
   int   n1 = ndisks(a, sz);
   int   n2 = ndisks(b, sz);
   int   n3 = ndisks(c, sz);
```

```
   assert(n1 >= 0 && n2 >= 0 && n3 >= 0);
   assert(n1 + n2 + n3 == sz - 1);
   if (is_out_of_order(a, sz) == yes)
      error_exit_wrong_order(a, sz);
   if (is_out_of_order(b, sz) == yes)
      error_exit_wrong_order(b, sz);
   if (is_out_of_order(c, sz) == yes)
      error_exit_wrong_order(c, sz);
}

no_yes is_out_of_order(tower a, int sz)
{
   int   i;

   for (i = top_index(a, sz); i < sz - 1; ++i) {
      if (a[i] >= a[i + 1])
         return yes;
   }
   return no;
}

int ndisks(tower a, int sz)
{
   return (sz - top_index(a, sz));
}

int top_index(tower a, int sz)
{
   int   i;

   for (i = 1; i < sz && a[i] == 0; ++i)
      ;
   return i;
}
```

In file wrt.c

```
#include "hanoi.h"

void wrt(tower a, tower b, tower c, disk d, int sz)
{
   cchr*        fct_name = "wrt()";
   int          fw = 26;                          /* field width */
   int          i;
   tower_tag    t;                         /* 'A', 'B', or 'C' */
```

```
   if (cnt == 0)
      printf("%5d%-*s", cnt, fw, ": Start:");
   else
      printf("%5d%s%d%s%c%s%c%s",  cnt,
      ": Move disk ", d, " from ", a[0], " to ", c[0], ":");

   // CAUTION:
   //    Towers a, b, c need not be named A, B, C, respectively.
   //    Find A and print it, then find B and print it, .....

   for (t = 'A'; t <= 'C'; ++t) {
      if (a[0] == t)
         wrt_tower(a, sz);
      else if (b[0] == t)
         wrt_tower(b, sz);
      else if (c[0] == t)
         wrt_tower(c, sz);
      else
         error_exit_cannot_get_here(fct_name);
   }
   putchar('\n');
}

void wrt_tower(tower a, int sz)
{
   int   fw;                                       /* field width */
   int   i;

   if (a[0] == 'C')
      printf("  ");
   for (i = 1; i < sz; ++i) {
      fw = (a[i] < 10) ? 2 : 3;
      if (a[i] == 0)
         printf("%*s", fw, "");
      else
         printf("%*d", fw, a[i]);
   }
}
```

In wrt(), we use the call printf("%5d%-*s", cnt, fw, ": Start:"). The format %-*s needs to be explained. The minus sign means to left-adjust in the field, and the * means that the integer value that goes here should be taken from the list of corresponding arguments. In this case the * takes its value from fw, the field width. See Chapter 13, "Input/Output and Files," for details about printf().

11.6 Style

For most common uses of recursion there is a simple, equivalent iterative program. Recursion simplifies the coding by suppressing the need for local variables that keep track of different indices; iteration is often a more efficient method of solution. Which method to code is frequently a matter of taste.

Let us write a simple recursive program that computes the average value of an array.

```
double average(double a[], int n)    /* n is size of a[] */
{
   if (n == 1)
      return a[0];
   else
      return ((a[n - 1] + (n - 1) * average(a, n - 1))/n);
}
```

In such cases, where the recursion is elementary, there is a simple transformation to an iterative form using a `while` or `for` loop. Here is the iterative form of the function `average()`:

```
double average(double a[], int n)    /* n is size of a[] */
{
   double   sum = 0.0;
   int      i;

   for (i = 0; i < n; ++i)
      sum += a[i];
   return (sum / n);
}
```

In this case the iterative form of the function is simpler. It also avoids $n - 1$ function calls, where n is the size of the array being averaged. A common programming style is to choose the iterative version over the recursive version of a function if both versions are simple. Nonetheless, many algorithms are commonly coded using recursion. One such algorithm is "quicksort." Another is the greatest common divisor algorithm given in exercise 8 on page 385.

11.7 Common Programming Errors

The most common errors in recursive functions lead to infinite loops. We use the recursive definition of factorial to illustrate several common pitfalls.

For a nonnegative integer n, the factorial of n, written $n!$, is defined by

$$0! = 1, \qquad n! = n(n-1)\cdot\cdots\cdot 3\cdot 2\cdot 1 \quad \text{for } n > 0$$

or equivalently,

$$0! = 1, \qquad n! = n((n-1)!) \quad \text{for } n > 0$$

Thus, for example, $5\cdot 4\cdot 3\cdot 2\cdot 1 = 120$. Using the recursive definition of factorial, it is easy to write a recursive version of the factorial function.

```
int factorial(int n)      /* recursive version */
{
   if (n <= 1)
      return 1;
   else
      return (n * factorial(n - 1));
}
```

This code is correct and works properly within the limits of integer precision available on a given system. However, because the numbers $n!$ grow large very fast, the function call `factorial(n)` yields a valid result only for a few values of `n`. On our system, the function call `factorial(12)` returns a correct value, but if the argument to the function is greater than 12, an incorrect value is returned. This type of programming error is common. Functions that are logically correct can return incorrect values if the logical operations in the body of the function are beyond the integer precision available to the system.

Suppose the programmer has incorrectly coded the factorial function, omitting the base case. This leads to an infinite loop.

```
long factorial_forever(long n)
{
   return (n * factorial_forever(n - 1));
}
```

Suppose the base case is coded, but only for `n` having the value 1. Now the function works properly with argument values in the range 1 to 12, but if the function is called with an argument that is zero or negative, an infinite loop occurs.

```
long factorial_positive(long n)
{
   if (n == 1)
      return 1;
   else
      return (n * factorial_positive(n - 1));
}
```

Another common error, not specifically tied to the use of recursion, is the incorrect use of the decrement operator. In many recursions a variable, say n, is used to pass an argument of lower value to the function in the recursion step. For some algorithms, --n is a correct argument; for others it is not. Consider

```
long factorial_decrement(long n)
{
   if (n <= 1)
      return 1;
   else
      return (n * factorial_decrement(--n));
}
```

In the second return statement we used the expression

```
n * factorial_decrement(--n)
```

which uses the variable n twice. Because the decrement operator has a side effect when it is applied to the second n, it may also affect the value of the first n. This type of programming error is common, especially when recursive functions are coded.

11.8 System Considerations

Recursive function calls require memory for each invocation. Because many invocations are active at the same time, the operating system may run out of available memory. Obviously, this is more likely to be a problem on small systems than on large ones. Of course, if you are writing code meant to run on many systems, you must know and respect all the system limitations.

Let us write a program that shows the depth of recursion that can occur on our Borland C system. The depth varies from one system to another and depends on the recursive function being used. Nonetheless, our experiment gives us some indication of our machine limits. We use the recursive function sum() presented in Section 11.1, "Recursive Problem Solving," on page 360, but modify it to use long integers. This modification avoids overflow problems for large values of n. The function call sum(n) activates n nested copies of the function. Thus n indicates the depth of recursion.

```
/* Test the depth of recursion for sum() */
#include <stdio.h>

long   sum(long);
int main(void)
{
   long   n = 0;

   for ( ; ; n += 100)
      printf("recursion test:  n = %ld  sum = %ld\n",
               n, sum(n));
   return 0;
}

long sum(long n)
{
   if (n <= 1)
      return n;
   else
      return (n + sum(n - 1));
}
```

Warning: This program may fail catastrophically and require you to reboot the system. Here are the last few lines printed by this program on our system:

```
 .....
recursion test:  n = 7900  sum = 31208950
recursion test:  n = 8000  sum = 32004000
recursion test:  n = %ld  sum = %ld
```

The program fails at this point without returning control to the operating system. This shows that failure occurs after the depth of the recursion exceeds 8000 calls to `sum()`. The system is allowing very deep recursions to occur before the system limit is reached. Note carefully that it is not the number of recursive calls per se that causes the failure; it is the depth of the recursion—more than 8000—that causes the problem.

11.9 Moving to C++

Recursion in C++ is no different from what it is in C. However, C++ libraries often have an extended precision package. The type `big_int`, an unbounded precision integer package, can be used by recursions such as `factorial()` to return correct, arbitrarily large, factorial computations. Of course, there are system limits.

Many C++ libraries have an ordered array type that can be used to illustrate the efficiency of binary lookup search. Although little different from its expression in C, the following program illustrates the importance of divide-and-conquer algorithms and their ready expression as recursive algorithms:

```
//Binary lookup in a sorted integer array
int bin_lookup(const sorted& keys, int size, int d)
{
   int index ;

   if ( size == 0) //failure
       return - 1;
   index = size - 1 / 2;
   if (keys[index] == d)
       return index;
   else if (keys[index] < d)
       return bin_lookup(keys, size- 1/2, d)
   else
       return bin_lookup(&keys[index + 1], size - 1/2, d)
}
```

The function `bin_lookup()` works in logarithmic time. Each recursion is guaranteed to cut the remaining search in half. The result is the index of the element containing value `d`, or `-1` if no such value is found.

Summary

- A function is said to be *recursive* if it calls itself, either directly or indirectly. Recursion is an advanced form of flow of control.
- Recursion typically consists of a base case or cases and a general case. It is important to make sure the function terminates.
- Any recursive function can be written in an equivalent iterative form. Due to system overhead in calling functions, a recursive function may be less efficient than an equivalent iterative one, but the difference is often very slight. When a recursive function is easier to code and maintain than an equivalent iterative one and the penalty is slight, the recursive form is preferable.

Exercises

1 The following program writes BLAST OFF first. Explain its behavior.

```
#include <stdio.h>

void count_down(int n)
{
   if (n) {
      count_down(n - 1);
      printf("%d !  ", n);
   }
   else
      printf("\nBLAST OFF\n");
}

int main(void)
{
   count_down(10);
   return 0;
}
```

2 Write a recursive function that tests whether a string is a palindrome, which is a string such as "abcba" or "otto" that reads the same in both directions. Write a program that tests your function. For comparison, write an iterative version of your program as well.

3 Consider the following recursive function. On some systems the function returns correct values; on others it returns incorrect values. Explain why. Write a test program to see what happens on your system.

```
int sum(int n)
{
   if (n <= 1)
      return n;
   else
      return (n + sum(--n));
}
```

4 Carefully examine the base case of the recursive function r_strncmp(). Does the following base case also work? Which is more efficient? Explain.

```
if (*s1 != *s2 || *s1 == '\0' || *s2 == '\0' || n == 1)
   return (*s1 - *s2);
```

Write a recursive version of the standard library function `strcmp()`. If `s1` and `s2` are strings, the function call `r_strcmp(s1, s2)` should return an integer value that is negative, zero, or positive, depending on whether `s1` is lexicographically less than, equal to, or greater than `s2`. Use `main()`, given in the following code, to test your function. Compile your program and put the executable code in the file *test*. If *infile* is a file containing many words, then use the command *test* < *infile* to test your program.

```
#include <string.h>
#include <stdio.h>

#define   MAXWORD   30    /* max characters in a word */
#define   N         50    /* number of words in array */

int   r_strcmp(char *, char *);

int main(void)
{
   int    i, j;
   char   word[N][MAXWORD],      /* an array of N words */
          temp[MAXWORD];

   for (i = 0; i < N; ++i)
      scanf("%s", word[i]);
   for (i = 0; i < N - 1; ++i)
      for (j = i + 1; j < N; ++j)
       if (r_strcmp(word[i], word[j]) > 0) {
          strcpy(temp, word[i]);
          strcpy(word[i], word[j]);
          strcpy(word[j], temp);
       }
   for (i = 0; i < N; ++i)
      printf("%s\n", word[i]);
   return 0;
}
```

5 Write a recursive version of the standard library function `strcpy()`. If `s1` and `s2` are strings, the function call `r_strcpy(s1, s2)` should overwrite whatever is in `s1` with the contents of `s2`, and the pointer value of the first argument, namely `s1`, should be returned. See Appendix A, "The Standard Library," for a description of `strcpy()`.

6 Although it is considered bad programming style to overwrite a constant string, we do it in this exercise to emphasize an important point. Consider the two statements

```
printf("%s\n", strcpy("try this", "and this"));
printf("%s\n", strcpy("and", "also this"));
```

One of these statements works correctly, whereas the other can be expected to cause difficulty. Why? Rewrite the function `r_strcpy()` that you wrote for the previous exercise so that if the type of error exhibited here occurs, an error message is printed and the program stops. Even though the function is recursive, make sure that you check for the error only once. Note also that some systems do not allow constant strings to be overwritten. *Hint:* Use a static variable.

7 A function that calls another function, which in turn calls the original function, is said to be *corecursive*. Note that corecursive functions occur in pairs. Write a program that counts the number of alphabetic characters in a string and sums the digits in the string. For example, the string `"A0is444apple7"` has eight alphabetic characters, and the digits in the string sum to 19. Write a pair of corecursive functions to help carry out the tasks. Use `count_alph()` to count the alphabetic characters, and use `sum_digit()` for summing the digits. These two functions should call each other. For comparison, write a noncorecursive function that performs the two tasks in a direct, more natural fashion. *Hint:* If necessary, use static variables.

8 The greatest common divisor of two positive integers is the largest integer that is a divisor of both of them. For example, 6 and 15 have 3 as their greatest common divisor, and 15 and 22 have 1 as their greatest common divisor. The following recursive function computes the greatest common divisor of two positive integers. First write a program to test the function; then write and test an equivalent iterative function.

```
int gcd(int a, int b)
{
   int   r;

   if ((r = a % b) == 0)
      return b;
   else
      return gcd(b, r);
}
```

9 Write a recursive lookup function to search an array in sorted order. Write a program to test your function. Use `random()` to fill an array `a[]` of size `n`, and use `bubble_sort()` to sort the array. The function call `look_up(v, a, n)` should be used to look for the value `v` in the array `a[]`. If just one of the elements of the array, say `a[i]`, has the value `v`, then `i` should be returned. If two or more of the elements of the array have the value `v`, then the index of any one of them is an acceptable answer. If none of the elements of the array has the value `v`, then -1 should be returned. The base case is to look at the

"middle" element a[n/2]. If this element has the value v, then n/2 is returned; otherwise recursion is used to look for v in whichever of the following is appropriate:

```
a[0], ..., a[n/2 - 1]   or   a[n/2 + 1], ..., a[n - 1]
```

For example, if the value of v is less than a[n/2], then v should be looked for in the first part of the array and the appropriate recursion would be

```
return (look_up(v, a, n/2));
```

10 The following code can be used to test the recursive function minmax() given in Section 11.4, "The Divide-and-Conquer Methodology," on page 367. The value of n is entered interactively; the function calloc() is used to create an array a[] of size n dynamically; the array is filled with randomly distributed integer values; and, finally, the minimum and maximum values of the array are computed in two ways: recursively, by calling minmax(), and iteratively. Because all of this occurs repeatedly inside a loop, we use the standard library function free() to give the storage pointed to by a back to the system at the end of the for loop.

```
#include <stdio.h>
#include <stdlib.h>

void   minmax(int *, int, int *, int *);

int main(void)
{
   int   *a, i,
         n,                    /* n is the size of a[] */
         r_min, r_max,         /* recursive min and max */
         i_min, i_max;         /* iterative min and max */

   printf("Input a power of 2:  ");
   while (scanf("%d", &n) == 1 && n > 0) {
      a = calloc(n, sizeof(int));
      for (i = 0; i < n; ++i)
         a[i] = rand();
      minmax(a, n, &r_min, &r_max);
      printf("\n%s%d%9s%d\n",
       "recursion:  min = ", r_min, "max = ", r_max);
      i_min = i_max = a[0];

      for (i = 1; i < n; ++i) {
         i_min = (i_min < a[i]) ? i_min : a[i];
         i_max = (i_max > a[i]) ? i_max : a[i];
      }
```

```
        printf("%s%d%9s%d\n\n",
         "iteration:  min = ", i_min, "max = ", i_max);
        free(a);
        printf("Input a power of 2:  ");
     }
     return 0;
  }
```

The value of n is the size of the array a[]. For each value of n that is a power of 2, the minimum and maximum values of the array are computed in two ways: recursively and iteratively. How many comparisons are used in each of these computations? *Hint:* Use manual simulation to find the answer when n takes on values that are powers of 2 of low order.

11 It is not at all obvious that the recursive algorithm minmax() is "best" in the sense of requiring the least number of comparisons. That there cannot exist a better algorithm is proved in the paper by Ira Pohl cited in Section 11.4, "The Divide-and-Conquer Methodology," on page 367. In this exercise we want to show how to modify the algorithm so that arrays of any size can be handled. The modified function may not have the property that it is the "best" possible, but nonetheless it is still a very efficient algorithm.

```
void minmax(int a[], int n, /* n is a the size of a[] */
            int *min_ptr, int *max_ptr)
{
   int   min1, max1, min2, max2;

   if (n == 1)
      *min_ptr = *max_ptr = a[0];
   else {
      minmax(a, n/2, &min1, &max1);
      minmax(a + n/2, n - n/2, &min2, &max2);
      if (min1 < min2)
         *min_ptr = min1;
      else
         *min_ptr = min2;
      if (max1 < max2)
         *max_ptr = max2;
      else
         *max_ptr = max1;
   }
}
```

Write a program to test this function. Notice that it is still a divide-and-conquer algorithm and that it handles arrays of all sizes correctly. The base case now occurs when n has value 1. In the best possible algorithm, given in Section 11.4, "The Divide-and-Conquer Methodology," on page 367, the base case occurs when n has the value 2. The value 2 is, of course, a power of 2. But 1 is also a power of 2. Can the original `minmax()` be modified so that `n` with value 1 is the base case and the algorithm still remains "best"? Perhaps the base case with `n` having value 2 was used to emphasize the "2-ness" of the algorithm. After all, when `n` has value 1, the algorithm is not too complicated. There is one more minor detail that needs to be considered. The algorithm in this exercise uses the argument `n - n/2`, whereas the comparable argument in the original algorithm is the expression `n/2`. Explain why.

12 Experiment with the *Towers of Hanoi* program. How many moves are required to solve a game that starts with *n* disks on tower A? If *n* is 64 and one disk is moved each day, how many billions of years does it take to move all the disks to tower C?

13 (Advanced) Write a nonrecursive version of the *Towers of Hanoi* program.

14 (Advanced) A knight is a chess piece that moves in the pattern of an "ell" (*L*). The chessboard has 64 squares; the knight can make two legal moves if placed at a corner square of the board and eight legal moves if placed in the middle square of the board. Write a function that computes the number of legal moves a knight can make when starting at a specific square on the board. Associate that number with the square. This is called the *connectivity* of the square as viewed by the knight. Write a program that finds and prints the number of legal moves associated with each square on the board. The numbers should be printed as an 8×8 array corresponding to the 64 squares on a chessboard, with each number representing the connectivity of its square. This array is the connectivity of the chessboard as viewed by the knight.

15 (Advanced; see the 1967 article, "A Method for Finding Hamiltonian Paths and Knight's Tours," by Ira Pohl, in *Communications of the ACM*, 10, no. 7). A knight's tour is a path the knight takes that covers all 64 squares without revisiting any square. Warnsdorf's rule states that to find a knight's tour, one starts from a corner square and goes to a square that has not yet been reached and has smallest connectivity. An *adjacent* square is one the knight can move to immediately. When a square is visited, all of the connectivity numbers of adjacent squares are decremented. Employ Warnsdorf's rule to find a knight's tour. Print out an 8×8 array corresponding to the chessboard, and in each position print the number of moves it took the knight to reach that square.

16 (Advanced) Pohl's improvement to Warnsdorf's rule was to suggest that ties be broken recursively (see the previous exercise). Warnsdorf's rule is called a *heuristic*. It is not guaranteed to work. Still, it is very efficient for a combinatorially difficult problem. Sometimes two squares have the same smallest connectivity. To break the tie, compute recursively which square leads to a further smallest connectivity and choose that square. On the ordinary 8×8

chessboard, from any starting square, the Warnsdorf-Pohl rule was always found to work. Implement this heuristic algorithm and run it for five different starting squares, printing each tour.

17 C++: Write a recursive function that computes Fibonacci numbers, which are defined as follows:

$$F_0 = 0, \quad F_1 = 1, \quad F_n = F_{n-1} + F_{n-2}$$

A Fibonacci recursion can quickly overflow the machine's stack frame. Compare an iterative to a recursive implementation in terms of running time. If it is available, use `big_int` and produce a table of the first 100 Fibonacci numbers.

18 Java: A method is said to be recursive if it calls itself, either directly or indirectly. In its simplest form the idea of recursion is straightforward. Rewrite the following Java program in C:

```
// Recur.java - recursive goodbye
//Java by Dissection page 124.
public class Recur {
   public static void main(String[] args) {
     sayGoodBye(5);
   }

   static void sayGoodBye(int n) {
      if (n < 1) //base case
         System.out.println("########");
      else {
         System.out.println("Say goodbye Gracie.");
         sayGoodBye(n - 1); //recursion
      }
   }
}
```

Structures and ADTs

Chapter 12

The structure type allows the programmer to aggregate components into a single, named variable. A structure has components that are individually named. These components are called *members*. Because the members of a structure can be of various types, the programmer can create aggregates of data that are suitable for a problem. Like arrays and pointers, structures are considered a derived type.

In this chapter we show how to declare structures and use them to represent a variety of familiar examples, such as a playing card or a student record. Critical to processing structures is accessing their members done with either the member operator "." or the structure pointer operator `->`. These operators, along with `()` and `[]`, have the highest precedence. After these operators are introduced, we provide a complete table of precedence and associativity for all the operators of C.

This chapter gives many examples to show how structures are processed. An example that implements a student record system is given to show the use of structures and the accessing of its members. The use of self-referential structures to create linked lists is explained, and the code necessary for the processing of linked lists is presented. These user implementations of a playing card, a student record, and a linked list are examples of user-defined types, or abstract data types (ADTs).

12.1 Declaring Structures

Structures are a means of aggregating a collection of data items of possibly different types. As a simple example, let us define a structure that describes a playing card. The spots on a card that represent its numeric value are called *pips*. A playing card, such as the three of spades, has a pip value, 3, and a suit value, spades. Structures allow us to group variables together. We can declare the structure type

```
struct card {
   int    pips;
   char   suit;
};
```

to capture the information needed to represent a playing card. In this declaration `struct` is a keyword, `card` is the structure tag name, and the variables `pips` and `suit` are members of the structure. The variable `pips` takes values from 1 to 13, representing ace to king, and the variable `suit` takes values from `'c'`, `'d'`, `'h'`, and `'s'`, representing clubs, diamonds, hearts, and spades.

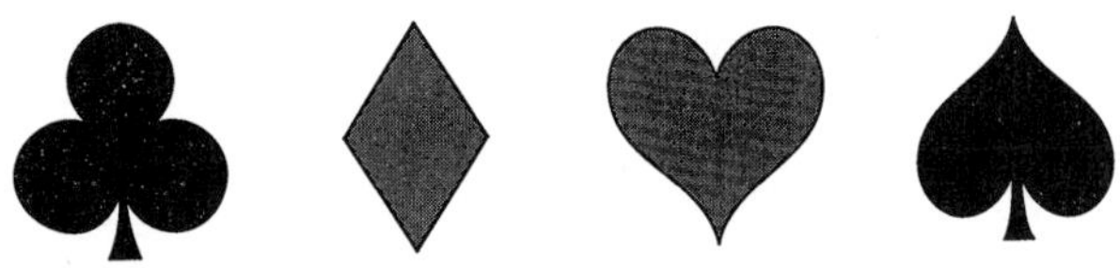

This declaration creates the derived data type `struct card`. The declaration can be thought of as a blueprint; it creates the type `struct card`, but no storage is allocated. The tag name can now be used to declare variables of this type. The declaration

```
struct card   c1, c2;
```

allocates storage for the identifiers `c1` and `c2`, which are of type `struct card`. To access the members of `c1` and `c2`, we use the structure member operator "`.`". Suppose we want to assign to `c1` the values representing the five of diamonds and to `c2` the values representing the queen of spades. To do this we can write

```
c1.pips = 5;
c1.suit = 'd';
c2.pips = 12;
c2.suit = 's';
```

A construct of the form

structure_variable . member_name

is used as a variable in the same way a simple variable or an element of an array is used. The member name must be unique within the specified structure. Because the member must always be prefaced or accessed through a unique structure variable identifier, there is no confusion between two members having the same name in different structures. An example is

```
struct fruit {
   char   name[15];
   int    calories;
};
```

```
struct vegetable {
   char   name[15];
   int    calories;
};

struct fruit        a;
struct vegetable    b;
```

Having made these declarations, we can access `a.calories` and `b.calories` without ambiguity.

Within a single declaration, it is possible to create a structure type and declare variables of that type at the same time. An example of this is

```
struct card {
   int    pips;
   char   suit;
} c, deck[52];
```

The identifier `card` is the structure tag name. The identifier `c` is declared to be a variable of type `struct card`, and the identifier `deck` is declared to be an array of type `struct card`. Another example of this is

```
struct {
   char   *last_name;
   int    student_id;
   char   grade;
} s1, s2, s3;
```

which declares `s1`, `s2`, and `s3` to represent three student records, but does not include a tag name for use in later declarations. Suppose we had instead written:

```
struct student {
   char   *last_name;
   int    student_id;
   char   grade;
};
```

This declaration, unlike the previous one, has `student` as a structure tag name, but no variables of this type are declared. It can be thought of as a blueprint. Now we can write

```
struct student    temp, class[100];
```

This declares `temp` and `class` to be of type `struct student`. Only at this point is storage allocated for these variables. The declaration of a structure type by itself does not cause storage to be allocated.

12.2 Accessing a Member

We have already seen the use of the member operator ".". In this section we give additional examples of its use and introduce the structure pointer operator ->.

Suppose we are writing a program called *class_info*, which generates information about a class of 100 students. We can begin by creating a header file. Note that we use the name *cl_info.h* to conform to MS-DOS length restrictions on file names. On systems without this limitation, *class_info.h* would be more mnemonic.

```
#define   CLASS_SIZE   100

struct student {
   char   *last_name;
   int    student_id;
   char   grade;
};
```

This header file can now be used to share information with the modules making up the program. Suppose in another file we write

```
#include "cl_info.h"

int main(void)
{
   struct student   temp, class[CLASS_SIZE];
   .....
```

We can assign values to the members of the structure variable `temp` by using statements such as

```
temp.grade = 'A';
temp.last_name = "Bushker";
temp.student_id = 590017;
```

Now suppose we want to count the number of failing students in a given class. To do this, we can write a function that accesses the `grade` member. Here is a function `fail()` that counts the number of F grades in the array `class[]`.

```
/* Count the failing grades. */

#include "cl_info.h"

int fail(struct student class[])
{
   int   i, cnt = 0;

   for (i = 0; i < CLASS_SIZE; ++i)
      cnt += class[i].grade == 'F';
   return cnt;
}
```

Dissection of the fail() Function

- ```
  int fail(struct student class[])
  {
     int   i, cnt = 0;
  ```

The parameter `class` is of type "pointer to `struct student`." We can think of it as a one-dimensional array of structures. Parameters of any type, including structure types, can be used in headers to function definitions.

- ```
  for (i = 0; i < CLASS_SIZE; ++i)
  ```

We are assuming that when this function is called, an array of type `struct student` and of size `CLASS_SIZE` is passed as an argument.

- ```
  cnt += class[i].grade == 'F';
  ```

An expression such as this demonstrates how concise C can be. C is operator rich; to be fluent in its use, the programmer must be careful about precedence and associativity. This statement is equivalent to

```
cnt += (((class[i]).grade) == 'F');
```

The member `grade` of the *i*th element (counting from zero) of the array of structures `class` is selected. A test is made to see if it is equal to `'F'`. If equality holds, then the value of the expression

```
class[i].grade == 'F'
```

is 1, and the value of `cnt` is incremented. If equality does not hold, then the value of the expression is 0, and the value of `cnt` remains unchanged. A clearer but more verbose equivalent is
```

```
    if (class[i].grade == 'F')
       ++cnt;
```

■ `return cnt;`

The number of failing grades is returned to the calling environment.

C provides the structure pointer operator -> to access the members of a structure via a pointer. This operator is typed on the keyboard as a minus sign followed by a greater than sign. If a pointer variable is assigned the address of a structure, then a member of the structure can be accessed by a construct of the form

pointer_to_structure -> *member_name*

An equivalent construct is given by

(**pointer_to_structure*) . *member_name*

The parentheses are necessary here. The operators -> and ".", along with () and [], have the highest precedence and associate from left to right. Because of this, the same construct without parentheses would be equivalent to

*(*pointer_to_structure* . *member_name*)

In complicated situations the two accessing modes can be combined in complicated ways. The following table illustrates their use in a straightforward manner.

Declarations and assignments

```
struct student temp, *p = &temp;
temp.grade = 'A';
temp.last_name = "Bushker";
temp.student_id = 590017
```

Expression	Equivalent expression	Conceptual Value
`temp.grade`	`p -> grade`	A
`temp.last_name`	`p -> last_name`	Bushker
`temp.student_id`	`p -> student_id`	590017
`(*p).student_id`	`p -> student_id`	590017

12.3 Operator Precedence and Associativity: A Final Look

We now want to display the entire precedence and associativity table for all the C operators. The operators "`.`" and `->` have been introduced in this chapter. These operators, together with `()` and `[]`, have the highest precedence.

Operators	Associativity
`()` `[]` `.` `->` `++` (*postfix*) `--` (*postfix*)	left to right
`++` (*prefix*) `--` (*prefix*) `!` `~` `sizeof` (*type*) `+` (*unary*) `-` (*unary*) `&` (*address*) `*` (*dereference*)	right to left
`*` `/` `%`	left to right
`+` `-`	left to right
`<<` `>>`	left to right
`<` `<=` `>` `>=`	left to right
`==` `!=`	left to right
`&`	left to right
`^`	left to right
`|`	left to right
`&&`	left to right
`||`	left to right
`?:`	right to left
`=` `+=` `-=` `*=` `/=` `%=` `>>=` `<<=` `&=` `^=` `|=`	right to left
`,` (*comma operator*)	left to right

The comma operator has the lowest precedence in C. The commas used in declarations and in argument lists to functions are not comma operators.

As we saw in Chapter 6, "The Fundamental Data Types," the unary operator `sizeof` can be used to find the number of bytes needed to store an object in memory. For example, the value of the expression `sizeof(struct card)` is the number of bytes needed by the system to store a variable of type `struct card`. On most systems the type of the expression is `unsigned`. Later in this chapter we see that the `sizeof` operator is used extensively when creating linked lists.

Although the complete table of operators is extensive, some simple rules apply. The primary operators are function parentheses, subscripting, and the two addressing operatiors for accessing a member of a structure. These four operators are of highest precedence. Unary operators come next, followed by the arithmetic operators. Arithmetic operators follow the usual convention—namely, multiplicative operators have higher precedence than additive operators. Assignments of all kinds are of lowest precedence, with the exception of the still lowlier comma operator. A programmer who does not know the rules of precedence and associativity in a particular situation should either look the rules up or use parentheses.

12.4 Structures, Functions, and Assignment

Traditional C systems allow a pointer to a structure type to be passed as an argument to a function and returned as a value. ANSI C allows structures themselves to be passed as arguments to functions and returned as values. In this environment, if `a` and `b` are variables of the same structure type, the assignment expression `a = b` is allowed. It causes each member of `a` to be assigned the value of the corresponding member of `b`. (See Section 12.15, "System Considerations," on page 415, for further remarks.)

To illustrate the use of structures with functions, we use the structure type `struct card`. For the remainder of this chapter, assume the header file *card.h* contains the declaration for this structure.

```
struct card {
   int    pips;
   char   suit;
};
```

Let us write functions that assign values to a card, extract the member values of a card, and print the values of a card. We assume that the header file *card.h* has been included wherever needed.

```
void assign_values(struct card *c_ptr, int p, char s)
{
   c_ptr -> pips = p;
   c_ptr -> suit = s;
}

void extract_values(struct card *c_ptr, int *p_ptr, char *s_ptr)
{
   *p_ptr = c_ptr -> pips;
   *s_ptr = c_ptr -> suit;
}
```

These functions access a card by using a pointer to a variable of type `struct card`. The structure pointer operator -> is used throughout to access the required member. Next, let us write a card-printing routine that takes a pointer to `struct card` and prints its values using `extract_values()`.

```
void prn_values(struct card *c_ptr)
{
   int    p;            /* pips value */
   char   s;            /* suit value */
   char   *suit_name;

   extract_values(c_ptr, &p, &s);
   switch (s) {
   case 'c' :
      suit_name = "clubs";
      break;
   case 'd' :
      suit_name = "diamonds";
      break;
   case 'h' :
      suit_name = "hearts";
      break;
   case 's' :
      suit_name = "spades";
      break;
   default:
      suit_name = "error";
   }
   printf("card:  %d of %s\n", p, suit_name);
}
```

Finally, we want to illustrate how these functions can be used. First, we assign values to a deck of cards, and then as a test we print out the heart suit.

```
void  assign_values(struct card *, int, char );
void  prn_values(struct card *);
void  extract_values(struct card *, int *, char *);

int main(void)
{
   int            i;
   struct card    deck[52];

   for (i = 0; i < 13; ++i) {
      assign_values(deck + i, i + 1, 'c');
      assign_values(deck + i + 13, i + 1, 'd');
      assign_values(deck + i + 26, i + 1, 'h');
      assign_values(deck + i + 39, i + 1, 's');
   }
   for (i = 0; i < 13; ++i)      /* print out the hearts */
      prn_values(deck + i + 26);
   return 0;
}
```

Notice how this code uses address arithmetic to assign and print values for the various suits. Thus the cards in the heart suit are printed by the statement

```
prn_values(deck + i + 26);
```

which is equivalent to

```
prn_values(&deck[i + 26]);
```

Functions can be designed to work with structures as parameters, rather than with pointers to structures. Let us rewrite the function `extract_values()`.

```
void extract_values(struct card  c,
                    int *p_ptr, char *s_ptr)
{
   *s_ptr = c.suit;
   *p_ptr = c.pips;
}
```

In C, the value of an argument that is passed to a function is copied when the function is invoked. This call-by-value mechanism was discussed in Section 4.12, "Invocation and Call-by-Value," on page 150, and Chapter 8, "Functions, Pointers, and Storage Classes." Because of this, when a structure is passed as an argument to a function, it is copied when the function is invoked. For this reason, passing the address of the structure is more efficient than passing the structure itself.

12.5 Problem Solving: Student Records

In C, structures, pointers, and arrays may be combined to create complicated data structures. Problem solving is greatly aided by matching a data structure to the information that is manipulated. Usually a real-world object, such as a student, is best described as a set of characteristics. In C, `struct` is an encapsulation mechanism for such a data aggregate. Once aggregated, the object is treated conceptually as a student, instead of as a collection of specific characteristics.

We start with our previous example of `struct student`, in Section 12.2, "Accessing a Member," on page 394, and develop it into a more comprehensive data structure for a student record. We begin by defining the various types needed.

```
#define   CLASS_SIZE   50
#define   NCOURSES     10      /* number of courses */
```

```
struct student {
   char   *last_name;
   int    student_id;
   char   grade;
};

struct date {
   short  day;
   char   month[10];
   short  year;
};

struct personal {
   char          name[20];
   struct date   birthday;
};

struct student_data {
   struct personal    p;
   int                student_id;
   char               grade[NCOURSES];
};
```

Notice that struct `student_data` is constructed with nested structures. One of its members is the structure `p`, which has as one of its members the `birthday` structure. After the declaration

```
struct student_data   temp;
```

has been made, the expression

```
temp.p.birthday.month[0]
```

has as its value the first letter of the month of the birthday of the student whose data is in `temp`. Structures such as `date` and `personal` are often used in database applications.

Let us write the function `read_date()` to enter data into a variable of type `struct date`. When the function is called, the address of the variable must be passed as an argument to the function.

```
#include "student.h"

void read_date(struct date *d)
{
   printf("Enter  day(int)  month(string)  year(int): ");
   scanf("%hd%s%hd", &d -> day, d -> month, &d -> year);
}
```

Dissection of the read_date() Function

■
```
void read_date(struct date *d)
{
   printf("Enter  day(int)  month(string)  year(int): ");
```

The parameter d has type "pointer to struct date." The printf() statement prompts the user for information.

■ `&d -> day`

This is an address. Because & is of lower precedence than ->, this expression is equivalent to

```
&(d -> day)
```

First the pointer d is used to access the member day. Then the address operator & is applied to this member to obtain its address.

■ `d -> month`

This is an address. The pointer d is used to access a member that is an array. An array name by itself is a pointer, or address; it points to the base address of the array.

■ `scanf("%hd%s%hd", &d -> day, d -> month, &d -> year);`

The function scanf() is used to read in three values and to store them at appropriate addresses. Recall that in the header file *student.h*, the two members day and year of struct date were declared to be of type short. The format %hd is used to convert characters in the standard input stream (keyboard) to a value of type short. (The h used to modify the conversion character d in the format comes from the second letter in the word *short*.)

The function read_date() can be used to read information into a variable of type struct student_data. For example, the code

```
struct student_data   temp;

read_date(&temp.p.birthday);
```

can be used to place information into the appropriate member of temp.

Here is a function to enter grades:

```
void read_grades(char g[])
{
   int   i;

   printf("Enter %d grades:  ", NCOURSES);
   for (i = 0; i < NCOURSES; ++i)
      scanf(" %c", &g[i]);
}
```

The control string " %c" is used to read in a single non-white space character. The blank just before the % matches optional white space in the input stream. This function could be called to read a list of grades into `temp` as follows:

```
read_grades(temp.grade);
```

The argument `temp.grade` is an address (pointer) because it refers to a member of a structure that is an array, and an array name by itself is the base address of the array. Thus, when the function is invoked, it causes the values of `temp.grade` in the calling environment to be changed.

Basically, understanding structures comes down to understanding how to access their members. As a further example, let us now write a function that takes data stored in the long form in `struct student_data` and converts it to the short form stored in `struct student`.

```
#include "student.h"

void extract( struct student_data    *s_data,
              int                    n,
              struct student         *undergrad)
{
   undergrad -> student_id = s_data -> student_id;
   undergrad -> last_name = s_data -> p.name;
   undergrad -> grade = s_data -> grade[n];
}
```

12.6 Initialization of Structures

All external and static variables, including structure variables, that are not explicitly initialized are automatically initialized by the system to zero. In traditional C, external and static structures can be initialized by the programmer. In ANSI C, we can initialize automatic structures as well. The syntax is similar to that used with arrays. A structure variable can be followed by an equal sign = and a list of constants contained within braces. If there are not enough values to assign to all the members of the structure, the remaining members are assigned the value zero by default. Some examples are

```
struct card   c = {12, 's'};    /* the queen of spades */

struct fruit   frt = {"plum", 150};

struct complex {
   double   real;
   double   imaginary;
}   m[3][3] = {
   {{1.0, -0.5}, {2.5, 1.0}, { 0.7, 0.7}},
   {{7.0, -6.5}, {-0.5, 1.0}, {45.7, 8.0}},
};   /* m[2][] is assigned zeroes */
```

12.7 The Use of typedef

In practice, the typedef facility is often used to rename a structure type. We see this in Section 12.9, "Linear Linked Lists," on page 407.

Let us illustrate the use of typedef by defining a small number of functions that operate on vectors and matrices.

```
#define   N   3   /* size of all vectors and matrices */

typedef   double   scalar;
typedef   scalar   vector[N];
typedef   scalar   matrix[N][N];
```

We have used the typedef mechanism to create the types scalar, vector, and matrix, which is both self-documenting and conceptually appropriate. Our programming language has been extended in a natural way to incorporate these new types as a domain. Notice how typedef can be used to build hierarchies of types. For example, we could have written

```
typedef   vector   matrix[N];
```

in place of

```
typedef   scalar   matrix[N][N];
```

The use of typedef to create type names such as scalar, vector, and matrix allows the programmer to think in terms of the application. Now we are ready to create functions that provide operations over our domain.

```
void add(vector x, vector y, vector z)      /* x = y + z */
{
   int i;

   for (i = 0; i < N; ++i)
      x[i] = y[i] + z[i];
}

scalar dot_product(vector x, vector y)
{
   int      i;
   scalar   sum = 0.0;

   for (i = 0; i < N; ++i)
      sum += x[i] * y[i];
   return sum;
}

void multiply(matrix a, matrix b, matrix c)    /* a=b*c */
{
   int   i, j, k;

   for (i = 0; i < N; ++i)
      for (j = 0; j < N; ++j) {
       a[i][j] = 0.0;
       for (k = 0; k < N; ++k)
          a[i][j] += b[i][k] * c[k][j];
      }
}
```

12.8 Self-Referential Structures

In this section we define structures with pointer members that refer to the structure type containing them. These are called *self-referential* structures. Self-referential structures often require storage management routines to explicitly obtain and release memory.

Let us define a structure with a member field that points at the same structure type. We wish to do this in order to have an unspecified number of such structures linked together.

```
struct list {
   int           data;
   struct list   *next;
};
```

Each variable of type `struct list` has two members, `data` and `next`. The pointer variable `next` is called a *link*. Each structure is linked to a succeeding structure by way of the member `next`. These structures are conveniently displayed pictorially, with links shown as arrows.

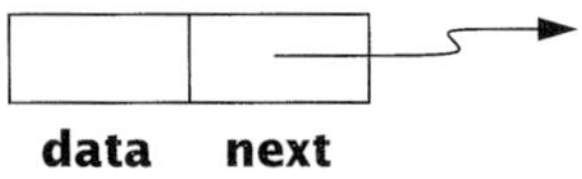

The pointer variable `next` contains an address of either the location in memory of the successor `struct list` element or the special value `NULL`, which is usually defined in *stdio.h* as a symbolic constant with value 0. The value `NULL` is used to denote the end of the list. To see how all this works, let us begin with the declaration

```
struct list   a, b, c;
```

We want to manipulate the structure variables `a`, `b`, and `c` to create a linked list. We begin by performing some assignments on these structures.

```
a.data = 1;
b.data = 2;
c.data = 3;
a.next = b.next = c.next = NULL;
```

The result of this code is described pictorially as follows:

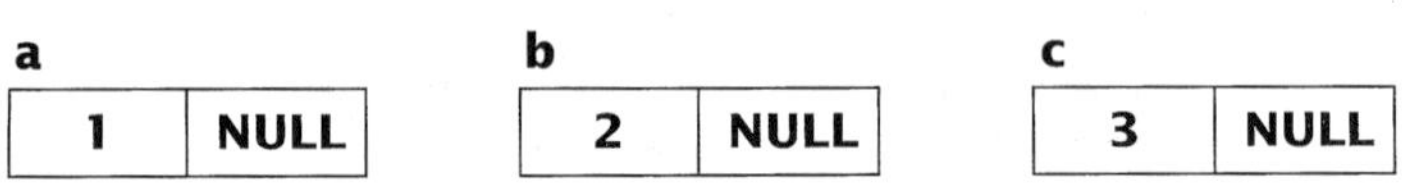

Next, let us chain the three structures together.

```
a.next = &b;
b.next = &c;
```

These pointer assignments result in linking `a` to `b` to `c`.

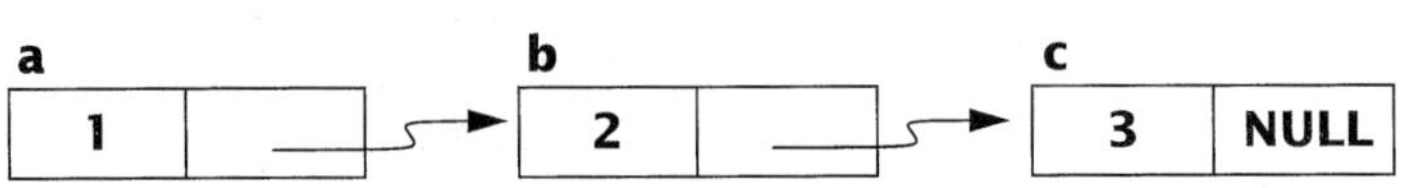

Now the links allow us to retrieve data from successive elements. For example,

`a.next -> data` *has value* 2
`a.next -> next -> data` *has value* 3

12.9 Linear Linked Lists

A *linear linked list* is like a clothesline on which the data structures hang sequentially. There is a head pointer that addresses the first element of the list, and each element points at a successor element, with the last element having a link value NULL. Typically, a linked list is created dynamically. In this section we show how this is done.

Let us begin by creating a header file that is included with the list processing functions we write in the sections that follow. This header file includes the file *stdio.h* because that is where NULL is defined.

In file list.h

```
#include <stdio.h>

typedef   char   DATA;      /* use char in examples */

struct linked_list {
   DATA                  d;
   struct linked_list    *next;
};

typedef   struct linked_list   ELEMENT;
typedef   ELEMENT *            LINK;
```

In the header file *list.h* we used typedef to create names of types that are more suggestive of their use. Notice that although DATA is simply the type char, conceptually it could be a more complicated type, such as an array or a structure (see exercise 11 on page 426).

Dynamic Storage Allocation

The declaration of struct linked_list in *list.h* does not allocate storage. It acts as a blueprint for the storage that the system allocates later when variables and arrays of this type are declared. We used the typedef facility to rename the type as ELEMENT because we wish to think of it as an element in our list. What makes self-referential structure types such as ELEMENT especially useful is that utility functions such as malloc() are provided in the standard library to allocate storage dynamically. If head is a variable of type LINK, then

```
head = malloc(sizeof(ELEMENT));
```

obtains from the system a piece of memory adequate to store an ELEMENT and assigns its base address to the pointer head. As in the preceding example, a function call to malloc() often uses the sizeof operator, which calculates the number of bytes required to store a particular object.

Suppose we want to dynamically create a linear linked list to store the three characters *n*, *e*, and *w*. The following code does this:

```
head = malloc(sizeof(ELEMENT));
head -> d = 'n';
head -> next = NULL;
```

This creates a single element list.

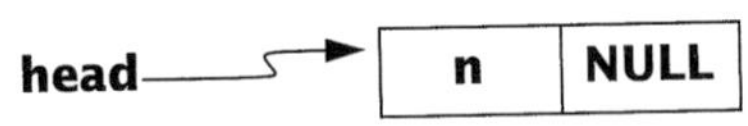

A second element is added by the assignments

```
head -> next = malloc(sizeof(ELEMENT));
head -> next -> d = 'e';
head -> next -> next = NULL;
```

Now there is a two-element list.

Finally we add the last element.

```
head -> next -> next = malloc(sizeof(ELEMENT));
head -> next -> next -> d = 'w';
head -> next -> next -> next = NULL;
```

Now we have a three-element list pointed at by head and ending with the sentinel value NULL.

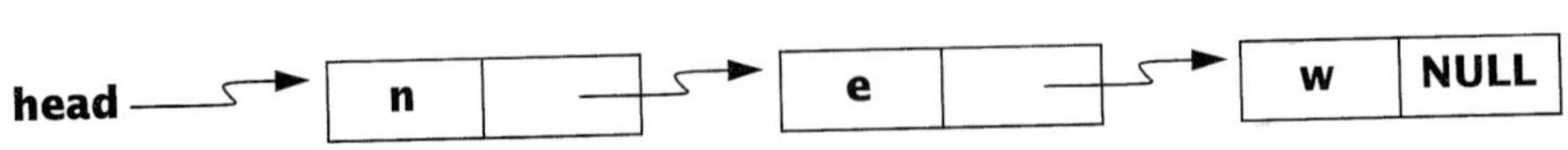

12.10 List Operations

The basic operations on linear linked lists include the following:

Basic List Operations

- Creating a list
- Counting the elements
- Looking up an element
- Inserting an element
- Deleting an element

We demonstrate the techniques for programming such operations on lists. The use of recursive functions is natural because lists are a recursively defined construct. Each routine requires the specifications in the header file *list.h*. Observe that d in these examples could be redefined as a more complicated data structure.

For our first example, we write a function that produces a list from a string. The function returns a pointer to the head of the resulting list. The heart of the function creates a list element by allocating storage and assigning member values.

```
/* List creation by recursion. */

#include "list.h"

LINK string_to_list(char s[])
{
   LINK   head;

   if (s[0] == '\0')      /* base case */
      return NULL;
   else {
      head = malloc(sizeof(ELEMENT));
      head -> d = s[0];
      head -> next = string_to_list(s + 1);
      return head;
   }
}
```

Dissection of the `string_to_list()` Function

■
```
LINK string_to_list(char s[])
{
   LINK   head;
```

When a string is passed as an argument, a linked list of the characters in the string is created. Because a pointer to the head of the list is returned, the type specifier in the header to this function definition is `LINK`.

■
```
if (s[0] == '\0')      /* base case */
   return NULL;
```

When the end-of-string sentinel is detected, `NULL` is returned, and, as we see, the recursion terminates. The value `NULL` is also used to mark the end of the linked list.

■
```
else {
   head = malloc(sizeof(ELEMENT));
```

If the string `s[]` is not the null string, then `malloc()` is used to retrieve enough bytes to store an object of type `ELEMENT`. The pointer variable `head` now points at the block of storage provided by `malloc()`.

■
```
head -> d = s[0];
```

The member `d` of the allocated `ELEMENT` is assigned the first character in the string `s[]`.

■
```
head -> next = string_to_list(s + 1);
```

The pointer expression `s + 1` points to the remainder of the string. The function is called recursively with `s + 1` as an argument. The pointer member `next` is assigned the pointer value that is returned by `string_to_list(s + 1)`. This recursive call returns as its value a `LINK` or, equivalently, a pointer to `ELEMENT`, which points to the remaining sublist.

■
```
return head;
```

The function exits with the address of the head of the list.

Notice once more how recursion has a base case, the creation of the empty list, and a general case, the creation of the remainder of the list.

12.11 Counting and Lookup

In this section we write two more recursive functions that perform list operations. The first is count(); it can be used to count the elements in a list. It involves recurring down the list and terminating when the NULL pointer is found. If the list is empty, the value 0 is returned; otherwise, the number of elements in the list is returned.

```
/* Count a list recursively. */

#include "list.h"

int count(LINK head)
{
   if (head == NULL)
      return 0;
   else
      return (1 + count(head -> next));
}
```

The next function searches a list for a particular element. If the element is found, a pointer to that element is returned; otherwise the NULL pointer is returned.

```
/* Lookup c in the list pointed to by head. */

#include "list.h"

LINK lookup(DATA c, LINK head)
{
   if (head == NULL)
      return NULL;
   else if (c == head -> d)
      return head;
   else
      return (lookup(c, head -> next));
}
```

12.12 Insertion and Deletion

One of the most useful properties of lists is that insertion takes a fixed amount of time once the position in the list is found. In contrast, if one wished to place a value in a large array, retaining all other array values in the same sequential order, the insertion would take, on average, time proportional to the length of the array. The values of all elements of the array that came after the newly inserted value would have to be moved over one element.

Let us illustrate insertion into a list by having two adjacent elements pointed at by `p1` and `p2` and by inserting between them an element pointed at by `q`.

Before

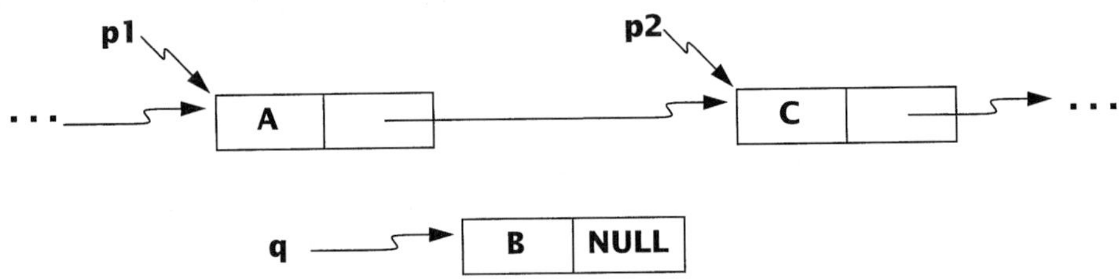

After insertion:

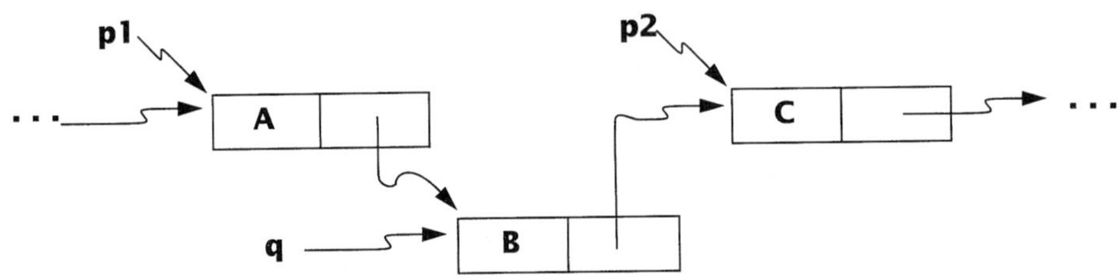

Here is a function that accomplishes the task:

```
/* Inserting an element in a linked list. */

#include "list.h"

void insert(LINK p1, LINK p2, LINK q)
{
   p1 -> next = q;     /* insertion */
   q -> next = p2;
}
```

Deleting an element is very simple in a linear linked list. The predecessor of the element to be deleted has its link member assigned the address of the successor to the deleted element. Let us first illustrate the situation before deletion

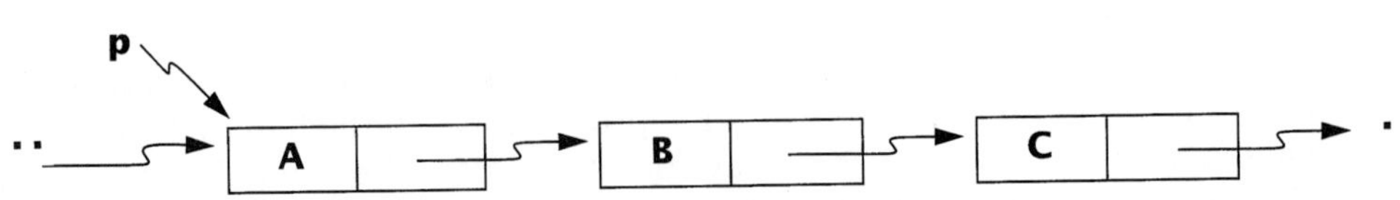

The next line of code

```
q = p -> next;
```

causes q to point at the element that we want to delete.

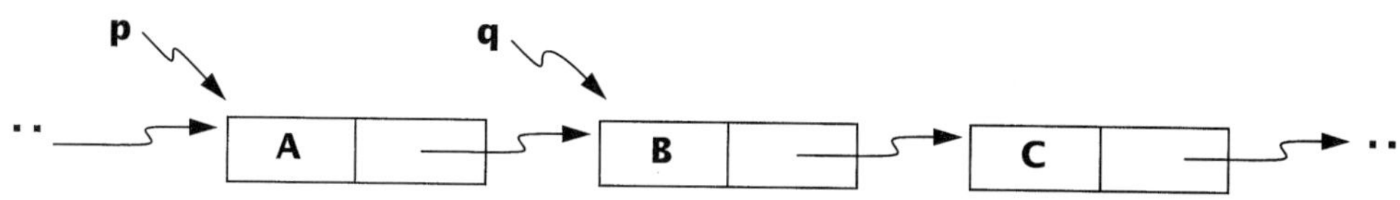

Now consider the statement

```
p -> next = q -> next;
```

After this statement is executed, we have

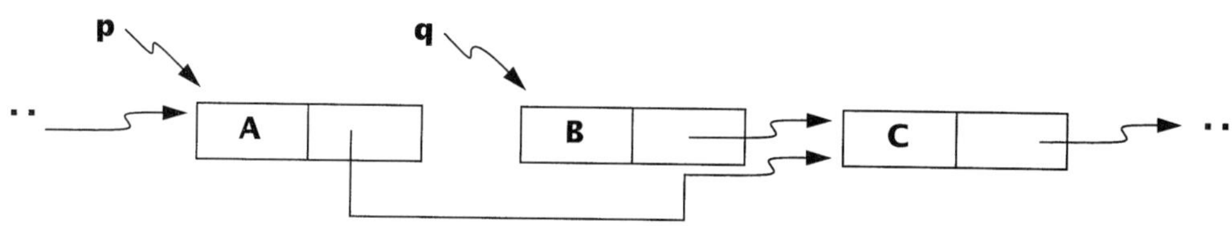

As the diagram shows, the element containing B is no longer accessible and is of no use. Such an inaccessible element is called *garbage*. Because memory is frequently a critical resource, it is desirable that this storage be returned to the system for later use. This may be done with the standard library function `free()`. Using `free()`, we write a deletion routine that returns dynamically allocated list storage to the system.

```
/* Recursive deletion of a list. */

#include "list.h"

void delete_list(LINK head)
{
   if (head != NULL) {
      delete_list(head -> next);
      free(head);                         /* release storage */
   }
}
```

12.13 Style

It is good programming style to aggregate related data into a structure. By declaring a structure, the programmer can create a data type suitable for a problem. The declaration should list each member on its own line, properly indented.

```
struct automobile {
   char      name[15];        /* example: buick   */
   int       year;            /* example: 1983    */
   double    cost;            /* example: 2390.95 */
};
```

It is usually good programming practice to associate a tag name with a structure type. It is convenient for both further declarations and documentation.

If extensive use is going to be made of a structure declaration, it is appropriate to use the `typedef` facility to create a new name for the type. In the case of `struct automobile`, we could use

```
typedef   struct automobile   CAR;
```

The new type name does not have to be in capital letters; we could just as well have used `Car` or `car`. In some styles, fully capitalized identifiers are reserved for preprocessor identifiers. The choice depends on personal taste.

A common programming style is to write structure declarations in header files that can then be included where needed. If the declaration of a structure type needs to be altered later, it is accomplished by changing its declaration in the header file. Perhaps later we discover that we want CAR to have a member describing the horsepower of an automobile. This is easily done by adding a line such as

```
int   horsepower;      /* example: 225 */
```

to the structure declaration in the header file.

12.14 Common Programming Errors

When working with self-referential structures, a common programming error is to access the wrong place in memory. For example, if a linear linked list is not properly terminated by a `NULL` pointer, some form of unexpected run-time error occurs.

Another common programming error is to mix up the order in the use of `typedef`. For example,

```
typedef   ELEMENT   struct linked_list;      /* wrong */
```

is incorrect because the identifier `ELEMENT` must follow, not precede, the `struct linked_list` type. Notice also that a `typedef` construction is followed by a semicolon.

Our last programming error involves the comparison of two variables of the same structure type—say, a and b. Although the assignment expression

```
a = b
```

is legal, the use of the expression

```
a == b        /* wrong */
```

to test for equality of two structures is not allowed. Because the operators = and == are so visually similar, beginning programmers sometimes make this mistake.

12.15 System Considerations

C has evolved with time. Traditional C systems allow pointers to structures to be passed as arguments to functions and returned as values. ANSI C compilers also allow structures themselves to be passed as arguments and returned as values. In addition, these compilers allow structure assignment. Programmers writing code that is meant to be backward-compatible must take into account restrictions that may be present in older compilers.

Traditional C does not allow the initialization of structure variables of storage class automatic. Maintaining compatibility with older systems requires that only static and external structure variables be initialized.

In database applications, structures often have tens, even hundreds, of members. If a structure is passed as an argument to a function, a copy of the structure is made when the function is invoked. If the structure is large, and a local copy really is not needed, then for the sake of efficiency it is better to pass a pointer to the structure rather than passing the structure itself.

Operating systems differ in their requirements for aligning storage on boundaries. For example, some systems may require that an `int` be aligned on a word boundary; others may not. Because of this, when space for a structure is allocated, it can happen that the space required for the structure as a whole is more than the sum of the space required for each of its members. Moreover, the space requirement for the structure as a whole may depend on the order of the members within the structure (see exercise 18 on page 427). This seldom concerns the programmer, except when memory is scarce.

12.16 Moving to C++

The concept of `struct` is augmented in C++ to allow functions to be members. The function declaration is included in the structure declaration and is invoked by using access methods for structure members. The functionality required by the `struct` data type should be directly included in the `struct` declaration.

We illustrate these ideas with code for a stack ADT. The *stack* is one of the most useful standard data structures. It allows insertion and deletion of data to occur only at a single restricted element, the top of the stack. This is the last-in-first-out (LIFO) discipline. Conceptually, it behaves like a pile of trays that pops up or is pushed down when trays are removed or added. The following is a stack with ABCD pushed on:

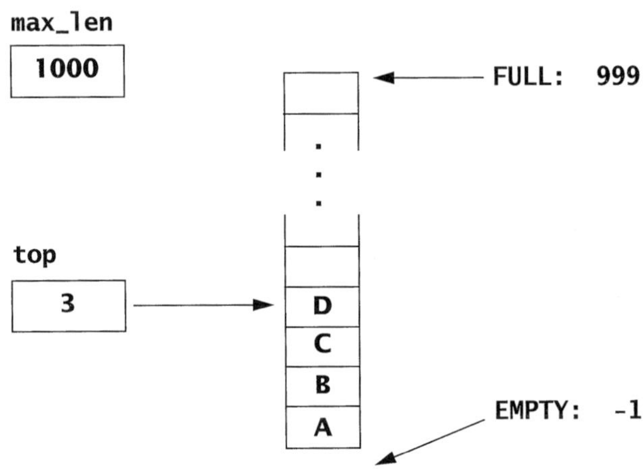

Typically, a stack allows the operations *push, pop, top, empty,* and *full.* The push operator places a value on the stack. The *pop* operator retrieves and deletes a value from the stack. The *top* operator returns the top value from the stack. The *empty* operator tests if the stack is empty. The *full* operator tests if the stack is full. The stack is a typical ADT.

We wish to implement a stack as a C++ data type using `struct` in its C form. An implementation choice is to use a fixed-length `char` array to store the contents of the stack. The top of the stack is an integer-valued member named `top`. The various stack operations are implemented as functions, each of whose argument lists includes a pointer to `stack` parameter. This allows the stack to be modified and avoids call-by-value copying of the stack.

```
//A C-like implementation of type stack.

const int  max_len = 1000;
enum boolean { false, true };
enum { EMPTY = -1, FULL = max_len - 1 };

struct stack {
   char  s[max_len];
   int   top;
};
```

We now code a set of functions to implement standard operations on the stac

```
//A standard set of stack operations.

void reset(stack* stk)
{
   stk -> top = EMPTY;
}

void push(char c, stack* stk)
{
   stk -> s[++stk -> top] = c;
}

char pop(stack* stk)
{
   return (stk -> s[stk -> top--]);
}

char top(stack* stk)
{
   return (stk -> s[stk -> top]);
}

boolean empty(const stack* stk)
{
   return (boolean(stk -> top == EMPTY));
}

boolean full(const stack* stk)
{
   return (boolean(stk -> top == FULL));
}
```

f the stack Functions

```
ıax_len = 1000;
ı { false, true };
' = -1, FULL = max_len - 1 };

{ {
ıax_len];
);
```

type boolean. In C++, the tag name of an enum type is a stant false is initialized to 0, and the constant true is ini- struct declaration creates the new type, stack. It has two y member s and the int member top.

```
stack* stk)

op = EMPTY;
```

sed for initialization. The member top is assigned the value ılar stack initialized is an argument passed as an address.

```
ıar c, stack* stk)

[++stk -> top] = c;

ack* stk)

stk -> s[stk -> top--]);
```

ion is implemented as a function of two arguments. The ıcremented. The value of c is shoved onto the top of the on assumes that the stack is not full. The pop operation is ke fashion; it assumes the stack is not empty. The value of k is returned, and the member top is decremented.

■
```
boolean empty(const stack* stk)
{
   return (boolean(stk -> top == EMPTY));
}

boolean full(const stack* stk)
{
   return (boolean(stk -> top == FULL));
}
```

These functions return an enumerated type `boolean` value. Each tests the `stack` member `top` for an appropriate condition. For example, before calling `push()`, the programmer can test that the stack is not full to ensure that `push()` works correctly. These functions do not modify the stack being pointed at. Therefore we can declare the pointer arguments to be `const`. In all functions the stack argument is passed as an address, and the structure pointer operator -> is used to access members.

Let us rewrite our stack example by declaring as member functions the various functions associated with the stack:

```
struct stack {
//data representation
   char  s[max_len];
   int   top;
   enum { EMPTY = -1, FULL = max_len - 1 };

//operations represented as member functions
   void  reset() { top = EMPTY; }
   void  push(char c) { top++; s[top] = c; }
   char  pop() { return s[top--]; }
   char  top_of() { return s[top]; }
   boolean  empty() { return (boolean(top == EMPTY)); }
   boolean  full() { return (boolean(top == FULL)); }
};
```

The member functions are written much as other functions. One difference is that they can use the data member names as is. Thus the member functions in `stack` use `top` and `s` in an unqualified manner. When invoked on a particular object of type `stack`, they act on the specified member in that object.

The following example illustrates these ideas. If two `stack` variables

```
stack data, operands;
```

are declared, then

```
data.reset();
operands.reset();
```

invoke the member function `reset`, which has the effect of setting both `data.top` and `operands.top` to EMPTY. If a pointer to `stack`

```
stack* ptr_operands = &operands;
```

is declared, then

```
ptr_operands -> push('A');
```

invokes the member function `push`, which increments `operands.top` and sets `operands.s[top]` to `'A'`. One last observation: Because of a naming conflict, the member `top_of()` had its name changed from the previous implementation.

Member functions that are defined within the `struct` are implicitly Cinline. As a rule, only short, heavily used member functions should be defined within the `struct`, as is the case for the example just given. To define a member function outside the `struct`, the scope resolution operator is used. Let us illustrate this by changing the definition of `push` to its corresponding function prototype within the `struct stack`. We write it out fully using the scope resolution operator. In this case the function is not implicitly inline.

```
struct stack {
//data representation

   char  s[max_len];
   int   top;
   enum { EMPTY = -1, FULL = max_len - 1 };

//operations represented as member functions
   void  reset() { top = EMPTY; }  //implicitly inline
   void  push(char c);              //function prototype
   .....
};

void stack::push(char c)            //definition not inline
{
   top++;
   s[top] = c;
}
```

The scope resolution operator `::` allows member functions from different `struct` types to have the same names. In this case, which member function is invoked depends on the type of object it acts upon. The declaration

```
stack  s, t, u;
```

creates three separate stack objects of `sizeof(stack)` bytes. Each of these variables has its own data members:

```
char  s[max_len];
int   top;
```

A member function is conceptually part of the type. There is no distinct member function for any of these three stack variables.

The concept of `struct` is augmented in C++ to allow functions to have `public` and `private` members. Inside a `struct`, the use of the keyword `private` followed by a colon restricts the scope of the members that follow this construct. The `private` members can be used only by a few categories of functions whose privileges include access to these members. These functions include the member functions of the `struct`. Other categories of functions that have access is discussed later in Section 15.3, "Overloading," on page 508.

We now modify our example of `stack` to hide its data representation.

```
struct stack {
public:
   void  reset() { top = EMPTY; }
   void  push(char c) { top++; s[top] = c; }
   char  pop() { return s[top--]; }
   char  top_of() { return s[top]; }
   boolean  empty() { return (boolean(top == EMPTY)); }
   boolean  full() { return (boolean(top == FULL)); }
private:
   char  s[max_len];
   int   top;
   enum { EMPTY = -1, FULL = max_len - 1 };
};
```

We now write `main()` to test these operations.

```
//Reverse a string with a stack.
int main(void)
{
   stack  s;
   char   str[40] = {"My name is Don Knuth!"};
   int    i = 0;
   cout << str << endl;
   s.reset();             //s.top = EMPTY; would be illegal
   while (str[i])
      if (!s.full())
       s.push(str[i++]);
   while (!s.empty())  //print the reverse
      cout << s.pop();
   cout << endl;
}
```

The output from this version of the test program is

```
My name is Don Knuth!
!htunK noD si eman yM
```

As the comment in `main()` states, access to the hidden variable `top` is controlled. It can be changed by the member function `reset()` but cannot be accessed directly. Also, notice how the variable `s` is passed to each member function using the structure member operator form.

The `struct stack` has a private part that contains its data description and a public part that contains member functions to implement stack operations. It is useful to think of the private part as restricted to the implementor's use and the public part as an interface specification that clients may use. The implementor could change the private part without affecting the correctness of a client's use of the stack type.

Hiding data is an important component of object-oriented programming. It allows for more easily debugged and maintained code because errors and modifications are localized. Client programs need only be aware of the type's interface specification.

Classes

Classes in C++ are introduced by the keyword `class`. They are a form of `struct` whose default privacy specification is `private`. Thus `struct` and `class` can be used interchangeably with the appropriate privacy specification.

Many scientific computations require complex numbers. Let us write an ADT for complex numbers.

```
struct complex {
public:
   void  assign(double r, double i);
   void  print() {cout << real << " + " << imag << "i "; }
private:
   double  real, imag;
};

inline void complex::assign(double r, double i = 0.0)
{
   real = r;
   imag = i;
}
```

Here is its equivalent `class` representation:

```
class complex {
public:
   void  assign(double r, double i);
   void  print() {cout << real << " + "<< imag << "i ";}
private:
   double  real, imag;
};

inline void complex::assign(double r, double i = 0.0)
{
   real = r;
   imag = i;
}
```

Also possible would have been

```
class complex {
   double  real, imag;
public:
   void  assign(double r, double i);
   void  print() {cout << real << " + " << imag << "i ";}
};
```

Here we are using the fact that the default access to `class` members is private. It is C++ style to prefer `class` to `struct` unless all members are data members with public access.

Summary

- A structure is an aggregation of subparts treated as a single variable. The subparts of the structure are called members.
- Structure members are accessed by the member operator "." and the structure pointer operator ->. If `s` is a structure variable with a member named `m`, then `s.m` refers to the value of the member `m` within `s`. If `p` is a pointer that points at `s`, then `p -> m` and `s.m` are equivalent expressions. Both "." and -> have the highest precedence among C operators.
- Structures can be members of other structures. Considerable complexity is possible when nesting structures, pointers, and arrays within one another. Care should be taken that the proper variables are being accessed.

- A self-referential structure uses a pointer member to address a structure of the same type. Self-referential structures can be used to create a linear linked list. Each element points to the next element, except the last, which has the value `NULL` for its pointer member.

- The function `malloc()` is used to dynamically allocate storage. It takes an argument of type `size_t` and returns a pointer to `void` that is the base address of the allocated storage. The type `size_t` is an unsigned integer type. It is defined in *stdlib.h*.

- Standard algorithms for list processing are naturally implemented recursively. Frequently, the base case is the detection of the `NULL` link. The general case recurs by moving one element over in the linked list.

Exercises

1 Suppose the following structure is used to write a dieting program:

```
structure food {
   char   name[15];
   int    portion_weight;
   int    calories;
};
```

What is the tag name of this structure? How would one declare an array `meal[10]` of this type? Let us say that a 4-ounce apple contains 200 calories. How would you assign values to the three members of `meal[0]` to represent such an apple?

2 Write a program that counts the number of calories in a given meal. The meal would be stored in the array `meal[]`. The program should write each course of the meal.

3 Create a structure that can describe a restaurant. It should have members that include the name, address, average cost, and type of food. Suppose an array of structures representing restaurants has been created. Write a function that prints out all restaurants of a given food type in order of cost, least expensive first.

4 The following function is supposed to assign values to a playing card, but does not work as expected. Describe what goes wrong.

```
#include "card.h"

struct card *assign_values (int    p,      /* pips value */
                            char   s       /* suit value */
 )
{
   card   *c_ptr;

   c_ptr -> pips = p;
   c_ptr -> suit = s;
   return c_ptr;
}
```

5 When playing poker and other card games, it is usual to arrange a hand to reflect its values. Write a program that arranges and prints out a hand of five cards in sorted order by pips value. Assume that an ace is highest in value, a king is next highest, and so forth.

6 Using the student record example in Section 12.2, "Accessing a Member," on page 394, write a function that prints the average for each student in a class. Let an A grade have value 4, a B grade have value 3, and so forth.

7 Write a function that prints out student data in order of their date of birth, oldest first. The original set of student records need not be in any order.

8 Write a function `prn_student_data()` that prints in a nice format all the information in a variable of type `struct student_data`.

9 Define a structure that contains the name of a food, its calories per serving, its food group (such as meat or fruit), and its cost. Write a program that is able to produce a balanced meal. The foods should be stored as an array of structures. Each meal the program constructs should contain four food groups and meet calorie and cost constraints. It should be capable of producing a large number of different menus.

10 The following declarations do not compile correctly. Explain what is wrong with the declarations and rewrite them.

```
struct husband {
   char          name[10];
   int           age;
   struct wife   spouse;
} a;
```

```
struct wife {
   char             name[10];
   int              age;
   struct husband   spouse;
} b;
```

11 Modify the header file *list.h* in Section 12.9, "Linear Linked Lists," on page 407, by replacing the `typedef` line with

```
struct data {
   char   name[10];
   int    age;
   int    weight;
};

typedef   struct data   DATA;
```

Write a function `create_list()` that transforms an array of type DATA into a linear linked list. Write another function that counts the number of people above both a given age and a given weight.

12 Given a linear linked list of the type found in the previous exercise, write a function `sort_by_age()` that sorts the list by age. Write another function `sort_by_name()` that sorts the list alphabetically by name.

13 Write an iterative version of the function `count()` that was presented in Section 12.10, "List Operations," on page 411.

14 Write an insertion function that inserts an element at the first position in the list following an element storing a particular DATA item. You should use `lookup()` to find the element. If the element is not present, the insertion should occur at the end of the list.

15 Explain why the parentheses are necessary in the construct

(**pointer_to_structure*) . *member_name*

Write a test program that uses this construct. Does your program compile if the parentheses are removed?

16 In simple situations a `typedef` can be replaced by a `#define`. Sometimes, however, this can lead to unexpected errors. Rewrite the header file *list.h* as follows:

```
#include <stdio.h>

#define   DATA   char      /* use char in examples */

struct linked_list {
   DATA                   d;
   struct linked_list   *next;
};

#define   ELEMENT   struct linked_list
#define   LINK      ELEMENT *
```

After you have done this, check to see that the functions `string_to_list()`, `count()`, and `lookup()` can all be compiled just as before. The function `insert()` does not compile. Explain why and modify the function so that it does.

17 The function `insert()`, which we wrote in Section 12.12, "Insertion and Deletion," on page 412, assumed that `p1` and `p2` were pointing to adjacent elements in a linked list. What happens if `p1` and `p2` are pointing to elements in the list that are not adjacent?

18 On some systems, the following two structures are not stored in the same number of bytes:

```
struct s1 {
   char   c1;
   char   c2;
   int    i;
};

struct s2 {
   char   c1;
   int    i;
   char   c2;
};
```

The statement

```
printf("%d\n%d\n", sizeof(struct s1),
       sizeof(struct s2));
```

causes system-dependent values to be printed. What are the space requirements for these structures on the C systems available to you? On some systems, such as Borland C, byte and word alignment options exist. On such systems, try this with both settings.

19 C++: Recode the stack example to use a linear linked list instead of an array as an implementation. The operations should remain abstractly the same.

20 Java: Java shares C++'s use of `class` but discards C's use of `struct`. In Java, everything is a `class`. Because of this, Java is considered a pure object-oriented language. Java uses garbage collection, and Java programmers do not use `malloc()` and `free()`. Furthermore, Java does not have pointers. Instead, `class` types are referential types, and instances of classes are created using `new`. Here is an example of implementing the ADT counter. `Counter` is a type that counts from 0 to 99 and then roll over like a car odometer back to 0. Convert the Java classes to appropriate C `structs` and the member functions to functions that act on pointers to `struct`.

```
// CounterTest.java - demonstration of class Counter
//Java by Dissection pages 200-201
class CounterTest {
  public static void main(String[] args) {
    Counter c1 = new Counter(); //create a Counter
    Counter c2 = new Counter(); //create another
    c1.click();  // increment Counter c1
    c2.click();  // increment Counter c2
    c2.click();  // increment Counter c2 again
    System.out.println("Counter1 value is " +
                        c1.get());
    System.out.println("Counter2 value is " +
                        c2.get());
    c1.reset();
    System.out.println("Counter1 value is " +
                        c1.get());
  }
}

class Counter {
  int value;                          //0 to 99
  void reset() { value = 0; }
  int get()    { return value;}     //current value
  void click() { value = (value + 1) % 100;}
}
```

Input/Output and Files

Chapter 13

In this chapter we explain how to use some of the input/output functions in the standard library, including the functions `printf()` and `scanf()`. Although we have used these functions throughout this text, many details still need to be explained. We present a number of tables showing the effects of various formats. The standard library provides functions related to `printf()` and `scanf()` that can be used for dealing with files and strings; their use is explained here.

General file input/output is important in applications in which data resides in files on disks and tapes. We show how to open files for processing and how to use a pointer to a file. Some applications need temporary files. Examples are given to illustrate their use.

13.1 The Output Function `printf()`

The `printf()` function has two nice properties that allow it a high level of flexibility. First, a list of arguments of arbitrary length can be printed, and second, the printing is controlled by simple conversion specifications, or formats. The function `printf()` delivers its character stream to the standard output file `stdout`, which is normally connected to the screen. The argument list to `printf()` has two parts:

control_string and *other_arguments*

In the example

```
printf("she sells %d %s for $%f", 99, "sea shells", 3.77);
```

we have

control_string: `"she sells %d %s for $%f"`
other_arguments: `99, "sea shells", 3.77`

The expressions in *other_arguments* are evaluated and converted according to the formats in the control string and are then placed in the output stream. Characters in the control string that are not part of a format are placed directly in the output stream. The % symbol introduces a conversion specification, or format. A single conversion specification is a string that begins with % and ends with a conversion character.

printf() conversion characters	
Conversion character	**How the corresponding argument is printed**
c	as a character
d, i	as a decimal integer
u	as an unsigned decimal integer
o	as an unsigned octal integer
x, X	as an unsigned hexadecimal integer
e	as a floating-point number; example: 7.123000e+00
E	as a floating-point number; example: 7.123000E+00
f	as a floating-point number; example: 7.123000
g	in the e-format or f-format, whichever is shorter
G	in the E-format or f-format, whichever is shorter
s	as a string
p	the corresponding argument is a pointer to void; its value is printed as a hexadecimal number
n	the corresponding argument is a pointer to an integer into which the number of characters written so far is printed; the argument is not converted
%	with the format %% a single % is written to the output stream; there is no corresponding argument to be converted

The function printf() returns as an int the number of characters printed. In the example

```
printf("she sells %d %s for $%f", 99, "sea shells", 3.77);
```

we can match the formats in the control string with their corresponding arguments in the argument list.

Format	Corresponding argument
%d	99
%s	"sea shells"
%f	3.77

Explicit formatting information may be included in a conversion specification; if it is not, defaults are used. For example, the format `%f` with corresponding argument `3.77` results in `3.770000` being printed. By default, the number is printed with six digits to the right of the decimal point.

Between the % that starts a conversion specification and the conversion character that ends it, the following may appear in order:

What May Appear in the Conversion Specification

- Zero or more flag characters that modify the meaning of the conversion specification. These flag characters are discussed in the next list.
- An optional positive integer that specifies the minimum *field width* of the converted argument. The place where an argument is printed is called its *field*, and the number of spaces used to print an argument is its *field width*. If the converted argument has fewer characters than the specified field width, then it is padded with spaces on the left or right, depending on whether the converted argument is right- or left-adjusted. If the converted argument has more characters than the specified field width, then the field width is extended to whatever is required. If the integer defining the field width begins with a zero and the argument being printed is right-adjusted in its field, then zeros rather than spaces are used for padding.
- An optional *precision*, which is specified by a period followed by a nonnegative integer. For `d`, `i`, `o`, `u`, `x`, and `X` conversions, it specifies the minimum number of digits to be printed.
- For `e`, `E`, and `f` conversions, it specifies the number of digits to the right of the decimal point. For `g` and `G` conversions, it specifies the maximum number of significant digits. For an `s` conversion, it specifies the maximum number of characters to be printed from a string, an optional `h` or `l`, which is a short or long modifier, respectively. If an `h` is followed by a `d`, `i`, `o`, `u`, `x`, or `X` conversion character, the conversion specification applies to a `short int` or `unsigned short int` argument; if an `h` is followed by an `n` conversion character, the corresponding argument is a pointer to a `short int` or `unsigned short int`. If an `l` is followed by a `d`, `i`, `o`, `u`, `x`, or `X` conversion character, the conversion specification applies to a `long int` or `unsigned long int` argument; if an `l` is followed by an `n` conversion character, the corresponding argument is a pointer to a `long int` or `unsigned long int`.
- An optional `L`, which is a long modifier. If an `L` is followed by an `e`, `E`, `f`, `g`, or `G` conversion character, the conversion specification applies to a `long double` argument.

"BOY-OH-BOY, HAVE YOU NOTICED HOW SNOOTY MELVYN HAS GOTTEN SINCE HE CONVERTED TO A DOUBLE?"

The Flag Characters in Conversion Specification

- A minus sign, which means the converted argument is to be left-adjusted in its field. If there is no minus sign, the converted argument is to be right-adjusted in its field.
- A plus sign, which means a nonnegative number that comes from a signed conversion is to have a + prepended. This works with the conversion characters `d`, `i`, `e`, `E`, `f`, `g`, and `G`. All negative numbers start with a minus sign.
- A space, which means that a nonnegative number that comes from a signed conversion is to have a space prepended. This works with the conversion characters `d`, `i`, `e`, `E`, `f`, `g`, and `G`. If both a space and a + flag are present, the space flag is ignored.
- A #, which means the result is converted to an "alternate form" depending on the conversion character. With the conversion character `o`, the # causes a zero to be prepended to the octal number being printed. In an `x` or `X` conversion, it causes `0x` or `0X` to be prepended to the hexadecimal number being printed. In a `g` or `G` conversion, it causes trailing zeros to be printed. In an `e`, `E`, `f`, `g`, or `G` conversion, it causes a decimal point to be printed, even with precision 0. The behavior is undefined for other conversions.
- A zero, which means zeros instead of spaces are used to pad the field. With `d`, `i`, `o`, `u`, `x`, `X`, `e`, `E`, `f`, `g`, and `G` conversion characters, this can result in numbers with leading zeros. Any sign and any `0x` or `0X` that is printed with a number precedes the leading zeros.

In a format, the field width, precision, or both may be specified by an asterisk instead of an integer, which indicates that a value is to be obtained from the argument list. Here is an example of how the facility can be used:

```
int      m, n;
double   x = 333.7777777;
.....                           /* get m and n from somewhere */
printf("x = %*.*f\n", m, n, x);
```

If the argument corresponding to the field width has a negative value, then it is taken as a minus flag followed by a positive field width. If the argument corresponding to the precision has a negative value, then it is considered to be missing.

The conversion specification %% can be used to print a single percent symbol in the output stream. It is a special case because there is no corresponding argument to be converted. For all the other formats, there should be a corresponding argument. If there are not enough arguments, the behavior is undefined. If there are too many arguments, the extra ones are evaluated but otherwise ignored.

The field width is the number of spaces used to print the argument. The default is whatever is required to properly display the value of the argument. Thus the integer value 255 (decimal) requires three spaces for decimal conversion `d` or octal conversion `o` but only two spaces for hexadecimal conversion `x`.

When an argument is printed, characters appropriate to the conversion specification are placed in a field. The characters appear right-adjusted unless a minus sign is present as a flag. If the specified field width is too short to properly display the value of the corresponding argument, the field width is increased to the default. If the entire field is not needed to display the converted argument, then the remaining part of the field is padded with blanks on the left or right, depending on whether the converted argument is right- or left-adjusted. The padding character on the left can be made a zero by specifying the field width with a leading zero.

Floating-point formats can specify precision with a nonnegative number that occurs to the right of the period. For string conversions, this is the maximum number of characters to be printed from the string. For `e`, `E`, and `f` conversions, it specifies the number of digits to appear to the right of the decimal point.

Examples of character and string formats are given in the next table. We use double quote characters to visually delimit the field. They are not printed.

Declarations and initializations			
`char   c = 'A', s[] = "Blue moon!";`			
Format	**Corresponding argument**	**How it is printed in its field**	**Remarks**
`%c`	`c`	`"A"`	field width 1 by default
`%2c`	`c`	`" A"`	field width 2, right-adjusted
`%-3c`	`c`	`"A  "`	field width 3, left-adjusted
`%s`	`s`	`"Blue moon!"`	field width 10 by default
`%3s`	`s`	`"Blue moon!"`	more space needed
`%.6s`	`s`	`"Blue m"`	precision 6
`%-11.8s`	`s`	`"Blue moo   "`	precision 8, left-adjusted

Examples of formats used to print numbers are given in the next table. Again we use double quote characters to visually delimit the field. They are not printed.

Declarations and initializations			
`int     i = 123;` `double  x = 0.123456789;`			
Format	**Corresponding argument**	**How it is printed in its field**	**Remarks**
`%d`	`i`	`"123"`	field width 3 by default
`%05d`	`i`	`"00123"`	padded with zeros
`%7o`	`i`	`"    173"`	right-adjusted, octal
`%-9x`	`i`	`"7b       "`	left-adjusted, hexadecimal
`%-#9x`	`i`	`"0x7b     "`	left-adjusted, hexadecimal
`%10.5f`	`x`	`"   0.12346"`	field width 10, precision 5
`%-12.5e`	`x`	`"1.23457e-01 "`	left-adjusted, e-format

13.2 The Input Function scanf()

The function scanf() has two nice properties that allow it flexibility at a high level. The first is that a list of arguments of arbitrary length can be scanned, and the second is that the input is controlled by simple conversion specifications, or formats. The function scanf() reads characters from the standard input file stdin. The argument list to scanf() has two parts:

control_string and *other_arguments*

In the example

```
char     a, b, c, s[100];
int      n;
double   x;

scanf("%c%c%c%d%s%lf", &a, &b, &c, &n, s, &x);
```

we have

control_string: "%c%c%c%d%s%lf"
other_arguments: &a, &b, &c, &n, s, &x

The arguments following the control string consist of a comma-separated list of pointer expressions, or addresses. Note that in this example, writing &s would be wrong; the expression s by itself is an address.

Directives in the Control String

The control string for scanf() is composed of three kinds of *directives*: ordinary characters, white space, and conversion specifications. We want to discuss each of these in detail.

Ordinary Characters

Characters in the control string other than white space characters and characters in a conversion specification are called *ordinary characters*. Ordinary characters must be matched in the input stream. Here is an example:

```
float   amount;

scanf("$%f", &amount);
```

The character $ is an ordinary character. An attempt is made to match a $ in the input stream. If the match succeeds, then white space, if any, is skipped, and characters that can be converted to a floating value are matched. The converted value are placed in memory at the address of amount.

In our next example, each of the three characters a, b, and c constitute an ordinary character directive.

```
scanf("abc");
```

First the character a is matched, then the character b, and finally the character c. If at some point scanf() fails to make a match, the offending character is left in the input stream and scanf() returns. If the call to scanf() succeeds, then the characters immediately following a, b, and c in the input stream are ready for processing.

White Space Characters

White space characters in the control string that are not in a conversion specification are matched with optional white space in the input stream. Consider the example

```
char   c1, c2, c3;

scanf(" %c %c %c", &c1, &c2, &c3);
```

If the input stream contains the letters *a*, *b*, and *c*, with or without leading white space and with or without intervening white space, then *a*, *b*, and *c* are read into c1, c2, and c3, respectively. A white space directive causes white space, if any, in the input stream to be skipped. Because of this, the following two statements are equivalent:

```
scanf(" %c %c %c", &c1, &c2, &c3);
scanf("\t%c  \t  %c\n%c", &c1, &c2, &c3);
```

Conversion Specifications

In a control string for scanf(), a conversion specification directive begins with a % and ends with a conversion character. It determines how characters in the input stream are matched and converted.

scanf() conversion characters		
Unmodified conversion character	**Characters in the input stream that are matched**	**Type of the corresponding argument**
`c`	any character, including white space	`char *`
`d`	an optionally signed decimal integer	`int *`
`i`	an optionally signed decimal, octal, or hexadecimal integer such as `77`, `077`, or `0x77`	`int *`
`u`	an optionally signed decimal integer	`unsigned *`
`o`	an optionally signed octal integer, leading `0` not needed	`unsigned *`
`x, X`	an optionally signed hexadecimal integer, leading `0x` or `0X` not allowed	`unsigned *`
`e, E, f, g, G`	an optionally signed floating-point number	`float *`
`s`	a sequence of non-white space characters	`char *`
`p`	what is produced by `%p` in `printf()`, usually an unsigned hexadecimal integer	`void **`
`n, %, [...]`	(*See the next table.*)	

Three conversion characters are of a special nature, and one of these, `[...]`, is not even a character although the construct is treated as such. We discuss these in the next table.

Special scanf() conversion characters	
Unmodified conversion character	**Remarks**
`n`	No characters in the input stream are matched. The corresponding argument is a pointer to `int`, into which is printed the number of characters read so far.
`%`	The conversion specification `%%` causes a single `%` character in the input stream to be matched. There is no corresponding argument.
`[...]`	The set of characters inside the brackets `[]` is called the *scan set.* It determines what is matched and read in. (See the following explanation.) The corresponding argument is a pointer to the base of an array of characters that is large enough to hold the characters that are matched, along with a terminating null character `\0` that is appended automatically.

Between the % and the Conversion Character There May Be

- An optional * that indicates assignment suppression, followed by an optional integer that defines a maximum scan width, followed by an optional h, l, or L that modifies the conversion character.
- The modifier h, which can precede a d, i, o, u, x, or X conversion character. It indicates that the converted value is to be stored in a `short int` or in an `unsigned short int`.
- The modifier l, which can precede either a d, i, o, u, x, or X conversion character or an e, E, f, g, or G conversion character. In the first case it indicates that the converted value is to be stored in a `long int` or in an `unsigned long int`. In the second case it indicates that the converted value is to be stored in a `double`.
- The modifier L, which can precede an e, E, f, g, or G conversion character. It indicates that the converted value is to be stored in a `long double`.

The characters in the input stream are converted to values according to the conversion specifications in the control string and placed at the address given by the corresponding pointer expression in the argument list. Except for character input, a scan field consists of contiguous non-white space characters that are appropriate to the specified conversion. The scan field ends when an inappropriate character is reached; the scan width, if specified, is exhausted; or the end-of-file mark is encountered, whichever comes first.

The scan width is the number of characters scanned to retrieve the argument value. The default is whatever is in the input stream. The specification %s skips white space and then reads in non-white space characters until a white space character or the end-of-file mark is encountered, whichever comes first. In contrast to this, the specification %5s skips white space, then reads in non-white space characters, stopping when a white space character is encountered, five characters have been read in, or the end-of-file mark is encountered, whichever comes first. When a string is read in, it is presumed that enough space has been allocated in memory to hold the string and an end-of-string sentinel \0, which is appended.

The format %*nc* can be used to read in the next *n* characters, including white space characters. It is presumed that enough space has been allocated in memory to hold them. The null character \0 is not appended.

Floating Numbers in the Input Stream

Floating numbers in the input stream are formatted as an optional sign followed by a digit string with an optional decimal point, followed by an optional exponential part. The exponential part consists of e or E, followed by an optional sign, followed by a digit string. Some examples are

```
77              /* is converted to a floating value */
+7.7e1          /* equivalent to 77 */
770.0E-1        /* equivalent to 77 */
+0.003
```

Remember: The input stream is not C code; different rules apply.

Using the Scan Set

A conversion specification of the form %[*string*] indicates that a special string is to be read in. The set of characters inside the brackets [] is called the *scan set*. If the first character in the scan set is not a circumflex character ^, then the string is to be made up only of the characters in the scan set. Thus the format %[abc] inputs a string containing only the letters a, b, and c and stops if any other character appears in the input stream, including a blank. In contrast to this, if the first character in the scan set is a circumflex, then the string is to be made up of all characters other than those in the scan set. Thus the format %[^abc] inputs a string terminated by any of a, b, or c but not by white space. Consider the code

```
char   store[30];

scanf("%29[AB \t\n]", store);
```

This reads into the character array store a string containing at most 29 characters. The string consists of the letters A and B and the white space characters blank, tab, and newline. Whatever is read into store is terminated with \0.

Programmers usually think of a line as a string of characters, including blanks and tabs, that ends with a newline character. One way to read a line into memory is to use an appropriate scan set. Consider the following code:

```
char   line[300];

while (scanf(" %[^\n]", line) == 1)
   printf("%s\n", line);
```

The effect of this code is to skip any blank lines and to remove leading white space from any other lines. Let us give an explicit example. We first create a program containing the preceding lines, compile it, and put the executable code in the file *pgm*. Then we put the following lines in *infile*:

```
A is for

   apple and
            alphabet pie.
```

When we give the command

pgm < infile > outfile

here is what we find in *outfile*:

```
A is for
apple and
alphabet pie.
```

In addition to the scanf() family of functions, C also provides the functions gets() and fgets() to read lines from a file (see exercise 9 on page 464).

The Return Value

When scanf() is invoked, an input failure or a matching failure can occur. An input failure occurs when there are no characters in the input stream. When this happens, EOF (typically, -1) is returned. When a matching failure occurs, the offending character is left in the input stream and the number of successful conversions up to that point is returned. This number is zero if no conversions have occurred. If scanf() succeeds, the number of successful conversions is returned; this number can also be zero.

A scanf() Example

We want to present an example that illustrates some of the capability of the scanf() function. We describe in detail the matching process that occurs with a particular input stream. Here is our example:

```
char   c, *cntrl_string, save[7], store[15];
int    a, cnt;

cntrl_string = "%d , %*s %% %c %[abc] %*s %5s %s";
cnt = scanf(cntrl_string, &a, &c, save, store, &store[5]);
```

With the following characters in the input stream:

```
23 , ignore_this  %  C  abacus  read_in_this**
```

the value 23 is placed in a; the comma is matched; the string "ignore_this" is ignored; the % is matched; the character C is placed in the variable c; the string "abac" is placed in save[0] through save[4], with the terminating \0 in save[4]; the "us" in abacus is ignored; the string "read_" is placed in store[0] through store[5], with the terminating \0 in store[5]; and finally the string "in_this**" is placed in store[5] through store[14], with the terminating \0 in store[14]. Because five successful conversions were made, the value 5 is returned by scanf().

scanf() examples			
Directive in control string	**Type of the corresponding argument**	**What is in the input stream**	**Remarks**
ab%2c	char *	abacus	ab is matched, ac is converted
%3hd	short *	-7733	-77 is converted
%4li	long *	+0x66	+0x6 is converted (hexadecimal)
-%2u	unsigned *	-123	- is matched, 12 is converted
+ %lu	unsigned long *	+-123	+ is matched, -123 is converted
+ %lu	unsigned long *	+ -123	+ is matched, -123 is converted
+ %lu	unsigned long *	+- 123	+ is matched, *error*, - cannot be converted
%3e	float *	+7e-2	+7e is converted
%4f	float *	7e+22	7e+2 is converted
%5lf	double *	-1.2345	-1.23 is converted
%4Lf	long double *	12345	1234 is converted
%p	void **	*system-dependent*	can read in what printf() with %p writes on output

13.3 The Functions sprintf() and sscanf()

The functions sprintf() and sscanf() are string versions of the functions printf() and scanf(), respectively. Their function prototypes, found in *stdio.h,* are

```
int   sprintf(char *s, const char *format, ...);
int   sscanf(const char *s, const char *format, ...);
```

The ellipsis indicates to the compiler that the function takes a variable number of arguments. A statement of the form

sprintf(*string*, *control_string*, *other_arguments*);

writes to the character array *string*. The conventions for *control_string* and *other_arguments* conform to those of printf(). In a similar fashion, a statement of the form

sscanf(*string*, *control_string*, *other_arguments*);

reads from the character array *string*.

Let us look at an example.

```
char   in_string[] = "1 2 3 go";
char   out_string[100], tmp[100];
int    a, b, c;

sscanf(in_string, "%d%d%d%s", &a, &b, &c, tmp);
sprintf(out_string, "%s %s %d%d%d\n", tmp, tmp, a, b, c);
printf("%s", out_string);
```

This is printed:

```
go go 123
```

First, the function sscanf() reads three integers and a string from in_string, putting them into a, b, c, and tmp, respectively. Then the function sprintf() writes to out_string. Finally, we use printf() to print out_string on the screen. *Caution:* It is the programmer's responsibility to provide adequate space in memory for the output of sprintf().

13.4 The Functions fprintf() and fscanf()

The functions fprintf() and fscanf() are file versions of the printf() and scanf() functions, respectively. Before we discuss their use, we need to know how C deals with files.

The header file *stdio.h* contains a number of constructs that pertain to files. Among these is the identifier FILE, which is a structure type whose members describe the current state of a file. To use files, the programmer need not know any details concerning the FILE structure type.

Also defined in *stdio.h* are the three file pointers: stdin, stdout, and stderr. We sometimes refer to them as files, even though they are actually pointers.

Standard C files in *stdio.h*		
Written in C	**Name**	**Remark**
`stdin`	standard input file	connected to the keyboard
`stdout`	standard output file	connected to the screen
`stderr`	standard error file	connected to the screen

The header file *stdio.h* contains function prototypes for many file-handling functions. Here are the prototypes for `fprintf()` and `fscanf()`:

```
int   fprintf(FILE *ofp, const char *format, ...);
int   fscanf(FILE *ifp, const char *format, ...);
```

The ellipsis indicates to the compiler that the function takes a variable number of arguments. A statement of the form

`fprintf(` *file_ptr*`,` *control_string*`,` *other_arguments*`);`

writes to the file pointed to by *file_ptr*. The conventions for *control_string* and *other_arguments* conform to those of `printf()`. In particular,

`fprintf(stdout, ...);`   is equivalent to   `printf...);`

In a similar fashion, a statement of the form

`fscanf(`*file_ptr*`,` *control_string*`,` *other_arguments*`);`

reads from the file pointed to by *file_ptr*. In particular,

`fscanf(stdin, ...);`   is equivalent to   `scanf(...);`

In the next section we show how to use `fopen()` to open files, how to use `fprintf()` and `fscanf()` to access them, and how to use `fclose()` to close files.

13.5 Accessing Files

Files have several important properties. They have a name. They must be opened and closed. They can be written to, or read from, or appended to. Conceptually, until a file is opened, nothing can be done to it. It is like a closed book. When it is opened, we have access to it at its beginning or end. To prevent accidental misuse, we tell the system which of the three activities—reading, writing, or appending—we perform on a file. When we are finished using the file, we close it.

Abstractly, a file can be thought of as a stream of characters. After a file has been opened, the stream can be accessed with file-handling functions in the standard library. Consider the following code:

```
#include <stdio.h>

int main(void)
{
   int    sum = 0, val;
   FILE   *ifp, *ofp;

   ifp = fopen("my_file", "r");      /* open for reading */
   ofp = fopen("outfile", "w");      /* open for writing */
   .....
```

This opens two files in the current directory: *my_file* for reading and *outfile* for writing. (The identifier `ifp` is an acronym for "infile pointer," and the identifier `ofp` is an acronym for "outfile pointer.") After a file has been opened, the file pointer is used exclusively in all references to the file. Suppose *my_file* contains integers. If we want to sum them and put the result in *outfile*, we can write

```
while (fscanf(ifp, "%d", &val) == 1)
   sum += val;
fprintf(ofp, "The sum is %d.\n", sum);
```

Note that `fscanf()`, like `scanf()`, returns the number of successful conversions. After we have finished using the files, we can close them by writing

```
fclose(ifp);
fclose(ofp);
```

A function call of the form `fopen(`*file_name*, *mode*`)` opens the named file in a particular mode and returns a file pointer. There are a number of possibilities for the mode.

Modes for opening files	
`"r"`	open text file for reading
`"w"`	open text file for writing
`"a"`	open text file for appending
`"rb"`	open binary file for reading
`"wb"`	open binary file for writing
`"ab"`	open binary file for appending

Each of these modes can end with a + character. This means the file is to be opened for both reading and writing; r+, for example, means "open text file for reading and writing."

Trying to open for reading a file that cannot be read, or does not exist, fails. In this case, fopen() returns a NULL pointer. Opening a file for writing causes the file to be created if it does not exist and overwritten if it does. Opening a file in append mode causes the file to be created if it does not exist and causes writing to occur at the end of the file if it does.

When a + occurs in the mode, the file is opened in update mode, for both reading and writing. Consider the code

```
FILE   *fp;

fp = fopen("my_file", "r+");        /* open for read and write*/
```

This opens *my_file* for input first, but both input and output may be performed on the file. However, input may not be directly followed by output unless the end-of-file mark has been reached or an intervening call to fseek(), fsetpos(), or rewind() has occurred. Similarly, output may not be directly followed by input without an intervening call to fflush(), fseek(), fsetpos(), or rewind().

In the UNIX operating system, there is no distinction between binary and text files, except in their contents; the file mechanism is the same for both. In MS-DOS and in some other operating systems, there are different file mechanisms for each of these file types (see exercise 22 on page 468).

A detailed description of the file-handling functions such as fopen() and fclose() can be found in Appendix A, "The Standard Library." Consult the appendix as necessary to understand how the various functions are used.

13.6 An Example: Double-Spacing a File

Let us illustrate the use of some file-handling functions by writing a program to double-space a file. In main(), we open files for reading and writing that are passed as command line arguments. After the files have been opened, we invoke double_space() to accomplish the task of double spacing.

```
#include <stdio.h>
#include <stdlib.h>

void   double_space(FILE *, FILE *);
void   prn_info(char *);
```

```
int main(int argc, char **argv)
{
   FILE   *ifp, *ofp;

   if (argc != 3) {
      prn_info(argv[0]);
      exit(1);
   }
   ifp = fopen(argv[1], "r");      /* open for reading */
   ofp = fopen(argv[2], "w");      /* open for writing */
   double_space(ifp, ofp);
   fclose(ifp);
   fclose(ofp);
   return 0;
}

void double_space(FILE *ifp, FILE *ofp)
{
   int  c;

   while ((c = getc(ifp)) != EOF) {
      putc(c, ofp);
      if (c == '\n')
         putc('\n', ofp); /* found newline - duplicate it */
   }
}

void prn_info(char *pgm_name)
{
   printf("\n%s%s%s\n\n%s%s\n\n",
      "Usage:  ", pgm_name, "  infile  outfile",
      "The contents of infile will be double-spaced ",
      "and written to outfile.");
}
```

Suppose we have compiled this program and put the executable code in the file *dbl_space*. When we give the command

dbl_space file1 file2

the program reads from *file1* and write to *file2*. The contents of *file2* are the same as those of *file1*, except every newline character has been duplicated.

Dissection of the dbl_space Program

- ```
  #include <stdio.h>
  #include <stdlib.h>

  void   double_space(FILE *, FILE *);
  void   prn_info(char *);
  ```

We have included *stdlib.h* because it contains the function prototype for `exit()`, which is used in `prn_info()`. The identifier `FILE` is a structure defined in *stdio.h*. To make use of files, we do not need to know system implementation details of how the file mechanism works. The function prototype for `double_space()` shows that it takes two file pointers as arguments.

- ```
  int main(int argc, char **argv)
  {
     FILE   *ifp, *ofp;

     if (argc != 3) {
        prn_info(argv[0]);
        exit(1);
     }
  ```

The identifiers `ifp` and `ofp` are file pointers. The names are acronyms for "infile pointer" and "outfile pointer," respectively. The program is designed to access two files entered as command line arguments. If there are too few or too many command line arguments, `prn_info()` is invoked to print information about the program, and `exit()` is invoked to exit the program. By convention, `exit()` returns a nonzero value when something has gone wrong.

- ```
  ifp = fopen(argv[1], "r");      /* open for reading */
  ofp = fopen(argv[2], "w");      /* open for writing */
  ```

We can think of `argv` as an array of strings. The function `fopen()` is used to open the file named in `argv[1]` for reading. The pointer value returned by the function is assigned to `ifp`. In a similar fashion, the file named in `argv[2]` is opened for writing.

- ```
  double_space(ifp, ofp);
  ```

The two file pointers are passed as arguments to `double_space()`, which then does the work of double spacing. Other functions of this form can be written to perform whatever useful work on files is needed.

■
```
fclose(ifp);
fclose(ofp);
```

The function `fclose()` from the standard library is used to close the files pointed to by `ifp` and `ofp`.

■
```
void double_space(FILE *ifp, FILE *ofp)
{
   int  c;
   .....
```

This is the start of the function definition for `double_space()`. The identifier `c` is an `int`. Although it is used to store characters obtained from a file, eventually it is assigned the value EOF, which is not a character.

■
```
while ((c = getc(ifp)) != EOF) {
   putc(c, ofp);
   if (c == '\n')
    putc('\n', ofp); /* found newline - duplicate it */
}
```

The macro `getc()` reads a character from the file pointed to by `ifp` and assigns the value to `c`. If the value of `c` is not EOF, then `putc()` writes `c` into the file pointed to by `ofp`. If `c` is a newline character, another newline character is written into the file as well. This has the effect of double spacing the output file. This process continues repeatedly until an EOF is encountered. The macros `getc()` and `putc()` are defined in *stdio.h*.

It is good programming style to close files explicitly in the same function in which they were opened. Any files not explicitly closed by the programmer are closed automatically by the system on program exit.

13.7 Using Temporary Files and Graceful Functions

In ANSI C, the programmer can invoke the library function `tmpfile()` to create a temporary binary file that is removed when it is closed or on program exit. The file is opened for updating with the mode `wb+`, meaning that the binary file is opened for both writing and reading. In MS-DOS, a binary file can also be used as a text file. In UNIX, there is only one mechanism for a file; except for their contents, binary and text files are the same.

In this section we want to write an elementary program that illustrates the use of `tmpfile()`. Our program also presents a graceful version of `fopen()`. We name our program *dbl_with_caps*. Here is what we want to accomplish:

What the dbl_with_caps Program Should Do

- Open a temporary file in update mode for writing and reading.
- Copy the contents of the first file into the temporary file, capitalizing any lowercase letters.
- Write a marker line at the bottom of the first file, so that we can easily distinguish what was already in the file from what we are going to add.
- Copy the contents of the temporary file to the bottom of the first file, thereby doubling its contents.

```
#include <ctype.h>
#include <stdio.h>
#include <stdlib.h>

FILE   *gfopen(char *filename, char *mode);

int main(int argc, char **argv)
{
   int    c;
   FILE   *fp, *tmp_fp;

   if (argc != 2) {
      fprintf(stderr, "\n%s%s%s\n\n%s%s\n\n",
       "Usage:  ", argv[0], "  filename",
       "The file will be doubled and some ",
       "letters capitalized.");
      exit(1);
   }
   fp = gfopen(argv[1], "r+");          /* open for read write */
   tmp_fp = tmpfile();                  /* open for write read */
   while ((c = getc(fp)) != EOF)
      putc(toupper(c), tmp_fp);        /* capitalize lowercase */
   fprintf(fp, "---\n");              /* print marker at bottom */
   rewind(tmp_fp);                        /* mv file pos to top */
   while ((c = getc(tmp_fp)) != EOF)          /* copy tmp file */
      putc(c, fp);                                /* at bottom */
   return 0;
}
```

```
/* A graceful version of fopen(). */

FILE *gfopen(char *fn, char *mode)
{
   FILE   *fp;

   if ((fp = fopen(fn, mode)) == NULL) {
      fprintf(stderr, "Cannot open %s - bye!\n", fn);
      exit(1);
   }
   return fp;
}
```

Before we explain the program, let us see its effects. Suppose in file *apple* we have

```
A is for apple and alphabet pie.
```

After we give the command

dbl_with_caps apple

the contents of the file *apple* are

```
A is for apple and alphabet pie.
---
A IS FOR APPLE AND ALPHABET PIE.
```

Dissection of the dbl_with_caps Program

- `fp = gfopen(argv[1], "r+");          /* open for read write */`

We are using a graceful version of `fopen()` to open a file for both reading and writing. If, for some reason, the file cannot be opened, a message is printed and the program exited. In contrast to this, consider the statement

```
fp = fopen(argv[1], "r+");      /* dangerous! */
```

If, for some reason, `argv[1]` cannot be opened, `fopen()` returns the `NULL` pointer. No warning is printed on the screen telling the user that something is wrong.

```
■ tmp_fp = tmpfile();                    /* open for write read*/
```

ANSI C provides the function `tmpfile()` to open a temporary file. The file mode is wb+; recall that it is a binary file that is opened for both writing and reading. A binary file can also be used as a text file. On program exit, the temporary file is removed by the system. Consult Appendix A, "The Standard Library," for the function prototype and other details.

```
■ while ((c = getc(fp)) != EOF)
     putc(toupper(c), tmp_fp);         /* capitalize lowercase */
```

The macros `getc()` and `putc()` are defined in *stdio.h*. They are used to read from one file and write to another. The function prototype for `toupper()` is given in *ctype.h*. If `c` is a lowercase letter, `toupper(c)` returns the corresponding uppercase letter; otherwise, it returns `c`. *Caution:* Some ANSI C compilers do not get this right (hopefully, they will improve with time). You may have to write

```
while ((c = getc(fp)) != EOF)
   if (islower(c))
      putc(toupper(c), tmp_fp);
   else
      putc(c, tmp_fp);
```

```
■ fprintf(fp, "---\n");
```

Because we encountered the end-of-file marker in the stream pointed to by `fp`, we can switch from reading to writing. Here, we are writing a marker line that serves to delineate the two parts of the file.

```
■ rewind(tmp_fp);
```

This causes the file position indicator for the stream pointed to by `tmp_fp` to be set to the beginning of the file. This statement is equivalent to

```
fseek(tmp_fp, 0, 0);
```

See Appendix A, "The Standard Library," for the function prototypes and for an explanation of `fseek()`.

```
■ while ((c = getc(tmp_fp)) != EOF)      /* copy TMP file */
     putc(c, fp);                             /* at bottom */
```

Now we are reading from the stream pointed to by `tmp_fp` and writing to the stream pointed to by `fp`. Note that a call to `rewind()` occurred before we switched from writing to reading on the stream pointed to by `tmp_fp`.

■
```
FILE *gfopen(char *fn, char *mode)
{
    .....
```

This is a graceful version of `fopen()`. If something goes wrong, a message is printed on the screen and the program is exited.

Note that we wrote to `stderr`. In this program, we could just as well have written to `stdout`. However, in other programs that use this function, there is an advantage to writing to `stderr` (see exercise 13 on page 466).

13.8 Accessing a File Randomly

In addition to accessing one character after another in a file (sequential access), we can access characters in different places (random access). The library functions `fseek()` and `ftell()` are used to access a file randomly. An expression of the form

`ftell(` *file_ptr* `)`

returns the current value of the file position indicator. The value represents the number of bytes from the beginning of the file, counting from zero. Whenever a character is read from the file, the system increments the position indicator by 1. Technically, the file position indicator is a member of the structure pointed to by *file_ptr*; the file pointer itself does not point to individual characters in the stream. This is a conceptual mistake that many beginning programmers make.

The function `fseek()` takes three arguments: a file pointer, an integer offset, and an integer that indicates the place in the file from which the offset should be computed. A statement of the form

`fseek(` *file_ptr* `,` *offset*`,` *place* `);`

sets the file position indicator to a value that represents *offset* bytes from *place*. The value for *place* can be 0, 1, or 2, meaning the beginning of the file, the current position, or the end of the file, respectively. *Caution:* The functions `fseek()` and `ftell()` are guaranteed to work properly only on binary files. In MS-DOS, if you want to use these functions, the file should be opened with a binary mode. In UNIX, because there is only one file mechanism, any file mode works.

A common exercise is to write a file backward. Let us write a program that does this by accessing the file randomly.

```
#include <stdio.h>

#define   MAXSTRING   100

int main(void)
{
   char   file_name[MAXSTRING];
   int    c;
   FILE   *ifp;

   fprintf(stderr, "\nInput a file name:  ");
   scanf("%s", file_name);
   ifp = fopen(file_name, "rb"); /* ms-dos binary mode */
   fseek(ifp, 0, 2);             /* move to end of file */
   fseek(ifp, -1, 1);            /* back one character */
   while (ftell(ifp) >= 0) {
      c = getc(ifp);             /* ahead one character */
      putchar(c);
      fseek(ifp, -2, 1);         /* back two characters */
   }
   return 0;
}
```

The prompt to the user is written to `stderr` so the program works properly with redirection (see exercise 13 on page 466). We open the file with mode `rb` so the program works in both MS-DOS and UNIX.

13.9 Style

In ANSI C, different conversion characters can have the same effect. When possible, we use lowercase instead of uppercase conversion characters. Also, for portability reasons, when dealing with decimal integers, we prefer `d` to `i`. The latter is unavailable in many traditional C systems.

A good programming style is to check that `fopen()` does its work as expected. In any serious program, such checks are essential. Suppose we want to open *my_file* for reading. A common programming style used to do this is

```
if ((ifp = fopen("my_file", "r")) == NULL) {
   printf("\nCannot open my_file - bye!\n\n");
   exit(1);
}
```

If, for some reason, `fopen()` is unable to open the named file, the pointer value `NULL` is returned. We test for this value, and if we find it, we print a message and exit.

Another stylistic issue concerns the indiscriminate opening of files for writing. If fopen() is used to open a file for writing that already exists, then the original contents of that file are destroyed. Because files are potentially valuable, the user should be warned if a file already exists. One way to do this is to first check to see if the file can be opened for reading. If it can, then the file exists. In this case, the user should be warned (see exercise 10 on page 465).

Most operating systems allow only a limited number of files to be open at one time. When writing a large program, it is essential that programmers keep track of which files are open. A good programming style is to close a file in the same function in which it was opened.

13.10 Common Programming Errors

Beginning programmers sometimes forget that the file mode is a string, not a character. If you type

```
ifp = fopen("my_file", 'r');      /* wrong */
```

your compiler should at least give you a warning. The programmer is well advised to pay attention to all pointer warnings.

When using printf() and scanf(), or the file and string versions of these functions, it is easy to improperly match formats in the control string with the arguments that follow—for example,

```
double   x;
FILE     *ifp, *ofp;

.....
fscanf(ifp, "%f", &x);             /* wrong, use %lf instead */
fprintf(ofp, "x = %lf\n", x);      /* wrong, use %f instead */
```

For functions in the printf() family, the format "%lf" does not exist.

Many common errors are related to the use of files. An error that beginning programmers often make is to use the file name instead of the file pointer. After a file has been opened, the file pointer is to be used to access the file, not the file name. Constructs such as

```
fprintf( file_name, ... );         /* wrong */
fclose( file_name);                /* wrong */
```

can cause unexpected run-time errors. Most compilers issue a message warning of suspicious pointer conversion. All such warnings should be heeded.

Some other common errors are opening a file that is already open, closing a file that is already closed, writing to a file that is open for reading, or reading from a file that is open for writing. What happens in such cases is system-dependent. The compiler cannot catch mistakes of this kind; it is the programmer's responsibility to open, use, and close files properly.

When using the functions `fprintf()`, `sprintf()`, `fscanf()`, and `sscanf()`, a common programming error is to forget to use a pointer to `FILE` or a string, as the case may be, as the first argument.

```
fprintf("k = %d\n", k);            /* wrong, file ptr missing */
```

This is a natural error to make, because the use of `fprintf()` is very similar to the use of `printf()`. Your compiler may warn you, but you may have difficulty interpreting what the warning is about.

Here is a mistake that can be very hard to find. The difficulty is that the compiler cannot help you at all.

```
char   msg[100], wrk[100];
int    val;

.....                              /* input msg and val  */
sprintf("%s %d\n", msg, val);      /* wrong arguments */
```

Because the programmer has used two strings as the first two arguments to `sprintf()`, the compiler is happy, even though these are the wrong strings to use. The programmer's intent was to use `sprintf()` to write into `wrk`, which should be the first argument to `sprintf()`.

When porting code to MS-DOS, there can be subtle problems. In UNIX, because all files are the same, it is common not to use the binary mode when opening a file. However, the functions `fseek()` and `ftell()` are guaranteed to work properly on binary files only.

The programmer often thinks of a file pointer as pointing to a stream of characters, which is certainly an acceptable mental image. The programmer should not, however, think of a file pointer as pointing to individual characters in the stream. This is not what happens. Technically, the file pointer points to a structure of type `FILE`, and the members of the structure keep track of what is happening in the file. (The programmer need not know the details concerning the structure itself.)

The Function sscanf() Is Different

We first discuss fscanf() and then show how sscanf() is different. Here is some code that we can use to read in non-white space characters one after another:

```
char   c;
FILE   *ifp;

.....
while (fscanf(ifp, " %c", &c) == 1) {
   .....                                   /* do something */
```

The file mechanism uses the file position indicator to keep track of the current position in the file. Because of this, every time fscanf() is called, we get the next character in the file.

The function sscanf() is different. Suppose line is a string, and we want to access the non-white space characters in line one after another. The following code fails!

```
while (sscanf(line, " %c", &c) == 1) {
   .....                                   /* do something */
```

Every time sscanf() is invoked, it accesses line from the beginning. There is no string position indicator mechanism that keeps track of where we are in the string (see exercise 5 on page 463). The correct C idiom is to use a pointer, say p, as follows:

```
for (p = line; *p != '\0'; ++p) {
   if (!isspace(*p))
      .....                                /* do something */
```

13.11 System Considerations

On any machine, the use of calloc() or malloc() to dynamically allocate memory fails if there is not enough memory. Because MS-DOS machines often have limited memory, the graceful versions of these functions are particularly useful in that environment.

Files are a limited resource. Only FOPEN_MAX files can be open at one time, including stdin, stdout, and stderr. The symbolic constant FOPEN_MAX is defined in *stdio.h*. A typical value for FOPEN_MAX is 20 although on some newer systems it is 64 or more.

In UNIX, there is only one file mechanism, whereas in MS-DOS, there is a difference between binary files and text files although both can be used to store text (see exercise 22 on page 468).

When a file is opened in append mode, the file position indicator can be repositioned by invoking `fseek()` or `rewind()`. In MS-DOS, what was already in the file cannot be overwritten; in UNIX, it can.

The need (or desire) to deal with larger files of all kinds seems to be increasing. ANSI C added the standard library functions `fgetpos()` and `fsetpos()` to access files that are potentially very large. An implementation can design these functions to access files that are too large to be handled by the traditional functions `ftell()` and `fseek()`. See Appendix A, "The Standard Library," for details.

13.12 Moving to C++

C systems have `stdin`, `stdout`, and `stderr` as standard files; in addition, systems may define other standard files, such as `stdprn` and `stdaux`. Abstractly, a file may be thought of as a stream of characters that are processed sequentially.

Standard files in C		
Written in C	**Name**	**Connected to**
`stdin`	standard input file	keyboard
`stdout`	standard output file	screen
`stderr`	standard error file	screen
`stdprn`	standard printer file	printer
`stdaux`	standard auxiliary file	auxiliary port

The C++ stream input/output ties the first three of these standard files to `cin`, `cout`, and `cerr`, respectively. Typically, C++ ties `cprn` and `caux` to their corresponding standard files `stdprn` and `stdaux`. There is also `clog`, which is a buffered version of `cerr`. Other files can be opened or created by the programmer. We show how to do this in the context of writing a program that double-spaces an existing file into an existing or new file. The file names are specified on the command line and passed into `argv`.

File I/O is handled by including *fstream.h*. This contains classes `ofstream` and `ifstream` for output and input file stream creation and manipulation. To properly open and manage an `ifstream` or `ofstream` related to a system file, you first declare it with an appropriate constructor. First we study the `ifstream` behavior.

```
ifstream();
ifstream(const char*, int = ios::in,int prot = filebuf::openprot);
```

The constructor of no arguments creates a variable that later is associated with an input file. The constructor of three arguments takes as its first argument the named file. The second argument specifies the file mode and the third is for file protection.

The file mode arguments are defined as enumerators in class `ios` as follows.

File mode arguments	
`ios::in`	input mode
`ios::app`	append mode
`ios::out`	output mode
`ios::ate`	open and seek to end of file
`ios::nocreate`	open but do not create mode
`ios::trunc`	discard contents and open
`ios::noreplace`	if file exists, open fails

Thus the default for an `ifstream` is input mode, and that for an `ofstream` is output mode. If file opening fails, the stream is put into a bad state. It can be tested with `operator!`.

Let us use this scheme to write a simple file-handling program.

```
//A program to double-space a file.
//Usage: executable  f1 f2
//f1 must be present and readable
//f2 must be writable if it exists

#include  <fstream.h>      //includes iostream.h
#include  <stdlib.h>

void double_space(ifstream& f, ofstream& t)
{
   char  c;

   while (f.get(c)) {
      t.put(c);
      if (c == '\n')
         t.put(c);
   }
}
```

```
int main(int argc, char** argv)
{
   if (argc != 3) {
      cout << "\nUsage: " << argv[0]
           << "  infile  outfile" << endl;
      exit(1);
   }

   ifstream  f_in(argv[1]);
   ofstream  f_out(argv[2]);

   if (!f_in) {
      cerr << "cannot open " << argv[1] << endl;
      exit(1);
   }
   if (!f_out) {
      cerr << "cannot open " << argv[2] << endl;
      exit(1);
   }
   double_space(f_in, f_out);
}
```

Dissection of the dbl_sp Program

- ```
  void double_space(ifstream& f, ofstream& t)
  {
     char  c;

     while (f.get(c)) {
        t.put(c);
        if (c == '\n')
           t.put(c);
     }
  }
  ```

  The `get` member function gets a character from an `ifstream`. The `put` member function puts a character to an `ofstream`. These functions do not ignore white space characters. The newline character is output twice, creating the desired double spacing in the output file.
  ```

■
```
ifstream  f_in(argv[1]);
ofstream  f_out(argv[2]);
```

The variable `f_in` is used for input, `f_out` for output. They are used to create corresponding `ifstream` and `ofstream` variables. The corresponding constructors are invoked on the names found in `argv[]` passed through the command line. If the input file opens, the `ifstream` `f_in` is constructed connected to the file named in `argv[1]`. If the output file opens, the `ofstream` `f_out` is constructed connected to the file named in `argv[2]`.

■
```
if (!f_in) {
   cerr << "cannot open " << argv[1] << endl;
   exit(1);
}
if (!f_out) {
   cerr << "cannot open " << argv[2] << endl;
   exit(1);
}
```

If the constructors for either `f_in` or `f_out` fail, they return a bad state tested by `operator!`, and then an error exit is executed. At this point, `f_in` can be used analogously to `cin`, and `f_out` can be used analogously to `cout`.

■
```
double_space(f_in, f_out);
```

The actual double spacing from the input file to the output file occurs here.

Other important member functions that are found in *fstream.h* include:

```
//opens ifstream file
void open(const char*, int = ios::in,
          int prot = filebuf::openprot);

//opens ofstream file
void open(const char*, int = ios::out,
          int prot = filebuf::openprot);

void close();
```

These functions can be used to open and close appropriate files. If you create a file stream with the default constructor, you normally use `open()` to associate it with a file. You can then use `close()` to close the file and open another file using the same stream. Additional member functions in other I/O classes allow for a full range of file manipulation.

Summary

- The functions printf() and scanf() and the related file and string versions of these functions use conversion specifications in a control string to deal with a list of arguments of variable length.

- The standard header file *stdio.h* must be included if files are to be used. It contains the definitions of the identifier FILE (a structure) and the file pointers stdin, stdout, and stderr. It also contains prototypes of many file-handling functions and definitions for the macros getc() and putc().

- A file can be thought of as a stream of characters. The stream can be accessed either sequentially or randomly. When a character is read from or written to a file, the file position indicator is incremented by 1.

- The system opens the three standard files stdin, stdout, and stderr at the beginning of each program. The function printf() writes to stdout. The function scanf() reads from stdin. The files stdout and stderr are usually connected to the screen; stdin is usually connected to the keyboard. Redirection causes the operating system to make other connections.

- The programmer can use fopen() and fclose() to open and close files, respectively. After a file has been opened, the file pointer is used to refer to the file.

- The macro call getc(ifp) reads the next character from the file pointed to by ifp. Similarly, the macro call putc(c, ofp) writes the value of c in the file pointed to by ofp.

- There are many kinds of file-handling errors that the compiler cannot catch. An example is trying to write to a file that has been opened for reading. It is the programmer's responsibility to open, use, and close files properly.

- Files are a scarce resource. The maximum number of files that can be open simultaneously is given by the symbolic constant FOPEN_MAX in *stdio.h*. For many systems this number is 20 although on some newer systems it is 64 or more. It is the programmer's responsibility to keep track of which files are open. On program exit, any open files are closed by the system automatically.

- The standard library provides a collection of functions that access a file through its file pointer. For example, the function call

```
fgets(line, MAXLINE, ifp)
```

reads the next line of characters from the file pointed to by `ifp`.

- In ANSI C, the function `tmpfile()` in the standard library can be used to open a temporary file. When a temporary file is closed, the system removes it.

Exercises

1 Write a program that uses the directive `%[\n]` in a control string in a `scanf()` statement to read lines from a file named on the command line. Print every other line to `stdout`. *Hint:* Use a counter and test to see if it is even or odd.

2 The conversion specification %n is available in ANSI C but not in traditional C. Can your compiler handle it correctly? Try the following code:

```
int   n1, n2;

printf("try %n me %n \n", &n1, &n2);
printf("n1 = %d  n2 = %d\n", n1, n2);
```

3 Can we give flag characters in a conversion specification in any order? The ANSI C document is not too specific about this point, but it seems that the intent is for any order to be acceptable. See what happens with your compiler when you try the following code:

```
printf("%0+17d\n", 1);
printf("%+017d\n", 1);
```

4 What is the effect of the following code?

```
char   s[300];

while (scanf("%*[^\n]%*[\n]%[^\n]%*[\n]", s) == 1)
   printf("%s\n", s);
```

Put these lines in a program, compile it, put the executable code in *pgm*, and then give the command

pgm < my_file

where the file *my_file* contains some lines of text. Do blank lines in *my_file* cause problems?

5 Accessing a string is not like accessing a file. When a file is opened, the file position indicator keeps track of where you are in the file. There is no comparable mechanism for a string. Write a program that contains the following lines and explain what is written in `tmp1` and `tmp2`:

```
char    c, s[] = "abc", *p = s;
int     i;
FILE    *ofp1, *ofp2;

ofp1 = fopen("tmp1", "w");
ofp2 = fopen("tmp2", "w");
for (i = 0; i < 3; ++i) {
   sscanf(s, "%c", &c);
   fprintf(ofp1, "%c", c);
}
for (i = 0; i < 3; ++i) {
   sscanf(p++, "%c", &c);
   fprintf(ofp2, "%c", c);
}
```

6 Compile the following program and put the executable code into the file *try_me*:

```
#include <stdio.h>

int main(void)
{
   fprintf(stdout, "A is for apple\n");
   fprintf(stderr, "and alphabet pie!\n");
   return 0;
}
```

Execute the program so you understand its effects. What happens when you redirect the output? Try the command:

try_me > temp

Make sure you read the file *temp* after you do this. If UNIX is available to you, try the command:

try_me > & temp

This causes the output that is written to `stderr` to be redirected, too. Make sure that you look at what is in *temp*. You may be surprised!

7 Write a program to number the lines in a file. The input file name should be passed to the program as a command line argument. The program should write to `stdout`. Each line in the input file should be written to the output file with the line number and a space prepended.

8 Modify the program you wrote in the previous exercise so that the line numbers are right-adjusted. The following output is *not* acceptable:

```
.....
9 This is line nine.
10 This is line ten.
```

If there are more than 10 lines but fewer than 100, the line numbers should be printed using the "%2d" format; if there are more than 100 lines but fewer than 1000, the line numbers should be printed using the "%3d" format; and so forth. If UNIX is available to you, try the command

nlines /usr/dict/words > outfile

where *nlines* is the name of your program. Examine the top and bottom of *outfile*, and a few places in between, to see if your program worked correctly. (The file is large—do not leave it lying around.)

9 Read about the functions `fgets()` and `fputs()` in Appendix A. Use `fgets()` to read lines from a program file named on the command line. If the first non-white space characters on the line are //, then remove the // characters, along with any blanks and tabs that immediately precede and follow the // characters, before writing the line to `stdout`. All other lines should be written to `stdout` without change. *Hint:* Use the following code:

```
char   line[MAXLINE], store[MAXLINE];
FILE   *ifp = stdin;

.....
while (fgets(line, MAXLINE, ifp) != NULL)
   if (sscanf(line, " // %[^\n]", store) == 1) {
      fputs(store, stdout);
      fputs("\n", stdout);      /* restore the newline */
   }
   else
      fputs(line, stdout);
}
```

10 Write a program called *wrt_rand* that creates a file of randomly distributed numbers. The file name is to be entered interactively. Your program should use three functions. Here is the first:

```
void get_info(char *filename, int *n_ptr)
{
   printf("\n%s\n\n%s",
      "This program creates a file of random numbers.",
      "How many random numbers would you like?  ");
   scanf("%d", n_ptr);
   printf("\nIn what file would you like them?  ");
   scanf("%s", filename);
}
```

The second function to be used in your program is a "careful" version of `fopen()`. Its purpose is to warn the user if the output file already exists. (There are other ways to do this.)

```
FILE *cfopen(char *filename, char *mode)
{
   char   reply[2];
   FILE   *fp;

   if (strcmp(mode, "w") == 0
      && (fp = fopen(filename, "r")) != NULL) {
       fclose(fp);
       printf("\nFile exists.  Overwrite it?  ");
       scanf("%1s", reply);
       if (*reply != 'y' && *reply != 'Y') {
          printf("\nBye!\n\n");
          exit(1);
       }
   }
   fp = gfopen(filename, mode);
   return fp;
}
```

The third function is `gfopen()`, the graceful version of `fopen()`. We discussed this function in Section 13.7, "Using Temporary Files and Graceful Functions," on page 450. *Hint:* To write your randomly distributed numbers neatly, use the following code:

```
for (i = 1; i <= n; ++i) {
   fprintf(ofp, "%12d", rand());
   if (i % 6 == 0 || i == n)
      fprintf(ofp, "\n");
}
```

11 In this exercise we examine a typical use of sscanf(). Suppose we are writing a serious interactive program that asks the user to input a positive integer. To guard against errors we can pick up as a string the line typed by the user. Here is one way to process the string:

```
char   line[MAXLINE];
int    error, n;

do {
   printf("Input a positive integer:  ");
   fgets(line, MAXLINE, stdin);
   error = sscanf(line, "%d", &n) != 1 || n <= 0;
   if (error)
      printf("\nERROR: Do it again.\n");
} while (error);
```

This catches some typing errors, but not all. If, for example, 23e is typed instead of 233, the error is not caught. Modify the code so that if anything other than a digit string surrounded by optional white space is typed, the input is considered to be in error. Use these ideas to rewrite the *wrt_rand* program you wrote in the previous exercise.

12 Our program that double-spaces a file can be invoked with the command

dbl_space infile outfile

But if *outfile* exists, it is overwritten; this is potentially dangerous. Rewrite the program so it writes to stdout instead. Then the program can be invoked with the command

dbl_space infile > outfile

This program design is safer. Of all the system commands, only a few are designed to overwrite a file. After all, nobody likes to lose a file by accident.

13 Make a further modification to the program *dbl_space* that you wrote in the previous exercise. Because the program is now intended to be used with redirection, it now makes sense to use

fprintf(stderr, ...)   rather than   printf(...)

in the function definition for prn_info(). Because printf() writes to stdout, which in turn is redirected, the user does not see the information on the screen. The symbol > is used to redirect what is written to stdout. It does not affect stderr. Rewrite your program two ways: with the error message being written first to stderr and then to stdout. Experiment with the two versions, with and without redirection, so you understand the different effects.

14 Make a further modification to the program *dbl_space* that you wrote in the previous exercise. Implement a command line option of the form *-n*, where *n* can be 1, 2, or 3. If *n* is 1, then the output should be single-spaced; that is, two or more contiguous newline characters in the input file should be written as a single newline character in the output file. If *n* is 2, the output file should be strictly double-spaced; that is, one or more contiguous newline characters in the input file should be rewritten as a pair of newline characters in the output file. If *n* is 3, the output file should be triple spaced.

15 Write the function `getwords(ifp, k, words)` so that it reads `k` words from the file pointed to by `ifp` and places them in the string `words`, separated by newlines. The function should return the number of words successfully read and stored in `words`. Write a program to test your function.

16 Write the function `putstring(s, ofp)` so that it writes the string `s` into the file pointed to by `ofp`. Use the macro `putc()` to accomplish the task. Write a program to test your function.

17 After three characters have been read from a file, can `ungetc()` be used to push them back onto the file (see Section A.12, "Character Input/Output," on page 542)? Write a program to test this.

18 Write a program that displays a file on the screen 20 lines at a time. The input file should be given as a command line argument. The program should display the next 20 lines after a carriage return has been typed. (This is an elementary version of the *more* utility in UNIX.)

19 Modify the program you wrote in the previous exercise. Your program should display one or more files given as command line arguments. Also, allow for a command line option of the form *-n*, where *n* is a positive integer specifying the number of lines that are to be displayed at one time.

20 The library function `fgets()` can be used to read from a file a line at a time (see Section A.12, "Character Input/Output," on page 540). Write a program called *search* that searches for patterns. If the command

search hello my_file

is given, then the string pattern *hello* is searched for in the file *my_file*. Any line that contains the pattern is printed. (This program is an elementary version of *grep*.) *Hint:* Use the following code:

```
char   line[MAXLINE], *pattern;
FILE   *ifp;

if (argc != 3) {
   .....
}

if ((ifp = fopen(argv[2], "r")) == NULL) {
   fprintf(stderr, "\nCannot open %s\n\n", argv[2]);
   exit(1);
}

pattern = argv[1];
while (fgets(line, MAXLINE, ifp) != NULL) {
   if (strstr(line, pattern) != NULL)
      .....
```

21 Modify the program that you wrote in the previous exercise. If the command line option *-n* is present, the line number should be printed as well.

22 In the early days of MS-DOS, a control-z character embedded in a file was used as an end-of-file mark. Although this is not done now, if a file has a control-z in it, and it is opened as a text file for reading, characters beyond the control-z may be inaccessible. Write a program with the following lines in it:

```
char   cntrl_z = 26;    /* decimal value for control-z */
int    c;
FILE   *ifp, *ofp;

ofp = fopen("tmp", "w");
fprintf(ofp, "%s%c%s\n",
   "A is for apple", cntrl_z, " and alphabet pie.");
fclose(ofp);
ifp = fopen("tmp", "r");             /* open as text file */
while ((c = getc(ifp)) != EOF)       /* print the file */
   putchar(c);
fclose(ifp);
printf("\n---\n");                   /* serves as marker */
ifp = fopen("tmp", "rb");            /* open as binary file */
while ((c = getc(ifp)) != EOF)       /* print the file */
   putchar(c);
```

What is printed? (Does the program act differently on a UNIX system?) Try the MS-DOS command

type tmp

Only the characters before the control-z are printed. How do you know there are more characters in the file? *Hint:* Try the *dir* command. Normally, control-z characters are not found in text files, but they certainly can occur in binary files. Subtle problems can occur if you open a binary file for processing with mode `r` instead of `rb`.

23 Examine the following program carefully. What is printed?

```
#include <stdio.h>

int main(void)
{
   printf("Hello!\n");
   fclose(stdout);
   printf("Goodbye!\n");
   return 0;
}
```

24 C++: Redo exercise 18 on page 467, using C++ file I/O.

25 Java: In the following Java example, we demonstrate how to detect an EOF with the standard Java class `BufferedReader`. The program opens the file specified on the command line and echoes its contents to the console. Rewrite this code as C.

```
// Echo.java - echo file contents to the screen
//Java by Dissection page 365.
import java.io.*;
class Echo {
  public static void main(String[] args) throws IOException
{
    if (args.length < 1){
      System.out.println("Usage: java Echo filename");
      System.exit(0);
    }

    BufferedReader input =
        new BufferedReader(new FileReader(args[0]));
    String line = input.readLine();
    while (line != null) {
      System.out.println(line);
      line = input.readLine();
    }
  }
}
```

Chapter 14

Software Tools

There are two kinds of software tools: general utilities provided by the operating system for everyone and specific utilities designed explicitly to aid the programmer in software development. Because operating system commands can be executed from within a C program, the programmer can use these commands as software tools to accomplish specific tasks.

Some software tools are provided in one operating system but not another. For example, *make* is available in UNIX, but in MS-DOS it is an add-on feature. Nonetheless, *make* is available on many MS-DOS systems.

Software tools vary with time. Debuggers on newer systems tend to be much better than what was available before. The C compiler itself can be considered a software tool. Today, most C compilers conform to the ANSI C standard.

In this chapter we first discuss how to execute an operating system command from within a program. Then a number of the more important tools for programmers are discussed, including the compiler, *make, touch, grep*, beautifiers, and debuggers.

14.1 Executing Commands from within a C Program

The library function `system()` provides access to operating system commands. Thus whatever tools are provided by the operating system are also available to the C programmer. In both MS-DOS and UNIX, the command *date* causes the current date to be printed on the screen. If we want this information printed on the screen from within a program, we can write

```
system("date");
```

The string passed to system() is treated as an operating system command. When the statement is executed, control is passed to the operating system, the command is executed, and then control is passed back to the program. The function prototype for system() is given in *stdlib.h.*

In UNIX, *vi* is a commonly used text editor. Suppose from inside a program we want to use *vi* to edit a file that has been given as a command line argument. We can write

```
#include <stdio.h>
#include <stdlib.h>

int main(int argc, char **argv)
{
   char   cmnd[MAXSTRING];

   printf("Opening %s for editing ...\n", argv[1]);
   sprintf(cmnd, "vi %s", argv[1]);
   system(cmnd);
   .....
```

If we wish to see the contents of the file sorted lexicographically by line, we can write

```
sprintf(cmnd, "sort %s", argv[1]);
system(cmnd);
```

A similar example works in MS-DOS, provided that we replace *vi* with an editor available on that system.

As a final example, let us suppose we are tired of looking at all those capital letters produced by the *dir* command on our MS-DOS system. We can write a program that interfaces with this command and writes only lowercase letters on the screen.

```
#include <ctype.h>
#include <stdio.h>
#include <stdlib.h>

#define   MAXSTRING   100

int main(void)
{
   char   cmnd[MAXSTRING];
   char   tfn[MAXSTRING];          /* tmp filename */
   int    c;
   FILE   *ifp;
```

```
    tmpnam(tfn);
    sprintf(cmnd, "dir > %s", tfn);
    system(cmnd);
    ifp = fopen(tfn, "r");
    while ((c = getc(ifp)) != EOF)
       putchar(tolower(c));
    remove(tfn);
    return 0;
}
```

First, we use the library function tmpnam() to create a temporary file name. Then we invoke system() to redirect the output of the *dir* command into the temporary file. Then we print on the screen the contents of the file, changing each uppercase letter to lowercase. Finally, when we are finished using the temporary file, we invoke the library function remove() to remove it. Consult Appendix A, "The Standard Library," for details about these functions.

14.2 Environment Variables

Environment variables are available in both UNIX and MS-DOS. The following program prints them on the screen:

```
#include <stdio.h>

int main(int argc, char *argv[], char *env[])
{
   int   i;

   for (i = 0; env[i] != NULL; ++i)
      printf("%s\n", env[i]);
   return 0;
}
```

Both of the parameters argv and env are of type pointer to pointer to char. We can think of them as arrays of pointers to char, or as arrays of strings. The system provides the strings and the space in which to store them. The last element in each of the arrays is a NULL pointer. In this program, we use only env. On our UNIX system, this program prints

```
BASE=/c/c/blufox/base
HOME=/c/c/blufox
SHELL=/bin/csh
TERM=xterm
USER=blufox
.....
```

To the left of the equal sign is the environment variable; to the right of the equal sign is its value, which should be thought of as a string. On our MS-DOS system, this program prints

```
COMSPEC=C:\COMMAND.COM
BASE=d:\base
INCLUDE=d:\msc\include
.....
```

Both MS-DOS and UNIX provide a command to display environment variables. In UNIX, the command is *env* or *printenv* (or both), and in MS-DOS, it is *set.* The output of the command is the same as the output of our program.

By convention, environment variables are usually capitalized. In a C program, we can access environment variables via the third parameter to `main()`, as we did in our last program, or we can use the function `getenv()` in the standard library. Its function prototype, which is in *stdlib.h*, is given by

```
char   *getenv(const char *name);
```

If the string passed as an argument is an environment variable, then the function returns the string (pointer to `char`) provided by the system that is the value of the variable. If the string passed as an argument is not an environment variable, then `NULL` is returned. Here is some code that illustrates the use of `getenv()`:

```
printf("%s%s\n%s%s\n%s%s\n%s%s\n%s%s\n",
   "    User's name: ", getenv("NAME"),
   "     Login name: ", getenv("LOGNAME"),
   "          Shell: ", getenv("SHELL"),
   "           Base: ", getenv("BASE"),
   "Home directory: ", getenv("HOME"));
```

On our UNIX system, this prints the following:

```
   User's name: Al Kelley
    Login name: blufox
         Shell: /bin/csh
          Base: /c/c/blufox/base
Home directory: /c/c/blufox/center
```

In UNIX, certain environment variables, such as `LOGNAME`, `SHELL`, and `HOME`, are provided by the system. To get others, we put lines such as

```
setenv  BASE  /c/c/blufox/base
setenv  NAME  "Al Kelley"
```

in our *.login* file.

14.3 The C Compiler

There are many C compilers, and an operating system may provide any number of them. Just a few of the possibilities are shown in the following table.

Compilers and their use	
Command	**The C compiler that is invoked**
cc	C compiler from Bell Laboratories
cc	C compiler from Cray Research running under UNICOS
cc	C compiler from Hewlett-Packard running under HP-UX
cc	C compiler from Silicon Graphics running under IRIX
cc	C compiler from Sun Microsystems running under Solaris
gcc	GNU C compiler from the Free Software Foundation
hc	High C compiler from Metaware
occ	Oregon C compiler from Oregon Software
qc	Quick C compiler from Microsoft
bc	Borland C compiler, integrated environment
bcc	Borland C compiler, command line version

In this section we explain the use of the compiler and discuss some of the options that are generally available for compilers in UNIX. Many of these options are available for compilers in the MS-DOS world as well.

If a complete program is contained in a single file, say *pgm.c*, then the command

```
cc pgm.c
```

translates the C code in *pgm.c* into executable object code and writes it in the file *a.out*. (In MS-DOS, the executable file is *pgm.exe*.) The command *a.out* executes the program. Now consider the command

```
cc -o pgm pgm.c
```

This causes the executable code to be written directly into the file *pgm*, overwriting the file if it already exists. Whatever is in *a.out* is not disturbed. (In MS-DOS, the option is *-e*, and no space can follow it.)

"NO, NO, DUDLEY. WHEN I SAY I WANT TO EXECUTE YOUR PROGRAM, THAT'S A GOOD THING!"

The *cc* command actually does its work in three stages: First the preprocessor is invoked, then the compiler, and finally the loader. The loader, or linker, is what puts all the pieces together to make the final executable file. The *-c* option can be used to compile only—that is, to invoke the preprocessor and the compiler but not the loader. This option is useful if we have a program written in more than one file. Consider the command

cc -c main.c file1.c file2.c

If there are no errors, corresponding object files ending in *.o* are created. (In MS-DOS, object files end in *.obj*.) To create an executable file, we can compile a mixture of *.c* and *.o* files. Suppose, for example, that we have an error in *main.c*. After correcting the error, we can give the command

cc -o pgm main.c file1.o file2.o

The use of *.o* files in place of *.c* files reduces compilation time. In addition to *.c* and *.o* files, we can also use *.s* files that have been created either by the assembler or by the compiler with the `-S` option, and we can use libraries created by the archiver (see Section 14.4, "Creating a Library," on page 477). Library file names typically end in *.a*. (Library file names end in *.lib* in MS-DOS.)

Some useful options to the compiler	
-c	Compile only; generate corresponding *.o* files.
-g	Generate code suitable for the debugger.
-o name	Put executable output code in *name*.
-p	Generate code suitable for the profiler.
-D name=def	Place at the top of each *.c* file the line `#define` *name def*
-E	Invoke the preprocessor but not the compiler.
-I dir	Look for `#include` files in the directory *dir*.
-M	Make a makefile.
-MM	Make a makefile but do not include any dependencies on the standard header files.
-O	Attempt code optimization.
-S	Generate assembler code in corresponding *.s* files.

Your compiler may not support all of these options, and it may provide others. Or it may provide an equivalent option under a different name (flag character). Compilers in MS-DOS usually support different memory models. Consult the documentation for your compiler for a detailed list of options.

14.4 Creating a Library

Many operating systems provide a utility to create and manage libraries. In UNIX, the utility is called the *archiver*, and it is invoked with the *ar* command. In the MS-DOS world, this utility is called the *librarian*, and it is an add-on feature. The Microsoft librarian, for example, is *lib*, whereas the Borland Turbo C librarian is *tlib*. By convention, library file names end in *.a* in UNIX and *.lib* in MS-DOS. We discuss the situation as it pertains to UNIX, but the general ideas apply to any librarian.

In UNIX, the archiver *ar* can be used to combine a group of files into a single file called a library. The standard C library is an example of such a file. On most UNIX systems, it is the file */usr/lib/libc.a*, but it can exist wholly or in part in other files as well. If UNIX is available to you, try the command

```
ar t /usr/lib/libc.a
```

The key *t* is used to display titles, or names, of files in the library. There are more titles than you care to look at. To count them, you can give the command

ar t /usr/lib/libc.a | wc

This pipes the output of the *ar* command to the input of the *wc* (word count) command, causing lines, words, and characters to be counted. It is not surprising that the standard library grows with time. On a DEC VAX 11/780 from the 1980s, the standard library contained 311 object files. On a Sun machine that was relatively new in 1990, the standard library contained 498 object files. On the Sun machine that we happen to be using today, the number of object files is 822.

Let us illustrate how programmers can create and use libraries of their own. We do this in the context of creating a "graceful library." In Section 13.6, "Using Temporary Files and Graceful Functions," on page 448, we presented `gfopen()`, a graceful version of `fopen()`. In a directory named *g_lib*, we have 17 such graceful functions, and we add more from time to time. These are functions such as `gfopen()`, `gfclose()`, `gcalloc()`, `gmalloc()`, and so forth. Each is written in a separate file, but for the purpose of building a library, they could just as well be in one file. To reinforce the idea of these functions, here is the code for `gcalloc()`:

```
#include <stdio.h>
#include <stdlib.h>

void *gcalloc(size_t n, size_t sizeof_something)
{
   void   *p;

   if ((p = calloc(n, sizeof_something)) == NULL) {
      fprintf(stderr, "\n%s\n%s%u%s%u\n\n",
         "ERROR: calloc(n, sizeof_something) has failed",
         "with n = ", n, " and sizeof_something = ",
         sizeof_something);
      exit(1);
   }
   return p;
}
```

To create our library, we must first compile the *.c* files to obtain corresponding *.o* files. After we have done this, we give the two commands

ar ruv g_lib.a gfopen.o gfclose.o gcalloc.o · · · · ·
ranlib g_lib.a

The letters *ruv* in the first command stand for replace, update, and verbose. This command causes the library *g_lib.a* to be created if it does not already exist. If it does exist, then the named *.o* files replace those of the same name already in the library. If any of the named *.o* files are not in the library, they are added to it. The *ranlib* command is used on older UNIX systems to randomize the library in a form that is useful for the loader. Newer UNIX systems do not need *ranlib* and do not provide it as a utility.

Suppose we are writing a program that consists of *main.c* and two other *.c* files. If our program invokes `gfopen()`, we need to make our library available to the compiler (loader). The following command does this:

```
cc -o pgm main.c file1.c file2.c g_lib.a
```

Suppose our program invokes a function but does not supply its function definition. The loader searches for this function first in *g_lib.a* and then in the standard library. The loader puts only those functions that are needed into the final executable file; it does not load the whole library.

If we write lots of programs, each consisting of many files, each program should be written in its own directory. Also, we should have a separate directory for our libraries such as *g_lib.a* and another directory for associated header files such as *g_lib.h*. For each function in *g_lib.a*, we put its prototype in *g_lib.h*. This header file must be included where needed. To manage all of this, we use the *make* utility (see Section 14.8, "The Use of *make*," on page 488).

14.5 Using the Profiler

In UNIX, if we use the *-p* option with the compiler, extra code is generated and placed in the object files and in the executable file (the program) produced by the compiler. When the program is invoked, the extra code produces information that can be used to generate a profile of the execution. The information for the profile is written automatically to the file *mon.out*. This file is not readable by humans. To obtain the information in *mon.out*, the programmer must give the command

```
prof pgm
```

where *pgm* is the name of the program.

We want to provide an example of how this all works. To get started, we write a program that uses sorting routines to sort two identical arrays of integers. By using the *-p* option when we compile the program, we obtain an execution profile that shows the relative efficiencies of two sorting routines.

We use two sorting routines: a transposition sort that we write ourselves and `qsort()`, which is provided by the standard library.

In file cmp_sorts.h:

```
#include <assert.h>
#include <stdio.h>
#include <stdlib.h>
#include "g_lib.h"

void   chk_arrays(int *a, int *b, int n);
int    compare(const void *p, const void *q);
void   prn_array(int *a, int n);
void   slow_sort(int *a, int n);
```

In file main.c:

```
#include "cmp_sorts.h"

int main(void)
{
   int   *a, *b, i, n;

   printf("\n%s\n\n%s",
      "Two identical arrays of integers will be sorted.",
      "Input the array size:  ");
   scanf("%d", &n);
   a = gcalloc(n, sizeof(int));    /* graceful calloc() */
   b = gcalloc(n, sizeof(int));
   for (i = 0; i < n; ++i)
      a[i] = b[i] = rand() % 1000;
   qsort(a, n, sizeof(int), compare);
   slow_sort(b, n);
   chk_arrays(a, b, n);
   if (n < 100)
      prn_array(a, n);
   return 0;
}
```

We prompt the user to get the array size, and then we use our graceful version of `calloc()` to allocate space dynamically (see Section 14.4, "Creating a Library," on page 478). After we fill the two arrays a and b with randomly distributed integers in the range 0 to 999, we use `slow_sort()` and `qsort()` to sort a and b, respectively. In `chk_arrays()`, we make certain that the arrays have been sorted in ascending order and that the two arrays are still identical. If the array size is less than 100, then we print the elements of a on the screen. During program development, this allows us to see that everything works as expected. When the array size is large, we do not bother printing the results. We only want to get a profile of the execution.

In file compare.c:

```
#include "cmp_sorts.h"

int compare(const void *vp, const void *vq)
{
   const int   *p = vp, *q = vq;

   return (*p - *q);
}
```

Because compare() is passed as an argument to qsort(), the function definition for compare() must be consistent with the function prototype of the corresponding parameter in the function prototype for qsort(). In particular, we need the type qualifier const (see Section 8.10, "The Type Qualifiers const and volatile," on page 286).

In file slow_sort.c:

```
#include "cmp_sorts.h"

void slow_sort(int *a, int n)
{
   int   i, j, tmp;

   for (i = 0; i < n; ++i)
      for (j = i + 1; j < n; ++j)
         if (a[i] > a[j]) {
            tmp = a[i];
            a[i] = a[j];
            a[j] = tmp;
         }
}
```

In file chk_arrays.c:

```
#include "cmp_sorts.h"

void chk_arrays(int *a, int *b, int n)
{
   int   i;

   for (i = 0; i < n - 1; ++i) {
      assert(a[i] == b[i]);
      assert(a[i] <= a[i+1]);
   }
   assert(a[i] == b[i]);
}
```

In file prn_array.c:

```
#include "cmp_sorts.h"

void prn_array(int *a, int n)
{
   int   i;

   for (i = 0; i < n; ++i) {
      if (i % 12 == 0)
         putchar('\n');
      printf("%5d", a[i]);
   }
   putchar('\n');
}
```

Now we want to get a profile of the execution of our program. To do this, we first have to compile our code with the *-p* option.

*gcc -p -o compare_sorts main.c chk_arrays.c compare.c \
    prn_array.c slow_sort.c g_lib.a*

The loader needs *g_lib.a* because that library contains `gcalloc()`. Next, we give the command

compare_sorts

and enter 1000 when prompted. Program execution causes the file *mon.out* to be created. Finally, to get an execution profile, we give the command

prof compare_sorts

This causes a profile of the execution of the program to be printed on the screen. Here are some of the lines:

```
%time  cumsecs  #call  ms/call  name
 96.6     2.84      1  2839.90  _slow_sort
  1.4     2.88  11291     0.00  _compare
  1.4     2.92      1    40.00  _qsort
  0.7     2.94      1    20.00  _main
  0.0     2.94      1     0.00  __doprnt
  0.0     2.94      2     0.00  _calloc
  0.0     2.94      1     0.00  _chk_arrays
  0.0     2.94      1     0.00  _exit
```

Note that `compare()` was called more than 11,000 times. This is because `qsort()` is recursive. If `qsort()` itself had been compiled with the *-p* option, we would have seen how many times it called itself. Not all of the functions in the list are user-defined; some of them, such as `_doprnt`, are system routines. This profile shows that 96.6 percent of the time was spent executing `slow_sort()` and only 1.4 percent of the time was spent executing `qsort()`. An execution profile such as this can be very useful when working to improve execution time efficiency. If you know which of your functions are using the most time, you can work on them to reduce execution time. Also, if you know that a function uses only a small percentage of the running time, then you know very little is gained by improving it.

14.6 How to Time C Code

Most operating systems provide access to the underlying machine's internal clock. In this section we show how to use some timing functions. Because our functions are meant to be used in many programs, we put them into the library *u_lib.a*, our utility library.

Access to the machine's clock is made available in ANSI C through a number of functions whose prototypes are in *time.h*. This header file also contains a number of other constructs, including the type definitions for `clock_t` and `time_t`, which are useful for dealing with time. Typically, the two type definitions are given by

```
typedef   long   clock_t;
typedef   long   time_t;
```

and in turn, these types are used in the function prototypes. Here are the prototypes for the three functions we use in our timing routines:

```
clock_t   clock(void);
time_t    time(time_t *p);
double    difftime(time_t time1, time_t time0);
```

When a program is executed, the operating system keeps track of the processor time that is being used. When `clock()` is invoked, the value returned is the system's best approximation of the time used by the program up to that point. The clock units can vary from one machine to another. The macro

```
#define   CLOCKS_PER_SEC   1000000     /* machine-dependent */
```

is provided in *time.h*. It can be used to convert the value returned by `clock()` to seconds.

The function `time()` returns the number of seconds that have elapsed since 1 January 1970. Other units and other starting dates are possible, but these are the ones typically used. If the pointer argument passed to `time()` is not `NULL`, then the value returned is assigned to what the argument is pointing to as well. One typical use of the function is

```
srand(time(NULL));
```

This seeds the random number generator. If the two values produced by `time()` are passed to `difftime()`, the difference expressed in seconds is returned as a `double`.

Following is a set of timing routines that can be used for many purposes, including the development of efficient code. We keep these functions in the file *time_keeper.c*.

In file time_keeper.c:

```
#include <stdio.h>
#include <stdlib.h>
#include <time.h>

#define   MAXSTRING   100

typedef struct {
   clock_t   begin_clock, save_clock;
   time_t    begin_time, save_time;
} time_keeper;

static time_keeper   tk;     /* known only to this file */

void start_time(void)
{
   tk.begin_clock = tk.save_clock = clock();
   tk.begin_time = tk.save_time = time(NULL);
}

double prn_time(void)
{
   char      s1[MAXSTRING], s2[MAXSTRING];
   int       field_width, n1, n2;
   double    clocks_per_sec = (double) CLOCKS_PER_SEC,
             user_time, real_time;

   user_time = (clock() - tk.save_clock) / clocks_per_sec;
   real_time = difftime(time(NULL), tk.save_time);
   tk.save_clock = clock();
   tk.save_time = time(NULL);
```

```
    /* Print the values found, and do it neatly. */

    sprintf(s1, "%.1f", user_time);
    n1 = strlen(s1);
    sprintf(s2, "%.1f", real_time);
    n2 = strlen(s2);
    field_width = (n1 > n2) ? n1 : n2;
    printf("%s%*.1f%s\n%s%*.1f%s\n\n",
       "User time: ", field_width, user_time, " seconds",
       "Real time: ", field_width, real_time, " seconds");
    return user_time;
}
```

Note that the structure tk is external to the functions and is known only in this file. It is used for communication between the functions in this file, and it cannot be accessed from some other file. Although we could have designed these functions so that tk is passed as an argument, this would have been inappropriate. If this were done, the user would have to allocate space for tk and then write start_time(tk) and prn_time(tk) to invoke these functions. But the user is not interested in the internal workings of start_time() and prn_time(). Thus it is best to hide tk from the user.

When start_time() is invoked, the values returned from clock() and time() are stored in tk. When prn_time() is invoked, new values from clock() and time() are used to compute and print the elapsed user time and the elapsed real time, and new values are stored in tk. User time is whatever the system allocates to the running of the program; real time is wall clock time. In a time-shared system, they need not be the same.

The function prn_total_time() is also in the file, but we have not shown it. It is similar to prn_time(), except that the elapsed times are computed relative to the last invocation of start_time() rather than the last invocation of any of the three functions.

Because our timing routines are meant to be used in a variety of programs, we put them into *u_lib.a*, our utility library. The following commands do this:

```
cc -c time_keeper.c;   ar ruv u_lib.a time_keeper.o
```

In the header file *u_lib.h*, we put the prototypes of the functions in *u_lib.a*. The header file must be included elsewhere as needed.

Now we want to demonstrate how our timing routines can be used. In certain applications, fast floating-point multiplication is desired. Should we use variables of type float or double? The following program can be used to test this:

```
/* Compare multiplication times. */

#include <stdio.h>
#include "u_lib.h"

#define   N   1000000

int main(void)
{
   long     i;
   float    a, b = 3.333, c = 5.555;  /*arbitrary values*/
   double   x, y = 3.333, z = 5.555;

   printf("\nNumber of multiplies: %d\n\n", N);
   printf("Type float:\n");
   start_time();                      /* start timing */
   for (i = 0; i < N; ++i)
      a = b * c;
   prn_time();                        /* print time info */
   printf("Type double:\n");
   for (i = 0; i < N; ++i)
      x = y * z;
   prn_time();                        /* print time info */
   return 0;
}
```

On an older machine with a traditional C compiler, we find, much to our surprise, that single precision multiplication is *slower* than double precision multiplication! Perhaps this is explained by the fact that in traditional C, any `float` is automatically promoted to a `double`. On a newer machine with an ANSI C compiler, we find that single precision multiplication is about 30 percent faster.

14.7 The Use of *dbx*

A debugger allows the programmer to step through the code a line at a time and see the values of variables and expressions at each step. This can be extremely helpful in discovering why a program is not acting as the programmer expected. The programming world is full of debuggers, and *dbx* is not a particularly good one. It just happens to be one that is generally available on UNIX systems. In this section we want to describe the basics of using *dbx*.

Steps to Follow to Start Using *dbx*

1 Go to a directory containing a C program.

2 Compile the program with the *-g* option (for debugging).

3 Give the command *dbx pgm*, where *pgm* is the name of the executable file. This invokes *dbx*. From now on, the commands we give are *dbx* commands.

4 Give a command such as *file main.c*. This sets the current file for *dbx*.

5 Give the command *list* to see the first ten lines in the file. Give the command again to see the next ten lines.

6 Give the command *stop at n*, where *n* is the line number of an executable line.

7 Give the command you would normally give to invoke *pgm*, but replace *pgm* with *run*. Example: *run 3*

8 At this point you can step through the program with the commands *step* and *next*. Use *step* to step into functions; use *next* to step over them. Use the command *print var* to print the current value of the variable *var*.

9 Give the command *quit* to quit.

This is just an outline of how to get started using *dbx*. Other useful commands are *alias* to see what aliases, if any, have been set; *continue* to continue program execution; and *help* to see a list of commands.

To cut down on the amount of typing needed to use *dbx*, the programmer can set aliases. Sometimes the system does this automatically. (There are slight variations in *dbx* from one system to another.) The programmer puts the aliases in the file *.dbxinit*, either in the current directory or in your home directory if the aliases are to be generally available. Here are the aliases we use:

```
alias a alias

a c cont;   a d delete;   a e edit;    a h help;   a l list;
a n next;   a p print;    a q quit;    a r run;    a j status;
a s step;   a w where;    a st stop;
```

In the MS-DOS world, debuggers are an add-on product. Both Microsoft and Borland, for example, provide excellent products. A UNIX workstation also may support add-on products. Although the programmer must expend some effort to learn to use a debugger, the effort can be well worth it.

14.8 The Use of *make*

For both the programmer and the machine, it is inefficient and costly to keep a moderate or large program entirely in one file that has to be recompiled repeatedly. A much better strategy is to write the program in multiple *.c* files, compiling them separately as needed. The *make* utility can be used to keep track of source files and provide convenient access to libraries and their associated header files. This utility is always available in UNIX and often in MS-DOS, where it is an add-on feature. Its use greatly facilitates both the construction and the maintenance of programs.

Suppose we are writing a program that consists of a number of *.h* and *.c* files. Typically, we would do this in a separate directory. The *make* command reads a file whose default name is *makefile*. This file contains the dependencies of the various modules, or files, making up the program, along with appropriate actions to be taken. In particular, it contains the instructions for compiling, or recompiling, the program. Such a file is called a *makefile*.

For simplicity, let us imagine that we have a program contained in two files, *main.c* and *sum.c*, and that a header file, *sum.h*, is included in each of the *.c* files. We want the executable code for this program to be in the file *sum*. Here is a simple makefile that can be used for program development and maintenance:

```
sum: main.o sum.o
	cc -o sum main.o sum.o

main.o: main.c sum.h
	cc -c main.c

sum.o: sum.c sum.h
	cc -c sum.c
```

The first line indicates that the file *sum* depends on the two object files *main.o* and *sum.o*. It is an example of a *dependency* line; it must start in column 1. The second line indicates how the program is to be compiled if one or more of the *.o* files have been changed. It is called an *action* line, or a *command*. There can be more than one action following a dependency line. A dependency line and the action lines that follow it make up what is called a *rule*. *Caution:* Each action line must begin with a tab character. (On the screen and on paper, a tab character looks like a sequence of blanks.)

By default, the *make* command makes the first rule it finds in the makefile. However, dependent files in that rule may themselves be dependent on other files, as specified in other rules, causing the other rules to be made first. These files, in turn, may cause still more rules to be made.

The second rule in our makefile states that *main.o* depends on the two files *main.c* and *sum.h.* If either of these files is changed, the action line shows what must be done to update *main.o.* After this makefile has been created, the programmer can compile or recompile the program *sum* by giving the command

make

With this command, *make* reads the file *makefile*, creates for itself a *dependency tree*, and takes whatever action is necessary.

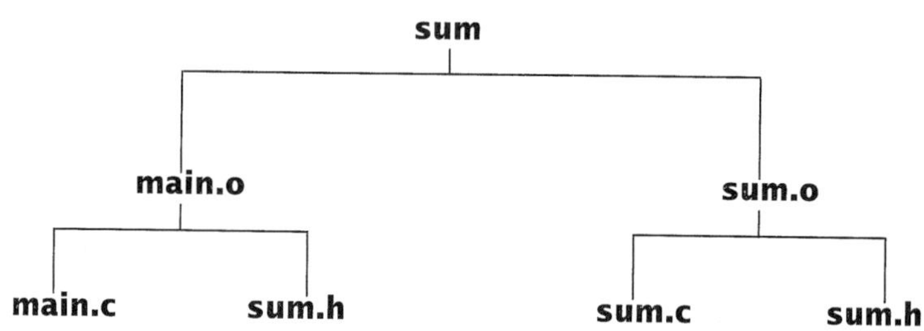

Certain rules are built into *make*, including the rule that the *.o* file depends on the corresponding *.c* file. Because of this, an equivalent makefile is given by

```
sum: main.o sum.o
        cc -o sum main.o sum.o

main.o: sum.h
        cc -c main.c

sum.o: sum.h
        cc -c sum.c
```

The *make* utility recognizes a number of built-in macros. Using one of them, we get yet another equivalent makefile.

```
sum: main.o sum.o
        cc -o sum main.o sum.o

main.o sum.o: sum.h
        cc -c $*.c
```

Here, the second rule states that the two *.o* files depend on *sum.h.* If we edit *sum.h*, both *main.o* and *sum.o* must be remade. The macro `$*.c` expands to `main.c` when *main.o* is being made, and it expands to `sum.c` when *sum.o* is being made.

To summarize, a makefile consists of a series of entries called *rules* that specify dependencies and actions. A rule begins in column 1 with a series of blank-separated target files, followed by a colon, followed by a blank-separated series of prerequisite files, also called *source* files. All the lines beginning with a tab that follow this are the actions, such as compilation, to be taken by the system to update the target files. The target files are dependent in some way on the prerequisite files and must be updated when the prerequisite files are modified.

In Section 14.5, "Using the Profiler," on page 480, we wrote a program that used two routines to sort two identical arrays. Then we showed how to compile the program with the *-p* option so that we could get an execution profile. In reality, we used a makefile for program development. Here is the one we used:

```
# Makefile for compare_sorts.
# After execution, use prof to get a profile.

BASE    =  /c/c/blufox
CC      =  gcc
CFLAGS  =  -p
EFILE   =  $(BASE)/bin/compare_sorts
INCLS   =  -I$(BASE)/include
LIBS    =  $(BASE)/lib/g_lib.a

OBJS  =  main.o   chk_arrays.o   compare.o  \
         prn_array.o  slow_sort.o

$(EFILE): $(OBJS)
        @echo "linking ....."
        @$(CC)  $(CFLAGS)  -o $(EFILE)  $(OBJS)  $(LIBS)

$(OBJS): compare_sorts.h
        $(CC)  $(CFLAGS)  $(INCLS)  -c  $*.c
```

Dissection of makefile for the compare_sorts Program

- ```
  # Makefile for compare_sorts.
  # After execution, use prof to get a profile.
  ```

Comments can be put in a makefile. A comment begins with a # and extends to the end of the line.

- ```
  BASE    = /c/c/blufox
  ```

This is an example of a macro definition. The general form of a macro definition is *macro_name* = *replacement_string*

By convention, macro names are usually capitalized, but they do not have to be. The replacement string can contain white space. If a backslash occurs at the end of the line, the replacement string continues to the next line. The macro BASE represents our base of operation on this particular machine (it need not be in our home directory).

■
```
CC     = gcc
CFLAGS = -p
```

The first macro specifies the C compiler we are using, in this case the GNU C compiler. The second macro specifies the options, if any, that are used with the *gcc* command.

■
```
EFILE  = $(BASE)/bin/compare_sorts
INCLS  = -I$(BASE)/include
LIBS   = $(BASE)/lib/g_lib.a
```

The first macro specifies the executable file, the second specifies a directory for include files, preceded by the *-I* option, and the third specifies our graceful library (see Section 14.4, "Creating a Library," on page 478). We need this library, because it contains the object code for `gcalloc()`, the graceful version of `calloc()`. Because our programs often invoke functions that are in *g_lib.a*, we routinely make this library available to the compiler (loader). The prototypes of the functions in *g_lib.a* are kept in *g_lib.h*, and we have to tell the compiler where to look for this header file.

■
```
OBJS  =  main.o     chk_arrays.o    compare.o  \
         prn_array.o  slow_sort.o
```

In this macro definition the replacement string is the list of object files that occurs on the right side of the equal sign. Note that we used a backslash to continue the line. Although we put *main.o* first and then list the others alphabetically, order is unimportant.

■
```
$(EFILE): $(OBJS)
        @echo "linking ....."
        @$(CC)  $(CFLAGS)  -o $(EFILE)  $(OBJS)  $(LIBS)
```

The first line is a dependency line, and the other two lines specify the actions to be taken. Note carefully that they begin with a tab. (It looks like eight blank spaces on the screen.) The @ symbol means that the action line itself is not to be echoed on the screen. Macro invocation has the form

```
$( macro_name )
```

Thus the construct `$(EFILE)` is replaced by

```
$(BASE)/bin/compare_sorts
```

which in turn is replaced by

```
/c/c/blufox/bin/compare_sorts
```

Similarly, `$(OBJS)` is replaced by the list of object files, and so forth. Thus the dependency line states that the executable file depends on the object files. If one or more of the object files has been updated, then the specified actions occur. The second action line is expanded to

```
@gcc  -p  -o /c/c/blufox/bin/compare_sorts  main.o    \
   chk_arrays.o  compare.o  prn_array.o  slow_sort.o  \
   /c/c/blufox/lib/g_lib.a
```

Although we have written it on three lines because of space limitations on the printed page, this is actually generated as a single line. The *-p* option causes the compiler to generate extra code suitable for the profiler. *Suggestion:* If *make* is new to you, build your makefiles without the @ symbol first. After you understand its effects, you can use it to prevent echoing.

■
```
$(OBJS): compare_sorts.h
        $(CC)  $(CFLAGS)  $(INCLS)  -c  $*.c
```

The dependency line says that all the object files depend on the header file *compare_sorts.h.* If the header file has been updated, then all the object files have to be updated, too. This is done through the action line. The construct `$*` that occurs at the end of the action line is a predefined macro called the *base file name macro.* It expands to the file name being built, excluding any extension. For example, if `main.o` is being built, then `$*.c` expands to `main.c`, and the action line becomes

```
gcc  -p  -I/c/c/blufox/include  -c  main.c
```

Certain dependencies are built into the *make* utility. For example, each *.o* file depends on the corresponding *.c* file. This means that if a *.c* file is updated, the actions specified for the corresponding *.o* file are taken. For the makefile we are discussing here, this means that the *.c* file is recompiled to produce a new *.o* file, which in turn causes all the object files to be relinked.

■ `-I/c/c/blufox/include`

An option of the form `-I`*dir* means "look in the directory *dir* for `#include` files." This option complements our use of libraries. At the top of each *.c* file making up this program, we have the line

```
#include "compare_sorts.h"
```

and near the top of *compare_sorts.h* we have the line

```
#include "g_lib.h"
```

This header file contains the function prototypes for the functions in our library *g_lib.a*. The `-I` option tells the compiler where to find the header file if it is not in the current directory.

The *make* utility is not specific to C. It can be used to maintain programs in any language. More generally, it can be used in any kind of project that consists of files with dependencies and associated actions.

14.9 The Use of *touch*

The *touch* utility is always available in UNIX, and it is sometimes available in MS-DOS. Typically, it is available anywhere *make* is. The *touch* utility is used to put a new time on a file. This is often necessary when using *make*, which compares file times to determine what has to be done.

To illustrate the use of *touch*, let us assume that we have the makefile discussed in the previous section, along with the relevant *.h*, *.c*, and *.o* files. To put the current date on the file *compare_sorts.h*, we can give the command

touch compare_sorts.h

This causes *compare_sorts.h* to have a more recent time than all the object files that depend on it. To recompile all the *.c* files and have the object files linked to create a new executable file, we give the command

make

14.10 Other Useful Tools

Operating systems provide many useful tools for the programmer. Here we list a few of the tools found on UNIX systems, along with some remarks. Comparable utilities are sometimes available in MS-DOS.

Useful tools	
cb	The C beautifier. It can be used to "pretty print" C code.
diff	Prints the lines that differ in two files.
grep	Searches for a pattern in one or more files.
indent	A C code "pretty printer" with lots of options.
wc	Counts lines, words, and characters in one or more files.

The *cb* utility reads from `stdin` and writes to `stdout`. It is not very powerful. To see what it can do, try the command

```
cb < pgm.c
```

where *pgm.c* is poorly formatted. The utility *indent* is more powerful. It can be found on Berkeley and Sun versions of UNIX. To make serious use of it, you need to read the online manual.

Tools such as *diff*, *grep*, and *wc* are of a general nature and are used by everyone, not just programmers. Although these are UNIX tools, they are often available in MS-DOS as well, especially *grep*, which is very useful to programmers.

Finally, let us mention that C can be used in conjunction with other high level tools, some of which are languages in their own right. Of particular importance are *lex* and *yacc*. More recent versions, called *flex* and *bison*, respectively, are available from the Free Software Foundation, Inc. They work in both MS-DOS and UNIX.

More tools	
awk	A pattern scanning and processing language.
csh	This shell, like *sh* and *ksh*, is programmable.
lex	Generates C code for lexical analysis.
sed	A stream editor that takes its commands from a file.
yacc	"Yet another compiler-compiler," used to generate C code.

14.11 Style

A good programming style is to use system commands rather than writing the comparable utility yourself. Suppose, for example, that you need to find all the lines in a file named *data* that contain the word *beautiful*. You can accomplish this with the statement

```
system("grep beautiful data > tmp");
```

Inside your program, the file *tmp* can then be opened for further processing.

The beginning programmer often has difficulty understanding error and warning messages generated by the compiler. For this reason, there is a tendency to disregard the warnings. A good programming style is to rewrite code until it compiles with no warnings.

An efficient programming style is to use the sophisticated tools that are available to the programmer. Tools such as debuggers, profilers, *make*, and *touch* are nearly universal. For the development of all but the smallest programs, these tools are extremely useful. Of course, some effort is involved in learning to use these utilities, but the payback is large.

14.12 Common Programming Errors

For the programmer, the compiler itself is the major software tool. A common error is to fail to set the warning level for the compiler at the highest level. All warnings should be heeded.

Beginning programmers often make the mistake of trying to write a program in a single file. A better strategy is to break the program into modules and use *make* to keep track of dependencies.

A common error in the use of *make* is to forget that each action line must be preceded by a single tab. This is an easy mistake to make because tabs are not visible.

When the programmer writes a makefile, it may have to be debugged. The "no action" option can be invoked with the command

```
make -n
```

This option causes *make* to print on the screen what its actions would have been, without actually doing them.

When the flow of control in a program is not working as the programmer thinks it should, a "pretty printer" can be used as a debugging tool. The idea of using a "pretty printer" for debugging is not widely appreciated, but in some situations it can help a lot (see exercise 9 on page 501).

14.13 System Considerations

In today's world, the programmer often works across a network rather than on a single machine. In our environment, we routinely use a number of machines on campus, machines at home, and various other machines around the country. One way to manage this complexity is to write code that depends on environment variables. Consider the following line from one of our *.login* files:

```
setenv BASE /c/c/blufox
```

This causes the environment variable BASE to have a string value that represents a certain directory on a particular machine. On another machine, the directory that we think of as "base" is different, but because we write our software so that it accesses the environment variable BASE, this does not matter.

Many compilers support a "verbose" *-v* option, which causes the compiler to print more information on the screen. The programmer should try this option to see if it has an effect.

In UNIX, the *make* utility reads instructions from the file named either *makefile* or *Makefile*. Some programmers prefer the name *Makefile* because it is listed earlier when the *ls* command is used. Because the MS-DOS operating system is not case-sensitive, this distinction does not apply.

In UNIX, each action line in a makefile must begin with a tab character. In MS-DOS, this can be one or more blanks or tabs.

In many operating systems the output of a command or program that writes to `stdout` can be "piped" to another command or program that reads from `stdin`. The output of the first command becomes the input of the second command. For example, in MS-DOS, the command *dir* writes the current directory to `stdout`, and the command *sort*, with no other command line arguments, reads from `stdin` and writes to `stdout`. The output of *dir* can be piped to the input of *sort* by giving the command

dir | sort

The symbol | represents a "pipe." In UNIX, a similar command works if we replace *dir* with *ls*. The concept of piping the output of one command to the input of another can be considered a way to get software tools to work together.

Throughout this text we have used *bc* and *bcc* as the commands that invoke the Borland C compiler. Before 1991, however, Borland compilers were invoked with the commands *tc* and *tcc* (the *t* stands for "Turbo").

Summary

- An operating system command can be executed from within a program by invoking `system()`. In MS-DOS, the statement

```
system("dir");
```

  causes a list of directories and files to be listed on the screen. In UNIX, we replace `"dir"` with `"ls"`.

- The programmer can use `getenv()` to access system environment variables.

- Most C compilers have myriad options. If you are doing serious work, it may pay to learn about all the options available on your compiler. Set the highest warning level. Heed all warnings.

- Many operating systems provide a utility to create and manage libraries. In UNIX, the utility is the *archiver*, and it is invoked with the *ar* command. In the MS-DOS world, this utility is the *librarian*, and it is an add-on feature.

- Using a library can save the programmer time and energy. The compilation process, however, then becomes more complex. The *make* utility can be used to help manage the complexity.

- UNIX systems provide the *prof* utility to profile the execution of a program. Often, other profilers are available as well. For example, the *gprof* utility from Berkeley can be found on many UNIX systems. A profiler is often available on an MS-DOS system although it is an add-on feature.

- Debuggers are available on many systems. The newer ones provide a graphical interface for the user. The debugger *dbx* is old technology, but it is generally available on UNIX systems. This utility, even though it is not spiffy, can be very useful to the programmer.

- The *make* utility can be used to keep track of source files and provide convenient access to libraries and their associated header files.

- The *touch* utility puts a new time on a file.

- Some software tools, such as *diff* and *grep*, are of a general nature; everyone uses them, not just programmers. The *grep* utility is available on all UNIX systems and on many MS-DOS systems. Programmers routinely use it for a variety of tasks.

Exercises

1 First, write a program that lists all the environment variables on your system. If you are working on a UNIX system, give the command

setenv ABC "Try me!"

This sets the environment variable *ABC*. In MS-DOS, the appropriate command is

set ABC="Try me!"

Now run your program again. Is your new environment variable listed among the others alphabetically, or is it at the end? How do you get double quotes in the string assigned as a value to an environment variable?

2 If UNIX is available to you, give the command

man sort

to read about the *sort* utility. Then experiment to see what the following program does:

```
#include <stdio.h>
#include <stdlib.h>

#define    MAXSTRING    100

int main(int argc, char **argv)
{
   char    command[MAXSTRING];

   sprintf(command, "sort -r %s", argv[1]);
   system(command);
   return 0;
}
```

Actually, the program needs improvement. Rewrite it so that it prints a prompt to the user.

3 Is the Turbo C compiler available to you? If so, try the command

tcc

This command by itself causes a list of all the options to be printed on the screen. This is a very nice feature. How many of the options do you know?

4 You already know how to write a bubble sort. Learn how to write quicksort; see, for example, *A Book on C* by Al Kelley and Ira Pohl (Menlo Park, Calif.: Benjamin/Cummings, 1990). Investigate the efficiency of each of these sorting routines by using the profiler. You may find the information provided by *prof* more interesting. With respect to efficiency, there is no contest between `qsort()` and a transposition sort, but between `qsort()` and `quicksort()`, there is.

5 In MS-DOS, the command to clear the screen is *cls*; in UNIX, it is *clear*. Try the command so that you understand its effect. Modify the *heads_or_tails* program that we presented in Section 4.10, "A Simulation: The Game of Heads or Tails," on page 147, so that the screen is cleared at the beginning of the program. Use the function call `system("cls")` or `system("clear")` to accomplish this. What happens when the output is redirected? Is the screen still cleared?

6 The last makefile presented in this chapter is a real one. Even though we dissected it, anyone who has not had experience with *make* may find the concepts difficult to grasp. If this utility is new to you, try the *make* command after you have created the following file:

```
# Experiment with the make command!

go: hello date list
        @echo Goodbye!
hello:
        @echo Hello!
date:
        @date; date; date
list:
        @pwd; ls
```

What happens if you remove the @ characters? What happens if a file named *hello* or *date* exists?

7 Create the following file, and then give the command *make*. What is printed? Write your answer first; then experiment to check it.

```
# Experiment with the make command!

Start: A1 A2
        @echo Start
A1: A3
        @echo A1
A2: A3
        @echo A2
A3:
        @echo A3
```

8 (Advanced) Along with many utilities, the UNIX operating system is distributed with a few games. Many installations remove the games because disk space is a scarce resource. It is, however, a common practice to leave one of the games on the system, the one that provides a random fortune. Sometimes the system administrator arranges for all users to get a fortune just prior to logout. (You can arrange for this yourself if you put the *fortune* command in your *.logout* file.) If UNIX is available to you, try the following command a number of times:

fortune

If this command has not been removed from the system, it prints a different fortune on the screen each time the command is invoked. If you give the command and see a fortune that you like, how can you capture it? (Perhaps you want to show it to your mother or to send it via e-mail to a friend in Paris.) If you give the *fortune* command again, you get a new fortune, not the one you had before. In this exercise you are to write a program that can capture a particular fortune. Begin by reading about the fortune command in the online manual. You can do this with the command

man fortune

Toward the end of the section, you see the name of the file where all the fortunes are stored. On most systems, this file is unreadable to the public. We know from experience, however, that one fortune begins with the line

```
There are three possible parts to a date, of which
```

and ends with the line

```
-Miss Manners' Guide to Excruciatingly Correct Behaviour
```

Your program should interactively ask the user to input a phrase to be searched for. Suppose the user types in "three possible parts to a date" when prompted. In your program you should do the following repeatedly:

1 Use the function call `system("fortune > tmp")` to capture a fortune in a file.

2 Search the file to see if it contains the desired phrase.

3 If it does, save the file, exit the loop, and send an e-mail to notify the user.

The program may take a while, so it should be run in background. That is why notification by e-mail is appropriate. The following code can be used to send a message by e-mail to the user:

```
char    command[MAXSTRING], file_name[MAXSTRING],
        message[MAXLINE], *user = getenv("USER");

sprintf(message, "%s\n%s%s\n\n",
   "Found a fortune!",
   "It was saved in the file ", file_name);
sprintf(command, "echo \"%s\" | mail %s",
         message, user);
system(command);
```

9 The fact that a "pretty printer" can be used as a debugging tool is not widely appreciated. Put the following lines in the file *try_cb.c*:

```
#include <stdio.h>

int main(void)
{
   int   a = 1, b = 2;

   if (a == 1)
      if (b == 2)
         printf("***\n");
   else
      printf("###\n");
   return 0;
}
```

Then give the command

cb < try_cb.c

You can see that the "pretty printer" *cb* aligns the code differently. Explain why.

Chapter 15

From C to C++

We use the terms *abstract data type (ADT)* and *object-oriented programming (OOP)* to refer to a powerful new programming approach. An ADT is a user-defined extension to the existing types available in the language. It consists of a set of values and a collection of operations that can act on those values. For example, Pascal and C do not have a complex number type, but C++ provides the class construct to add such a type and integrate it with existing types.

Objects are class variables. OOP allows ADTs to be created and used easily. OOP uses the mechanism of *inheritance* to conveniently derive a new type from an existing user-defined types and it allows the programmer to model the objects found in the problem domain by programming their content and behavior with a class.

The new class construct in C++ provides the *encapsulation* mechanism to implement ADTs. Encapsulation packages both the internal implementation details of the type and the externally available operations and functions that can act on objects of that type. The implementation details can be made inaccessible to code that uses the type. For example, stack might be implemented as a fixed-length array, whereas the publicly available operations would include *push* and *pop*. Changing the internal implementation to a linked list should not affect how *push* and *pop* are used externally. Code that uses the ADT is called *client* code for the ADT. The implementation of stack is hidden from its clients.

15.1 Why Switch to C++?

C has been the language of choice in the computer industry for more than a decade. Because C++ is based on C, it retains much of that language, including a rich operator set, nearly orthogonal design, terseness, and extensibility. C++ is a highly portable language, and translators for it exist on many machines and systems. C++ compilers are highly compatible with existing C programs, because maintaining such compatibility was a design objective. Unlike other object-oriented languages, such as Smalltalk, C++ is an extension of an existing language in wide use on many machines.

If C++ is viewed as an object-oriented language alternative to Smalltalk, it is a relatively inexpensive alternative. Programming in C++ does not require a graphics environment, and C++ programs do not incur run-time expense from type checking or garbage collection.

C++ improves on C in significant ways, especially in supporting strong typing. The function prototype syntax, as now required by Standard C (ANSI C), is a C++ innovation. C++ has stronger type rules than C, which makes it a safer language.

C++ is a marriage of the low level and the high level. C was designed to be a systems implementation language, a language close to the machine. C++ adds object-oriented features that are designed to allow a programmer to create or import a library appropriate to the problem domain. The user can write code at the level appropriate to the problem while still maintaining contact with the machine-level implementation details. Operators can be given new definitions based on the types of their arguments. Operator overloading supports the implementation of new types that may be operated upon transparently. Like operators, normal functions may be overloaded.

C++ relies less on the preprocessor. C programs often use the preprocessor to implement constants and useful macros. However, parameterized `#define` macros introduce insecurities. In C++, the `inline` keyword requests the compiler to produce inline code for a function having no more overhead than a macro. The inline function has precisely the semantics and syntactic usage of static functions. This preserves type checking while increasing run-time performance as compared with normal functions. Reliance on the preprocessor in C++ is further diminished by the `const` type modifier, which specifies that an object is nonmodifiable.

There are a large number of other improvements. A favorite of programmers is the addition of the // symbol for one-line comments. There is also a convenient new I/O library, *iostream.h*, that provides a very useful alternative to *stdio.h*, the C library. The `new` and `delete` operators provide convenient access to free store.

Abstract data types are implemented in C++ through the `class` mechanism. Classes allow a programmer to control the visibility of the underlying implementation. What is public is accessible, and what is private is hidden. Data hiding is one component of object-oriented programming. Classes have member functions, including those that overload operators. Member functions allow the programmer to code the appropriate functionality for the ADT. Classes can be defined through an inheritance mechanism that allows for improved code sharing and library development. Inheritance is another hallmark of object-oriented programming.

C is often criticized as being a weakly typed, unsafe language. However, C++ is strongly typed. Conversions between types are allowed, provided they are well defined. In fact, the language allows the programmer to create conversion functions between arbitrary types but not between two nonclass types.

By and large, the semantics of C++ are much more stringently defined than those of C. For example, type conversion and typing are more carefully implemented. The C need for preprocessor extensibility is curtailed: Function overloading and `inline` can be used to replace macros with arguments, and the `const` type modifier is sufficient for most named constants. The preprocessor's primary remaining uses are file inclusion and conditional compilation.

C++ supports the object-oriented programming style. This is a major advance over the structured programming style, but a chief cost is the increased complexity of the language; given C++'s objectives, this is hardly surprising. Although the benefits gained by living within the C family and adding improved interface schemes outweigh this cost, the complexity that C++ adds to the C language is one of its biggest drawbacks. Though this increase reflects the large number of necessary new ideas, it makes mastery more difficult.

Several reasons exist for the C programmer to learn about C++.

Why the C Programmer Should Learn About C++

- C++ and C are increasingly being used together.
- With little additional effort, the C programmer can take advantage of several features that make C++ a "better C."
- C++ is increasingly being used in colleges and industry, especially in advanced applications, where it is beginning to displace C.

"I DUNNO, ASHLEY, BUT EVEN FOR A C PROGRAMMER, I THINK DUDLEY IS A LITTLE TOO OBJECT-ORIENTED!"

This chapter cannot give more than a taste of OOP concepts. A good introduction to these concepts is given in *Object-Oriented Programming Using C++* by Ira Pohl (Redwood City, Calif.: Benjamin/Cummings, 1993).

15.2 Classes and Abstract Data Types

What is novel about C++ is its aggregate type `class`. A `class` is an extension of the idea of `struct` in traditional C. This is similar to a Pascal `record` type. A `class` provides the means for implementing a user-defined data type and associated functions and operators. Therefore, a `class` can be used to implement an ADT. Let us write a `class` called `string` that implements a restricted form of string.

```
//An elementary implementation of type string.
#include  <string.h>
#include  <iostream.h>

const int  max_len = 255;

class string {
public:                    //universal access
   void assign(const char* st)
         { strcpy(s, st); len = strlen(st); }
   int length() const { return len; }
   void print() const
         { cout << s << "\nLength:  " << len << endl;}
private:                   //restricted access
   char  s[max_len];  //implement as a character array
   int   len;
};
```

In C++, classes have two additions to the `struct` concept in C, as seen in this example: (1) members that are functions, such as `assign()`, and (2) public and private members. The keyword `public` indicates access of the members that follow it. Without this keyword, members are private to the class. Private members are available for use only by other member functions of the class. Public members are available to any function within the scope of the class declaration. Privacy allows part of the implementation of a class type to be hidden, which prevents unanticipated modifications to the data structure. Restricted access, or *data hiding*, is a feature of object-oriented programming.

The declaration of member functions allows the ADT to have particular functions act on its private representation. For example, the member function `length()` returns the length of the string defined to be the number of characters up to but excluding the first zero value character. The member function `print()`

outputs both the string and its length. The member function `assign()` stores a character string into the hidden variable `s` and computes and stores its length in the hidden variable `len`. Member functions that do not modify the values of member variables are declared `const`.

We can now use this data type `string` as if it were a basic type of the language. Code that uses this type is its *client*. The client can use only the public members to act on variables of type `string`.

```
//Test of the class string.

int main(void)
{
   string  one, two;
   char    three[40] = {"My name is Charles Babbage."};

   one.assign("My name is Alan Turing.");
   two.assign(three);
   cout << three;
   cout << "\nLength: " << strlen(three) << endl;
   //print the shorter of one and two
   if (one.length() <= two.length())
      one.print();
   else
      two.print();
   return 0;
}
```

Variables `one` and `two` are of type `string`. The variable `three` is of type pointer to `char` and is not compatible with `string`. The following diagram shows the contents of `len`, `max_len`, and `s` for the variable `two` and their relationships.

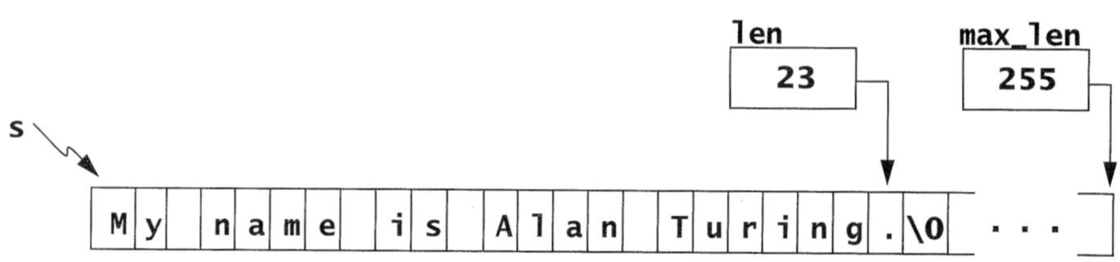

The output of this example program is

```
My name is Charles Babbage.
Length: 27
My name is Alan Turing.
Length: 23
```

15.3 Overloading

Overloading is the practice of giving several meanings to an operator or a function. The meaning selected depends on the types of the arguments used by the operator or function. Let us overload the function `print` in the previous example. This is a second definition of the `print` function.

```
class string {
public:                         //universal access
   .....
   void  print() const
           { cout << s << "Length: " << len << endl;}
   void  print(int n) const
           { for (int i = 0; i < n; ++i)
                   cout << s << endl; }
   .....
}
```

This version of `print()` takes a single argument of type `int`. It prints the string *n* times.

```
three.print(2);          //print string three twice
three.print(-1);         //string three is not printed
```

It is possible to overload most of the C++ operators. For example, we overload + to mean "concatenate two strings." To do this we need two new keywords: `friend` and `operator`. The keyword `operator` precedes the operator token and replaces what would otherwise be a function name in a function declaration. The keyword `friend` gives a function access to the private members of a class variable. A `friend` function is not a member of the class but has the privileges of a member function in the class in which it is declared.

```
//Overloading the operator+.

#include  <string.h>
#include  <iostream.h>
const int  max_len = 255;

class string {
public:
   void  assign(const char* st){ strcpy(s, st); len = strlen(st);}
   int  length() const { return len; }
   void  print() const  cout << s << "\nLength: " << len << endl;}
   friend string operator+(const string& a, const string& b);
private:
   char  s[max_len];
   int   len;
};
```

```
//overload +
string operator+(const string& a, const string& b)
{
   string  temp;

   temp.assign(a.s);
   temp.len = a.len + b.len;
   if (temp.len < max_len)
      strcat(temp.s, b.s);
   else
      cerr << "Max length exceeded in concatenation."
           << endl;
   return temp;
}

void print(const char* c)  //file scope print definition
{
   cout << c << "\nLength: " << strlen(c) << endl;
}

int main(void)
{
   string  one, two, both;
   char    three[40] = {"My name is Charles Babbage."};

   one.assign("My name is Alan Turing.");
   two.assign(three);
   print(three);          //file scope print called
                          //Print shorter of one and two
   if (one.length() <= two.length())
      one.print();        //member function print called
   else
      two.print();
   both = one + two;      //plus overloaded as concatenate
   both.print();
   return 0;
}
```

Dissection of the operator+() Function

■ `string operator+(const string& a, const string& b)`

Plus is overloaded. Both of its arguments are strings. The arguments are called by reference. The declaration *type& identifier* declares the identifier to be a reference variable. Use of `const` indicates that the arguments cannot be modified. This allows call-by-reference as found in languages such as Pascal.

■
```
string temp;
```

The function needs to return a value of type `string`. This local variable is used to store and return the concatenated string value.

■
```
temp.assign(a.s);
temp.len = a.len + b.len;
if (temp.len < max_len)
   strcat(temp.s, b.s);
```

The string `a.s` is copied into `temp.s` by calling `string::assign()`, which uses the `strcpy()` library function. The length of the resulting concatenated string is tested to see that it does not exceed the maximum length for strings. If the length is acceptable, the standard library function `strcat()` is called with the hidden string members `temp.s` and `b.s`. The references to `temp.s`, `a.s`, and `b.s` are allowed because this function is a friend of class `string`.

■
```
cerr << "Max length exceeded in concatenation."
     << endl;
```

The standard error stream `cerr` is used to print an error message, and no concatenation takes place. Only the first string is returned.

■
```
return  temp;
```

The operator was given a return type of `string`, and `temp` has been assigned the appropriate concatenated string.

The ternary conditional operator `?:`, the scope resolution operator `::`, and the two member operators "`.`" and "`.*`" cannot be overloaded.

15.4 Constructors and Destructors

In OOP terminology, a variable is called an *object.* A *constructor* is a member function whose job it is to initialize an object of its class. In many cases this involves dynamic storage allocation. A constructor is invoked whenever an object of its class is created. A *destructor* is a member function whose job is to *finalize* a variable of its class. In many cases this involves dynamic storage deallocation. The destructor is called implicitly when an automatic object goes out of scope.

Let us change our `string` example by dynamically allocating storage for each `string` variable. We replace the private array variable with a pointer. The remodeled class uses a constructor to allocate an appropriate amount of storage dynamically using the `new` operator.

```
//An implementation of dynamically allocated strings.

class string {
public:
   //constructor
   string(int n) { s = new char[n + 1]; len = n; }
   void  assign(const char* st)
           { strcpy(s, st); len = strlen(st); }
   int  length() const { return len; }
   void  print() const
           { cout << s << "\nLength: " << len << endl; }
   friend string  operator+(const string& a,
                            const string& b);
private:
   char*  s;
   int    len;
};
```

A constructor's name is the same as the class name. In allocating storage for initializing objects, the constructor typically uses new. The keyword new is a unary operator that takes as an argument a data type that can include an array size. It allocates the appropriate amount of memory to store this type and returns the pointer value that addresses this memory. In the preceding example, `n + 1` bytes would be allocated from free store. Thus, the declaration

```
string  a(40), b(100);
```

would allocate 41 bytes for the variable a, pointed at by `a.s`, and 101 bytes for the variable b, pointed at by `b.s`. We add one byte for the end-of-string value 0. Storage obtained by new is persistent and is not automatically returned on block exit. When storage return is desired, a destructor function must be included in the class. A destructor is written as an ordinary member function whose name is the same as the class name preceded by the tilde symbol ~. Typically, a destructor uses the unary operator `delete`, another addition to the language, to automatically deallocate storage associated with a pointer expression.

```
//Add as a member function to class string.
~string() { delete []s; }       //destructor
```

It is usual to overload the constructor, writing a variety of such functions to accommodate more than one style of initialization. Consider, for example, initializing a string with a pointer to `char` value. This constructor would be

```
string(const char* p)
{
   len = strlen(p);
   s = new char[len + 1];
   strcpy(s, p);
}
```

A typical declaration invoking this version of the constructor would be

```
char*   str = "I came on foot.";
string  a("I came by bus."), b(str);
```

It would also be desirable to have a constructor of no arguments

```
string() { len = 255; s = new char[255]; }
```

This would be invoked by declarations without parenthesized arguments and would, by default, allocate 255 bytes of memory. All three constructors would then be invoked in the following declaration:

```
string  a, b(10), c("I came by horse.");
```

The overloaded constructor is selected by the form of each declaration. The variable a has no parameters and so is allocated 255 bytes. The variable b has an integer parameter and so is allocated 11 bytes. The variable c has a pointer parameter to the literal string `"I came by horse."`, and so is allocated 17 bytes, with this literal string copied into its private s member.

15.5 Inheritance

The central element of OOP is the encapsulation of an appropriate set of data types and their operations. The class construct, with its member functions and data members, provides an appropriate coding tool. Class variables are the *objects* to be manipulated. Pascal uses the type `record` to encapsulate variables.

Classes also provide data hiding. Access privileges can be managed and limited to whatever group of functions needs access to implementation details. This promotes modularity and robustness.

Another important concept in OOP is the promotion of code reuse through the inheritance mechanism. This is the mechanism of *deriving* a new class from an existing one, called the *base* class. The base class can be added to or altered to create the derived class. This allows the creation of a hierarchy of related data types that share code.

Many types are variants of one another, and developing new code for each is frequently tedious and error-prone. A derived class inherits the description of the base class. Hierarchy is a method for coping with complexity. It imposes classifications on objects. For example, the periodic table of elements has elements that are gasses. These have properties that are shared by all elements in that classification. The inert gasses are an important subclassification. The hierarchy is that an inert gas, such as argon, is a gas, which in turn is an element. This provides a convenient way to understand the behavior of inert gasses. We know they are composed of protons and electrons, as this description is shared by all elements. We know they are in a gaseous state at room temperature, as this behavior is shared by all gasses. We know they do not combine in ordinary chemical reactions with other elements, as this behavior is shared by all inert gasses.

Consider designing a database for a college. The registrar must track different types of students. The base class we need to develop captures a description of student. Two main categories of student are graduate and undergraduate.

OOP Design Methodology

1 Decide on an appropriate set of types.

2 Design their relatedness into the code, using inheritance.

An example of deriving a class is

```
enum support { ta, ra, fellowship, other };
enum year { fresh, soph, junior, senior, grad };

class student {
public:
   student(char* nm, int id, double g, year x);
   void  print() const;
private:
   int     student_id;
   double  gpa;
   year    y;
   char    name[30];
};

class grad_student : public student {
public:
   grad_student(char* nm, int id, double g,
                year x, support t, char* d, char* th);
   void print() const;
private:
   support  s;
   char     dept[10];
   char     thesis[80];
};
```

In this example, `grad_student` is the derived class, and `student` is the base class. The use of the keyword `public` following the colon in the derived class header means that the public members of `student` are to be inherited as public members of `grad_student`. Private members of the base class cannot be accessed in the derived class. Public inheritance also means that the derived class `grad_student` is a subtype of `student`.

An inheritance structure provides a design for the overall system. For example, a database that contained all the people at a college could be derived from the base class `person`. The `student` base class could be used to derive law students, as a further significant category of objects. Similarly, `person` could be the base class for a variety of employee categories.

15.6 Polymorphism

A *polymorphic* function or operator has many forms. For example, in C++, the division operator is polymorphic. If the arguments to the division operator are integral, then integer division is used. However, if one or both arguments are floating-point, then floating-point division is used.

In C++, a function name or operator is overloadable. A function is called based on its *signature*, defined as the list of argument types in its parameter list.

For example, in the division expression

```
a / b    //type is determined by native coercions
```

the result depends on the arguments being automatically coerced to the widest type. So if both arguments are integer, the result is an integer division. However, if one or both arguments are floating-point, the result is floating-point.

Another example is the output statement

```
cout << a;  //polymorphism via function overloading
```

where the shift operator << is invoking a function that is able to output an object of type `a`. So if a is an integer, the output is integer. But if a is floating-point, the output is floating-point.

Polymorphism localizes responsibility for behavior. The client code frequently requires no revision when additional functionality is added to the system through ADT-provided code improvements.

A technique for implementing a package of routines to provide an ADT shape could rely on a comprehensive structural description of any shape. For instance,

```
struct shape {
   enum { CIRCLE, RECTANGLE, ..... } e_val;
   double  center, radius;
   .....
};
```

would have all the members necessary for any shape currently drawable in our system. It would also have an enumerator value so it could be identified. The area routine would then be written as

```
double area(shape* s)
{
   switch(s -> e_val) {
   case CIRCLE: return (PI * s -> radius * s -> radius);
   case RECTANGLE: return (s -> height * s -> width);
   .....
}
```

What is involved in revising this code to include a new shape? An additional case in the code body and additional members in the structure are needed. Unfortunately, these would have ripple effects throughout our entire code body because each routine so structured has to have an additional case, even when that case is just adding a label to a preexisting case. Thus what is conceptually a local improvement requires global changes.

OOP coding techniques in C++ for the same problem use a shape hierarchy. The hierarchy is the obvious one, in which circle and rectangle are derived from shape. The revision process is one in which code improvements are provided in a new derived class, so additional description is localized. The programmer overrides the meaning of any changed routines—in this case, the new area calculation. Client code that does not use the new type is unaffected; client code that is improved by the new type is typically minimally changed.

C++ code following this design uses `shape` as an *abstract base class.* This is a class containing one or more pure virtual functions.

```
//shape is an abstract base class.
class shape {
public:
   virtual double  area() = 0;           //pure virtual function
};

class rectangle : public shape {
public:
   rectangle(double h, double w) : height(h), width(w) { }
   double

area() { return (height * width); }    //override
private:
   double  height, width;
};

class circle : public shape {
public:
   circle(double r) : radius(r) { }
   double  area() { return ( 3.14159 * radius * radius); }
private:
   double  radius;
};
```

Client code for computing an arbitrary area is polymorphic. The appropriate `area()` function is selected at run-time.

```
shape*  ptr_shape;
   .....
   cout << " area = " << ptr_shape -> area();
   .....
```

Now imagine improving our hierarchy of types by developing a `square` class.

```
class square : public rectangle {
public:
   square(double h) : rectangle(h,h) { }
   double  area() { return (rectangle::area()); }
};
```

The client code remains unchanged. This was not the case with the non-OOP code.

15.7 Templates

C++ uses the keyword `template` to provide *parametric polymorphism.* Parametric polymorphism allows the same code to be used with respect to different types, where the type is a parameter of the code body. The code is written generically. An especially important use for this technique is in writing generic *container classes.* A container class is used to contain data of a particular type. Stacks, vectors, trees, and lists are all examples of standard container classes. We develop a `stack` container class as a parameterized type.

```
//template stack implementation
template <class TYPE>
class stack {
public:
   stack(int size = 1000) : max_len(size)
            { s = new TYPE[size]; top = EMPTY; }
   ~stack() { delete []s; }
   void
```

```
reset() { top = EMPTY; }
   void  push(TYPE c) { s[++top] = c; }
   TYPE  pop() { return s[top--]; }
   TYPE  top_of() { return s[top]; }
   boolean  empty() { return boolean(top == EMPTY); }
   boolean  full() { return boolean(top == max_len - 1); }
private:
   enum    {EMPTY = -1};
   TYPE*   s;
   int     max_len;
   int     top;
};
```

The syntax of the class declaration is prefaced by

template <class *identifier*>

This identifier is a template argument that essentially stands for an arbitrary type. Throughout the class definition, the template argument can be used as a type name. This argument is instantiated in the actual declarations. An example of a `stack` declaration using this is

```
stack<char>     stk_ch;           // 1000 char stack
stack<char*>    stk_str(200);     // 200 char* stack
stack<complex>  stk_cmplx(100);   // 100 complex stack
```

This mechanism saves us rewriting class declarations in which the only variation would be type declarations.

When processing such a type, the code must always use the angle brackets as part of the declaration. Here are two functions using the `stack` template:

```
//Reversing a series of char* represented strings
void reverse(char* str[], int n)
{
   stack<char*>  stk(n);         //this stack holds char*
   for (int i = 0; i < n; ++i)
      stk.push(str[i]);
   for (i = 0; i < n; ++i)
      str[i] = stk.pop();
}
```

In function reverse(), a stack<char*> is used to insert *n* strings and then pop them in reverse order.

```
//Initializing a stack of complex numbers from an array
void init(complex c[], stack<complex>& stk, n)
{
   for (int i = 0; i < n; ++i)
      stk.push(c[i]);
}
```

In function init(), a stack<complex> variable is passed by reference, and n complex numbers are pushed onto this stack.

15.8 C++ Exceptions

C++ introduces an exception-handling mechanism that is sensitive to context. The context for raising an exception is a try block. Handlers declared using the keyword catch are found at the end of a try block.

An exception is raised by using the throw expression. The exception is handled by invoking an appropriate handler selected from a list of handlers found immediately after the handler's try block. A simple example of all this is

```
//stack constructor with exceptions
stack::stack(int n)
{
   if (n < 1)
      throw (n);                  //want a positive value
   p = new char[n];               //create a stack of characters
   if (p == 0)                    //new returns 0 when it fails
      throw ("FREE STORE EXHAUSTED");
   else
      top = EMPTY;
      max_len = n;
}

void g()
{
   try {
      stack  a(n), b(n);
      .....

   }
   catch (int n) {.....}          //an incorrect size
   catch (char* error) {.....}   //free store exhaustion
}
```

The first `throw()` has an integer argument and matches the `catch(int n)` signature. This handler is expected to perform an appropriate action, where an incorrect array size has been passed as an argument to the constructor. For example, printing an error message and aborting are appropriate handler actions. The second `throw()` has a pointer to `char` argument and matches the `catch(char* error)` signature.

15.9 Benefits Of Object-Oriented Programming

OOP programming is frequently more difficult than normal procedural programming as found in C or Pascal. At least one extra design step is necessary before we begin coding algorithms. This step involves designing types that are appropriate for the specific problem at hand.

Frequently one is solving the problem more generally than is strictly necessary. The belief is that a more general solution pays dividends in several ways. The solution is more encapsulated and thus more robust and easier to maintain and change. Also, the solution is more reusable. For example, where the code needs a stack, that stack is easily borrowed from existing code. In an ordinary procedural language, such a data structure is frequently "wired into" the algorithm and cannot be exported.

OOP is many things to many people. Attempts at defining it are reminiscent of the blind sages, attempts at describing the elephant. Consider one more equation:

OOP = type-extensibility + polymorphism

15.10 Style

There are two commenting styles: the new one begins with // and the comment continues to the end of the line, and the other is the old comment style `/* old style */`. The new style is definitely favored by C++ programmers. In situations where copious commenting is in order, the new style comments are easier to write and easier to read.

In this chapter we have usually followed the more common C++ style of writing * and & next to the type. Examples of this are `char* c` instead of `char *c` and `float& x` instead of `float &x`.

In C++, a function declaration with no parameters is equivalent to using `void`. Thus, for example,

```
int f();        is equivalent to        int f(void);
```

15.11 Common Programming Errors

As with any new language, there are lots of possibilities for errors. Here we mention two errors that can be quite difficult to debug. The first error is caused by a comment in a #define:

```
#define   LIMIT   77                 // danger - watch out!

for (i = 0; i < LIMIT; ++i)
   .....                             // do something
```

This error is system-dependent. Some preprocessors remove comments; others do not. If the preprocessor does not remove comments, every occurrence of LIMIT is replaced by

```
77             // danger - watch out!
```

Thus the for loop becomes

```
for (i = 0; i < 77                   // danger - watch out! ; ++i)
   .....
```

Naturally, the compiler is not too happy with this. Unfortunately, because of the nature of this error, the compiler error message is not very helpful.

For computational work, it is common to overload the ^ operator so that m^n yields the value of m raised to the power n. After this has been done, we might write

```
cout << "2 raised to the power 3 is " << 2^3 << "\n";
```

The difficulty here is that we have forgotten that << has higher precedence than ^. Again, because of the nature of the error, the compiler error message is not very helpful. The correct way to write the line is

```
cout << "2 raised to the power 3 is " << (2^3) << "\n";
```

15.12 System Considerations

ANSI C has borrowed a number of constructs from C++, including the function prototype and the const qualifier. Consider the code

```
const int   n = 7;

int   a[n];
```

This is legal in C++, but not in C. In C, an array size must be a constant. Even though `n` is `const` qualified, it is a nonmodifiable variable but not a constant in C.

ANSI C may be in the process of inheriting another feature from C++—namely, the // commenting style. The latest C compilers from both Borland and Microsoft support the new commenting style. One striking example of its use is in the Microsoft C code that supports windows. This code is heavily commented, and most of the comments are in the new style.

Summary

- What is truly novel about C++ is the aggregate type `class`, which is introduced by the language. A `class` is an extension of the idea of `struct` in traditional C. Its use is a way of implementing a data type and associated functions and operators. Therefore a `class` is an implementation of an abstract data type (ADT). There are two important additions to the structure concept: (1) It includes members that are functions, and (2) it employs a new keyword, `public`. This keyword indicates the visibility of the members that follow it. Without this keyword, the members are private to the class. Private members are available for use only by other member functions of the class. Public members are available to any function within the scope of the class declaration. Privacy allows part of the implementation of a class type to be "hidden."

- The term *overloading* refers to the practice of giving several meanings to an operator or a function. The meaning selected depends on the types of the arguments used by the operator or function.

- The keyword `operator` introduces the operator token and replaces what would otherwise be a function name in a function declaration. The keyword `friend` gives a function access to the private members of a class variable. A `friend` function is not a member of the class but has the privileges of a member function in the class in which it is declared.

- A constructor is a member function whose job it is to initialize a variable of its class. In many cases this involves dynamic storage allocation. A constructor is invoked whenever an object of its associated class is created, typically when a variable is declared.

- A destructor is a member function whose job it is to deallocate a variable of its class. Where an object has been allocated dynamically, its associated memory can be deallocated (returned to free store) by a destructor. This is done by implicitly invoking the destructor upon block exit for any class variables declared inside the block.

- The central element of object-oriented programming (OOP) is the encapsulation of an appropriate set of data types and their operations. These user-defined types are ADTs. The class construct with its member functions and data members provides an appropriate coding tool. Class variables are the *objects* to be manipulated.

- Another important concept in OOP is the promotion of code reuse through the *inheritance* mechanism. This is the mechanism of *deriving* a new class from an existing one, called the *base* class. The base class can be added to or altered to create the derived class. In this way a hierarchy of related data types can be created that share code. This typing hierarchy can be used dynamically by `virtual` functions. Virtual member functions in a base class are overloaded in a derived class. These functions allow for dynamic, or run-time, typing. A pointer to the base class can also point at objects of the derived classes. When such a pointer is used to point at the overloaded virtual function, it dynamically selects which version of the member function to call.

Exercises

1 Take a working program such as the following, omit each line in turn, and run it through the compiler. Record the error messages that each line deletion causes.

```
#include <iostream.h>

int main(void)
{
   int   m, n, k;

   cout << "\nEnter two integers: ";
   cin  >> m >> n;
   k = m + n;
   cout << "\nTheir sum is " << k << ".\n";
   return 0;
}
```

2 Write a program that asks interactively for your *name* and *age* and responds with

`Hello` *name*`, next year you will be` *next_age*`.`

where *next_age* is *age* + 1.

3 Write a program that prints out a table of squares, square roots, and cubes. Use either tabbing or strings of blanks to get a neatly aligned table like the following:

```
Integer       Square      Square root     Cube
----------------------------------------------
1             1           1.00000         1
2             4           1.41421         8
 .....
```

4 In ANSI C, the traditional swapping function is

```
void swap(int *p, int  *q)
{
   int  tmp;

   tmp = *p;
   *p = *q;
   *q = tmp;
}
```

Rewrite this in C++ using reference parameters. Then write a program to test it. Note that in C we used `p` and `q` as identifiers to indicate pointer usage. With reference parameters, other identifiers are more appropriate. For example,

```
void swap(int& i, int& j)
{
   .....
```

5 Add to the class `string` a member function `reverse()` (see Section 15.2, "Classes and Abstract Data Types," on page 506). This function reverses the underlying representation of the characters in the private member `s`.

6 Add to the class `string` a member function `void print(int k)`. This function overloads `print()` and is meant to print the first `k` characters of the string.

7 Overload the operator * in class `string`. Its member declaration should be

```
string operator*(string& a, int n);
```

The `string` represented by `a` should be copied back into `a` `n` times. Check that this does not overrun storage.

Appendix A

The Standard Library

The standard library provides functions that are available for use by the programmer. Associated with the library are standard header files provided by the system. These header files contain prototypes of functions in the standard library, macro definitions, and other programming elements. If a programmer wants to use a particular function from the library, the corresponding header file should be included. Here is a complete list of the header files.

C header files			
<assert.h>	<limits.h>	<signal.h>	<stdlib.h>
<ctype.h>	<locale.h>	<stdarg.h>	<string.h>
<errno.h>	<math.h>	<stddef.h>	<time.h>
<float.h>	<setjmp.h>	<stdio.h>	

These files may be included in any order. Also, they may be included more than once, with the effect being the same as if they were included only once. In this appendix we organize our discussion by header file.

A.1 Diagnostics: <assert.h>

This header file defines the assert() macro. If the macro NDEBUG is defined at the point where <assert.h> is included, then all assertions are effectively discarded.

- `void assert(int expr);`

If expr is zero (*false*), then diagnostics are printed and the program is aborted. The diagnostics include the expression, the file name, and the line number in the file.

A.2 Character Handling: <ctype.h>

This header defines several macros that are used to test a character argument. In addition, there are function prototypes for two functions used to map a character argument.

Testing a Character

```
int isalnum(int c);        /* is alphanumeric */
int isalpha(int c);        /* is alphabetic */
int iscntrl(int c);        /* is control */
int isdigit(int c);        /* is digit: 0-9 */
int isgraph(int c);        /* is graphic */
int islower(int c);        /* is lowercase */
int isprint(int c);        /* is printable */
int ispunct(int c);        /* is punctuation */
int isspace(int c);        /* is white space */
int isupper(int c);        /* is uppercase */
int isxdigit(int c);       /* is hex digit 0-9, a-f, A-F */
```

These character tests are typically implemented as macros; see *ctype.h* in your installation for details. If the argument `c` satisfies the test, then a nonzero value (*true*) is returned; otherwise zero (*false*) is returned. These macros should also be available as functions.

The printing characters are implementation-defined, but each occupies one printing position on the screen. A graphic character is any printing character, except for a space. Thus a graphic character puts a visible mark on a single printing position on the screen. A punctuation character is any printing character other than a space or a character `c` for which `isalnum(c)` is true. The standard white space characters are space, form feed (`'\f'`), newline (`'\n'`), carriage return (`'\r'`), horizontal tab (`'\t'`), and vertical tab (`'\v'`). The control characters are the audible bell (`'\a'`), backspace (`'\b'`), any character `c` for which `isspace(c)` is true other than space, and control-c, control-h, and so on.

Mapping a Character

The two functions `tolower()` and `toupper()` are used to map a character argument. *Caution:* Early versions of many ANSI C compilers did not implement these functions correctly.

```
int tolower(int c);
```

If `c` is an uppercase letter, the corresponding lowercase letter is returned; otherwise `c` is returned.

■ `int toupper(int c);`

If `c` is a lowercase letter, the corresponding uppercase letter is returned; otherwise `c` is returned.

The next three macros often occur on ASCII machines. The first two are related to, but not the same as, `tolower()` and `toupper()`.

```
#define   _tolower(c)    ((c) + 'a' - 'A')
#define   _toupper(c)    ((c) + 'A' - 'a')
#define   toascii(c)     ((c) & 0x7f)
```

The hexadecimal constant `0x7f` is a mask for the low-order 7 bits.

A.3 Errors: <errno.h>

The identifier `errno` is defined here, along with several macros that are used to report error conditions.

```
extern int   errno;
```

Typically, there are lots of macros in *errno.h*. Which macros occur is system-dependent, but all names must begin with E. Various library functions use these macros for error reporting.

Two macros are common to all systems. These are used by the mathematical functions in the library.

```
#define   EDOM     33       /* domain error */
#define   ERANGE   34       /* range error */
```

Values other than 33 and 34 could be used here, but these values are typical.

The *domain* of a mathematical function is the set of argument values for which it is defined. For example, the domain of the square root function is the set of all nonnegative numbers. A *domain error* occurs when a mathematical function is called with an argument not in its domain. When this happens, the system assigns the value `EDOM` to `errno`. The programmer can use `perror()` and `strerror()` to print a message associated with the value stored in `errno`.

A *range error* occurs when the value to be returned by the function is defined mathematically but cannot be represented in a `double`. When this happens, the system assigns the value `ERANGE` to `errno`.

A.4 Floating Limits: <float.h>

Macros that define various floating characteristics and limits are defined here. There are many of them. Some examples are

```
#define   DBL_MAX          1.7976931348623157e+308
#define   FLT_MAX          3.40282347e+38F
#define   LDBL_MAX         1.7976931348623157e+308

#define   DBL_MIN          2.2250738585072014e-308
#define   FLT_MIN          1.17549435e-38F
#define   LDBL_MIN         2.2250738585072014e-308

#define   DBL_EPSILON      2.2204460492503131e-16
#define   FLT_EPSILON      1.19209290e-07F
#define   LDBL_EPSILON     2.2204460492503131e-16
```

The constants are system-dependent. We are assuming that a `long double` is implemented as a `double`. Not all systems do this. Some provide more precision and range; see *float.h* on your system.

A.5 Integral Limits: <limits.h>

Macros that define various integral characteristics and limits are defined here. There are many of them. Some examples are

```
#define   CHAR_BIT   8       /* number of bits in a byte */
#define   CHAR_MAX   127
#define   CHAR_MIN   (-128)
#define   SHRT_MAX   32767
#define   SHRT_MIN   (-32768)
#define   INT_MAX    2147483647
#define   INT_MIN    (-2147483648)
```

The constants are system-dependent.

A.6 Localization: <locale.h>

This header contains programming constructs that can be used to set or access properties suitable for the current locale. The following structure type is defined:

```
struct lconv {
   char   *decimal_point;
   char   *thousands_sep;
   char   *currency_symbol;
   .....
};
```

The members allow for local variations, such as using a comma instead of a period for a decimal point. At least six symbolic constants are defined.

```
#define LC_ALL        1 /* all categories */
#define LC_COLLATE    2 /*strcoll() and strxfrm */
#define LC_CTYPE      3 /*character handling functions */
#define LC_MONETARY   4 /* monetary info in localeconv() */
#define LC_NUMERIC    5 /*decimal point in lib fcts */
#define LC_TIME       6 /*strftime()*/
```

The values of the symbolic constants are system-dependent. Other macros beginning with LC_ can be specified. These macros can be used as the first argument to the `setlocale()` function.

■ `char *setlocale(int category, const char *locale);`

The first argument is typically one of the above symbolic constants. The second argument is "C", "", or some other string. The function returns a pointer to a string of static duration, supplied by the system, that describes the new locale, if it is available; otherwise the NULL pointer is returned. At program startup, the system behaves as if

```
setlocale(LC_ALL, "C");
```

has been executed. This specifies a minimal environment for C translation. The statement

```
setlocale(LC_ALL, "");
```

specifies the native environment, which is system-dependent. Using a macro other than LC_ALL affects only part of the locale. For example, LC_MONETARY affects only that part of the locale dealing with monetary information.

■ `struct lconv *localeconv(void);`

A pointer to a structure provided by the system is returned. It is of static duration and contains numeric information about the current locale. Further calls to the function `setlocale()` can change the values stored in the structure.

A.7 Mathematics: <math.h>

This header file contains prototypes for the mathematical functions in the library. It also contains one macro definition.

```
#define    HUGE_VAL    1.7976931348623157e+308
```

The value of the macro is system-dependent.

The *domain* of a mathematical function is the set of argument values for which it is defined. A *domain error* occurs when a mathematical function is called with an argument not in its domain. When this happens, the function returns a system-dependent value, and the system assigns the value EDOM to errno.

A *range error* occurs when the value to be returned by the function is defined mathematically but cannot be represented in a double. If the value is too large in magnitude (overflow), then either HUGE_VAL or -HUGE_VAL is returned. If the value is too small in magnitude (underflow), zero is returned. On overflow, the value of the macro ERANGE is stored in errno. What happens on underflow is system-dependent. Some systems store ERANGE in errno; others do not.

■
```
double cos(double x);
double sin(double x);
double tan(double x);
```

These are the cosine, sine, and tangent functions, respectively.

■
```
double acos(double x);                   /* arccosine of x */
double asin(double x);                   /* arcsine of x */
double atan(double x);                   /* arctangent of x */
double atan2(double y, double x);        /* arctangent of y/x */
```

These are inverse trigonometric functions. The angle *theta* returned by each of them is in radians. The range of the acos() function is $[0, \pi]$. The range of the asin() and atan() functions is $[-\pi/2, \pi/2]$. The range of the atan2() function is $[-\pi, \pi]$. Its principal use is to assist in changing rectangular coordinates into polar coordinates. For the functions acos() and asin(), a domain error occurs if the argument is not in the range [-1, 1]. For the function atan2(), a domain error occurs if both arguments are zero and y/x cannot be represented.

■
```
double cosh(double x);
double sinh(double x);
double tanh(double x);
```

These are the hyperbolic cosine, hyperbolic sine, and hyperbolic tangent functions, respectively.

```
■ double exp(double x);
  double log(double x);
  double log10(double x);
```

The exp() function returns e^x. The log() function returns the natural logarithm (base e) of x. The log10() function returns the base ten logarithm of x. For both log functions, a domain error occurs if x is negative. A range error occurs if x is zero and the logarithm of zero cannot be represented. (Some systems can represent infinity.)

```
■ double ceil(double x);
  double floor(double x);
```

The ceiling function returns the smallest integer not less than x. The floor function returns the largest integer not greater than x.

```
■ double fabs(double x);        /* floating absolute value */
```

Returns the absolute value of x. *Caution:* The related function abs() is designed for integer values, not floating values. Do not confuse abs() with fabs().

```
■ double fmod(double x, double y);          /* floating modulus
  */
```

Returns the value x (mod y). More explicitly, if y is nonzero, the value x - i * y is returned, where i is an integer such that the result is zero or has the same sign as x and magnitude less than the magnitude of y. If y is zero, what is returned is system-dependent, but zero is typical. In this case a domain error occurs on some systems.

```
■ double pow(double x, double y);           /* power function */
```

Returns x raised to the y power. A domain error occurs if x is negative and y is not an integer.

```
■ double sqrt(double x);                    /* square root */
```

Returns the square root of x, provided x is nonnegative. A domain error occurs if x is negative.

```
■ double frexp(double value, int *exp_ptr); /* free exponent */
```

This is a primitive used by other functions in the library. It splits value into mantissa and exponent. The statement

```
x = frexp(value, &exp);
```

causes the relationship

```
value = x * 2^exp
```

to hold, where the magnitude of x is in the interval [1/2, 1) or x is zero.

■ `double ldexp(double x, int exp);                /* load exponent */`

The value x * 2^{exp} is returned.

■ `double modf(double value, double *i_ptr);`

Breaks `value` into integer and fractional parts. The function call `modf(value, &i)` returns the value *f*, and indirectly the value `i`, so that

```
value = i + f
```

A.8 Nonlocal Jumps: <setjmp.h>

This header provides one type definition and two prototypes. These declarations allow the programmer to make nonlocal jumps. A nonlocal jump is like a `goto` but with the flow of control leaving the function in which it occurs. The type definition is system-dependent. The following is an example:

```
typedef   long   jmp_buf[16];
```

An array of type `jmp_buf` is used to hold system information that is used to restore the calling environment.

■ `int setjmp(jmp_buf env);`

Saves the current calling environment in the array `env` for later use by `longjmp()` and returns zero. Although on many systems this is implemented as a function, in ANSI C, it is supposed to be implemented as a macro.

■ `void longjmp(jmp_buf env, int value);`

The function call `longjmp(env, value)` restores the environment saved by the most recent invocation of `setjmp(env)`. If `setjmp(env)` was not invoked, or if the function in which it was invoked is no longer active, the behavior is undefined. A successful call causes program control to jump to the place following the previous call to `setjmp(env)`. If `value` is nonzero, the effect is as if `setjmp(env)` were called again, with value being returned. If value is zero, the effect is as if set-jmp(env) were called again, with one being returned.

A.9 Signal Handling: <signal.h>

This header contains constructs used by the programmer to handle exceptional conditions, or signals. The following macros are defined in this header:

```
#define   SIGINT    2     /* interrupt */
#define   SIGILL    4     /* illegal instruction */
#define   SIGFPE    8     /* floating-point exception */
#define   SIGSEGV   11    /* segment violation */
#define   SIGTERM   15    /* asynchronous termination */
#define   SIGABRT   22    /* abort */
```

The constants are system-dependent, but these are commonly used. Other signals are usually supported; see the file *signal.h* on your system.

The macros in the next set may be used as the second argument of the function signal().

```
#define   SIG_DFL   ((void (*)(int)) 0)     /* default */
#define   SIG_ERR   ((void (*)(int)) -1)    /* error */
#define   SIG_IGN   ((void (*)(int)) 1)     /* ignore */
```

A system may supply other such macros. The names must begin with SIG_ followed by a capital letter.

■ `void (*signal(int sig, void (*func)(int)))(int);`

The function call signal(sig, func) associates the signal sig with the signal handler func(). If the call is successful, the pointer value func of the previous call with first argument sig is returned, or NULL is returned if there was no previous call. If the call is unsuccessful, the pointer value SIG_ERR is returned.

The function call signal(sig, func) instructs the system to invoke func(sig) when the signal sig is raised. If the second argument to signal() is SIG_DFL, default action occurs; if it is SIG_IGN, the signal is ignored. When program control returns from func(), it returns to the place where sig was raised.

■ `int raise(int sig);`

Causes the signal sig to be raised. If the call is successful, zero is returned; otherwise a nonzero value is returned. This function can be for testing purposes.

A.10 Variable Arguments: <stdarg.h>

This header file provides the programmer with a portable means of writing functions such as printf() that have a variable number of arguments. The header file contains one typedef and three macros. How these are implemented is system-dependent, but here is one way it can be done:

```
typedef   char *   va_list;

#define   va_start(ap, v)  \
             ((void) (ap = (va_list) &v + sizeof(v)))
#define   va_arg(ap, type)    (*((type *)(ap))++)
#define   va_end(ap)          ((void) (ap = 0))
```

In the macro va_start(), the variable v is the last argument that is declared in the header to your variable argument function definition. This variable cannot be of storage class register, and it cannot be an array type or a type such as char that is widened by automatic conversions. The macro va_start() initializes the argument pointer ap. The macro va_arg() accesses the next argument in the list. The macro va_end() performs any cleanup that may be required before function exit. The following program illustrates the use of these constructs:

```
#include   <stdio.h>
#include   <stdarg.h>

int   va_sum(int cnt, ...);

int main(void)
{
   int      a = 1, b = 2, c = 3;

   printf("First call:  sum = %d\n", va_sum(2, a, b));
   printf("Second call: sum = %d\n", va_sum(3, a, b, c));
   return 0;
}

int va_sum(int cnt, ...)               /* sum the arguments */
{
   int       i, sum = 0;
   va_list   ap;

   va_start(ap, cnt);                  /* startup */
   for (i = 0; i < cnt; ++i)
      sum += va_arg(ap, int);          /* get next argument */
   va_end(ap);                         /* cleanup */
   return sum;
}
```

A.11 Common Definitions: <stddef.h>

This header file contains some type definitions and macros that are commonly used in other places. How they are implemented is system-dependent, but here is one way of doing it:

```
typedef   char       wchar_t;
typedef   int        ptrdiff_t;
typedef   unsigned   size_t;

#define   NULL       ((void *) 0)
#define   offsetof(s_type, m)  \
             ((size_t) &(((s_type *) 0) -> m))
```

Here, we defined the wide character type `wchar_t` as a plain `char`. A system can define it to be any integral type. It must be able to hold the largest extended character set of all the locales that are supported. The type `ptrdiff_t` is the type obtained when two pointers are subtracted. The type `size_t` is the type obtained with use of the `sizeof` operator. A macro call of the form `offsetof(`*s_type*`, m)` computes the offset in bytes of the member `m` from the beginning of the structure *s_type*. The following program illustrates its use:

```
#include   <stdio.h>
#include   <stddef.h>

typedef struct {
   double   a, b, c;
} data;

int main(void)
{
   printf("%d %d\n",
         offsetof(data, a), offsetof(data, b));
   return 0;
}
```

On most systems this program causes 0 and 8 to be printed.

A.12 Input/Output: <stdio.h>

This header file contains macros, type definitions, and prototypes of functions used by the programmer to access files. Here are some example macros and type definitions:

```
#define   BUFSIZ          1024    /*buf size for all I/O*/
#define   EOF             (-1)    /*returned on EOF*/
#define   FILENAME_MAX    255     /*max filename chars */
#define   FOPEN_MAX       20      /*max open files*/
#define   L_tmpnam        16      /*size tmp filename*/
#define   NULL            0       /*null pointer value */
#define   TMP_MAX         65535   /*max unique filenames*/

typedef   long        pos_t;      /*used with fsetpos() */
typedef   unsigned    size_t;     /*type from sizeof op*/
typedef   char *      va_list;    /*used with vfprintf()*/
```

The structure type FILE has members that describe the current state of a file. The name and number of its members are system-dependent. Here is an example:

```
typedef struct {
    int            cnt;        /* size of unused part of buf */
    unsigned char  *b_ptr;     /* next buffer loc to access */
    unsigned char  *base;      /* start of buffer */
    int            bufsize;    /* buffer size */
    short          flag;       /* info stored bitwise */
    char           fd;         /* file descriptor */
} FILE;

extern FILE   _iob[];
```

An object of type FILE should be capable of recording all the information needed to control a stream, including a file position indicator, a pointer to its associated buffer, an *error indicator* that records whether a read/write error has occurred, and an *end-of-file indicator* that records whether the end-of-file mark has been reached. How this is implemented is system-dependent. For example, the error indicator and the end-of-file indicator might be encoded bitwise in the structure member flag.

Typically, the type fpos_t is given by

```
typedef   long   fpos_t;
```

An object of this type is supposed to be capable of recording all the information needed to uniquely specify every position in a file.

Macros are used to define stdin, stdout, and stderr. Although we think of them as files, they are actually pointers.

```
#define   stdin    (&_iob[0])
#define   stdout   (&_iob[1])
#define   stderr   (&_iob[2])
```

Unlike other files, `stdin`, `stdout`, and `stderr` do not have to be opened explicitly by the programmer.

A few macros are intended for use with functions.

```
#define   _IOFBF     0      /* setvbuf(): full buffering */
#define   _IOLBF     0x80   /* setvbuf(): line buffering */
#define   _IONBF     0x04   /* setvbuf(): no buffering */
#define   SEEK_SET   0      /* fseek(): file beginning */
#define   SEEK_CUR   1      /* fseek(): current file pos */
#define   SEEK_END   2      /* fseek(): EOF */
```

When a file is opened, the operating system associates it with a *stream* and keeps information about the stream in an object of type `FILE`. A pointer to `FILE` can be thought of as being associated with the file or the stream or both.

Opening, Closing, and Conditioning a File

■ `FILE *fopen(const char *filename, const char *mode);`

Performs the necessary housekeeping to open a buffered file. A successful call creates a stream and returns a pointer to `FILE` that is associated with the stream. If `filename` cannot be accessed, `NULL` is returned. The basic file modes are `"r"`, `"w"`, and `"a"`, corresponding to read, write, and append, respectively. The file position indicator is set at the beginning of the file if the file mode is `"r"` or `"w"`, and it is set at the end of the file if the file mode is `"a"`. If the file mode is `"w"` or `"a"` and the file does not exist, it is created. An update mode (both reading and writing) is indicated with a `+`. A binary file is indicated with a `b`. For example, the mode `"r+"` is used to open a text file for both reading and writing. The mode `"rb"` is used to open a binary file for reading. The mode `"rb+"` or `"r+b"` is used to open a binary file for reading and writing. Similar conventions apply to `"w"` and `"a"` (see Section 13.4, "Accessing Files," on page 443). In update mode, input may not be directly followed by output unless the end-of-file mark has been reached or an intervening call to one of the file-positioning functions `fseek()`, `fsetpos()`, or `rewind()` has occurred. In a similar fashion, output may not be directly followed by input unless an intervening call to `fflush()` or to one of the file-positioning functions `fseek()`, `fsetpos()`, or `rewind()` has occurred.

■ `int fclose(FILE *fp);`

Performs the necessary housekeeping to empty buffers and break all connections to the file associated with fp. If the file is successfully closed, zero is returned. If an error occurs or the file was already closed, EOF is returned. Open files are a limited resource. At most FOPEN_MAX files can be open simultaneously. System efficiency is improved by keeping only needed files open.

■ `int fflush(FILE *fp);`

Any buffered data is delivered. If the call is successful, zero is returned; otherwise EOF is returned.

■
```
FILE *freopen(const char *filename,
              const char *mode, FILE *fp);
```

Closes the file associated with fp, opens filename as specified by mode, and associates fp with the new file. If the function call is successful, fp is returned; otherwise NULL is returned. This function is useful for changing the file associated with stdin, stdout, or stderr.

■ `void setbuf(FILE *fp, char *buf);`

If fp is not NULL, the function call setbuf(fp, buf) is equivalent to

```
setvbuf(fp, buf, _IOFBF, BUFSIZ)
```

except that nothing is returned. If fp is NULL, the mode is _IONBF.

■ `int setvbuf(FILE *fp, char *buf, int mode, size_t n);`

Determines how the file associated with fp is to be buffered. The function must be invoked after the file has been opened but before it is accessed. The modes _IOFBF, _IOLBF, and _IONBF cause the file to be fully buffered, line buffered, and unbuffered, respectively. If buf is not NULL, the array of size n pointed to by buf is used as a buffer. If buf is NULL, the system provides the buffer. A successful call returns zero. *Caution:* If an array of storage class automatic is used as a buffer, the file should be closed before the function is exited.

■ `FILE *tmpfile(void);`

Opens a temporary file with mode "wb+" and returns a pointer associated with the file. If the request cannot be honored, NULL is returned. The system removes the file after it is closed or on program exit.

■ `char *tmpnam(char *s);`

Creates a unique temporary name that is typically used as a file name. If `s` is not `NULL`, the name is stored in `s`, which must be of size `L_tmpnam` or larger. If `s` is `NULL`, the system provides an array of static duration to store the name. Further calls to `tmpnam()` can overwrite this space. In all cases the base address of the array in which the name is stored is returned. Repeated calls to `tmpnam()` generate at least `TMP_MAX` unique names.

Accessing the File Position Indicator

Functions in this section are used by the programmer to access a file randomly. The traditional functions for this purpose are `fseek()`, `ftell()`, and `rewind()`. ANSI C has added `fgetpos()` and `fsetpos()`. An implementation can design these functions to access files that are too large to be handled by the traditional functions. However, early versions of many ANSI C compilers have not taken advantage of this opportunity.

■ `int fseek(FILE *fp, long offset, int place);`

Sets the file position indicator for the next input or output operation. The position is `offset` bytes from `place`. The value of `place` can be `SEEK_SET`, `SEEK_CUR`, or `SEEK_END`, which correspond to the beginning of the file, the current position in the file, or the end of the file, respectively. If the function call is successful, the end-of-file indicator is cleared and zero is returned.

■ `long ftell(FILE *fp);`

Returns the current value of the file position indicator for the file associated with `fp`. On a binary file, this value is a count of the number of bytes from the beginning of the file. For text files on some systems, this value is a "magic cookie." In any case, by saving the value returned, `fseek()` can be used to reset the file position indicator. An unsuccessful call returns -1 and stores a system-dependent value in `errno`.

■ `void rewind(FILE *fp);`

Sets the file position indicator to the beginning of the file and clears the end-of-file and error indicators. The function call `rewind(fp)` is equivalent to

```
(void) fseek(fp, 0L, SEEK_SET)
```

except that `fseek()` clears only the end-of-file indicator.

■ `int fgetpos(FILE *fp, fpos_t *pos);`

Gets the current value of the file position indicator for the file associated with `fp` and stores it in the object pointed to by `pos`. The stored value can be used later by `fsetpos()` to reset the file position indicator. A successful call returns zero; otherwise a system-dependent value is stored in `errno` and a nonzero value is returned.

■ `int fsetpos(FILE *fp, const fpos_t *pos);`

Sets the file position indicator to the value pointed to by `pos`. A successful call clears the end-of-file indicator and returns zero; otherwise a system-dependent value is written to `errno` and a nonzero value is returned.

Error Handling

■ `void clearerr(FILE *fp);`

Clears the error and end-of-file indicators for the file associated with `fp`.

■ `int feof(FILE *fp);`

Returns a nonzero value if the end-of-file indicator has been set for the file associated with `fp`.

■ `int ferror(FILE *fp);`

Returns a nonzero value if the error indicator has been set for the file associated with `fp`.

■ `void perror(const char *s);`

Prints an error message associated with `errno` on `stderr`. First the string `s` is printed, followed by a colon and a space. Then the associated error message is printed, followed by a newline. (The function call `strerror(errno)` prints only the associated error message.)

Character Input/Output

■ `int getc(FILE *fp);`

Equivalent to `fgetc()`, except that it is implemented as a macro. Because `fp` may be evaluated more than once in the macro definition, a call with an argument that has side effects, such as `fgetc(*p++)`, may not work correctly.

■ `int getchar(void);`

The call `getchar()` is equivalent to `getc(stdin)`.

■ `char *gets(char *s);`

Reads characters from `stdin` and stores them in the array pointed to by `s` until a newline is read or the end-of-file is reached, whichever occurs first. At this point, any newline is discarded and a null character is written. (In contrast, `fgets()` preserves the newline.) If any characters are written, `s` is returned; otherwise `NULL` is returned.

■ `int fgetc(FILE *fp);`

Gets the next character from the file associated with `fp` and returns the value of the character read. If the end-of-file is encountered, the end-of-file indicator is set and `EOF` is returned. If an error occurs, the error indicator is set and `EOF` is returned.

■ `char *fgets(char *line, int n, FILE *fp);`

Reads at most `n - 1` characters from the file associated with `fp` into the array pointed to by `line`. As soon as a newline is read into the array or an end-of-file is encountered, no additional characters are read from the file. A null character is written into the array to end the process. If an end-of-file is encountered right at the start, the contents of `line` are undisturbed and `NULL` is returned; otherwise `line` is returned.

■ `int fputc(int c, FILE *fp);`

Converts the argument `c` to an `unsigned char` and writes it into the file associated with `fp` . If the call `fputc(c)` is successful, it returns

```
(int) (unsigned char) c
```

otherwise it sets the error indicator and returns `EOF`.

■ `int fputs(const char *s, FILE *fp);`

Copies the null-terminated string `s` into the file associated with `fp`, except for the terminating null character itself. (The related function `puts()` appends a newline.) A successful call returns a nonnegative value; otherwise `EOF` is returned.

■ `int putc(int c, FILE *fp);`

Equivalent to `fputc()`, except that it is implemented as a macro. Because `fp` may be evaluated more than once in the macro definition, a call with an argument that has side effects, such as `putc(*p++)`, may not work correctly.

■ `int putchar(int c);`

The call `putchar(c)` is equivalent to `putc(c, stdout)`.

■ `int puts(const char *s);`

Copies the null-terminated string `s` to the standard output file, except for the terminating null character itself. Then a newline is written. (The related function `fputs()` does not append a newline.) A successful call returns a nonnegative value; otherwise `EOF` is returned.

■ `int ungetc(int c, FILE *fp);`

Pushes the value `(unsigned char) c` back onto the stream associated with `fp`, provided the value of `c` is not `EOF`. At least one character can be pushed back. (Most systems allow more.) Pushed-back characters are read from the stream in the reverse order in which they were pushed back. Once they have been read, they are forgotten; they are not placed permanently in the file. *Caution:* An intervening call to one of the file-positioning functions `fseek()`, `fsetpos()`, or `rewind()` causes any pushed-back characters to be lost. Also, until the pushed-back characters have been read, `ftell()` may be unreliable.

Formatted Input/Output

■ `int fprintf(FILE *fp, const char *cntrl_string, ...);`

Writes formatted text into the file associated with `fp` and returns the number of characters written. If an error occurs, the error indicator is set and a negative value is returned. Conversion specifications, or formats, can occur in `cntrl_string`. They begin with a % and end with a conversion character. The formats determine how the other arguments are printed (see Section , "The Output Function printf()," on page 429).

■ `int printf(const char *cntrl_string, ...);`

A function call of the form `printf(cntrl_string,` *other_arguments*`)` is equivalent to

`fprintf(stdout, cntrl_string,` *other_arguments* `)`

■ `int sprintf(char *s, const char *cntrl_string, ...);`

This is the string version of `printf()`. Instead of writing to `stdout`, it writes to the string pointed to by `s`.

■
```
int vfprintf(FILE *fp, const char *cntrl_string,
             va_list ap);
int vprintf(const char *cntrl_string, va_list ap);
int vsprintf(char s*, const char *cntrl_string,
             va_list ap);
```

These functions correspond to `fprintf()`, `printf()`, and `sprintf()`, respectively. Instead of a variable-length argument list, they have a pointer to an array of arguments as defined in *stdarg.h*

■ `int fscanf(FILE *fp, const char *cntrl_string, ...);`

Reads text from the file stream associated with `fp` and processes it according to the directives in the control string. There are three kinds of *directives*: ordinary characters, white space, and conversion specifications. Ordinary characters are matched, and white space is matched with optional white space. A conversion specification begins with a % and ends with a conversion character; it causes characters to be read from the input stream, a corresponding value to be computed, and the value to be placed in memory at an address specified by one of the other arguments. If the function is invoked and the input stream is empty, `EOF` is returned; otherwise, the number of successful conversions is returned (see Section 13.2, "The Return Value," on page 440).

■ `int scanf(const char *cntrl_string, ...);`

A function call of the form `scanf(cntrl_string,` *other_arguments* `)` is equivalent to

`fscanf(stdin, cntrl_string,` *other_arguments* `)`

■ `int sscanf(const char *s, const char *cntrl_string, ...);`

This is the string version of `scanf()`. Instead of reading from `stdin`, it reads from the string pointed to by `s`. Reading from a string is unlike reading from a file in the sense that if we use `sscanf()` to read from `s` again, then the input starts at the beginning of the string, not from where we left off before.

Direct Input/Output

The functions `fread()` and `fwrite()` are used to read and write binary files, respectively. No conversions are performed. In certain applications, the use of these functions can save considerable time.

```
■ size_t fread(void *a_ptr, size_t el_size, size_t n,
               FILE *fp);
```

Reads at most `n * el_size` bytes (characters) from the file associated with `fp` into the array pointed to by `a_ptr`. The number of array elements successfully written is returned. If an end-of-file is encountered, the end-of-file indicator is set and a short count is returned. If `el_size` or `n` is zero, the input stream is not read and zero is returned.

```
■ size_t fwrite(const void *a_ptr, size_t el_size,
               size_t n, FILE *fp);
```

Reads `n * el_size` bytes (characters) from the array pointed to by `a_ptr` and writes them to the file associated with `fp`. The number of array elements successfully written is returned. If an error occurs, a short count is returned. If `el_size` or `n` is zero, the array is not accessed and zero is returned.

Removing or Renaming a File

```
■ int remove(const char *filename);
```

Removes the file with the name `filename` from the file system. If the call is successful, zero is returned; otherwise -1 is returned. (This is the `unlink()` function in traditional C.)

```
■ int rename(const char *from, const char *to);
```

Changes the name of a file. The old name is in the string pointed to by `from`. The new name is in the string pointed to by `to`. If a file with the new name already exists, what happens is system-dependent; typically, in UNIX, however, the file is overwritten. On most systems, the old and new names can be either files or directories. If one of the arguments is a directory name, the other one must be too. Zero is returned if the call is successful; otherwise -1 is returned and a system-dependent value is written to `errno`.

A.13 General Utilities: `<stdlib.h>`

This header file contains prototypes of functions for general use, along with related macros and type definitions. Here are some examples of the macros and type definitions:

```
#include <stddef.h>                        /* for size_t and wchar_t */

#define   EXIT_SUCCESS   0                 /* for use with exit() */
#define   EXIT_FAILURE   1                 /* for use with exit() */
#define   NULL           0                 /* null pointer value */
#define   RAND_MAX       32767             /* 2^15 - 1 */

typedef struct {
   int   quot;                             /* quotient */
   int   rem;                              /* remainder */
} div_t;

typedef struct {
   long quot;                              /* quotient */
   long rem;                               /* remainder */
} ldiv_t;
```

Dynamic Allocation of Memory

■ `void *calloc(size_t n, size_t el_size);`

Allocates contiguous space in memory for an array of `n` elements, with each element requiring `el_size` bytes. The space is initialized with all bits set to zero. A successful call returns the base address of the allocated space; otherwise `NULL` is returned.

■ `void *malloc(size_t size);`

Allocates a block of space in memory consisting of `size` bytes. The space is not initialized. A successful call returns the base address of the allocated space; otherwise `NULL` is returned.

■ `void *realloc(void *ptr, size_t size);`

Changes the size of the block pointed to by `ptr` to `size` bytes. The contents of the space is unchanged up to the lesser of the old and new sizes. Any new space is not initialized. The function attempts to keep the base address of the block the same, but if this is not possible, it allocates a new block of memory, copying the relevant portion of the old block and deallocating it. If `ptr` is `NULL`, the effect is the same as calling malloc(). If ptr is not NULL, it must be the base address of space previously allocated by a call to calloc(), malloc(), or realloc() that has not yet been deallocated by a call to free() or realloc(). A successful call returns the base address of the resized (or new) space; otherwise NULL is returned.

■ `void free(void *ptr);`

Causes the space in memory pointed to by ptr to be deallocated. If ptr is NULL, the function has no effect. If ptr is not NULL, it must be the base address of space previously allocated by a call to calloc(), malloc(), or realloc() that has not yet been deallocated by a call to free() or realloc(). Otherwise the call is in error. The effect of the error is system-dependent.

Searching and Sorting

■
```
void *bsearch(const void *key_ptr, const void *a_ptr,
              size_t n_els, size_t el_size,
              int compare(const void *, const void *));
```

Searches the sorted array pointed to by a_ptr for an element that matches the object pointed to by key_ptr. If a match is found, the address of the element is returned; otherwise NULL is returned. The number of elements in the array is n_els, and each element is stored in memory in el_size bytes. The elements of the array must be in ascending sorted order with respect to the comparison function compare(). The comparison function takes two arguments, each one being an address of an element of the array. The comparison function returns an int that is less than, equal to, or greater than zero, depending on whether the element pointed to by its first argument is considered to be less than, equal to, or greater than the element pointed to by its second argument. (The function bsearch() uses a binary search algorithm.)

■
```
void qsort(void *a_ptr, size_t n_els, size_t el_size,
           int compare(const void *, const void *));
```

Sorts the array pointed to by a_ptr in ascending order with respect to the comparison function compare(). The number of elements in the array is n_els, and each element is stored in memory in el_size bytes. The comparison function takes two arguments, each one being an address of an element of the array. The comparison function returns an int that is less than, equal to, or greater than zero, depending on whether the element pointed to by its first argument is considered to be less than, equal to, or greater than the element pointed to by its second argument. (By tradition, the function qsort() implements a "quicker-sort" algorithm.)

Pseudorandom Number Generator

■ `int rand(void);`

Each call generates an integer and returns it. Repeated calls generate what appears to be a randomly distributed sequence of integers in the interval [0, RAND_MAX].

■ `void srand(unsigned seed);`

Seeds the random number generator, causing the sequence generated by repeated calls to `rand()` to start in a different place each time. On program startup, the random number generator acts as if `srand(1)` had been called. The statement

```
srand(time(NULL));
```

can be used to seed the random number generator with a different value each time the program is invoked.

Communicating with the Environment

■ `char *getenv(const char *name);`

Searches a list of environment variables provided by the operating system. If `name` is one of the variables in the list, the base address of its corresponding string value is returned; otherwise `NULL` is returned (see Section 14.1, "Environment Variables," on page 473).

■ `int system(const char *s);`

Passes the string `s` as a command to be executed by the command interpreter (the shell) provided by the operating system. If `s` is not `NULL` and a connection to the operating system exits, the function returns the exit status returned by the command. If `s` is `NULL`, the function returns a nonzero value if the command interpreter is available via this mechanism; otherwise it returns zero.

Integer Arithmetic

■
```
int  abs(int i);
long labs(long i);
```

Both functions return the absolute value of `i`.

```
■ div_t  div(int numer, int denom);
  ldiv_t ldiv(long numer, long denom);
```

Both functions divide `numer` by `denom` and return a structure that has the quotient and remainder as members. The following is an example:

```
div_t   d;

d = div(17, 5);
printf("quotient = %d, remainder = %d\n", d.quot, d.rem);
```

When executed, this code prints the line

```
quotient = 3, remainder = 2
```

String Conversion

Members of the two families `ato...()` and `strto ...()` are used to convert a string to a value. The conversion is conceptual; it interprets the characters in the string, but the string itself does not change. The string can begin with optional white space. The conversion stops with the first inappropriate character. For example, both of the function calls

`strtod("123x456", NULL)` and `strtod("\n 123 456", NULL)`

return the `double` value 123.0. The `strto ...()` family provides more control over the conversion process and provides for error checking.

```
■ double atof(const char *s); /* ascii to floating number */
```

Converts the string `s` to a `double` and returns it. Except for error behavior, the function call

`atof(s)` is equivalent to `strtod(s, NULL)`

If no conversion takes place, the function returns zero.

```
■ int atoi(const char *s);    /* ascii to integer */
```

Converts the string `s` to an `int` and returns it. Except for error behavior, the function call

`atoi(s)` is equivalent to `(int) strtol(s, NULL, 10)`

If no conversion takes place, the function returns zero.

■ `long atol(const char *s);    /* ascii to long */`

Converts the string `s` to a `long` and returns it. Except for error behavior, the function call

```
atol(s)      is equivalent to      strtol(s, NULL, 10)
```

If no conversion takes place, the function returns zero.

■ `double strtod(const char *s, char **end_ptr);`

Converts the string `s` to a `double` and returns it. If no conversion takes place, zero is returned. If `end_ptr` is not `NULL` and conversion takes place, the address of the character that stops the conversion process is stored in the object pointed to by `end_ptr`. If `end_ptr` is not `NULL` and no conversion takes place, the value `s` is stored in the object pointed to by `end_ptr`. On overflow, either `HUGE_VAL` or `-HUGE_VAL` is returned and `ERANGE` is stored in `errno`. On underflow, zero is returned and `ERANGE` is stored in `errno`.

■ `long strtol(const char *s, char **end_ptr, int base);`

Converts the string `s` to a `long` and returns it. If `base` has a value from 2 to 36, the digits and letters in `s` are interpreted in that base. In base 36, the letters `a` through `z` and `A` through `Z` are interpreted as 10 through 35, respectively. With a smaller base, only those digits and letters with corresponding values less than the base are interpreted. If `end_ptr` is not `NULL` and conversion takes place, the address of the character that stops the conversion process is stored in the object pointed to by `end_ptr`. Here is an example:

```
char   *p;
long   value;

value = strtol("12345", &p, 3);
printf("value = %ld, end string = \"%s\"\n", value, p);
```

When executed, this code prints the line

```
value = 5, end string = "345"
```

Because the base is 3, the character `3` in the string `"12345"` stops the conversion process. Only the first two characters in the string are converted. In base 3, the characters `12` get converted to decimal value 5. In a similar fashion, the code

```
value = strtol("abcde", &p, 12);
printf("value = %ld, end string = \"%s\"\n", value, p);
```

prints the line

```
value = 131, end string = "cde"
```

Because the base is 12, the character c in the string "abcde" stops the conversion process. Only the first two characters in the string are converted. In base 12, the characters ab get converted to decimal value 131.

If base is zero, s is interpreted as either a hexadecimal, octal, or decimal integer, depending on the leading nonwhite characters in s. With an optional sign and 0x or 0X, the string is interpreted as a hexadecimal integer (base 16). With an optional sign and 0, but not 0x or 0X, the string is interpreted as an octal integer (base 8). Otherwise, it is interpreted as a decimal integer.

If no conversion takes place, zero is returned. If end_ptr is not NULL and no conversion takes place, the value s is stored in the object pointed to by end_ptr. On overflow, either LONG_MAX or -LONG_MAX is returned and ERANGE is stored in errno.

■
```
unsigned long strtoul(const char *s,
                      char **end_ptr, int base);
```

Similar to strtol(), but returns an unsigned long. On overflow, either ULONG_MAX or -ULONG_MAX is returned.

Multibyte Character Functions

Multibyte characters are used to represent members of an extended character set. How the members of an extended character set are defined is locale-dependent.

■
```
int mblen(const char *s, size_t n);
```

If s is NULL, the function returns a nonzero or zero value, depending on whether multibyte characters do or do not have a state-dependent encoding. If s is not NULL, the function examines at most n characters in s and returns the number of bytes that comprise the next multibyte character. If s points to the null character, zero is returned. If s does not point to a multibyte character, the value -1 is returned.

■
```
int mbtowc(wchar_t *p, const char *s, size_t n);
```

Acts the same as mblen() but with the following additional capability: If p is not NULL, the function converts the next multibyte character in s to its corresponding wide character type and stores it in the object pointed to by p.

■ `int wctomb(char *s, wchar_t wc);`

If `s` is `NULL`, the function returns a nonzero or zero value, depending on whether multibyte characters do or do not have a state-dependent encoding. If `s` is not `NULL` and `wc` is a wide character corresponding to a multibyte character, the function stores the multibyte character in `s` and returns the number of bytes required to represent it. If `s` is not `NULL` and `wc` does not correspond to a multibyte character, the value -1 is returned.

Multibyte String Functions

■ `size_t mbstowcs(wchar_t *wcs, const char *mbs, size_t n);`

Reads the multibyte string pointed to by `mbs` and writes the corresponding wide character string into `wcs`. At most, `n` wide characters are written, followed by a wide null character. If the conversion is successful, the number of wide characters written is returned, not counting the final wide null character; otherwise -1 is returned.

■ `int wcstombs(char *mbs, const wchar_t *wcs, size_t n);`

Reads the wide character string pointed to by `wcs` and writes the corresponding multibyte string into `mbs`. The conversion process stops after `n` wide characters have been written or a null character is written, whichever comes first. If the conversion is successful, the number of characters written is returned, not counting the null character (if any); otherwise -1 is returned.

Leaving the Program

■ `void abort(void);`

Causes abnormal program termination, unless a signal handler catches `SIGABRT` and does not return. Whether any open files are properly closed and any temporary files are removed depends on the implementation.

■ `int atexit(void (*func)(void));`

Registers the function pointed to by `func` for execution on normal program exit. A successful call returns zero; otherwise a nonzero value is returned. At least 32 such functions can be registered. The execution of the registered functions occurs in the reverse order of registration. Only global variables are available to these functions.

■ `void exit(int status);`

Causes normal program termination. The functions registered by `atexit()` are invoked in the reverse order in which they were registered, buffered streams are flushed, files are closed, and temporary files that were created by `tmpfile()` are removed. The value `status`, along with control, is returned to the host environment. If the value of `status` is zero or `EXIT_SUCCESS`, the host environment assumes that the program executed successfully; if the value is `EXIT_FAILURE`, it assumes that the program did not execute successfully. The host environment may recognize other values for `status`.

A.14 Memory and String Handling: `<string.h>`

This header file contains prototypes of functions in two families. The functions `mem ...()` are used to manipulate blocks of memory of a specified size. These blocks can be thought of as arrays of bytes (characters). They are like strings, except that they are not null-terminated. The functions `str ...()` are used to manipulate null-terminated strings. Typically, the following line is at the top of the header file:

```
#include <stddef.h>          /* for NULL and size_t */
```

Memory-Handling Functions

■ `void *memchr(const void *p, int c, size_t n);`

Starting in memory at the address `p`, a search is made for the first unsigned character (byte) that matches the value `(unsigned char)c`. At most, `n` bytes are searched. If successful, a pointer to the character is returned; otherwise `NULL` is returned.

■ `int memcmp(const void *p, const void *q, size_t n);`

Compares two blocks in memory of size `n`. The bytes are treated as unsigned characters. The function returns a value that is less than, equal to, or greater than zero, depending on whether the block pointed to by `p` is lexicographically less than, equal to, or greater than the block pointed to by `q`.

■ `void *memcpy(void *to, void *from, size_t n);`

Copies the block of `n` bytes pointed to by `from` to the block pointed to by `to`. The value `to` is returned. If the blocks overlap, the behavior is undefined.

■ `void *memmove(void *to, void *from, size_t n);`

Copies the block of `n` bytes pointed to by `from` to the block pointed to by `to`. The value `to` is returned. If the blocks overlap, each byte in the block pointed to by `from` is accessed before a new value is written in that byte. Thus a correct copy is made, even when the blocks overlap.

■ `void *memset(void *p, int c, size_t n);`

Sets each byte in the block of size `n` pointed to by `p` to value `(unsigned char)c`. The value `p` is returned.

String-Handling Functions

■ `char *strcat(char *s1, const char *s2);`

Concatenates the strings `s1` and `s2`. That is, a copy of `s2` is appended to the end of `s1`. The programmer must ensure that `s1` points to enough space to hold the result. The string `s1` is returned.

■ `char *strchr(const char *s, int c);`

Searches for the first character in `s` that matches the value `(char) c`. If the character is found, its address is returned; otherwise `NULL` is returned. The call `strchr(s, '\0')` returns a pointer to the terminating null character in `s`.

■ `int strcmp(const char *s1, const char *s2);`

Compares the two strings `s1` and `s2` lexicographically. The elements of the strings are treated as unsigned characters. The function returns a value that is less than, equal to, or greater than zero, depending on whether `s1` is lexicographically less than, equal to, or greater than `s2`.

■ `int strcoll(const char *s1, const char *s2);`

Compares the two strings `s1` and `s2` using a comparison rule that depends on the current locale. The function returns a value that is less than, equal to, or greater than zero, depending on whether `s1` is considered less than, equal to, or greater than `s2`.

■ `char *strcpy(char *s1, const char *s2);`

Copies the string `s2` into the string `s1`, including the terminating null character. Whatever exists in `s1` is overwritten. The programmer must ensure that `s1` points to enough space to hold the result. The value `s1` is returned.

■ `size_t strcspn(const char *s1, const char *s2);`

Computes the length of the maximal initial substring in `s1` consisting entirely of characters *not* in `s2`. For example, the function call

```
strcspn("April is the cruelest month", "abc")
```

returns the value 13 because `"April is the "` is the maximal initial substring of the first argument having no characters in common with `"abc"`. (The character `c` in the name `strcspn` stands for "complement," and the letters `spn` stand for "span.")

■ `char *strerror(int error_number);`

Returns a pointer to an error string provided by the system. The contents of the string must not be changed by the program. If an error causes the system to write a value in `errno`, the programmer can invoke `strerror(errno)` to print the associated error message. (The related function `perror()` can also be used to print the error message.)

■ `size_t strlen(const char *s);`

Returns the length of the string `s`. The length is the number of characters in the string, not counting the terminating null character.

■ `char *strncat(char *s1, const char *s2, size_t n);`

At most `n` characters in `s2`, not counting the null character, are appended to `s1`. Then a null character is written in `s1`. The programmer must ensure that `s1` points to enough space to hold the result. The string `s1` is returned.

■ `int strncmp(const char *s1, const char *s2, size_t n);`

Compares at most `n` characters lexicographically in each of the two strings `s1` and `s2`. The comparison stops with the *n*th character or a terminating null character, whichever comes first. The elements of the strings are treated as unsigned characters. The function returns a value that is less than, equal to, or greater than zero, depending on whether the compared portion of `s1` is lexicographically less than, equal to, or greater than the compared portion of `s2`.

■ `char *strncpy(char *s1, const char *s2, size_t n);`

Precisely `n` characters are written into `s1`, overwriting whatever is there. The characters are taken from `s2` until `n` of them have been copied or a null character has been copied, whichever comes first. Any remaining characters in `s1` are assigned the value `'\0'`. If the length of `s2` is `n` or larger, `s1` is not null-terminated. The programmer must ensure that `s1` points to enough space to hold the result. The value `s1` is returned.

■ `char *strpbrk(const char *s1, const char *s2);`

Searches for the first character in `s1` that matches any one of the characters in `s2`. If the search is successful, the address of the character found in `s1` is returned; otherwise `NULL` is returned. For example, the function call

```
strpbrk("April is the cruelest month", "abc")
```

returns the address of `c` in `cruelest`. (The letters `pbrk` in the name `strpbrk` stand for "pointer to break.")

■ `char *strrchr(const char *s, int c);`

Searches from the right for the first character in `s` that matches the value `(char) c`. If the character is found, its address is returned; otherwise `NULL` is returned. The call `strchr(s, '\0')` returns a pointer to the terminating null character in `s`.

■ `size_t strspn(const char *s1, const char *s2);`

Computes the length of the maximal initial substring in `s1` consisting entirely of characters in `s2`. For example, the function call

```
strspn("April is the cruelest month", "A is for apple")
```

returns the value 9 because all the characters in the first argument preceding the `t` in `the` occur in the second argument, but the letter `t` does not. (The letters `spn` in the name `strspn` stand for "span.")

■ `char *strstr(const char *s1, const char *s2);`

Searches in `s1` for the first occurrence of the substring `s2`. If the search is successful, a pointer to the base address of the substring in `s1` is returned; otherwise `NULL` is returned.

■ `char *strtok(char *s1, const char *s2);`

Searches for tokens in `s1`, using the characters in `s2` as token separators. If `s1` contains one or more tokens, the first token in `s1` is found, the character immediately following the token is overwritten with a null character, the remainder of `s1` is stored elsewhere by the system, and the address of the first character in the token is returned. Subsequent calls with `s1` equal to `NULL` return the base address of a string supplied by the system that contains the next token. If no additional tokens are available, `NULL` is returned. The initial call `strtok(s1, s2)` returns `NULL` if `s1` contains no tokens. The following is an example:

```
char   s1[] = " this is,an    example ; ";
char   s2[] = ",; ";
char   *p;

printf("\"%s\"", strtok(s1, s2));
while ((p = strtok(NULL, s2)) != NULL)
   printf(" \"%s\"", p);
putchar('\n');
```

When executed, this code prints the line

```
"this" "is" "an" "example"
```

■ `size_t strxfrm(char *s1, const char *s2, size_t n);`

Transforms the string `s2` and places the result in `s1`, overwriting whatever is there. At most, `n` characters, including a terminating null character, are written in `s1`. The length of `s1` is returned. The transformation is such that when two transformed strings are used as arguments to `strcmp()`, the value returned is less than, equal to, or greater than zero, depending on whether `strcoll()` applied to the untransformed strings returns a value less than, equal to, or greater than zero. (The letters `xfrm` in the name `strxfrm` stand for "transform.")

A.15 Date and Time: <time.h>

This header file contains prototypes of functions that deal with date, time, and the internal clock. Here are examples of some macros and type definitions:

```
#include <stddef.h>                      /* for NULL and size_t */

#define   CLOCKS_PER_SEC   1000000   /* machine-dependent */

typedef   long   clock_t;
typedef   long   time_t;
```

Objects of type `struct tm` are used to store the date and time.

```
struct tm {
   int   tm_sec;      /* seconds after the minute: [0, 60] */
   int   tm_min;      /* minutes after the hour: [0, 59]   */
   int   tm_hour;     /* hours since midnight: [0, 23]     */
   int   tm_mday;     /* day of the month: [1, 31]         */
   int   tm_mon;      /* months since January: [0, 11]     */
   int   tm_year;     /* years since 1900                  */
   int   tm_wday;     /* days since Sunday: [0, 6]         */
   int   tm_yday;     /* days since 1 January: [0, 365]    */
   int   tm_isdst;    /* Daylight Savings Time flag        */
};
```

Note that the range of values for `tm_sec` has to accommodate a "leap second," which occurs only sporadically. The flag `tm_isdst` is positive if Daylight Savings Time is in effect, zero if it is not, and negative if the information is not available.

Accessing the Clock

On most systems, the `clock()` function provides access to the underlying machine clock. The rate at which the clock runs is machine-dependent.

■ `clock_t clock(void);`

Returns an approximation to the number of CPU "clock ticks" used by the program up to the point of invocation. To convert it to seconds, the value returned can be divided by `CLOCKS_PER_SEC`. If the CPU clock is not available, the value -1 is returned (see Section 14.5, "How to Time C Code," on page 483).

Accessing the Time

In ANSI C, time comes in two principal versions: a "calendar time," expressed as an integer, which on most systems represents the number of seconds that have elapsed since 1 January 1970, and a "broken-down time," expressed as a structure of type `struct tm`. The calendar time is encoded with respect to Universal Time Coordinated (UTC). The programmer can use library functions to convert one version of time to the other. Also, functions are available to print the time as a string.

■ `time_t time(time_t *tp);`

Returns the current calendar time, expressed as the number of seconds that have elapsed since 1 January 1970 (UTC). Other units and other starting dates are possible, but these are the ones typically used. If `tp` is not `NULL`, the value also is stored in the object pointed to by `tp`. Consider the following code:

```
time_t   now;

now = time(NULL);
printf("\n%s%ld\n%s%s%s%s\n",
  "                        now = ", now,
  "                ctime(&now) = ", ctime(&now),
  "asctime(localtime(&now)) = ",asctime(localtime(&now)));
```

When executed on our system, this code printed the lines:

```
                     now = 685136007
             ctime(&now) = Tue Sep 17 12:33:27 1991
asctime(localtime(&now)) = Tue Sep 17 12:33:27 1991
```

■ `char *asctime(const struct tm *tp);`

Converts the broken-down time pointed to by `tp` to a string provided by the system. The function returns the base address of the string. Later calls to `asctime()` and `ctime()` overwrite the string.

■ `char *ctime(const time_t *t_ptr);`

Converts the calendar time pointed to by `t_ptr` to a string provided by the system. The function returns the base address of the string. Later calls to `asctime()` and `ctime()` overwrite the string. The two function calls

`ctime(&now)` and `asctime(localtime(&now))`

are equivalent.

■ `double difftime(time_t t0, time_t t1);`

Computes the difference `t1 - t0` and, if necessary, converts this value to the number of seconds that have elapsed between the calendar times `t0` and `t1`. The value is returned as a `double`.

■ `struct tm *gmtime(const time_t *t_ptr);`

Converts the calendar time pointed to by `t_ptr` to a broken-down time, and stores it in an object of type `struct tm` that is provided by the system. The address of the structure is returned. The function computes the broken-down time with respect to Universal Time Coordinated (UTC). This used to be called Greenwich Mean Time (GMT); hence the name of the function. Later calls to `gmtime()` and `localtime()` overwrite the structure.

■ `struct tm *localtime(const time_t *t_ptr);`

Converts the calendar time pointed to by `t_ptr` to a broken-down local time, and stores it in an object of type `struct tm` that is provided by the system. The address of the structure is returned. Later calls to `gmtime()` and `localtime()` overwrite the structure.

■ `time_t mktime(struct tm *tp);`

Converts the broken-down local time in the structure pointed to by `tp` to the corresponding calendar time. If the call is successful, the calendar time is returned; otherwise -1 is returned. For the purpose of the computation, the `tm_wday` and `tm_yday` members of the structure are disregarded. Before the computation, other members can have values outside their usual range. After the computation, the members of the structure may be overwritten with an equivalent set of values in which each member lies within its normal range. The values for `tm_wday` and `tm_yday` are computed from those for the other members. For example, the following code can be used to find the date 1000 days from now:

```
struct tm    *tp;
time_t       now, later;

now = time(NULL);
tp = localtime(&now);
tp -> tm_mday += 1000;
later = mktime(tp);
printf("\n1000 days from now: %s\n", ctime(&later));
```

■ `size_t strftime(char *s, size_t n,`
`                const char *cntrl_str, const struct tm *tp);`

Writes characters into the string pointed to by `s` under the direction of the control string pointed to by `cntrl_str`. At most, `n` characters are written, including the null character. If more than `n` characters are required, the function returns zero and the contents of `s` are indeterminate; otherwise the length of `s` is returned. The control string consists of ordinary characters and conversion specifications, or formats, that determine how values from the broken-down time in the structure pointed to by `tp` are to be written. Each conversion specification consists of a % followed by a conversion character.

Using strftime()		
Conversion specification	**What is printed**	**Example**
%a	abbreviated weekday name	Fri
%A	full weekday name	Friday
%b	abbreviated month name	Sep
%B	full month name	September
%c	date and time	Sep 01 02:17:23 1993
%d	day of the month	01
%H	hour of the 24-hour day	02
%h	hour of the 12-hour day	02
%j	day of the year	243
%m	month of the year	9
%M	minutes after the hour	17
%p	AM or PM	AM
%s	seconds after the hour	23
%U	week of the year (Sun-Sat)	34
%w	day of the week (0-6)	5
%x	date	Sep 01 1993
%X	time	02:17:23
%y	year of the century	93
%Y	year	1993
%Z	time zone	PDT
%%	percent character	%

Consider the following code:

```
char     s[100];
time_t   now;

now = time(NULL);
strftime(s, 100, "%H:%M:%S on %A, %d %B %Y",
        localtime(&now));
printf("%s\n\n", s);
```

When we executed a program containing these lines, the following line was printed:

```
13:01:15 on Tuesday, 17 September 1991
```

A.16 Miscellaneous

In addition to the functions specified by ANSI C, the system may provide other functions in the library. In this section we describe some of the non-ANSI C functions that are widely available. Some functions, such as `execl()`, are common to most systems. Other functions, such as `fork()` or `spawnl()`, are generally available in one operating system but not another. The name of the associated header file is system-dependent.

Using File Descriptors

■ `int open(const char *filename, int flag, ...);`

Opens the named file for reading and/or writing, as specified by the information stored bitwise in `flag`. If a file is being created, a third argument of type `unsigned` is needed; it sets the file permissions for the new file. If the call is successful, a nonnegative integer called the *file descriptor* is returned; otherwise `errno` is set and -1 is returned. Values that can be used for `flag` are given in the header file that contains the prototype for `open()`. These values are system-dependent.

■ `int close(int fd);`

Closes the file associated with the file descriptor `fd`. If the call is successful, zero is returned; otherwise `errno` is set and -1 is returned.

■ `int read(int fd, char *buf, int n);`

Reads at most `n` bytes from the file associated with the file descriptor `fd` into the object pointed to by `buf`. If the call is successful, the number of bytes written in `buf` is returned; otherwise `errno` is set and -1 is returned. A short count is returned if the end-of-file character is encountered.

■ `int write(int fd, const char *buf, int n);`

Writes at most `n` bytes from the object pointed to by `buf` into the file associated with the file descriptor `fd`. If the call is successful, the number of bytes written in the file is returned; otherwise `errno` is set and -1 is returned. A short count can indicate that the disk is full.

Creating a Concurrent Process

■ `int fork(void);`

Copies the current process and begins executing it concurrently. The child process has its own process identification number. When `fork()` is called, it returns zero to the child and the child's process ID to the parent. If the call fails, `errno` is set and -1 is returned. This function is not available in MS-DOS.

■ `int vfork(void);`

Spawns a new process in a virtual memory-efficient way. The child process has its own process identification number. The address space of the parent process is not fully copied, which is very inefficient in a paged environment. The child borrows the parent's memory and thread of control until a call to `exec ...()` occurs or the child exits. The parent process is suspended while the child is using its resources. When `vfork()` is called, it returns zero to the child and the child's process ID to the parent. If the call fails, `errno` is set and -1 is returned. This function is not available in MS-DOS.

Overlaying a Process

In this section we describe the two families `exec...()` and `spawn...()`. The first is generally available on both MS-DOS and UNIX systems, the second only on MS-DOS systems. On UNIX systems, `fork()` can be used with `exec...()` to achieve the effect of `spawn...()`.

■
```
int execl(char *name, char *arg0, ..., char *argN);
int execle(char *name, char *arg0, ..., char *argN,
           char **envp);
int execlp(char *name, char *arg0, ..., char *argN);
int execlpe(char *name, char *arg0, ..., char *argN,
            char **envp);
int execv(char *name, char **argv);
int execve(char *name, char **argv, char **envp);
int execvp(char *name, char **argv);
int execvpe(char *name, char **argv, char **envp);
```

These functions overlay the current process with the named program. There is no return to the parent process. By default, the child process inherits the environment of the parent. Members of the family with names that begin with `execl` require a list of arguments that are taken as the command line arguments for the child process. The last argument in the list must be the `NULL` pointer. Members of the family with names that begin with `execv` use the array `argv` to supply command line arguments to the child process. The last element of `argv` must have the value NULL. Members of the family with names ending in e use the array envp to supply environment variables to the child process. The last element of envp must have the value NULL. Members of the family with p in their name use the path variable specified in the environment to determine which directories to search for the program.

- `int spawnl(int mode, char *name, char *arg0,..., char *argN);`
  `.....`

This family of functions corresponds to the exec...() family, except that each member has an initial integer argument. The values for mode are 0, 1, and 2. The value 0 causes the parent process to wait for the child process to finish before continuing. With value 1, the parent and child processes should execute concurrently, except that this has not been implemented yet. The use of this value causes an error. The value 2 causes the child process to overlay the parent process.

Interprocess Communication

- `int pipe(int pd[2]);`

Creates an input/output mechanism called a *pipe*, and puts the associated file descriptors (pipe descriptors) in the array pd. If the call is successful, zero is returned; otherwise errno is set and -1 is returned. After a pipe has been created, the system assumes that two or more cooperating processes created by subsequent calls to fork() use read() and write() to pass data through the pipe. One descriptor, pd[0], is read from; the other, pd[1], is written to. The pipe capacity is system-dependent but is at least 4096 bytes. If a write fills the pipe, it blocks until data is read out of it. As with other file descriptors, close() can be used to explicitly close pd[0] and pd[1]. This function is not available in MS-DOS.

Suspending Program Execution

- `void sleep(unsigned seconds);`

Suspends the current process from execution for the number of seconds requested. The time is only approximate.

Appendix B

The Preprocessor

The C language uses the preprocessor to extend its power and notation. In this appendix we present a detailed discussion of the preprocessor, including new features added by the ANSI C committee. We begin by explaining the use of `#include`, then thoroughly discuss the use of the `#define` macro facility. Macros can be used to generate inline code that takes the place of a function call. Their use can reduce program execution time.

Lines that begin with a # are called *preprocessing directives.* These lines communicate with the preprocessor. In ANSI C, the # can be preceded on the line by white space, whereas in traditional C, it must occur in column 1. The syntax for preprocessing directives is independent of the rest of the C language. The effect of a preprocessing directive starts at its place in a file and continues until the end of that file or until it is negated by another directive. It is always helpful to keep in mind that the preprocessor does not "know" C.

B.1 The Use of #include

A preprocessing directive of the form

`#include "`*filename*`"`

causes the preprocessor to replace the line with a copy of the contents of the named file. A search for the file is made first in the current directory and then in other system-dependent places. With a preprocessing directive of the form

`#include <`*filename*`>`

the preprocessor does not look for the file in the current directory; it looks only in system-dependent places. In UNIX systems, the standard header files such as *stdio.h* and *stdlib.h* are typically found in */usr/include.* In general, where the standard header files are stored is system-dependent.

There is no restriction on what the `#include` file can contain. In particular, it can contain other preprocessing directives that are expanded by the preprocessor in turn. *Caution*: Beginning programmers sometimes confuse the standard header files with the standard library. Although the include files provide an interface to the standard library, they are not themselves the library.

B.2 The Use of #define

Preprocessing directives with `#define` occur in two forms:

#define *identifier* *token_string*$_{opt}$
#define *identifier*(*identifier*, · · · · · , *identifier*) *token_string*$_{opt}$

The *token_string* is optional. A long definition of either form can be continued to the next line by placing a backslash \ at the end of the current line. If a simple `#define` of the first form occurs in a file, the preprocessor replaces every occurrence of *identifier* by *token_string* in the remainder of the file, except in quoted strings. Consider the example

```
#define   SECONDS_PER_DAY   (60 * 60 * 24)
```

In this example the token string is `(60 * 60 * 24)`, and the preprocessor replaces every occurrence of the symbolic constant `SECONDS_PER_DAY` by that string in the remainder of the file.

The use of simple `#define`s can improve program clarity and portability. For example, if special constants such as π or the speed of light c are used in a program, they should be defined.

```
#define   PI   3.14159
#define   C    299792.458    /* speed of light in km/sec */
```

Other special constants that are used in programs are also best coded as symbolic constants.

```
#define   EOF      (-1)         /* typical end-of-file value */
#define   MAXINT   2147483647   /* largest 4-byte integer */
```

Program limits that are programmer decisions can also be specified symbolically.

```
#define   ITERS   50         /* number of iterations */
#define   SIZE    250        /* array size */
#define   EPS     1.0e-9     /* a numerical limit */
```

In general, symbolic constants aid documentation by replacing what might otherwise be a mysterious constant with a mnemonic identifier. They aid portability by allowing constants that may be system-dependent to be altered once. They aid reliability by restricting to one place the check on the actual representation of the constant.

Mathematical Cow

Syntactic Sugar

Although it is not considered good programming practice to do so, the programmer can use the preprocessor to alter the syntax of C. For example, because the use of = in place of == is a frequent programming error, a programmer could use

```
#define   EQ   ==
```

to defend against such a mistake. This superficial alteration of the programming syntax is called *syntactic sugar.* Another example of this is to change the form of the `while` statement by introducing `do`, which is an ALGOL-style construction.

```
#define   do   /* blank */
```

With these two `#define` lines at the top of the file, the code

```
while (i EQ 1) do {
   .....
```

becomes, after the preprocessor pass,

```
while (i == 1) {
   .....
```

Keep in mind that because `do` disappears from anywhere in the file, the `do-while` statement cannot be used.

B.3 Macros with Arguments

In modern programming methodology, macros are considered inherently unsafe because they are implemented by the preprocessor, and the preprocessor does not "know" C. Macros with arguments are especially dangerous. Nonetheless, because they save the overhead of a function call, macros with arguments have been used extensively at the system level. (In C++, inline functions can be used instead of macros with arguments.) The general form of a macro with arguments is given by

`#define` *identifier*(*identifier*, ··· , *identifier*) $token\_string_{opt}$

There can be no space between the first identifier and the left parenthesis. Zero or more identifiers can occur in the parameter list—for example,

```
#define   SQ(x)   ((x) * (x))
```

The identifier `x` in the `#define` is a parameter that is substituted in later text. The substitution is one of string replacement without consideration for syntactic correctness. For example, with the argument `7 + w`, the macro call

`SQ(7 + w)` expands to `((7 + w) * (7 + w))`

In a similar fashion

`SQ(SQ(*p))` expands to `((((*p) * (*p))) * (((*p) * (*p))))`

This seemingly extravagant use of parentheses is to protect against the macro expanding an expression that would then lead to an unanticipated order of evaluation. We want to explain fully why all the parentheses are necessary. First, suppose we had defined the macro as

```
#define   SQ(x)   x * x
```

With this definition,

`SQ(a + b)` expands to `a + b * a + b`

which, because of operator precedence, is not the same as

```
((a + b) * (a + b))
```

Now suppose we had defined the macro as

```
#define   SQ(x)   (x) * (x)
```

With this definition,

`4 / SQ(2)` expands to `4 / (2) * (2)`

which, because of operator precedence, is not the same as

```
4 / ((2) * (2))
```

Finally, let us suppose we had defined the macro as

```
#define   SQ (x)   ((x) * (x))
```

With this definition,

`SQ(7)` expands to `(x)   ((x) * (x)) (7)`

which is not even close to what was intended. If, in the macro definition, there is a space between the macro name and the left parenthesis that follows, the rest of the line is taken as replacement text.

Even when a macro is written in a robust fashion, as in the example

```
#define   SQ(x)   ((x) * (x))
```

things can go wrong. If, for example, we were to write `SQ(++k)`, the macro call would be expanded to

```
((++k) * (++k))
```

which is certainly not what we intended. If SQ(++k) were a function call instead of a macro call, there would be no problem. The expression ++k would be evaluated, and a copy of that value would be passed to the function.

Another common programming error is to end a #define line with a semicolon, making it part of the replacement string when that is not wanted. As an example of this, consider

```
#define   SQ(x)    ((x) * (x));
```

The semicolon here was typed by mistake—a mistake that is made easily because programmers often end a line of code with a semicolon. When used in the body of a function, the line

```
x = SQ(y);
```
expands to
```
x = ((y) * (y));;
```

The last semicolon creates an unwanted null statement. If we were to write

```
if (x == 2)
   x = SQ(y);
else
   ++x;
```

we would get a syntax error caused by the unwanted null statement. The extra semicolon does not allow the else to be attached to the if statement.

Although macros with arguments, in many cases, act like functions, they are different because the preprocessor expands them into inline code. Because of this, the programmer can make mistakes. Consider the following macro:

```
#define   PRN(array, size)   printf("\n");                \
                             for (i = 0; i < size; ++i) \
                                printf("%5d", array[i])
```

Suppose we want to use this macro to print an array five times. To accomplish this, we might write

```
for (j = 0; j < 5; ++j)
   PRN(a, n);
```

This, however, does not produce the desired results. The preprocessor expands these two lines of code into new code that is equivalent to

```
for (j = 0; j < 5; ++j)
   printf("\n");
for (i = 0; i < n; ++i)
   printf("%5d", a[i]);
```

We get five newlines and a single printout of the array. If an error such as this occurs, it can be quite mystifying. To guard against this type of error, one can use braces in the macro definition.

Debugging code that contains macros with arguments can be very difficult. Most C compilers provide the -E option to show the output of the preprocessor pass.

```
cc -E pgm.c > tmp
```

Because the output tends to be voluminous, the programmer typically redirects the output into a temporary file and then looks at what is in the file with the help of an editor.

Macros are frequently used to replace function calls with inline code, which is more efficient. For example, instead of writing a function to find the minimum of two values, a programmer could write

```
#define   min(x, y)   (((x) < (y)) ? (x) : (y))
```

After this definition, an expression such as

```
m = min(u, v)
```

is expanded by the preprocessor to

```
m = (((u) < (v)) ? (u) : (v))
```

The arguments of `min()` can be arbitrary expressions of compatible type. Also, we can use `min()` to build another macro. For example, if we need to find the minimum of four values, we can write

```
#define   min4(a, b, c, d)   min(min(a, b), min(c, d))
```

A macro definition can use both functions and macros in its body. Here are some examples:

```
#define   SQ(x)       ((x) * (x))
#define   CUBE(x)     (SQ(x) * (x))
#define   F_POW(x)    sqrt(sqrt(CUBE(x)))
                                          /* fractional power: 3/4 */
```

B.4 The Use of #undef

A preprocessing directive of the form

`#undef` *identifier*

undefines a macro. It causes the previous definition of a macro to be forgotten. Consider, for example, the following code:

```
#undef PI

#define   PI   "I like apple."
```

If `PI` has been defined previously, the `#undef` preprocessing directive undefines it for the remainder of the file, or up to the point where `PI` is defined again. If `PI` has not been defined previously, then the preprocessing directive has no effect.

Programmers sometimes need to use the `#undef` facility unexpectedly. Here is an example. In many C systems on Sun machines, the following program fails:

```
#include <stdio.h>

int main(void)
{
   int   earth = 1, moon = 2, sun = 3;

   printf("sum = %d\n", earth + moon + sun);
   return 0;
}
```

The difficulty occurs because the system treats the identifier `sun` as a `#define` symbolic constant. If your compiler complains about this code, you can see that the error message produced is completely uninformative. You can use the `-E` option of the compiler to see the output from the preprocessor. To fix the problem, put the following line at the top of the file:

```
#undef sun
```

Caution: This kind of problem can occur on other machines. (Does the use of `dec` as an identifier on a DEC machine cause problems? Or `cray` on a Cray machine?) The problem is both compiler- and machine-dependent.

B.5 Conditional Compilation

The preprocessor has directives for conditional compilation. The directives can be used for program development and for writing code that is more easily portable from one machine to another. Each preprocessing directive of the form

```
#if       constant_integral_expression
#ifdef    identifier
#ifndef   identifier
```

provides for conditional compilation of the code that follows until the preprocessing directive

```
#endif
```

is reached. For the intervening code to be compiled, after `#if`, the constant expression must be nonzero (*true*), and after `#ifdef` or `#if defined`, the named identifier must have been defined previously in a `#define` line, without an intervening

```
#undef identifier
```

having been used to undefine the macro. After `#ifndef`, the named identifier must be currently undefined.

The integral constant expression used in a preprocessing directive cannot contain the `sizeof` operator or a cast. It may, however, use the `defined` preprocessing operator. This operator is available in ANSI C but not necessarily in traditional C. The expression

`defined identifier`   is equivalent to   `defined(identifier)`

It evaluates to one if the identifier is currently defined, and to zero otherwise. Here is an example of how it can be used:

```
#if defined(HP9000) || defined(SUN4) && !defined(VAX)
   .....      /* machine-dependent code */
#endif
```

Sometimes `printf()` statements are useful for debugging purposes. Suppose at the top of a file we write

```
#define   DEBUG   1
```

then throughout the rest of the file we write lines such as

```
#if DEBUG
   printf("debug:  a = %d\n", a);
#endif
```

Because the symbolic constant DEBUG has nonzero value, the printf() statements are compiled. Later, these lines can be omitted from compilation by changing the value of the symbolic constant DEBUG to zero.

An alternate scheme is to define a symbolic constant having no value. Suppose at the top of a file we write

```
#define    DEBUG
```

Then we can use the #ifdef or #if defined forms of conditional compilation. For example, if we write

```
#ifdef DEBUG
   .....
#endif
```

the intervening lines of code are compiled. When we remove the #define line that defines DEBUG at the top of the file, the intervening lines of code are not compiled.

Suppose we are writing code in a large software project. We may be expected to include at the top of all our code certain header files supplied by others. Our code may depend on some of the function prototypes and on some of the macros in these header files, but because the header files are for the project as a whole, our code might not use everything. Moreover, we may not even know all the things that eventually will be in the header files. To prevent the clash of macro names, we can use the #undef facility.

```
#include "everything.h"

#undef     PIE
#define    PIE    "I like apple."
  .....
```

If PIE happens to be defined in *everything.h*, then we have undefined it. If it is not defined in *everything.h*, then the #undef directive has no effect.

Here is a common use of conditional compilation. Imagine that you are in the testing phase of program development and that your code has the form

statements
more statements
and still more statements

For debugging or testing purposes, you may wish to temporarily disregard, or block out, some of your code. To do this, you can put the code into a comment.

```
statements
/*
more statements
*/
and still more statements
```

However, if blocked-out code contains comments within it, this method results in a syntax error; the use of conditional compilation solves this problem.

```
statements
#if 0
more statements
#endif
and still more statements
```

The preprocessor has control structures that are similar to the `if-else` statement in C. Each of the `#if` forms can be followed by any number of lines, possibly containing preprocessing directives of the form

```
#elif    constant_integral_expression
```

possibly followed by the preprocessing directive

```
#else
```

and, finally, followed by the preprocessing directive

```
#endif
```

Note that `#elif` is a contraction for "else-if." The flow of control for conditional compilation is analogous to that provided by `if-else` statements.

B.6 Predefined Macros

In ANSI C, there are five predefined macros. They are always available and cannot be undefined by the programmer. Each of these macro names includes two leading and two trailing underscore characters.

Predefined macro	Value
`__DATE__`	A string containing the current date.
`__FILE__`	A string containing the file name.
`__LINE__`	An integer representing the current line number.
`__STDC__`	If the implementation follows ANSI Standard C, then the value is a nonzero integer.
`__TIME__`	A string containing the current time.

B.7 The Operators # and

The preprocessing operators # and ## are available in ANSI C but not in traditional C. The unary operator # causes "stringization" of a formal parameter in a macro definition. Here is an example of its use:

```
#define   message_for(a, b)  \
          printf(#a " and " #b ": We love you!\n")

int main(void)
{
   message_for(Carole, Debra);
   return 0;
}
```

When the macro is invoked, each parameter in the macro definition is replaced by its corresponding argument, with the # causing the argument to be surrounded by double quotes. Thus, after the preprocessor pass, we obtain

```
int main(void)
{
   printf("Carole" " and " "Debra" ": We love you!\n");
   return 0;
}
```

Because string constants separated by white space are concatenated, this printf() statement is equivalent to

```
printf("Carole and Debra: We love you!\n");
```

The next section shows how to use the "stringization" operator # in assertions.

The binary operator ## is used to merge tokens. Here is an example of how the operator is used:

```
#define   X(i)   x ## i

X(1) = X(2) = X(3);
```

After the preprocessor pass, we are left with the line

```
x1 = x2 = x3;
```

B.8 The assert() Macro

ANSI C provides the `assert()` macro in the standard header file *assert.h*. This macro can be used to ensure that the value of an expression is what you expect it to be. Suppose you are writing a critical function and you want to be sure that the arguments satisfy certain conditions. Here is an example of how `assert()` can be used to do this:

```
#include <assert.h>

void f(char *p, int n)
{
   .....
   assert(p != NULL);
   assert(n > 0 && n < 5);
   .....
```

If an assertion fails, the system prints out a message and abort the program. Although the `assert()` macro is implemented differently on each system, its general behavior is always the same. Here is one way the macro might be written:

```
#if defined(NDEBUG)
   #define   assert(ignore)   ((void) 0)   /* ignore it */
#else
   #define   assert(expr)                          \
      if (!(expr)) {                               \
       printf("\n%s%s\n%s%s\n%s%d\n\n",            \
          "Assertion failed: ", #expr,             \
          "in file ", __FILE__,                    \
          "at line ", __LINE__);                   \
       abort();                                    \
      }
#endif
```

Note that if the macro `NDEBUG` is defined, all assertions are ignored. This allows the programmer to use assertions freely during program development and to effectively discard them later by defining the macro `NDEBUG`. The function `abort()` is in the standard library (see Appendix A, "The Standard Library").

B.9 The Use of #error and #pragma

ANSI C has added the #error and #pragma preprocessing directives. The following code demonstrates how #error can be used:

```
#if A_SIZE < B_SIZE
   #error "Incompatible sizes"
#endif
```

If, during compilation, the preprocessor reaches the #error directive, then a compile-time error occurs, and the string following the directive is printed on the screen. In our example, we used the #error macro to enforce the consistency of two symbolic constants. In an analogous fashion, the directive can be used to enforce other conditions.

The #pragma directive is provided for implementation-specific uses. Its general form is

#pragma   *tokens*

It causes a behavior that depends on the particular C compiler. Any #pragma that is not recognized by the compiler is ignored.

B.10 Line Numbers

A preprocessing directive of the form

#line   *integral_constant*   "*filename*"

causes the compiler to renumber the source text so that the next line has the specified constant and to believe that the current source file name is *filename*. If no file name is present, then only the renumbering of lines takes place. Normally, line numbers are hidden from the programmer and occur only in reference to warnings and syntax errors.

B.11 Corresponding Functions

In ANSI C, many of the macros with parameters that are given in the standard header files are supposed to have corresponding functions in the standard library. As an example, suppose we want to access the function isalpha() instead of the macro. One way to do this is to write

```
#undef isalpha
```

somewhere in the file before `isalpha()` is invoked. This discards the macro definition, forcing the compiler to use the function instead. We would still include the header file *ctype.h* at the top of the file because, in addition to macros, the file contains function prototypes.

Another way to obtain the function instead of the macro is to write

```
(isalpha)(c)
```

The preprocessor does not recognize this construct as a macro. The compiler, however, recognizes it as a function call.

Appendix C

Bitwise Operators

In this appendix, we discuss the bit operators, with which the programmer can access the individual bits in a byte. These low-level data structures are often nonportable. They are important to systems programming and programming in which optimal storage utilization and efficiency are priorities.

C.1 Bitwise Operators and Expressions

The bitwise operators act on integral expressions represented as strings of binary digits. These operators are explicitly system-dependent. We restrict our discussion to machines having 8-bit bytes, 4-byte words, the two's complement representation of integers, and ASCII character codes.

Bitwise operators		
Logical operators	(unary) bitwise complement	~
	bitwise and	&
	bitwise exclusive or	^
	bitwise inclusive or	|
Shift operators	left-shift	<<
	right-shift	>>

The operator ~ is unary; all the other bitwise operators are binary. They operate on integral expressions. Like other operators, the bitwise operators have rules of precedence and associativity that determine precisely how expressions involving them are evaluated (see Appendix E, "ASCII Character Codes").

Bitwise Complement

The operator ~ is called the *complement operator*, or the *bitwise complement operator*. It inverts the bit string representation of its argument; the zeroes become ones, and the ones become zeroes. Consider, for example, the declaration

```
int    a = 70707;
```

The binary representation of a is

```
00000000 00000001 00010100 00110011
```

The expression ~a is the bitwise complement of a, and this expression has the binary representation

```
11111111 11111110 11101011 11001100
```

The `int` value of the expression ~a is -70708.

Two's Complement

The *two's complement representation* of a nonnegative integer *n* is the bit string obtained by writing *n* in base 2. If we take the bitwise complement of the bit string and add 1 to it, we obtain the two's complement representation of -*n*. The next table gives some examples. To save space, we show only the two low-order bytes.

Value of *n*	Binary representation	Bitwise complement	Two's complement representation of −*n*	Value of −*n*
7	00000000 00000111	11111111 11111000	11111111 11111001	-7
8	00000000 00001000	11111111 11110111	11111111 11111000	-8
9	00000000 00001001	11111111 11110110	11111111 11110111	-9
-7	11111111 11111001	00000000 00000110	00000000 00000111	7

The preceding table is read from left to right. If we start with a positive integer *n*, consider its binary representation, and add 1 to its bitwise complement, then we obtain the two's complement representation of -*n*. A machine that uses the two's complement representation as its binary representation in memory for integral values is called a *two's complement machine.*

On a two's complement machine, if we start with the binary representation of a negative number -*n* and add 1 to its bitwise complement, we obtain the two's complement representation, or binary representation, of *n*. This is illustrated in the last line in our previous table.

The two's complement representations of both 0 and -1 are special. The value 0 has all bits off; the value -1 has all bits on. Note that if a binary string is added to its bitwise complement, then the result has all bits on, which is the two's complement representation of -1. Negative numbers are characterized by having the high bit on.

On a two's complement machine, the hardware that does addition and bitwise complementation can be used to implement subtraction. The operation `a - b` is the same as `a + (-b)`, and `-b` is obtained by taking the bitwise complement of `b` and adding 1.

Bitwise Binary Logical Operators

The three operators & (and), ^ (exclusive or), and | (inclusive or) are binary operators. They take integral expressions as operands. The two operands, properly widened, are operated on bit position by bit position. The following table shows the bitwise operators acting on 1-bit fields.

a	b	a & b	a ^ b	a | b
0	0	0	0	0
1	0	0	1	1
0	1	0	1	1
1	1	1	0	1

The next table contains examples of the bitwise operators acting on `int` variables.

Declaration and initializations		
`int    a = 33333, b = -77777;`		
Expression	**Representation**	**Value**
`a`	`00000000 00000000 10000010 00110101`	33333
`b`	`11111111 11111110 11010000 00101111`	-77777
`a & b`	`00000000 00000000 10000000 00100101`	32805
`a ^ b`	`11111111 11111110 01010010 00011010`	-110054
`a | b`	`11111111 11111110 11010010 00111111`	-77249
`~(a | b)`	`00000000 00000001 00101101 11000000`	77248
`(~a & ~b)`	`00000000 00000001 00101101 11000000`	77248

Left- and Right-Shift Operators

The two operands of a shift operator must be integral expressions. The integral promotions are performed on each of the operands. The type of the expression as a whole is that of its promoted left operand. An expression of the form

expr1 << *expr2*

causes the bit representation of *expr1* to be shifted to the left by the number of places specified by *expr2*. On the low-order end, zeroes are shifted in.

Declaration and initialization		
`char c = 'Z';`		
Expression	**Representation**	**Action**
`c`	`00000000 00000000 00000000 01011010`	unshifted
`c << 1`	`00000000 00000000 00000000 10110100`	left-shifted 1
`c << 4`	`00000000 00000000 00000101 10100000`	left-shifted 4
`c << 31`	`00000000 00000000 00000000 00000000`	left-shifted 31

Even though `c` is stored in one byte, in an expression it is promoted to an `int`. When shift expressions are evaluated, integral promotions are performed on the two operands separately, and the type of the result is that of the promoted left operand. Thus the value of an expression such as `c << 1` is stored in four bytes.

The right-shift operator >> is not quite symmetric to the left-shift operator. For unsigned integral expressions, zeroes are shifted in at the high end. For the signed types, some machines shift in zeroes, whereas others shift in sign bits (see exercise 9 on page 597). The sign bit is the high-order bit; it is zero for nonnegative integers and one for negative integers.

Declarations and initializations		
`int a = 1 << 31; /* shift 1 to the high bit */` `unsigned b = 1 << 31;`		
Expression	**Representation**	**Action**
`a`	`10000000 00000000 00000000 00000000`	unshifted
`a >> 3`	`11110000 00000000 00000000 00000000`	right-shifted 3
`b`	`10000000 00000000 00000000 00000000`	unshifted
`b >> 3`	`00010000 00000000 00000000 00000000`	right-shifted 3

Note that on our machine, sign bits are shifted in with an `int`. On another machine, zeroes might be shifted in. To avoid this difficulty, programmers often use unsigned types when using bitwise operators.

If the right operand of a shift operator is negative or has a value that equals or exceeds the number of bits used to represent the left operand, then the behavior is undefined. It is the programmer's responsibility to keep the value of the right operand within proper bounds.

Our next table illustrates the rules of precedence and associativity with respect to the shift operators. To save space, we show only the two low-order bytes.

Declaration and initializations			
`unsigned a = 1, b = 2;`			
Expression	**Equivalent expression**	**Representation**	**Value**
`a << b >> 1`	`(a << b) >> 1`	`00000000 00000010`	128
`a << 1 + 2 << 3`	`(a << (1 + 2)) << 3`	`00000000 01000000`	64
`a + b << 12 * a >> b`	`((a + b) << (12 * a)) >> b`	`00001100 00000000`	3072

C.2 Masks

A mask is a constant or variable that is used to extract desired bits from another variable or expression. Because the `int` constant 1 has the bit representation

```
00000000 00000000 00000000 00000001
```

it can be used to determine the low-order bit of an `int` expression. The following code uses this mask and prints an alternating sequence of zeroes and ones:

```
int   i, mask = 1;

for (i = 0; i < 10; ++i)
   printf("%d", i & mask);
```

If we wish to find the value of a particular bit in an expression, we can use a mask that is one in that position and zero elsewhere. For example, we can use the expression `1 << 2`, as a mask for the third bit, counting from the right. The expression

```
(v & (1 << 2)) ? 1 : 0
```

has the value one or zero depending on the third bit in `v`.

Another example of a mask is the constant value 255, which is $2^8 - 1$. It has the following bit representation:

```
00000000 00000000 00000000 11111111
```

Because only the low-order byte is turned on, the expression

```
v & 255
```

yields a value having a bit representation with its high-order bytes zero and its low-order byte the same as the low-order byte in v. We express this by saying, "255 is a mask for the low-order byte."

C.3 Printing an int Bitwise

The `bit_print()` function we discuss in this section is a typical example of a system software program. For anyone writing software that deals with the machine at the bit level, the `bit_print()` utility is essential; it allows the programmer to see what is happening. For the beginning programmer, exploration with `bit_print()` helps to provide a conceptual framework that is very useful.

Our `bit_print()` function uses a mask to print out the bit representation of an `int`. The function can be used to explore how values of expressions are represented in memory.

```
/* Bit print an int expression. */

#include <limits.h>

void bit_print(int a)
{
   int   i;
   int   n = sizeof(int) * CHAR_BIT;        /* in limits.h */
   int   mask = 1 << (n - 1);               /* mask = 100·····0 */

   for (i = 1; i <= n; ++i) {
      putchar(((a & mask) == 0) ? '0' : '1');
      a <<= 1;
      if (i % CHAR_BIT == 0 && i < n)
         putchar(' ');
   }
}
```

Dissection of the bit_print() Function

■ `#include <limits.h>`

In ANSI C, the symbolic constant `CHAR_BIT` is defined in *limits.h*. In traditional C, this header file is not usually available. The value of `CHAR_BIT` on most systems is 8. It represents the number of bits in a `char` or, equivalently, the number of bits in a byte. ANSI C requires at least eight bits in a byte.

■ `int    n = sizeof(int) * CHAR_BIT;    /* in limits.h */`

Because we want this function to work on machines having either 2- or 4-byte words, we use the variable `n` to represent the number of bits in a machine word. We expect the value of the expression `sizeof(int)` to be either 2 or 4, and we expect the symbolic constant `CHAR_BIT`, which is defined in the standard header file *limits.h*, to be 8. Thus we expect `n` to be initialized to either 16 or 32, depending on the machine.

■ `int    mask = 1 << (n - 1);        /* mask = 100·····0 */`

Because of operator precedence, the parentheses are not needed in the initialization. We put them there to make the code more readable. Because `<<` has higher precedence than `=`, the expression `1 << (n - 1)` is evaluated first. Suppose `n` has value 32. The constant 1 has only its low-order bit turned on. The expression `1 << 31` shifts that bit to the high-order end. Thus `mask` has all of its bits off except for its high-order bit (sign bit), which is on.

■
```
for (i = 1; i <= n; ++i) {
   putchar(((a & mask) == 0) ? '0' : '1');
   a <<= 1;
   .....
```

First, consider the expression

```
(a & mask) == 0
```

If the high-order bit in `a` is off, the expression `a & mask` has all of its bits off, and the expression `(a & mask) == 0` is *true*. Conversely, if the high-order bit in `a` is on, the expression `a & mask` has its high-order bit on, and the expression `(a & mask) == 0` is *false*. Now consider the expression

```
((a & mask) == 0) ? '0' : '1'
```

If the high-order bit in a is off, the conditional expression has the value '0'; otherwise it has the value '1'. Thus putchar() prints a 0 if the high-order bit is off, and a 1 if it is on.

■
```
putchar(((a & mask) == 0) ? '0' : '1');
a <<= 1;
```

After the high-order bit in a has been printed, we left-shift the bits in a by one and place the result back in a. Recall that

`a <<= 1;` is equivalent to `a = a << 1;`

The value of the expression `a << 1` has the same bit pattern as a, except that it has been left-shifted by one. The expression by itself does not change the value of a in memory. In contrast to this, the expression `a <<= 1` does change the value of a in memory. Its effect is to bring the next bit into the high-order position, ready to be printed the next time through the loop.

■
```
if (i % CHAR_BIT == 0 && i < n)
   putchar(' ');
```

If we assume that the value of the symbolic constant CHAR_BIT is 8, this code causes a blank to be printed after each group of eight bits has been printed.

This bit_print() function printed a space between each group of CHAR_BIT bits. It is not necessary to do this, but it certainly makes the output easier to read.

C.4 Packing and Unpacking

The use of bitwise expressions allows for data compression across byte boundaries. This is useful in saving space, but it can be even more useful in saving time. On a machine with 4-byte words, each instruction cycle processes 32 bits in parallel. The following function can be used to pack four characters into an int. It uses shift operations to do the packing byte by byte.

```
/* Pack 4 characters into an int. */

#include <limits.h>

int pack(char a, char b, char c, char d)
{
   int   p = a;      /* p will be packed with a, b, c, d */

   p = (p << CHAR_BIT) | b;
   p = (p << CHAR_BIT) | c;
   p = (p << CHAR_BIT) | d;
   return p;
}
```

To test our function, we write a program with the lines

```
printf("abcd = ");
bit_print(pack('a', 'b', 'c', 'd'));
putchar('\n');
```

in `main()`. Here is the output of our test program:

```
abcd = 01100001 01100010 01100011 01100100
```

Observe that the high-order byte has value 97, or `'a'`, and that the values of the remaining bytes are 98, 99, and 100. Thus `pack()` did its work properly.

Having written `pack()`, we now want to be able to retrieve the characters from within the 32-bit `int`. Again, we can use a mask to do this.

```
/* Unpack a byte from an int. */

#include <limits.h>

char unpack(int p, int k)          /* k = 0, 1, 2, or 3 */
{
   int        n = k * CHAR_BIT;    /* n = 0, 8, 16, or 24 */
   unsigned   mask = 255;          /* low-order byte */

   mask <<= n;
   return ((p & mask) >> n);
}
```

Dissection of the unpack() Function

■ `#include <limits.h>`

We have included this header file because it contains the definition of the symbolic constant CHAR_BIT. It represents the number of bits in a byte. On most machines its value is 8.

■
```
char unpack(int p, int k)        /* k = 0, 1, 2, or 3 */
{
    .....
```

We think of the parameter p as a packed int, with its bytes numbered 0 through 3. The parameter k indicates which byte we want: if k has value 0, then we want the low-order byte; if k has value 1, then we want the next byte; and so forth.

■
```
int          n = k * CHAR_BIT;  /* n = 0, 8, 16, or 24 */
```

If we assume that CHAR_BIT is 8 and that k has value 0, 1, 2, or 3, then n is initialized with the value 0, 8, 16, or 24.

■
```
unsigned    mask = 255;         /* low-order byte */
```

The constant 255 is special; to understand it, first consider 256. Because $256 = 2^8$, the bit representation of 256 has all 0 bits except for a 1 in the ninth bit, counting from the low-order bit. Because 255 is one less than 256, the bit representation of 255 has all 0 bits, except for the first eight bits, which are all 1 (see exercise 1 on page 595). Thus the binary representation of mask is

```
00000000 00000000 00000000 11111111
```

■
```
mask <<= n;
```

Let us assume that CHAR_BIT is 8. If n has value 0, the bits in mask are not changed. If n has value 8, the bits in mask are left-shifted by 8. In this case we think of mask stored in memory as

```
00000000 00000000 11111111 00000000
```

If `n` has value 16, then the bits in `mask` are left-shifted by 16. In this case we think of `mask` stored in memory as

```
00000000 11111111 00000000 00000000
```

In a similar fashion, if `n` has value 24, then `mask` has only the bits in its high-order byte turned on.

■ `(p & mask) >> n`

Parentheses are needed because & has lower precedence than >>. Suppose `p` has value -3579753 (which we chose because it has a suitable bit pattern), and `n` has value 16. The following table illustrates what happens.

Expression	Binary	Decimal
`p`	11111111 11001001 01100000 10010111	-3579753
`mask`	00000000 11111111 00000000 00000000	16711680
`p & mask`	00000000 11001001 00000000 00000000	13172736
`(p & mask) >> n`	00000000 00000000 00000000 11001001	201

■ `return ((p & mask) >> n);`

Because the type for `unpack()` is `char`, the `int` expression `(p & mask) >> n` is converted to a `char` before it is passed back to the calling environment. When an `int` is converted to a `char`, only the low-order byte is retained; the other bytes are discarded.

Imagine wanting to keep an abbreviated employee record in one integer. We suppose an "employee identification number" can be stored in nine bits and a "job type" can be stored in six bits, which provides for a total of up to 64 job types. The employee's "gender" can be stored in one bit. These three fields require 16 bits, which on a machine with 4-byte words is a `short` integer. We can think of the three bit fields as follows:

Identification	Job type	Gender
bbbbbbbbb	bbbbbb	b

The following function can be used in a program designed to enter employee data into a `short`. The inverse problem of reading data out of the `short` would be accomplished with the use of masks.

```
/* Create employee data in a short int. */

short create_employee_data(int id_no, int job_type,
                           char gender)
{
   short   employee = 0;     /* start with all bits off */

   employee |= (gender == 'm' || gender == 'M') ? 0 : 1;
   employee |= job_type << 1;
   employee |= id_no << 7;
   return employee;
}
```

C.5 Common Programming Errors

A common error is caused by the programmer confusing & with && and | with ||. Like the use of = instead of ==, this kind of error is easy to make. For the most part, the resulting expressions do not lead to syntax errors, so your compiler cannot tell you that an error has been made. To illustrate these ideas, let us suppose a, b, and c are `int` variables. Then each of the expressions

```
a == b && c          a == b & c          a = b & c
```

is legal and can be used, for example, to control an `if` statement or a loop.

When using bitwise operators, the programmer must take into account the type of the expression. Here is an innocuous looking initialization that results in a difficult bug:

```
unsigned   lo_byte = ~0 >> 24;  /* turn the low byte on */
```

The programmer is trying to create a mask for the low-order byte. Because `0` has all bits off, the expression `~0` has all bits on. Then the bits are right-shifted by 24 with the intention of shifting in zeroes at the high end. The programmer remembered that with `unsigned` types, zeroes are always shifted in. But this initialization failed. When the `bit_print()` function was used to see what happened, the programmer discovered that all bits were on! The problem is that `0` is of type `int`, and the operations `~0 >> 24` do not change that type. The final result is assigned to `lo_byte`, which is of type `unsigned`, but that does not help. The correct initialization is

```
unsigned   lo_byte = ~((unsigned) 0) >> 24;
```

The outer parentheses are not necessary, but they make the code more readable.

On any machine, a mask of type `long` is acceptable. However, when we tried the following initialization on a 2-byte machine, our code did not work as expected:

```
long   mask = 1 << 31;            /* turn the high bit on */
```

We made an egregious error. The expression `1` is of type `int`, and therefore stored in two bytes. When `1` is left-shifted by 31, all bits are turned off, so that `mask` effectively is assigned the value zero, which is not what was intended. Here is the correct initialization:

```
long   mask = (long) 1 << 31;     /* turn the high bit on */
```

C.6 System Considerations

The fact that some machines right-shift in zeroes and other machines shift in sign bits can cause trouble. Suppose the machine you are working on always shifts in zeroes. Then using an `int` produces the same result as using an `unsigned`. If you later move the code to a machine that shifts in sign bits, then the use of an `int` may cause unwanted results.

In C, any expression of type `char` or `short` is promoted to an `int`, and this is done in a way that preserves values. Any `unsigned char` or `unsigned short` gets 0s padded on the left, whereas sign extension occurs on signed quantities. This means that the sign bit is propagated. The following table illustrates this.

Expression	Binary representation	Value
`128`	`00000000 00000000 00000000 10000000`	`128`
`(char) 128`	`11111111 11111111 11111111 10000000`	`-128`
`-1 ^ 128`	`11111111 11111111 11111111 01111111`	`-129`
`(char) (-1 ^ 128)`	`00000000 00000000 00000000 01111111`	`127`
`255`	`00000000 00000000 00000000 11111111`	`255`
`(unsigned char) 255`	`00000000 00000000 00000000 11111111`	`255`

On our system, a plain `char` is implemented as a `signed char`. When an `int` is cast to a `char`, only the low-order byte is retained; all the other bytes are discarded. But then the expression as a whole is promoted to an `int`. For signed quantities, the eighth bit (sign bit) in the `char` determines what is padded to the left. In contrast to this, an `unsigned char` is padded with zeroes irrespective of the sign bit.

The ideas of promotion and sign extension explain why using a `char` to test against `EOF` can fail on some systems (see exercise 19 on page 599).

The programmer has to be cautious when using multicharacter character constants. On most systems, constants such as `'ab'` can be used, but how the bytes are actually stored in a word is system-dependent.

Summary

- The bitwise operators provide the programmer with a means of accessing the bits in an integral expression. Typically, we think of the operands of these operators as bit strings.

- The use of bitwise expressions allows for data compression across byte boundaries. This capability is useful in saving space, but it can be even more useful in saving time. On a machine with 4-byte words, each instruction cycle processes 32 bits in parallel.

- Most machines use the two's complement representation for integers. In this representation the high-order bit is the sign bit. It is one for negative integers and zero for nonnegative integers.

- Bitwise operations are explicitly system-dependent. A left-shift causes zeroes to be shifted in. The situation for a right-shift is more complicated. If the integral expression is `unsigned`, then zeroes are shifted in. If the expression is one of the signed types, then what is shifted in is system-dependent. Some machines shift in sign bits. This means that if the sign bit is zero, then zeroes are shifted in, and if the sign bit is one, then ones are shifted in. Some machines shift in zeroes in all cases.

- Masks are particular values that are typically used with the | operator to set a series of bits, and with the & operator to extract a series of bits.

- Packing is the act of placing a number of distinct values into various subfields of a given variable. Unpacking extracts these values.

- The function `bit_print()` is a software tool. The programmer can use it to see what is happening in memory at the bit level.

Exercises

1 Use the `bit_print()` function to create a table containing n, the binary representation for 2^n, and the binary representation for $2^n - 1$, for $n = 0, 1, 2, \ldots, 32$. If your machine has 2-byte words, then the output of your program should look like this:

```
 0:  00000000 00000001   00000000 00000000
 1:  00000000 00000010   00000000 00000001
 2:  00000000 00000100   00000000 00000011
 .....
15:  10000000 00000000   01111111 11111111
 .....
```

After you have done this, write down a similar table by hand that contains n, 10^n, and $10^n - 1$ for $n = 0, 1, 2, \ldots, 7$. Write the numbers in base 10 in your table. Do you see the similarity between the two tables? *Hint:* Use the following code:

```
int   i, power = 1;

for (i = 0; i < 32; ++i) {
   printf("%2d:  ", i);
   bit_print(power);
   printf("   ");
   bit_print(power - 1);
   putchar('\n');
   power *= 2;
}
```

2 Write a function that takes as its input a string of decimal integers. Each character in the string can be thought of as a decimal digit. The digits should be converted to 4-bit binary strings and packed into an `int`. If an `int` has 32 bits, then as many as eight digits can be packed into it. When you test your function, here is what you might see on the screen:

```
Input a string of decimal digits:  12345678

12345678 = 0001 0010 0011 0100 0101 0110 0111 1000
```

Also, write an inverse function. It should unpack an `int` and return the original string. *Hint:* Here is one way to begin a conversion function:

```
int convert(char *s)
{
   char   *p;
   int    a = 0;          /* turn all bits off */

   for (p = s; *p != '\0'; ++p) {
      a <<= 4;
      switch (*p) {
      case '1':
         a |= 1;
       break;
      case '2':
      .....
```

3 Some of the binary representations of the numbers in this chapter are easy to check for correctness, and some are not. Use `bit_print()` to check some of the more difficult representations. Try, for example, 70707 and its bitwise complement. Did we really get it right in the text?

4 Suppose integers have a 16-bit two's complement representation. Write down the binary representation for -1, -5, -101, -1023. *Hint:* Recall that the two's complement representation of negative integers is obtained by taking the bit representation of the corresponding positive integer, complementing it, and adding 1.

5 Carole, Barbara, and Debra all vote on 16 referendums. Assume that each individual's vote is stored bitwise in a 16-bit integer. Write a function definition that begins

```
short majority(short a, short b, short c)
{
   .....
```

This function should take as input the votes of Carole, Barbara, and Debra stored in `a`, `b`, and `c`, respectively. It should return the bitwise majority of `a`, `b`, and `c`.

6 Write a function definition that begins

```
int circular_shift(int a, int n)
{
   .....
```

This function should left-shift `a` by `n` positions, where the high-order bits are reintroduced as the low-order bits. Here are two examples of a circular shift operation defined for a `char` instead of an `int`:

```
10000001   circular shift 1 yields   00000011
01101011   circular shift 3 yields   01011011
```

Write a program that uses `bit_print()` to test your function.

7 Write a function that reverses the bit representation of an `int`. Here are two examples of a reversing operation defined for a `char` instead of an `int`:

```
01110101   reversed yields   10101110
10101111   reversed yields   11110101
```

8 Write a function that extracts every other bit position from a 32-bit expression. The result should be returned as a 16-bit expression. Your function should work on machines having either 2- or 4-byte words.

9 Does your machine shift in sign bits? Here is some code that can help you to determine this:

```
int         i = -1;      /* turn all bits on */
unsigned    u = -1;

if (i >> 1 == u >> 1)
   printf("Zeros are shifted in.\n");
else
   printf("Sign bits are shifted in.\n");
```

Explain why this code works.

10 A 20th-century date can be written with integers in the form *day/month/year.* An example is 1/7/33, which represents 1 July 1933. Write a function that stores the day, month, and year compactly. Because we need 31 values for the day, 12 different values for the month, and 100 values for the year, we can use five bits to represent the day, four bits to represent the month, and seven bits to represent the year. Your function should take as input the day, month, and year as integers, and it should return the date packed into a 16-bit integer. Write another function that does the unpacking. Write a program to test your functions.

11 Write a function that acts directly on a packed date (see the previous exercise) and produces the next calendar day in packed form. Contrast this with the program you wrote in exercise 2 on page 595.

12 Rewrite the program given in Section 3.12, "Problem Solving: Boolean Variables," on page 97. Use the five low-order bits in the `char` variable `b` to represent the five boolean variables `b1`, . . . , `b5`.

13 Rewrite the program from the previous exercise to take advantage of machine arithmetic. Show by hand simulation that the effect of adding one to the bit representation for `b` is equivalent to the effect of the nested `for` statements. In this exercise, your program should generate the table using a single unnested `for` statement.

14 Write an interactive program that asks the user to input an integer n. Use `bit_print()` to write out the binary representation of n, $2 \times n$, $4 \times n$, and $8 \times n$. Can you explain what happens? *Hint:* In base ten, what happens to a number when you multiply it by 10^k for $k = 1, 2, 3$?

15 Suppose you are on a two's complement machine that does not provide bitwise complementation. Write a function `bit_complement()` to implement the operation that only uses arithmetic operations. *Hint:* If `a` is a variable of type `int`, and binary complementation is available, then the expressions

`-a` and `~a + 1`

have the same value.

16 Consider the function `pack()` (see Section C.4, "Packing and Unpacking," on page 588). The body of the function consists of four statements. Rewrite the function so that these four statements are collapsed into a single `return` statement.

17 Rewrite the function `pack()` so that only arithmetic operations are used.

18 Most machines implement a plain `char` as either a `signed char` or as an `unsigned char`. How is a plain `char` implemented on your machine? Try the following code:

```
char            c  = 128;     /* turn the high bit on */
signed char     sc = 128;
unsigned char   uc = 128;

printf("c = %d  sc = %d  uc = %d\n", c, sc, uc);
```

Although a variable of type `char` is stored in memory in a single byte, as an expression, it is promoted to an `int`. Change the %d formats to %u. Do you see the effects of the promotion?

19 Suppose a system implements a plain `char` as an `unsigned char`. Explain the effect of the following code:

```
char   c = EOF;

if (c == EOF)
   printf("Truth!\n");
else
   printf("This needs to be explained!\n");
```

We are assuming that *stdio.h* has been included. If your system implements a plain `char` as a `signed char`, then to see how this code would run on a different system, just change the declaration to

```
unsigned char   c = EOF;
```

Hint: Look in *stdio.h* to find the value of `EOF`. Then read Section C.6, "System Considerations," on page 593, carefully. If you are still mystified, use `bit_print()` to see what is happening.

Appendix D

ANSI C Compared to Traditional C

In this appendix we list the major differences between ANSI C and traditional C. Where appropriate, we have included examples. The list is not complete. Only the major changes are noted.

D.1 Types

- The keyword `signed` has been added to the language.
- Three types of characters are specified: plain `char`, `signed char`, and `unsigned char`. An implementation may represent a plain `char` as either a `signed char` or an `unsigned char`.
- The keyword `signed` can be used in declarations of any of the signed integral types and in casts. Except with `char`, its use is always optional.
- In traditional C, the type `long float` is equivalent to `double`. Because `long float` was rarely used, it has been removed from ANSI C.
- The type `long double` has been added to ANSI C. Constants of this type are specified with the suffix `L`. A `long double` may provide more precision and range than a `double`, but it is not required to do so.
- The keyword `void` is used to indicate that a function takes no arguments or returns no value.
- The type `void *` is used for generic pointers. For example, the function prototype for `malloc()` is given by

```
void *malloc(size_t size);
```

A generic pointer can be assigned a pointer value of any type, and a variable of any pointer type can be assigned a generic pointer value. Casts are not needed. In contrast, the generic pointer type in traditional C is `char *`. Here, casts are necessary.

- Enumeration types are supported. An example is

```
enum day {sun, mon, tue, wed, thu, fri, sat};
```

The enumerators in this example are `sun`, `mon`, . . . , `sat`. Enumerators are constants of type `int` and can be used in `case` labels in `switch` statements.

D.2 Constants

- String constants separated by white space are concatenated. Thus

```
"abc"
"def" "ghi"        is equivalent to        "abcdefghi"
```

- String constants are not modifiable. (Not all compilers enforce this.)

- The type of a numeric constant can be specified by letter suffixes. Some examples are

```
123L      /* long          */
123U      /* unsigned      */
123UL     /* unsigned long */
1.23F     /* float         */
1.23L     /* long double   */
```

Suffixes may be lower- or uppercase. A numeric constant without a suffix is a type big enough to contain the value.

- The digits 8 and 9 are no longer considered octal digits. They may not be used in an octal constant.

- Hexadecimal escape sequences beginning with `\x` have been introduced. As with octal escape sequences beginning with `\0`, they are used in character and string constants.

D.3 Declarations

- The type qualifier `const` has been added. It means that variables so declared are not modifiable. (Compilers do not always enforce this.)

- The type qualifier `volatile` has been added. It means that variables so declared are modifiable by an agent external to the program. For example, some systems put the declaration

  ```
  extern volatile int   errno;
  ```

  in the header file *errno.h*.

D.4 Initializations

- In ANSI C, automatic aggregates such as arrays and structures can be initialized. In traditional C, they must be external or of storage class `static`.

- Unions can be initialized. An initialization refers to the union's first member.

- Character arrays of size *n* can be initialized using a string constant of exactly *n* characters. An example is

  ```
  char   today[3] = "Fri";
  ```

  The end-of-string sentinel `\0` in `"Fri"` is not copied into `today`.

D.5 Expressions

- For reasons of symmetry, a unary plus operator has been added to the language.

- In traditional C, expressions involving one of the commutative binary operators such as + or * can be reordered at the convenience of the compiler, even though they have been parenthesized in the program. For example, in the statement

  ```
  x = (a + b) + c;
  ```

  the variables can be summed by the compiler in some unspecified order. In ANSI C, this is not true. The parentheses must be honored.

- A pointer to a function can be dereferenced either explicitly or implicitly. If, for example, `f` is a pointer to a function that takes three arguments, then the expression

  `f(a, b, c)` is equivalent to `(*f)(a, b, c)`

- The `sizeof` operator yields a value of type `size_t`. The type definition for `size_t` is given in *stddef.h.*

- A pointer of type `void *` cannot be dereferenced without first casting it to an appropriate type. However, it can be used in logical expressions, where it is compared to another pointer.

D.6 Functions

- ANSI C provides a new function definition syntax. A parameter declaration list occurs in the parentheses following the function name. An example is

```
int f(int a, float b)
{
    .....
```

  In contrast, the traditional C style is

```
int f(a, b)
int     a;
float   b;
{
    .....
```

- ANSI C provides the function prototype, which is a new style of function declaration. A parameter type list occurs in the parentheses following the function name. Identifiers are optional. For example,

  `int f(int, float);` and `int f(int a, float b);`

  are equivalent function prototypes. In contrast, the traditional C style is

```
int f();
```

  If a function takes no arguments, then `void` is used as the parameter type in the function prototype. If a function takes a variable number of arguments, then the ellipsis is used as the rightmost parameter in the function prototype.

- Redeclaring a parameter identifier in the outer block of a function definition is illegal. The following code illustrates the error:

```
void f(int a, int b, int c)
{
   int   a;     /* error: a cannot be redefined here */
   .....
```

  Although this is legal in traditional C, it is almost always a programming error. Indeed, it can be a difficult bug to find.

- Structures and unions can be passed as arguments to functions, and they can be returned from functions. The passing mechanism is call-by-value, which means that a local copy is made.

D.7 Conversions

- An expression of type `float` is not automatically converted to a `double`.

- When arguments to functions are evaluated, the resulting value is converted to the type specified by the function prototype, provided the conversion is compatible. Otherwise, a syntax error occurs.

- Arithmetic conversions are more carefully specified (see Section 6.9, "Conversions and Casts," on page 216). In ANSI C, the basic philosophy for conversions is to preserve values, if possible. Because of this, the rules require some conversions on a machine with 2-byte words to be different from those on a machine with 4-byte words.

- The resulting type of a shift operation is not dependent on the right operand. In ANSI C, the integral promotions are performed on each operand, and the type of the result is that of the promoted left operand.

D.8 Array Pointers

- Many traditional C compilers do not allow the operand of the address operator & to be an array. In ANSI C, because this is legal, pointers to multidimensional arrays can be used. Here is an example:

```
int   a[2][3] = {2, 3, 5, 7, 11, 13};
int   (*p)[][3];                /* the first dimension
                                   need not be specified */
p = &a;
printf("%d\n", (*p)[1][2]);     /* 13 is printed */
```

D.9 Structures and Unions

- Structures and unions can be used in assignments. If `s1` and `s2` are two structure variables of the same type, the expression `s1 = s2` is valid. Values of members in `s2` are copied into corresponding members of `s1`.

- Structures and unions can be passed as arguments to functions, and they can be returned from functions. All arguments to functions, including structures and unions, are passed call-by-value.

- If `m` is a member of a structure or union and the function call `f()` returns a structure or union of the same type, then the expression `f().m` is valid.

- Structures and unions can be used with the comma operator and in conditional expressions. Some examples are

```
int        a, b;
struct s   s1, s2, s3;

.....
(a, s1)          /* comma expression having structure type
*/
a < b ? s1 : s2  /* conditional expression struct type */
```

- If *expr* is a structure or union expression and `m` is a member, then an expression of the form *expr*`.m` is valid. However, *expr*`.m` can be assigned a value only if *expr* can. Even though expressions such as

```
(s1 = s2).m    (a, s1).m    (a < b ? s1 : s2).m    f().m
```

are valid, they cannot occur on the left side of an assignment operator.

D.10 Preprocessor

- Preprocessing directives do not have to begin in column 1.
- The following predefined macros have been added:

  `__DATE__` `__FILE__` `__LINE__` `__STDC__` `__TIME__`

  They may not be redefined or undefined (see Section B.6, "Predefined Macros," on page 575).
- A macro may not be redefined without first undefining it. Multiple definitions are allowed, provided they are the same.
- The preprocessor operators # and ## have been added. The unary operator # causes the "stringization" of a formal parameter in a macro definition. The binary operator ## merges tokens (see Section B.7, "The Operators # and ##," on page 576)).
- The preprocessor operator `defined` has been added (see Section B.5, "Conditional Compilation," on page 573).
- The preprocessing directives `#elif`, `#error`, and `#pragma` have been added (see Section B.5, "Conditional Compilation," on page 573, and Section B.9, "The Use of #error and #pragma," on page 578).
- In traditional C, `toupper()` and `tolower()` are defined as macros in *ctype.h* as follows:

```
#define   toupper(c)   ((c)-'a'+'A')
#define   tolower(c)   ((c)-'A'+'a')
```

  The macro call `toupper(c)` works properly only when `c` has the value of a lowercase letter. Similarly, the macro call `tolower(c)` works properly only when `c` has the value of an uppercase letter. In ANSI C, `toupper()` and `tolower()` are implemented either as functions or as macros, but their behavior is different. If `c` has the value of a lowercase letter, then `toupper(c)` returns the value of the corresponding uppercase letter. If `c` does not have the value of a lowercase letter, then the value `c` is returned. Similar remarks hold with respect to `tolower()`.
- In ANSI C, every macro is also available as a function. Suppose *stdio.h* has been included. Then `putchar(c)` is a macro call but `(putchar)(c)` is a function call.

D.11 Header Files

- ANSI C has added new header files. The header file *stdlib.h* contains function prototypes for many of the functions in the standard library.

- The header files *float.h* and *limits.h* contain macro definitions describing implementation characteristics. ANSI C requires that certain minimum values and ranges be supported for each arithmetic type.

D.12 Miscellaneous

- In traditional C, the operators += and =+ are synonymous, although the use of =+ is considered old-fashioned. In ANSI C, the use of =+, =*, and so on is not allowed.

- An ANSI C compiler treats an assignment operator such as += as a single token. In traditional C, because it is treated as two tokens, white space can occur between the + and =. Thus the expression `a + = 2` is legal in traditional C but illegal in ANSI C.

- Each of the following has a distinct name space: label identifiers, variable identifiers, tag names, and member names for each structure and union. All tags for `enum`, `struct`, and `union` comprise a single name space.

- Two identifiers are considered distinct if they differ within the first *n* characters, where *n* must be at least 31.

- The expression controlling a `switch` statement can be any integral type. Floating types are not allowed. The constant integral expression in a `case` label can be any integral type, including an enumerator.

- Pointers and `int`s are not interchangeable. Only the integer 0 can be assigned to a pointer without a cast.

- Pointer expressions may point to one element beyond an allocated array.

- External declarations and linkage rules are more carefully defined.

- Many changes have been made to the standard library and its associated header files.

Appendix

E

ASCII Character Codes

American Standard Code for Information Interchange										
	0	**1**	**2**	**3**	**4**	**5**	**6**	**7**	**8**	**9**
0	nul	soh	stx	etx	eot	enq	ack	bel	bs	ht
1	nl	vt	np	cr	so	si	dle	dc1	dc2	dc3
2	dc4	nak	syn	etb	can	em	sub	esc	fs	gs
3	rs	us	sp	!	"	#	$	%	&	'
4	(	)	*	+	,	-	.	/	0	1
5	2	3	4	5	6	7	8	9	:	;
6	<	=	>	?	@	A	B	C	D	E
7	F	G	H	I	J	K	L	M	N	O
8	P	Q	R	S	T	U	V	W	X	Y
9	Z	[	\	]	^	_	`	a	b	c
10	d	e	f	g	h	i	j	k	l	m
11	n	o	p	q	r	s	t	u	v	w
12	x	y	z	{	|	}	~	del		

How to Read the Table

- Observe that the character A is in row 6, column 5. This means that the character A has value 65.

Some Observations

- Character codes 0 through 31 and 127 are nonprinting.
- Character code 32 prints a single space.
- Character codes for digits 0 through 9 are contiguous, letters A through Z are contiguous, and letters a through z are contiguous.
- The difference between a capital letter and the corresponding lowercase letter is 32.

The meaning of some of the abbreviations			
bel	audible bell	ht	horizontal tab
bs	backspace	nl	newline
cr	carriage return	nul	null
esc	escape	vt	vertical tab

Note: On most UNIX systems the command *man ascii* causes the ASCII table to be printed on the screen in decimal, octal, and hexadecimal.

Appendix F

Operator Precedence and Associativity

The table below shows precedence and associativity for all the C++ operators. In case of doubt, parenthesize.

<table>
<tr><th>Operators</th><th>Associativity</th></tr>
<tr><td>() [] -> . ++ (postfix) -- (postfix)</td><td>left to right</td></tr>
<tr><td>++ (prefix) -- (prefix) ! ~ sizeof(type)
+ (unary) - (unary) & (address) * (indirection)</td><td>right to left</td></tr>
<tr><td>* / %</td><td>left to right</td></tr>
<tr><td>+ -</td><td>left to right</td></tr>
<tr><td><< >></td><td>left to right</td></tr>
<tr><td>< <= > >=</td><td>left to right</td></tr>
<tr><td>== !=</td><td>left to right</td></tr>
<tr><td>&</td><td>left to right</td></tr>
<tr><td>^</td><td>left to right</td></tr>
<tr><td>|</td><td>left to right</td></tr>
<tr><td>&&</td><td>left to right</td></tr>
<tr><td>||</td><td>left to right</td></tr>
<tr><td>?:</td><td>right to left</td></tr>
<tr><td>= += -= *= /= *= >>= <<= &= ^= |=</td><td>right to left</td></tr>
<tr><td>, (comma operator)</td><td>left to right</td></tr>
</table>

Index

Symbols

A

G

P

U

V

W

X

Y

Z